The End of Culture

Books by Eric Gans

At the University of California Press:

The Discovery of Illusion: Flaubert's Early Works, 1835–1837. 1971.

The Origin of Language. 1981.

In French.

Un pari contre l'histoire: Les premières nouvelles de Mérimée. Paris: Minard, 1972.

Musset et le drame tragique. Paris: José Corti, 1974.

Le paradoxe de Phèdre, suivi de Le paradoxe constitutif du roman. Paris: Nizet, 1975.

Essais d'esthétique paradoxale. Paris: Gallimard, 1977.

THE END OF CULTURE
Toward a Generative Anthropology

Eric Gans

UNIVERSITY OF CALIFORNIA PRESS
Berkeley • Los Angeles • London

University of California Press
Berkeley and Los Angeles, California

University of California Press, Ltd.
London, England

Library of Congress Cataloging in Publication Data

Gans, Eric Lawrence, 1941-
  The end of culture.

  Sequel to: The origin of language.
  Bibliography: p. 331
  Includes index.
  1. Culture—Origin. 2. Anthropology—Philosophy.
3. Civilization, Occidental—History. 4. Greek
literature—History and criticism. I. Title.
GN357.5.G36 1985   306   84-16180
ISBN 0-520-05181-5

Printed in the United States of America

1 2 3 4 5 6 7 8 9

To my parents, Irving and Pearl Gans

Si j'écris leur histoire, ils descendront de moi.

Contents

Preface

The End of Culture may strike the reader as a somewhat peculiar title for a work that attempts to describe the origins of our cultural heritage. The present volume is, in reality, the first of two, the second of which, currently in preparation, will deal with the cultural problems of modernity. In a broader sense, *The End of Culture* is a sequel to *The Origin of Language* (University of California Press, 1981), although it is complete in itself and does not presuppose knowledge of the previous book. Also related to its overall theme is a forthcoming work entitled *Le centre lumineux: Anthropologie de la révélation*, which deals specifically with the religious element of Western culture. In all these texts, I have attempted to provide the basis for a general anthropology, conceived as a theory of human representation founded on the principle of the originary hypothesis that is presented in the opening chapters of the present work.

This anthropology is meant to have universal application; but, as the reader will find, it is unabashedly occidentocentric. Such civilizations as those of India and China are certainly worthy of interest in themselves, but it seems to me undeniable that today all societies, however ferociously their leaders and ideologues may deny it, are constituted on Western modes. The triumph of Marxism in China and the persistence of parliamentary government in India are clear indications of this, as is the adoption of rational market-oriented production methods by those Asian countries, Japan in particular, that have been able to avoid or overcome "third-world" status. If Mohammed and Marx are understood, as they should be, as heirs of the Judeo-Christian tradition, there is virtually no nation in the world today in whose reigning ideology this tradition is not dominant, however much it may be tempered with or colored by a par-

ticular regional heritage. Those countries that are the least successful
are precisely those that have found the assimilation of Western culture most difficult.

Cultural relativism has its virtues, for the varieties of social organization all have something to teach us, but its dogmatic status
among anthropologists corresponds to a self-interested romanticism
(self-interested because only they in the West have access to the
revelations that non-Western cultures hold in store for us) that operates by denying the unique and unprecedented success of the
Western tradition in permeating the totality of the world's societies.
Some may talk of "imperialism," but I would claim that the economic
and military superiority of Western civilization is grounded not on
a materialistic degradation of the human spirit but, on the contrary,
on a superior ethic. This should by no means be taken to imply the
racial or national superiority of the West over the rest of the world.
There is nothing here to suggest that the future advances of civilization cannot come from Asia or even Africa. Once Western culture
has been fully assimilated, it becomes world culture; and the future
of world culture lies with the world, not with Europe or North
America.

Some of the theoretical developments of this volume, as is perhaps
inevitable, are more rigorous and, to my mind at least, more satisfactory than others. The originary hypothesis itself and the more
immediate deductions from it are the real core of the book. It has
been difficult, in the absence of broadly based dialogue concerning
these theories, to elaborate them with equal proficiency in all areas.
What I am proposing is a new set of principles for the conduct of
human science, and the working-out of results from such principles
is a lengthy task. I think that on the basis of what is presented here,
as well as in the other works mentioned above, the reader can begin
to see the advantages of the originary hypothesis as a foundation for
the human sciences. This would still hold true if someone should
succeed, on the basis of an improved understanding of this hypothesis, in refuting every concrete analysis in this book. Just as the West
should feel only pride if it is one day surpassed in productivity by
Japan or China, I would be fully satisfied to have supplied a basic
principle by means of which others were able to renew and deepen
our understanding of cultural phenomena.

E. G.

Los Angeles
September 1983

Introduction

Primitive societies have no culture as distinct from ritual and economic activities. Thus one often speaks of these societies as a whole as "cultures." Even early civilizations allow for no distinction between ritual and secular culture; and Judaism ignores, not to say rejects, this distinction. If Western civilization is looked upon as a product of the interaction of Judaic and Hellenic elements, then "culture" as we know it is given to us by the Greeks. Because the secular perspective of modern society derives rather from the Greek than from the Judaic side of its heritage, the "anticultural," iconoclastic component of this heritage tends to go unnoticed, and indeed to be repressed. The Greek contribution to modernity scarcely needs elucidation. The state, authoritarian or democratic, the generalized international exchange-system, science and its technological by-products, as well as the arts and "humanities," all have clearly visible Greek antecedents. The Judaic side seems scarcely visible; one might wonder what this Middle Eastern tribe has contributed to the greatness of Western civilization.

To understand this contribution is truly to understand the fusion that constituted our civilization. This fusion is not one of *Geister* or *Weltanschauungen*, but of principles of social organization. True, in their continuity, these principles can only be expressed as ideas, and religioethical ideas at that, but this does not mean that their chief meeting ground is or ever was in the debates of philosophers and theologians—or, for that matter, of social scientists. These principles, incarnated in the realities of social organization, preside over its evolution. The synchronic state of social (self-)consciousness, and even the pseudodiachronic series of such states,[1] as might be elaborated by a historian of *mentalités*, is not the primary locus of the interaction and realization of these principles. Our own understand-

1

ing of them, while of necessity taking its place within this series, is not determined by earlier understandings, nor can it fruitfully consist of reflection upon them. The Hegelian idea that the true philosophy of history is the history of philosophy is inadequate, and it remains inadequate even in its Marxian inversion wherein "historical materialism" is the history of material relations. There is no simple pathway from a historical hypothesis to its concrete realization in the course of time; a series of synchronic cuts may corroborate such a hypothesis but cannot furnish sufficient grounds for its formulation. All historical, cultural, or, in a word, *anthropological* hypotheses must be *transcendental:* they must *precede* the analysis of any specific historical-cultural artifacts. "Empiricism" in such cases is only unconscious traditionalism.

From this perspective, it is not necessary that the Judaic principle of social organization be reflected in any specific institution. The institutions of Western society are derived from those of Greco-Roman antiquity. What is of Judaic origin is rather the conception of the community as moral rather than sacrificial, a conception incorporated, albeit imperfectly, in the rites of the Christian church, the redistributive functions of which are mediated by the moral obligation of charity.[2] The exchange-system is thus deritualized at its base, as it never was for the Greeks, and becomes free to develop its own dynamic. But this is not a merely negative development, a simple liberation of the economic/rational from its "irrational" ties to ritual, as the various materialist theories from Marx to Marvin Harris would have it. This separation reflects a truly universal morality that is in the last analysis independent of any ritual reaffirmation.

The nonviolent communal presence originally assumed only by ritual forms of redistribution is now made coextensive with the virtual presence of human (linguistic) communication. The primacy of the *word* in the Judeo-Christian tradition, from the creation story to "In the beginning was the word (*logos*)," reflects this emergent coextensiveness. But because it is therein expressed in theological rather than sociological terms, its deritualizing and hence ultimately detheologizing effect is necessarily hidden. The substitution of an interpersonal ethic, as democratic as speech, for the tyranny of ritual is not perceived as a sociological phenomenon because it expresses itself as the subordination of all to the will of an all-powerful deity. Yet only thus can this ethic function as a social principle. This is not to deny the role of the church, both in Christianity and even in postexilic Judaism. But the institutionalized church, however much it may uphold or disturb the social order per se, is never other than a guarantee of the essentially nonritual, ethical, *secular* nature of this order. The fundamental contribution of the Judaic tradition to Western civilization is its institutionalization of the supplementary nature of ritual with respect to the principles of interpersonal relations, the fundamental model for which is the nonviolent nonritual presence of linguistic communication.

The church incarnates, no doubt, this institutionalization; but merely to oppose it on the Judaic side of the ledger to the "Greek" institutions of the state, the free market, and the sciences would prevent any understanding of the different natures of the two contributing traditions, as well as of the regression of this Judaic element from social self-consciousness once the institutional functions of the church began to decline. The church is certainly not a "modern" institution—but it would be equally a mistake to consider it an "ancient" one. Within the ancient-modern continuum, it is rather best seen as transitional; and this is really to say that it is rather an anti-institution of Western society, destined to decline as this society develops toward maturity. This does not imply by any means, however, that the Judeo-Christian element in Western society is gradually being eliminated. On the contrary, the decline of the church is the real triumph of this element, the basic institutional model for which partakes of the spiritual nature of language rather than of the material one of ritual.

Modern secular culture arises with the decline of the institutional power of the church in the early modern era in the face of the growing autonomy of the bourgeois exchange-system. As the term "Renaissance" explicitly indicates, the rebirth of secular culture was equated with a rebirth of the Greek at the expense of the Judeo-Christian element—a rebirth that stands in defiant contrast with the atemporal rebirth proclaimed by Christianity. The very deliberateness of the Renaissance program—albeit more deliberate in retrospect than it appeared to its participants—is a sign that the classical roots of Western civilization, unlike its Judaic ones, are *not* simply incarnate in its sociopolitical institutions, however "Greek" these may appear, but must be continually reaffirmed. This is not to deny the sociological aspect of the Renaissance itself, which was as much a struggle for "Greek" institutions (the free market, the independent commercial city) as for Greek letters. But the sociological equation of "Greek" and "bourgeois" that takes the classical past as a fortunate accident, a given seized upon by a new class to bolster its prestige, is no less arbitrary than the romantic doctrine for which the classical contribution to the West is no more than a thin veneer upon a "Germanic" base. The revival of the forms of a partly deritualized classical culture under the conditions of a radical separation from its original ritual base is anything but an epiphenomenon. It is the hallmark of Western civilization, which is to say, the only universal civilization the world has ever known, or is likely ever to know.

"Culture" is not so much a body of representations (such a definition would obliterate the distinction between culture and the ritually based corpus of primitive and preclassical societies) as an open and dynamic *system* of representations. Within this system are painting, architecture, music, and so on, but the exemplary cultural form is discourse. Yet it is no accident that the earliest serious reflection on the phenomenon of culture, and in particular of its (re)birth in the Renaissance, took the plastic arts as its privileged domain. This is not merely the reflection of the value scale of the (particularly Italian) Renaissance itself. The plastic arts offer an apparently clear-cut mimetic *telos* that nineteenth-century art could be said not merely to have attained but to have understood, and even to have "transcended." To a society that had at least begun to take the measure of man, the ideal of "man as the measure of all things" could become transparent. Thus the genius of the individual artist appeared at once as free and as oriented along a more or less linear scale; the history of art approached the progressive form of the history of science. In this view, man's self-understanding through culture is ultimately a matter of clearing away obstacles to a clear and objective vision. The variants in objectivity that in the second moment of the analysis cannot be denied are then to be explained structurally on the basis of diverse sociohistorical factors (for example, Wölfflin's exemplary opposition between Renaissance and Baroque pictorial modes).

If such analyses, by their very explanatory power, promote a division within esthetic consciousness between form and content, "style" and "iconography," this is because the lack of integration of these elements is a necessary feature, if not of the artworks themselves, at least of their understanding in discursive terms. Iconography can be fascinating in itself, but the very term implies that the artist's choice of subject matter—in contrast with his style—is arbitrary and transparently conventional. The classical contribution to culture thus becomes seen as twofold: in the first place, a "humanistic" drive toward an objective vision of man and his surroundings, and, in a rather distant second place, a set of mythological and historical figures that, alone or in combination with Christian and mimetic motifs (portraiture, landscape), constitute the ostensible subject matter of artworks—it being understood that their "real" subject matter, one made explicit in Postimpressionist art, is simply the artist's vision. This analysis is no doubt generally faithful to the artist's own intention, which only in the case of supreme achievements placed formal perfection in the service of interpreting the content; and these supreme achievements were almost never attained with classical subject matter. It is therefore not surprising that the understanding of culture promoted by a primary orientation to the plastic arts has been unproblematically artist-centered, treating social structures as at best the inspiration for structural variants that reflect the needs of dominant elements of these structures (as, for example, the Baroque style reflects the needs of the post-Tridentine Catholic Church). Yet the link between the phenomenon of culture and the social relations of emerging bourgeois society is far more fundamental as well as far more problematic. The social order is not merely a supportive or repressive backdrop to the creativity of the artist; this very creative urge, with the corresponding receptivity on the part of its audience, is an intimate part of this order.

It is the discursive element of culture—that is, literature—that most clearly displays the problematic nature of cultural creativity. The truths uncovered by literature cannot at any point be assimilated to a mechanical objectivity in the partial but not trivial sense that the mimetic fidelity of Renaissance painting can be assimilated *post factum* to that of photography. Literary content can rarely be studied "iconographically"; a new treatment of an old myth is always a reinterpretation that in the most favorable cases sheds new light on its underlying anthropological significance. Because language is not only the chief vehicle of social communication but the original cultural act and the omnipresent archetype of nonviolent communal presence, cultural discourse, however far removed from its ritual origins, always makes a visible appeal to communal solidarity, if only in its use of openly "arbitrary" signs unassimilable to the "second nature"—whether individual or material, objective or subjective—of esthetic vision.

It is in discourse that the creative, processual nature of culture approaches most closely its linguistic archetype, as well as, more specifically, its Greek antecedents. In the Jewish tradition, the character of discourse as we define it is reserved for a determinate set of sacred texts, all further significant writings being not even authoritative commentary on these texts so much as the report of dialogues

concerning them. In contrast, the classical tradition contains no really
sacred texts but includes various genres of secular discourse, many
of which—forensic, philosophical, historical—are peculiarly Greek
inventions. In secular discourse, the sacred authority of the hypos-
tasized collective Subject of ritual becomes invested in an individual
employing language for a secular end—albeit one that, in the classical
world, always remained outside the domain of the secular institution
par excellence which is the economic exchange-system. The specifically Greek contribution to Western culture is thus, in the broadest
sense, like that of the Jews, a substitution of linguistic for ritual
models of intersubjective relations. But whereas the originally linguistic structure of what we call "virtual presence" was significant
for the Jews as an *ethical* structure and was only peripherally reflected
in linguistic forms per se—most notable in the dialogic tradition of
rabbinical exegesis—the Greeks made language, in the place of ritual,
into a new principle of social interaction, the ethical nature (and
origin) of which was for them only implicit. This discursive freedom,
in the absence of insight into its interpersonal foundations, could
not lead to a fully radical deritualization; and indeed, unexaminable
ritual restraints—as personified by Socrates' *daimon*—are omnipresent in Greek culture. The familiar explanations for the decline of
classical civilization—dependence on slave labor, external pressures
from "barbarians," insufficient incentives for technological or man-
agerial improvements—cite specific examples of the inadequate radicality of classical deritualization-through-discourse.[3] Classical
civilization was founded on a principle of exclusion that could ultimately be justified only on ritual grounds. What is of particular
interest to us is that this arbitrary differential element is not merely
a sociopolitical reality but a constraint on discourse as well. It is this
incompletely deritualized difference that is the source of the ineluctable ambiguity and instability of what we here term "culture."

This difference is present in philosophy as well as in literature.
At his least authoritarian, the philosopher seeks, through the *elenchos*,
the "true" meaning of words, but he never goes beyond the words
to the anthropological origin of the concepts they represent. Plato's
authoritarian ontology is the only possible outcome of a Socratic
search that accepts without historical justification the reality of concepts. To seek to know "the good" is to posit a priori a social order
productive of essential unanimity as to its values and at the same
time to avoid any possible consideration of the representational basis
for this unanimity. Just as viewing culture from the perspective of
the plastic arts leads to an exaggerated faith in the objectivity of

"vision," so seeing it from that of philosophy leads to an exaggerated faith—exemplified by Hegel—in the omnipotence of logic. Neither of these faiths can well survive the demystification of our era. The visions of modern art inspire cynicism or metaphoric mysticism, and modern philosophy is either nihilistic or narrowly mathematical. It is doubtless true that, as discourse, philosophy judges itself, is itself metaphilosophy. But precisely here it attempts too much, for it can never examine its own anthropological basis without ceasing to be philosophy. And this pretension places philosophy at the margin of cultural discourse. It is rather *fiction*, literature "proper," that above all else functions as the central cultural institution.

Literature too is an essentially Greek invention, although the popularizing tendency of modern culture has led to the forgetting of this fact. Traditional "folk" storytelling is closer to myth than to literature, and to overemphasize the continuity of Greek literature with its mythical basis is to refuse to confront its essential features. Homer is no simple storyteller, and the Greeks are the only ancient people to choose a literary work as their fundamental text. Homer and the Bible, literature and sacred history, sum up better than anything else the complementary contribution of Greek and Jew to Western civilization. All biblical narration is made to justify a sacred law, which is always ultimately an ethical law. Homeric narration has a very different orientation. Discursive—desiring—identification with the characters is prior to any relation to transcendental values. The primary mediation that binds the community of hearers of the Homeric text is that provided by the fictional discourse itself, and transcendental values are relevant only insofar as they are incarnated within this discourse. To be sure, the hearers already form an implicit community bound by ritually derived values, but the continued success of the Homeric poems as literature attests to the fact that becoming a part of this implicit community requires no prior agreement or even reflection upon the nature of these values. Discourse is for the Greeks a self-contained phenomenon, an institution without explicit institutional constraints. Fictional discourse better exemplifies this institution than philosophy, because its audience requires no motivation extraneous to the discourse itself. "Esthetic pleasure" is sufficient reason for joining this audience, and any inquiry into the nature of this pleasure is *post factum*. The biblical text is designed to inspire fear of God, that is, respect for ethical constraints. The Homeric text contents itself with inspiring a love for the text itself, or more precisely, for the position of hearer subordinated to the reciting Subject.

The Greeks had no "culture" in the modern sense. Homer and Sophocles were part of their native tradition, and a "cultured" Greek was not unlike a "cultured" African or Indian tribesman in knowing his tradition better than his neighbor. Yet the Greek tradition requires to develop into a culture only enough time for the wearing away of its ritual underpinnings—a development historically inevitable, given that discourse-in-itself as invented by the Greeks precisely forgoes the explicit appeal to any specific set of ritual constraints. Greek discourse is built to survive the tradition that fathered it, and this survival, already apparent by Hellenic times, becomes in Rome the first definitive example of "culture." The Roman student of Greek letters already partook of the delicious alienation that fueled the diligent ardors of the scholars of the Renaissance.

But the culture of late antiquity died out without being transformed, the early mixtures of Greco-Roman with Judeo-Christian elements having led to no durable fusion. Such fusion could only take place within a society whose ritual hierarchy was founded on universalist Judeo-Christian morality rather than on the still-primitive traditional ethic of antiquity. The unquestioned authority of the Subject of discourse drives the culture of antiquity ever further from lived experience into a "higher" realm. The mythical sources of the content of this culture—the careers of gods and warriors—incarnate this distance, but it would be facile to let this incarnation serve as an explanation. What made the heights of antique culture ever more inapproachable from below, so that "low" content could no longer be integrated within it and it exhausted itself in sterile conventionality, was not its ritual origins but the absence of any thoroughgoing transcendence of them. The a priori authority of the Subject-of-discourse precludes the universalization within the discourse itself of its ethical basis, the definitive transcendence of ritual violence and dissimulation. Christianity arrived too late to revitalize the ancient forms—forms primarily not of discourse but of social organization. The real cultural synthesis was not to occur until the Renaissance. Here culture was recreated with the power to adapt itself to the changing world of experience and, in the process, to work through its functionality as a historical phenomenon. The decline of culture in the modern world is not a collapse, but a dilution through universalization. The dialogue of high and low has not led to uncomprehending silence; it has rather been so successful that the partners can no longer be distinguished from each other.

The foregoing discussion suggests that culture as it has existed in the West since the Renaissance is a unique phenomenon irreducible to any of the general definitions of the word "culture" offered by anthropologists or sociologists. We particularly refer to the unique centrality of esthetic—and above all, literary—works in both the everyday activity and the self-consciousness of the various national groupings that have moved in the orbit of Western civilization, which today includes virtually the entire world. The esthetic subverts and replaces ritual at the center of communal activity, establishes and expresses both hierarchies of social worth and universal ethical values. If it is possible to speak today of a decline in this culture, it consists in an exhaustion of the innovative possibilities of high culture rather than in a diminution of the general importance of cultural phenomena. The key question, one on which any general anthropology must take its stand, is whether this decline in radicality, which reflects the quasi-total assimilation of the cultural into the exchange-system, presages the eventual decline of the phenomenon of culture itself.

The notion of "popular culture" is as oxymoronic and derivative as the wearing of blue jeans by upper-class city-dwellers. Culture is originally high culture, cut off from the direct expression of everyday experience by a barrier of "taste" or "breeding" that is easier to define sociologically than to understand anthropologically. The height of culture is not a mere derivative of that of ritual. The continual reinforcement of the high/low, cultured/uncultured distinction down to the semipopular arts of the present day (for example, cinema, jazz) bespeaks its structural importance. Despite its rough correlation with social status, it is not a mere reflection of other hierarchies, a fact which lends the points of difference between the cultural and sociopolitical hierarchies a particular interest. The original tension was not between high and low culture but between culture and religious tradition; low culture is a latter-day mediating element. Culture was classical, expressed in learned tongues and dealing with a no longer extant ritual universe; tradition was Christian and expressed in the vernacular. The exploitation of the new high culture by social snobbery should not mask its suprasocial, anthropological importance: the classical faith in discourse, or more generally, in the self-sufficiency of the esthetic creative Subject, was presented in the Renaissance not as an ethic opposed to that of Christianity but as a higher aspiration within it.

In the self-consciousness of its promoters, the Renaissance was a revival of interest in the human in contrast with the sterility of scholastic textualism and of the church ritual in general. The contemporaneity of Renaissance and Reformation was scarcely acciden-

tal. In either case, appeal was made to a direct, noninstitutional
reading of texts in their application to the exemplary status of individuals. The communal basis of medieval Catholicism was attacked
from both sides. The Protestants proposed a transcendental harmony
unknowable to mankind within which the individual had to find his
way without the benefit of positive ritual guidance. To this transcendental interpretation of the deritualized Judeo-Christian ethic,
Renaissance humanism opposed an optimistic vision of the earthly
harmony of human desires, as realized in the various utopias of the
era. But this aspect of the Renaissance is not centrally cultural, and
its contrast with the Reformationist perspective is incompletely drawn.
If the Renaissance vision were primarily that expressed in utopias,
we would be hard pressed to explain how it gave rise to the modern
problem of culture. To be sure, the inhabitants of Renaissance utopias were, generally speaking, "cultured" people, but the faith in
culture they incarnate cannot be abstracted from its discursive-es-
thetic basis without falling into the facile optimism of the utopians
themselves, whose attempts at anthropological synthesis were all too
painfully premature.

Becoming cultured or "cultivated" may appear, then, to be the
end of culture, and at least through the Enlightenment this view of
culture prevails. But the evident continuity of Renaissance culture
with that of the present day can only be understood if we abandon
the naive instrumentalism of early modern cultural ideology to con-
centrate on the nature of the instrument. The latter is primarily and
archetypally literary discourse. The cultural ideal of *Bildung* can be
seen as a partially misguided attempt to implant the purgative functionalism of Aristotle's *Poetics* into a deritualized Judeo-Christian
universe. The cultural experience purges the passions, not momentarily as in Aristotle, whose analogy remains close to its ritual-sac-
rificial model, but progressively; it educates to conformity with a
universal ethic. But this education lacks the concrete social integration of classical *paideia*. From Montaigne to Rousseau—the latter's
ostensible hostility to esthetic discourse and to "culture" in general
remaining still, as recent criticism (Derrida) has delighted in pointing
out, within the framework of "metaphysical," that is, Greek dis-
cursiveness—the educational ideal is to produce conformity with the
transcendental, deritualized morality that is the specifically Jewish
contribution to modern culture. That in Rousseau this ethical ideal
appears to *oppose* itself to the esthetic basis of culture is by no means
the sign of any loss of vigor on the part of the esthetic. The whole
post-Rousseauean evolution of culture demonstrates rather the con-

trary, that the educational ideal—though not its ethical basis—was only an accretion upon the esthetico-discursive body of culture. The contemporary debates about the ethics of violent and/or pornographic works in the cinema and elsewhere demonstrate how little we have to say about cultural *Bildung* two hundred years after the *Emile*. But all the while, discursive culture has gone from victory to victory, reaching the very masses whose folkways had served Rousseau as a counterexample to the high culture he deplored. It is all too obvious today that the ethical basis of culture cannot be sought in any specific "purgative" or "educational" effect of cultural works.

The classical sources of modern culture were not so much exemplary as alien, exemplary because they were alien. Alienation guaranteed the universality of a rediscovered, self-substantive cultural discourse. The Greek's faith in discourse could be wedded to the Jewish ethic only on a terrain defined by the Greeks. Yet this is not a proof of the more fundamental nature of the Greek contribution to modernity, but the opposite. The Judeo-Christian ethic could effectively absorb the pagan ritual content because its premises were in fact more universal, less particularistic than the Greek cultural heritage, however much the restorers of the latter believed the contrary. This illusory belief was not, however, an accidental mystification. Nor can it be explained by a critique of a medieval, ritualized Christianity that had so betrayed its founding ethical insights that they could only be revived in the figures of pre-Christian religion. The alienation, the tension, of high culture was anything but a necessary evil.

Our anthropological hypothesis concerning the phenomenon of "culture" is the following: in submitting ourselves to the esthetic (in particular, the discursive) Subject, we accept the localization of our desire within a self-contained universe of discourse, and *at the same time* experience this sacrificial acceptation of constraint as a sign of our integration into a universal ethical community. This synthesis— tentative, problematic, indeed, essentially paradoxical—is, in effect, that of the "Greek" and the "Jewish," the discursive and the moral, elements of modern Western society. But if we take an interest in the phenomenon of culture for its own sake, it is not simply in order to reduce it to a combination, however problematic, of preexistent components. The anthropological importance of culture is precisely that it dissolves the difference between Jew and Greek in its paradoxical effort to reground human society on a foundation anterior to both ethical reflection and discourse. "Culture," like all religious and secular cultural forms, is an attempt to understand and to come to terms with the origin of the human community. Not that the diversity of cultural products is by any means a mere epiphenomenon, a surface glitter overlying their single fundamental theme. On the contrary, this diversity is itself a value—the supreme cultural value. But the richness of culture, as we are now in the process of discovering, is not infinite, and our admiration for it should not blind us to the underlying unity of all cultural aspirations. Only thus, in our newfound awareness of the limits of culture, may we fruitfully pursue its goal on the theoretical plane.

In a previous work, *The Origin of Language*,[4] we proposed an *evenemential originary hypothesis* to explain the origin of representational form. Our analysis of culture will proceed on a similar basis. But rather than merely referring the reader to this earlier volume, we shall begin again from the beginning with a revised version of the hypothesis. The modifications that we have seen fit to make in our first version of the originary hypothesis do not affect the substance of our earlier presentation of the genesis of linguistic form; this presentation will, consequently, not be repeated. But where these modifications do indeed shed new light on matters touched on in the earlier work, reference will be made to it in the text.

The Originary Hypothesis

The fundamental principle of the originary hypothesis is the following: the origin of the specifically human category of formal representation cannot be understood as a gradual process but only as an *event*. Human representation proper, as opposed to the protorepresentational forms of animal language, takes place on a scene the origin of which can only be understood as itself a "scene," that is, an event participated in by the nascent human community. Theories that attempt to trace a continuous evolution of human language or culture from animal forms are doomed to failure because they cannot construct such a scene.

In *The Origin of Language* we followed René Girard[1] in supposing the original scene to be the outcome of a "mimetic crisis" in which the protohuman society is beset by violent rivalry over an attractive object. In such a crisis the original object would be abandoned as attention is focused on the rivalry itself. The crisis would be resolved by the selection of a single victim on whom the violence of the entire group would be concentrated. The model for this "violent unanimity" is the scapegoat mechanism, the universality of which in all cultures is affirmed by Girard. In the latter's version of the hypothesis, the collective murder of this "emissary victim" creates the original scene of culture. The group of murderers surrounding the body experience a sudden release of tension, their violence spent, and they contemplate the body as the source of this miraculous transformation of violence into peace. The body of the victim thus becomes for Girard the object of "the first noninstinctive attention,"[2] which turns it into a *sacred* object, the first signifier and the source of all signification.

It is here that our exposition of the hypothesis departed from that of Girard. For if the scene we were describing was truly the original scene of representation, then the object of attention cannot itself be the first sign. The sign we postulated was rather an "abortive gesture of appropriation" designating the "sacred" object that appeared to each member of the group as both infinitely desirable and infinitely dangerous because it was the object of the appetites of all the others. The group of murderers surrounding the body are transformed into a community, not by the mere fact of the passage of violence to peace, but through their renouncement of appetitive appropriation of the remains. The hands reaching out toward the object hesitate in mid-course through the fear of each that he will fall victim to the reprisals of all the others. This hesitation turns the gesture of appropriation into a gesture of designation, and the locus of the body into the original scene of representation.

In a work devoted essentially to the evolution of linguistic forms, the foregoing version of the original event was sufficient. But the concept of desire it implies was inadequate for a theory of culture, and indeed led to conclusions concerning esthetic and cultural phenomena that we now find in need of revision. The source of the difficulty is that the choice of the "emissary victim" as the original significant object has no appetitive motivation. The desire felt by each member of the nascent community toward the remains of their victim is already wholly "metaphysical," that is, motivated exclusively by the similar desire of the others. This is not because of any specific quality of a human victim (as opposed, for example, to a beast of prey); it is a function of the crisis-resolution scheme borrowed from Girard. For, in this scene, the victim is not set upon by the group because he is attractive to their appetite—sexual or alimentary—but because he is through some visible sign of vulnerability identified as a suitable outlet for purely destructive mimetic aggression. Even if we reject ethical motivations, the mimetic rivalry that turns into a unanimous attack on the victim is by the nature of this theory (and it is explicitly so presented by Girard) distinct from appetite and, indeed, opposed to it. The crisis begins with a fight over an appetizing object, but the strength of mimetic tendencies is such that, as increasing numbers are drawn to the conflict, the original object is lost in the shuffle.

The shift in focus between (1) the original appetitive object and (2) the emissary victim effectively defines the moment of humanization—the "nature/culture" dichotomy—in Girard's theory, even if the realization of this shift by the collectivity must await the calm that follows the violent resolution of intracommunal conflict. But by positing such a shift, this theory obliges us to eliminate altogether the appetitive element of desire. Culture is founded on a purely arbitrary, violent choice of the first significant object. This theory takes as its given an intensity of "mimetic tendency" such that the appetitive is altogether forgotten; but, in effect, such an intensity must itself be explained, and the only conceivable explanation is the preexistence of collective representation, that is, of human culture. If we forgo this explanation, we are forced to begin our theory of representation with an absolutely arbitrary significance. The original community is then altogether blind to the nature of its desire for the "sacred" object, and, by the same token, altogether devoid of an ethical basis for its newly achieved peaceful reciprocity. The only cultural act that can legitimately follow from such beginnings is the repetition of the emissary murder in ritual.

It is true that by including in our model a scene of representation, we were able to define a state of "ritual presence" of the members of the community to each other within which linguistic forms could develop. But the *content* of these forms could be derived from the (violent) original event only by way of ritual. And because this content is in its origins *absolutely* unmotivated, no explanation could be given of attempts to motivate it. Thus the very question of "explanation," that is, the search for motivations of the original event, can never be posed. If, in its origin, representation on the one hand creates significance *ex nihilo* and, on the other, presents its object as absolutely significant in itself, then the problem of *truth*, of correspondence between sign and referent-independent-of-sign, could never arise. For its users, the "truth" of representation would be self-evident, so to speak tautological; for us (but whence could "we" have evolved?) representation would be necessarily false; and no mediating factor could be legitimately brought forward to break the impasse.

These are radical conclusions, more rigorous than those of *The Origin of Language*, where we were obliged to postulate a number of secondary causes of the evolution of linguistic forms: a "lowering of the threshold of significance" as society became more peaceful, a mnemonic-explanatory function for discourse within ritual. But the progress of our theory of representation requires that it become increasingly rigorous precisely in the sense of situating the origin of all determining elements of the evolution of human representation within our hypothetical scene. It is this necessity that differentiates what we have elsewhere called "human science" or "radical anthropology" from the natural as well as the empirical social sciences.[3] Because we seek not merely to observe the regularities of human conduct as though from without but to reconstruct the significant moments of its evolution, we cannot accept any institutionally given form as an inexplicable *donnée*. And if this was already true in the case of the formal structures of language, it is still more radically so in that of culture. For the essential evolution of language is prehistoric; the declarative sentence completes the dialectic of linguistic forms. The evolution of culture is, on the contrary, only today reaching its critical point. If we would understand this evolution, in the sense of being able both to predict and to participate in its future course, we must be able to situate all the essential determinants of the cultural situation within the domain of our hypothesis. The cultural significance of hypothetical construction is precisely that it constitutes an attempt to understand the fundamental human institutions "nonculturally," that is, without the benefit of *fictions*. Our models, although lacking the concrete verifiability of those of the natural sciences, are neither mythical nor esthetic: they make a claim of truth. The substantiation of this claim cannot well be made directly; it must come from the application of our hypothetical model to the explanation of historical phenomena, particularly those of the present. And to judge the value of such applications, our only possible overall criterion must be that of simplicity. The less we need to introduce elements extraneous to our original hypothetical model, the more our analyses carry conviction.

The reader may here make what appears to be an unanswerable objection. If the sole *essential* epistemological basis for our theory is its simplicity—if, in other words, the rigor and thence the truth-value of the theory depend upon the closeness of fit between the hypothesis of origin and analyses of cultural phenomena for which this same hypothesis serves as the point of reference—then how can we prevent these analyses from simply reducing the phenomena to the categories of the hypothesis? Our response to this objection is that, precisely in the case of representations, the significant elements are effectively irreducible because our understanding of them involves our grasp of these elements. The very fact that such an understanding is always in principle possible can indeed be *explained* only by positing a common origin of all representational phenomena. But even if one forgoes any explanation, one cannot very well refuse to accept the intuitive sense of understanding with which we confront such phenomena; and our common faith in this sense serves to guarantee the pertinence of our analyses.

As soon as the phenomenon of representation is no longer accepted as a given, either "natural" like the genetic and other "codes," or miraculous and incapable of explanation, then it is obvious that any explanation of categories of representation, let alone individual acts of representation, must refer at least implicitly to an explanation, that is, a theory, a hypothesis concerning the phenomenon of representation-in-general. And the only hypothesis that can in any sense explain representation as a historically given activity peculiar to our species must be a generative one that proposes a model of its emergence from an earlier state in which it was absent. These are, indeed, not difficult concepts. They are nonetheless revolutionary, because they contradict and indeed refute the bases of the philosophical and social-scientific thought—both equally "metaphysical"—that our culture has produced until now. The ease with which these ideas can now be developed, as well as the resistance to them which, although powerful, must be looked upon as merely residual, are crucial matters that must be dealt with in a separate work.

1

The Originary Scene of Representation

THE MINIMAL HYPOTHESIS

Instead of presupposing a "mimetic crisis" as a precondition for the original act of representation, we shall consider a weaker hypothesis—bearing in mind, of course, that the "weakness" of our presuppositions makes the hypothesis proportionally more powerful. We shall suppose only the scene of representation as such as the minimal state of our hypothesis: the members of the group surrounding an object, attractive for whatever reason, and designating it by means of an abortive gesture of appropriation. Even the duration of this designation need not be specified. We are not obliged to postulate a lengthy stasis resulting from a durable impossibility of appropriating the object. The constitution of the act of representation is alone sufficient: the recognition by each member of the group that both he and his fellows are in fact designating the object *for the moment* without actively attempting to appropriate it.

The advantage of this minimal hypothesis is that it cannot be attacked, as earlier versions could be, as an unwarranted extrapolation from historically given data. We need not give even the appearance of creating yet another "myth of origin." The hypothesis of an original scene of representation merely abstracts the central element of all experiences of representation and situates it on the only "scene" that can conceivably exist in the prior absence of representation: that of collective presence. "Presence" here acquires, through the act of representation, its potential for becoming a the-

19

ological, and thence a metaphysical, concept; it does not possess this potential at the outset, where it is merely the presence of mutual confrontation before an object of potentially conflicting appetites. Appetite alone can render this object worthy of attention in the absence of structures of signification. The appetitive element is not, indeed, so much added on as a causal explanation of the scene of representation as it is abstracted from it, for appetite is always the ultimate ground of significance, just as "use value" is the ground of "exchange value." The only conceivable fundamental objection to our hypothesis can come from one who refuses the very notion of an origin of representation, who affirms either that it "always already" existed or that it was created by a divine miracle. But neither of these is an argument worthy of scientific consideration.

The original scene of representation as here presented requires no external motivation, although such activities as hunting generate plausible settings. Fear of conflict is the sole necessary motivation for the abortion of the original gesture of appropriation. The minimality of our hypothesis indeed requires that this "abortion" be in its origin no more than a *hesitation* sufficiently marked to designate the object. The activity of appropriation can then proceed, but on a new basis. For the hesitation will have sufficed to make each member aware not merely of the appropriative intentions of the others but of their renouncement, expressed in the designating gestures, of *merely* appetitive (that is, "instinctual") appropriation. Thus the act of representation, however brief, must lead to a nonviolent communal division or sharing of the object. For if the act of appropriation still led to conflict, the hesitation would serve no function for the group and would therefore not be preserved. Or still more simply, if the time of the hesitation were insufficient to prevent conflict, it would necessarily increase. The prevention of conflict by means of the (temporarily) aborted gesture already suffices to define this gesture as representing, for the attainment of a peaceful resolution can only be explained as the result of the newly achieved awareness of the common intention to appropriate coupled with the renouncement of immediate appropriation as stated above. This awareness is not itself "instinctive"; it is brought about by the creation of a scene of representation wherein the attractive object, for the moment inaccessible, is signified by the gesture.

It should be noted that, although the collective nature of the original scene is essential, the numbers involved do not figure in the hypothesis. Thus those who retain an affection for the Condillacian scene of two boys alone on an island need not reject our theory.

More to the point, this indifference to number permits the assimilation to the original scene of all acts of representation involving more than one individual. The only absolute requirement, which precludes the enlargement of our hypothetical scene to include solitary self-communication (as in the gestural theory of Trân Duc Thao[1] or the expressive theory of Herder), is that we always derive internal representation from external, mental scenes from interpersonal ones.

CONSEQUENCES OF THE HYPOTHESIS

The original scene is by definition the hypothetical origin of the fundamental categories of human culture. The specificity of these categories and the degree to which they may be considered as autonomous sets of phenomena must be constructed rigorously on the basis of the hypothesis alone; care must be taken to avoid commonsense or empirical justifications.

Presence and the Scene of Representation

The anthropological category of presence must be distinguished from the metaphysical notion of the "presence" of a representation as well as from the natural category that applies to the spatial awareness of sentient beings. Once a spatial range of activity is defined by a specific perceptual apparatus, it becomes possible to distinguish between "interesting" and "uninteresting" objects according to their value—positive or negative—in ensuring the animal's (or even the plant's) well-being. Depending on the level of evolutionary complexity, the perceptual apparatus may either be specifically programed to take cognizance of the object or be subject to the influence of learned responses. In the original scene under consideration, the desired object (for example, a beast of prey) is at first present to all merely in this prehuman sense. But the designative gesture adds a specifically human element to this dual relation: presence in the anthropological sense includes not merely a subject and an object but an Other. Each individual designates the object not merely as one attractive to his own appetites but as one worthy of interest on the part of the other members of the group. The object is not merely present to each, it is made present or "presentified" to all.

But this supplementary presentification is a re-presentation on an "other scene." In the original event, this scene of representation may be of short duration, but it serves to establish among the participants a communal presence before the object that is never altogether lost. For it is precisely the memory of this presence that leads to the peaceful division of the object and to the eventual reproduction of the designating gesture on a future occasion. This memory is by no means "collective"; it is strictly individual. What is collective is rather the *significant content* of this memory: the gesture-as-designating-the-object and the-object-as-designated-by-the-gesture. In *The Origin of Language* we used the term "significant memory" to refer to the retention by each individual of collectively established signs and their meanings. But this memory is not merely a catalogue of signs; in order for the meaning of signs to be retained, there must first be retained the memory of the presence within which the sign was first associated with its object. This memory establishes between the members of the nascent human community a *virtual presence* that is transmitted to each newly admitted member of this community. In the original scene, it is the presence of the referent that guarantees the meaning of the sign; but as we showed in *The Origin of Language*, once virtual presence is established and the meaning of signs is retained in significant memory, forms of signification (that is, of language) can evolve in which the reproduction of the sign is sufficient to evoke in a present other the (remembered) image of its referent.

The scene of representation as a whole, as retained in the memories of the participants in the original event, is thus broken down into its component relations: that between sign and object, that between signifying self and receiving other. This is possible because the scene, as the locus for all significant interpersonal communication, came into being from the outset as a form separate from its referential content. This is, indeed, why we are justified in employing the theatrical metaphor "scene." Instead of the gesture of appropriation's making its originally intended contact with the object, it is transformed, if only momentarily, into a gesture of designation by the very fact that the object is for the moment inaccessible, not for "natural" but for *communal* reasons. Instead of a part of the natural world immediately subject to appetitive interest, the object becomes the center of a scene in which the relation of primary interest—an interest of a new sort, a *significant interest*—is not the appetitive one between man and object but the communal one between man and man.

Thus the scene of representation may be said to have an *ethical* origin, although the specific category of the ethical—the human relation without consideration of any specific object—is only latent in the original scene. But, as virtual presence, this interpersonal relation provides from the outset the general form of significant communication, for henceforth the mutual presence of members of the community will reestablish the conditions for the reproduction of the gesture. The object itself, however much it may be valorized or sacralized by its position at the center, is there—*present* in the anthropological sense—only because it has been *renounced* as an appetitive object for the sake of the collectivity. Its essential separability from the scene on which it appears is thus attributed to it from the beginning; and the evolution of language alongside the elaboration of specifically sacred forms is the historical proof of this separation.

Nothing in our exposition requires that we posit a thematic awareness of this separability on the part of the participants; on the contrary, our minimal hypothesis specifically excludes any such nonfunctional element. The scene need not and undoubtedly cannot be remembered in abstraction from its central object; the impossibility of this abstraction explains the universality of the phenomenon of the sacred, which we shall discuss presently as what we may call a "separable" category derived from the original hypothesis. But the establishment of virtual presence does not require that memory itself be analytical. It suffices that, of the two relations of the remembered scene—the significant and the interpersonal—the more fundamental, interpersonal relation be *functionally* anterior to the other. However powerful the sacred valorization of the object-in-itself, the sacred can only function as a hypostasis of, and a mask for, the interpersonal category of the significant.

Desire and the Imaginary

The problem of desire is no doubt the most difficult of human science. One could claim that the solution to this problem would be the veritable end of culture, that once human desire was wholly predictable, cultural phenomena would either disappear or degenerate into the application of wholly mastered manipulative technique. The fearful premonition of such a solution indeed informs many of the dystopias so current in modern literature. Man is perceived as motivated by desire and therefore as infinitely vulnerable to the understanding of it; the manipulations of consumer society are often cited as ominous signs of a growing capacity to generate desires for objects of no real value to the desirer.

We have already touched on this subject in the final chapter of *The Origin of Language* and will deal with it more thoroughly in a future volume. At this point, we shall merely attempt to pose the problem. But the question arises whether this problem is not a function of the complexity of the world and of the experiences it generates rather than of desire per se. It would be a metaphysical exercise of little value to deal with this question as one of definition of terms. The Freudian theory of desire, for example, cannot simply be dismissed by charging Freud with equating desire to the over-simplified "energetic" concept of the libido. Unless the specifically human or cultural element of desire is clarified—thereby structurally distinguishing desire from instinctual appetite—we have no means of understanding the relationship between desire and the totality of social institutions that can variously be seen as functioning to generate it, to control it, or to repress it. There is need, therefore, of a structural definition. But if this definition were so rigorous as to permit of precise practical application, so that a specific cultural component could be extracted from—or injected into—a given object-relation, then the "final solution" would indeed be upon us. The conceptual problem of desire, in other words, is a model of the practical problem. But, by the same token, for a complete conceptualization to be possible, society must contain institutions that make it possible to extract and observe the cultural component of desire at first hand. In this sense, the progress of the modern exchange-system, with its increasingly direct effect on individual desire, is the ultimate source of our theoretical construction of desire, and, albeit indirectly, of our hypothesis as a whole.

The foregoing considerations should make us wary of an over-simple, purely cultural model of desire that treats as inessential its appetitive component. Such a model, like structural models of signification, cannot avoid defining the cultural as the purely arbitrary, a radically inexplicable condition amenable only to either structuralist (or poststructuralist) stoicism or faith in divine intervention.[2] Our minimal hypothesis avoids the necessity of a change in the central object from an appetitive to a mimetic-aggressive one, or even of the transformation of the victim from object of aggression to object of desire (as in *The Origin of Language*). The object is from the beginning appetitive; it is excess of appetite that presents the danger, and it is this excess that, as a result of the creation of the scene of representation, is converted into desire.

We thus define desire as appetite mediated by the appearance of its object on the scene of representation. In the original event, the participants have an appetitive relation to the object. This relation is *already* partly mimetic: it suffices that an animal be able to be redirected to (or away from) a new object through perceiving the action of a cospecific for mimesis to come into play. But if we would distinguish a specifically human quality in desire, this can occur only as a result of the establishment of the scene of representation. In the context of our hypothetical original event, the relation of desire can only be said to exist upon the execution of the abortive gesture of appropriation. At this moment, each becomes aware of the interest in the object on the part of the others. This awareness is what constitutes communal presence. It must definitely be considered as *conscious*, but not as *thematic*, for it is awareness of the general form of representation and not of the represented content. The thematization of this awareness of presence is, indeed, precisely the subject matter of the theory of representation as we have defined it.

Now the object is already a conscious one—for it is already "present" in the prehuman sense of perceivable. The question of narrow and broad definitions of consciousness is nevertheless more problematic than the similar question with regard to presence. It is no doubt useful to refer to an animal "consciousness" or awareness of objects; we should specify a *contingent* awareness that takes place on a neutral ground, so that the object's existence for consciousness implies a perceptual scene upon which the object is not *necessarily* present. Human consciousness may then be more narrowly defined as implying a scene of representation. The objects of consciousness in this sense, real or imaginary, would be perceived within a context of potential representation—one in which, therefore, the power of the perceiving subject, not merely to observe the object passively but to re-present it to himself, is always latent. In this sense, the awareness of communal presence falls between the two forms of consciousness just defined and can only be understood on the basis of the concrete experience of the original event. And this should not surprise us. For the distinction just made between animal and human consciousness owes nothing essential to an originary hypothesis; it is compatible with a metaphysical view of human difference. It is, in contrast, the nature of our consciousness of human presence that must be formulated in terms of a hypothetical event, because this consciousness is precisely at the origin of representation and, consequently, not directly visible on the (cultural) scene of representation itself.

The object is thus already a conscious one before the act of representation. What this act does is transform irrevocably the nature of this consciousness. For the purely individual scene of perception is now transformed into the *communal* scene of representation. As a consequence, the merely appetitive relation (however it may be mediated by mimesis) must now take place before the community. During the moment of hesitation in which the gesture of designation is made and understood, each observes not merely the object but the gestures of the others, which express the same appetitive attraction as his own. For the duration of the scene of representation, the object is not merely wanted but *desired* precisely insofar as it has become, for this duration, inaccessible. The scene of representation is real, but it is also reproduced in the mind of each participant as the origin of what we may call his *desiring imagination*. The public significance attributed to the object makes his private representation of it a form of imaginary possession that not merely augments its appetitive attraction (as would be the case in simple—precultural—mimesis) but radically transforms this attraction into a phenomenon of potentially general significance.

The gesture of signification is an original gesture of appropriation the normal termination of which is suspended, but at the same time realized in the imagination as something unrealizable in reality. To possess the object is for the moment infinitely impossible, but it is, for that very reason, infinitely desirable. Each designating gesture is expressive of a desire that fills not only the field of perception but the communal field of representation. Each participant sees in the hesitation of the others the impossible chance of success for his own desire. The solitude of the object admits of no *real* possession but, by the same token, permits each member of the group to prolong his gesture into an *imaginary* possession. But in order for this imaginary possession to take place, each must take into himself, secretly as it were, the collective scene of representation. The hypothetical scene is thus the origin of the private world of the imagination precisely because of its communal, public nature. For the "private" (as the French word *privé* suggests) can only be constituted as the abstracting of the individual self from an originally public situation.

But the radicality of the shift from the scene of (appetitive) perception to the scene of (desiring) representation does not render unimportant the appetitive value of the object. It is this value alone that guarantees the success of the operation and assures its future repetition. The original representation would lead to nothing if it did not result in a satisfactory peaceful sharing of the object—or, at least, to one more peaceful and satisfactory than before. Insofar as the origin of culture is the origin of representation, it must lead to increased appetitive satisfaction from the represented object.[3] Deferral of immediate satisfaction through representation can survive only if it leads to increased long-term satisfaction. For the duration of this deferral, the desire-object may be said to be in a purely cultural context, since its appetitive value cannot be tested, and in its place stands only the communal designation of the object as significant. But this designation must be subsequently justified by the appetitive satisfaction derived from the object. The subsequent evolution of human culture will strengthen deferral and will permit not merely its prolongation with respect to appetitive objects but its application to mediate objects in themselves devoid of appetitive satisfaction. But appetitive satisfaction—as Freud well knew—remains the ultimate goal of representation and of the desire it engenders.

The origin of desire is directly linked to that of the imaginary. The imaginary prolongation of the designative gesture toward the object constitutes the original experience of desire. This prolongation takes place on the imaginary scene of representation, which it exploits to create an impossible image. For the object is *necessarily* inaccessible, and it is precisely this that permits each individual to imagine himself as alone acceding to it. The imagination thus originates as essentially paradoxical. Even if, in the original scene, the paradox is removed by the eventual collective appropriation and sharing of the object, it is never really abolished, because shared possession or even complete possession under the aegis of the group as a whole cannot realize the image of desire that is formulated prior to the existence of any such possibility.

The perversity of desire stems from its compensatory status during the time of deferral of appropriation. It is not that the end of desire is merely greater than the end of appetite but that it is necessarily unrealizable. This must be taken in its most radical sense; not only does the image contain elements incompatible with the communal configuration (the necessary solitude of the object, the self as its sole proprietor), but it is fundamentally paradoxical because incompatible with its own conditions of emission (the self as away from the object, the self as possessing the object). This paradox of desire may be presented in a very simple manner. We are here only stating an obvious truth, but one whose obviousness has always blinded theoreticians of desire to its problematic character and therefore to its unsettling consequences. The desiring image is paradoxical not because the *others* would prevent its realization but because the self, insofar as it desires, remains on the (imaginary) scene of representation and not on the (real) scene where the object is situated. The image, even if it represents a wholly possible *future* fulfillment, cannot represent a *real* fulfillment because its conception is possible only under conditions of nonfulfillment. The member of the original community cannot possess the desired object, because his desire arises only when the object is not possessed.

Thus formulated, our theory of desire may appear tautological. Desire is unfulfillable because, in order for it to be formulated, it must be unfulfilled. But far from being a tautology, this formula is the only one sufficient to stand as a basis for a general theory of representation. Its radicality, which will become clear in what follows, is perhaps the most convincing of all demonstrations of the usefulness of the originary hypothesis. For without the concrete scene required by this hypothesis, it would have been virtually inconceivable that such a theory of desire could have been formulated. Only a theory that situates the origin of signification in an *event*— that is, in a specific moment in time—can go beneath the temporal continuity that virtual presence provides for all members of human culture. For what appears tautological in our formulation is simply this: desire is experienced in time, and the temporal distance between its constitution as an image and its real fulfillment (allowing for the moment that the image be altogether realizable) is not felt as modifying the essence of the desire. If I formulate at 10:30 the desire for a candy bar and I purchase one at 11:00, I consider myself to have fulfilled my desire: the candy bar in my hand is a realization of the image formed a half hour earlier. This imagined satisfaction is felt as fully realized; there is no need to speak here of the inevitable disappointment that comes with obtaining the object of one's desire. In comparison with this example, the fatal desires portrayed in tragedy or the impossible ones revealed on the psychoanalyst's couch appear as perversions in no way implicit in the essence of desire. But from our originary perspective, what is essential even in the desire for the candy bar is the contrast between the imaginary satisfaction, which appears to me as *significant*, and the real satisfaction, which, precisely to the extent that it is unproblematic, is also, from the communal standpoint, insignificant. Of course, even during the deferral of satisfaction I knew there was nothing significant about possessing or eating a candy bar; but to the extent that I actively desired it, its imaginary possession gave meaning to my temporal existence.[4] The very fact that such an example resists testing through introspection or even experiment only confirms the necessity for an originary hypothesis. For only on the basis of such a theory can we unify our understanding of desire and grasp the common element between our experience with the candy bar and the most tragic or pathological desire-experiences. Indeed, the existence of commercially accessible desire-objects, often more costly by several orders of magnitude than candy bars, is a most significant phenomenon in its own right. For desires oriented toward and realizable in the marketplace are the dominant feature of modern consumer society and are the crucial determinant in the evolution of modern culture.

The Esthetic Moment

We have defined desire in the original event as the prolongation of the gesture toward the object on the individual's imaginary scene of representation. The image of desire is not the public representation itself but a private image of satisfaction. This private image is, nevertheless, dependent on the public scene that confronts each individual. We shall define as *esthetic* the spectator's relation to the image(s) of desire insofar as they are dependent on the contemplation of this public scene. The object is, insofar as it is contemplated by the members of the group, an *esthetic object*, and their experience of desire during the period of deferral, an *esthetic experience*.

At first glance, these definitions may be felt to be too broad to grasp the specificity of what is normally called the esthetic. The contemplation of an art-object may arouse desire, but this desire can never be followed by appetitive satisfaction, even if it leads to the appropriation (for example, purchase) of the object. But to honor this objection in our theory would result in the relegation of the esthetic to an epiphenomenal status—one that could be explained at all only as a derivative of the sacralization of the object. The esthetic object would become a mere simulacrum of the real object, and our experience of it a substitute for the real experience. This is in fact how we shall describe the emergence, within ritual, of the art-object. But in order for the specificity of our experience of art-objects to have a legitimate place in our theory, it is necessary that the origin of this experience be comprehended as a moment of the original event. This is not a *parti pris* but a rigorous consequence of the originary hypothesis. For if we assert the essential unity of all cultural phenomena—that is, those phenomena that are dependent on the specifically human practice of representation—then the roots of all the fundamental categories of cultural experience must be found in the original event. To exclude the esthetic from this event can then only be to make it a derivative of some other element—for example, the sacred. But such a derivative status, although not logically impossible, contradicts the generally held intuition that the esthetic is a fundamental category of human experience independent of the sacred, an intuition substantiated by the existence of the arts as secular esthetic institutions. To avoid the apparent difficulty of encompassing the esthetic in the original event, we would be forced to declare it a secondary phenomenon for all eternity. This position seems to us indefensible, in particular given the enormous expansion of the esthetic domain in our own time.

The central object is not yet an art-object, that is, an object destined exclusively for esthetic contemplation. But this does not prevent us from referring to it as acting during the time of deferral as an esthetic object. The members of the group have, by means of the gesture of designation, placed the object on the momentarily inaccessible scene of representation. As they designate it, they perceive each other's designation, and their gesture thus becomes the first protolinguistic sign. But, at the same time, they observe the object, and not only perceive it but *contemplate* it. Contemplation has no doubt an appetitive function (keeping the object in sight in preparation for appropriation) as well as a purely representational or (proto)linguistic function (verification of the referent of the sign emitted by the others), but it exceeds the necessities of both these functions. And this, very simply, because these functions are essentially instantaneous—as defined, needless to say, in the context of human perception—whereas the contemplation has a certain duration, that of deferral. During this period, the object is separated from the desiring spectator not merely by a physical distance but by a communally instituted formal barrier that is the source of the explicit and permanent barrier that will later surround art-objects. It is not simply that the fear of retribution from the others makes the isolation of the object absolute, for transgression of the implicit interdiction is always at least conceivable. What is truly absolute is the distinction between the scene of representation as such and the real situation. So long as the object is contemplated *within* the scene of representation, this contemplation itself is not appetitive.

It is evident from the foregoing that desire and the esthetic are inseparable. Desire arises from the same contemplation of the object on the scene of representation that we have just spoken of as the original esthetic experience. But although the two categories of ex-

perience are and remain inseparable, they correspond to two different moments of the same experience. Esthetic contemplation is
inevitably accompanied by desire. But the specifically esthetic moment is the contemplation itself, in which not the "private" image
of desired satisfaction but the "public" image of the desire-object is
perceived. The desire that attaches to esthetic contemplation, however it may distort this public configuration, returns to it as its
guarantee, its formally objective correlative, in a characteristic oscillation of imaginary content. It is the equilibrium of this oscillation,
as opposed to the movement of desire from public to private, from
objective reality to subjective satisfaction, that characterizes the esthetic experience and for which specifically esthetic objects eventually come to be fabricated.

In the hypothesized originary event, we cannot distinguish between an esthetic and a desiring moment as such. This implies that
henceforth the two moments can never be wholly distinguished.
Our analysis of the phenomenon of "culture" will remain faithful to
this premise. There is, nevertheless, a difference of polarity that
accounts for the intuitively perceived difference between desire and
esthetic pleasure as well as for the specificity not only of art-objects
but of (commercial) desire-objects. For the time of deferral is followed in the minimal hypothesis by actual appropriation of the
object. Hence this period is bounded at the beginning by the temporary renouncement of appropriation that transforms the original
acquisitive gesture into one of representation, and at the end by a
resumption of appropriative activity. The period of deferral may
thus be said to be polarized by its two boundaries, and to constitute
in fact a transition from one to the other. At the beginning, inactive
contemplation replaces action; at the end, this transformation is reversed. At the beginning of the period, the relation to the object
may then be said to be primarily esthetic; the object's central place
on the scene of representation, in contradistinction to that of appetitive action, cannot be established prior to the imaginary prolongation of representation by desire. At the end, as the process is
reversed, the images of desire take precedence over the contemplation
of the object, with the result that this contemplation is abolished as
desire becomes the basis for what we shall call a *praxis* of appropriation.

Within the period of deferral we cannot define, even speculatively,
the private oscillation between contemplation and desiring imagination; the polarity thus established is demonstrable only at its end
points. (This objectification of the esthetic/desire polarity is a further

confirmation of the superiority of the minimal hypothesis over previous versions that posit an absolute discontinuity between the originary scene and appetitive object-relations.) This demonstration is, however, sufficient to account for the future institutional divergence between what we may call "worldly" desire and the esthetic. For this purpose, it is not necessary to distinguish each movement that composes the oscillation between the perceived object and the images of desire it provokes. For the precise nature of this oscillation, beyond the question of its mere existence or nonexistence, is not formalized, or indeed formalizable, in an institutional structure of representation.[5] It suffices that the polarity be present for esthetic contemplation to be, on the one hand, maintained as such within the scene of representation, and on the other, converted into a practical desiring imagination leading to a worldly praxis. The choice of one pole or the other depends on whether the desire-object is seen with respect to its potential for deferring mimetic conflict or for peaceful sharing of appetitive satisfaction. The differentiation of desire-objects, or more properly, objects of significance, will lead to the institutionalization of this polarity—for example, in the opposition between merely figurable transcendental divinities and their worldly—and edible—representatives.

Praxis and the Origin of the Exchange-System

We shall reserve the Aristotelian term *praxis* for "practical"—that is, humanly useful—actions performed on worldly objects and mediated by a system of representations. The act of the members of the original community in appropriating and sharing the desire-object is thus the originary praxial act. In praxis, desire is turned to practical use; its imaged satisfaction becomes a model for action.

This is an area where much has been made of prehuman accomplishments. The fabrication by higher apes of simple *ad hoc* tools (chimpanzees stripping branches of leaves to make termiting sticks), or their solution of simple practical problems (Köhler's ape discovering how to reach a suspended banana with a stick by using a box as a stepladder), or even such stereotyped activities as a cat's anticipating in his pounce the forward motion of the mouse have often been taken as proof that animals too are capable of formulating projects, and thus, presumably, of creating anticipatory images of future actions. We have no need to deny the possibility of an animal practical imagination of some kind. But what we do claim is that the human practical imagination, based as it is on the public scene of representation, is not merely vastly more powerful but contains an additional component essential to its functioning. The members of the nascent community, in transforming their impossible desire into the imaginary anticipation of the praxis of appropriation that follows the period of deferral, are not simply anticipating appetitive satisfaction. Their individual acts of appropriation are henceforth performed in the presence of the group as a whole. The desire-image as a praxis-model is continually modified not only by the individual's changing perception of the object but by his perception of the other members of the group as they likewise approach it.

Human praxis is not reducible to the formulation and execution of a (new or repeated) pattern of behavior; it is from the outset a *social* phenomenon. Its techniques are learned not from the simple imitation of others but through explicit cooperation with them. No doubt, a man placed in a cage with a box, a stick, and a banana hung out of reach would go about the appropriation of the banana in much the same way as Köhler's ape. But it is a mistake to see this situation, typical as it may be of animal practical thought, as equally typical of the human. If humans are capable of carrying out tasks far beyond the capacity of apes, it is not simply because they are more "intelligent" but because these tasks are conceived in the first place as communal ones. The original imaginations of desire are corrected continuously by the perception of the actions of the others. The ape learns few techniques from others, and this only by un-organized imitation; his greatest feats of intelligence are accomplished alone, and by chance transmitted to his fellows. Man, in contrast, even without taking into account the advantage conferred on him by his possession of systems of representation, possesses from the outset a sense of the potential danger in attempting to convert desire into praxis that makes him attentive to similar attempts on the part of others. Human praxis, even when carried out alone, is an essentially collective activity. In the original event, he who acts to realize his desire before the end of the period of deferral will be made all too well aware of the collective constraint on desire. But this constraint is also the source of a capacity for practical learning from others not comparable to mere appetitive mimesis.

The first praxis, according to our hypothesis, is the collective distribution of the desire-object. However unequal this division may in fact have been, it must have demonstrably reduced the level of violence from that provoked by immediate grasping for the object. Each individual can realize only partially his desire for the (whole) object, but as a result of his renouncement he is able to enjoy his portion of the object in communal peace. This sharing of the object is the first act of *exchange*.

We need not assume for our purpose here that any exchange of material objects (for example, pieces of meat) took place. The term "exchange" is justified nonetheless. It is no accident that communal sharing of this sort in ritual/sacrificial feasts is the focus of economic activity in many primitive societies, or that the origin of money in historical times can be traced to such rituals.[6] For already in the distribution of the object in the originary event, each individual's portion, taken with the accord of the others, becomes a socially legitimated piece of property with not merely a qualitative but a quantitative (or at least quantifiable) value. The comparability of these portions follows immediately from the communal presence in which the apportioning is carried out.

It is at this stage of our discussion of the original event that we leave the strict confines of the scene of representation. The actual consumption or appetitive use of the object, whether alimentary or, for example, sexual, is not a necessary element of the scene itself. The appropriative praxis and apportioning of the desire-object have been included in our minimal hypothesis because only thus can the scene acquire a selective value, the fundamental premise of such a hypothesis being that the scene of representation must have originally occurred as a temporary deferral of appetitive acts. Consumption, although the normal consequence of appropriation, is not its necessary conclusion; it can be delayed for a variety of reasons. Although the development of culture as we know it involves the elaboration of activities of consumption directly linked to the scene of representation—activities the anticipation of which will influence the later evolution of the scene itself—we cannot include these activities within our minimal hypothesis. The primary consequence of this exclusion is that the element of ritual that becomes associated with the scene as a result of its being carried to a consumptive conclusion—for example, the sacrificial feast—remains separable from it. The separability of the ritual element that characterizes our own secular experience is explicable only if it is posited at the outset; and we have just seen this to be a direct consequence of the minimal nature of the hypothesis.

MINIMALITY AND GENERATIVITY:
A NOTE ON EPISTEMOLOGY

It may well be objected that no obvious connection exists between the structure of an original hypothetical scene and the later evolution of human institutions. Since in any case we have no means of directly confirming the hypothesis, how can the inclusion or exclusion of specific elements serve as an explanation of phenomena such as "de-ritualization" that occur in historical time tens or hundreds of millennia after the originary event may be supposed to have taken place? This question becomes crucial in the case of ritual and the sacred, because it is not at all certain that these phenomena can be eliminated even from the most rigorously scientific discourse, not to speak of human representation taken as a whole. The relevance of this question to the "end" and possible future of culture is apparent; it may be expressed by such subsidiary questions as: Is a wholly nonritual culture possible? or: What is the place, if any, of the sacred in existing secular culture? But beyond the matter of ritual and the sacred is the more fundamental matter of the general epistemological foundation of our anthropological discourse.

To the naive reader, the hypothesis is merely a construct formulated as a substitute for an unknown reality. In this view, "had we been there," or could we somehow reproduce the origin of culture in the laboratory, as the origin of life may shortly be reproduced, the formulation of originary hypotheses would become unnecessary. What is lacking in this view is consideration for the fact that the phenomenon of representation, unlike that of life, cannot be transported to a scene other than its own. Our theory concerning the scene of representation takes place on that same scene, and even to speak of its "inherent limitations"—in comparison, for example, with divine intellect—is meaningless. The only means we have to conceive of this scene in itself—that is, as something other than the very scene on which we conceive it—is to imagine it in its nascent state—that is, as the locus of an act not yet representational but in the process of becoming so. The hypothesis we thus formulate cannot demonstrate the limits of representation, but it can provide for it a set of preconditions the plausibility of which may be verified by the examination of real institutions.

What distinguishes an anthropological hypothesis from a myth of origin, religious or heuristic, is that criteria are provided by which its plausibility may be determined. It is easy enough to postulate that language and custom were given to men by the gods, and whatever we may think of this explanation, history has shown that in most times and places it has been found altogether plausible. But a believer in such an explanation can give no reasons *why* he finds it plausible. Thus not only is it unfalsifiable—in any case, Popper's criterion cannot apply here directly—but its plausibility cannot even be compared with that of another explanation. For the believer, this transcendental explanation appears plausible-in-itself, founded on unquestionable, culturally significant representations. *Our* gods are the *real* ones because their significance has been demonstrated within our culture. This is an argument that can be refuted only within a discourse that holds no representations to be significant-in-themselves. And this plausibility can be measured only by the *minimality* of the hypothesis. This criterion alone suffices to confirm the intuition, present in all prescientific hypotheses—and in those scientific ones formulated before structuralist agnosticism discouraged social scientists from so doing—that the hypothesis must be *originary*.

The prestige of synchronic analysis in fields like linguistics has unfortunately terrorized several generations of thinkers into rejecting out of hand as unscientific the universal intuition that an institution is best explained at its origin. The search for the origin of life or of the cosmos, carried out by impeccably scientific biologists and astrophysicists, has only slowly begun to make its impact felt on the social sciences, always fearful of repeating the epistemological horrors of mythologists and precritical philosophers. But just as modern cosmologists need not shy away from the subjects of the speculations of the pre-Socratics, so modern anthropologists need not fear those of Vico or Rousseau. We would claim that if one thing is perfectly scientific about the speculations of philosophers, or even of the authors of Genesis, it is precisely the originary nature of the hypotheses they propose.

For to explain a structure of any kind by proposing a hypothesis of its origin is to minimalize this hypothesis with respect to the temporal existence of the structure. Before explaining a structure that has already maintained itself for a certain time, such a hypothesis explains it in its first moments, the younger structure being a lesser hypothetical object than the older. The simplicity of this truth can best be illustrated in the trivially minimal case where no particular hypothesis need be formulated because the "structure" in question is fully explicable in terms of already-accepted models. In that case, we do not even speak of a synchronic structure but of an *event* the course of which can be explained on the basis of previously existing theory. To demonstrate that nothing really new is involved, we explain away the *origin* of the phenomenon and thereby do away with the apparent substantiality of its historical reality. Reductionism is always at least implicitly diachronic.

Quite evidently, however, temporal minimalization is not a sufficient criterion of plausibility for a hypothesis. The new structure must be reduced as far as possible to preexistent structures, leaving only a minimal difference to be accounted for. The particular difficulty of the application of this criterion to human science is in the definition of this difference; for if man is defined, as we have defined him, by his use of representations, then the difference we are seeking is that of difference itself. The minimal difference of man is his capacity to create a minimal significant difference. We include here the second sense of Jacques Derrida's term *différance*—that of *deferral*.[7] The scene of representation differs from the real precisely because it defers the real, which is to say, the appetitive.

The minimality of a hypothesis is a universal touchstone of scientific epistemology (Occam's razor). But here it is not simply a matter, as in the natural sciences, of finding the simplest model that fits the data. Because we are attempting to explain the origin of significance, our hypothetical scene must take the form of a significant event—one that will be signified by its participants and held in memory through the preservation of its sign. To minimalize the hypothesis is to reduce to a minimum the significant elements of this event. But since, by the hypothesis, all representations are derived from this event either directly or by structural analogy (we may say, heuristically, by "metonomy" or "metaphor"), the minimal hypothesis will coincide with what are conceived at the time of its formulation to be the most general or universal features of representation.

Thus an originary hypothesis is not merely a heuristically efficient nominalist model in the spirit of Occam but a realist one—in short, an ontology. Any element that we include in our hypothesis is by this inclusion affirmed as an essential element of representation-in-general. In particular, to include a ritual or sacred element would be to affirm its permanent inseparability from the scene of representation. But our exclusion is not founded merely on the undesirability of this consequence. As soon as the minimality of the hypothesis is made a criterion of its plausibility, the insertion of the scene of representation into a prehuman appetitive context must correspond to a minimal time of deferral, and not, for example, to the indefinite deferral affirmed by the hypothesis of *The Origin of*

Language. We should note that the requirement of minimality also excludes the possibility of linking representation to the instinctual deferrals of animal ritual. If these genetically transmitted and, consequently, very slowly evolving methods could have sufficed for man, he would never have been obliged to invent representation. The latter can only come into being as a result of the breakdown of the instinctive constraints of animal ritual, in the crisis brought about by the return to a purely appetitive context. Mythical formulations of the originary hypothesis express the justified intuition that man's origin was revolutionary, not evolutionary.

2

The Universal Structures of
Human Culture

The hypothesis as here formulated includes as essential the elements of desire, esthetic contemplation, and exchange, in addition to the communal presence (form) and signifying gesture (content) of the scene of representation itself. It thus suggests a model of culture composed of language, art, and a system of socioeconomic exchange, but from which the element of ritual is absent. Yet no culture corresponding to this model has ever existed. Even the most advanced social systems of today have preserved sacred ritual forms. The model of culture of which we speak may perhaps appear plausible as a projection of present trends into the future. But the related projection of this model into the past, as a model for the original human community, must itself acquire plausibility. Because all known societies possess the category of the sacred, a secondary hypothesis must be formulated to explain its origin.

The inelegance of a second hypothesis is compensated for by its secondary character. Because ritual and the sacred are not situated within the original scene of representation, their origin takes place within culture as already constituted. The phenomenon of the sacred may thus be seen from without, as a feature of historically existing societies, but not necessarily of all future ones. What is thus created is a model of what might be called the "ritual epoch" in human history, corresponding to the period of traditional (preindustrial) society; modern society would then appear as a transitional phase toward a hypothetical "postritual" epoch. The interest of such a model lies less in its futurist implications than in its application to contemporary society, the essentially postritual character of which has often been affirmed, but nearly always in the perspective of a historical progressivism that situates religion at the beginning and science at the end of the historical continuum. In our theory, the scene of representation is a transhistorical constant that is inhabited by the sacred—or, more precisely, by the sacred/profane distinction—during a certain period of its existence. In contrast, the phenomenon of the esthetic, condemned by Hegel to the same ultimate *Aufhebung* as religion, is for us an essential element of the scene of representation. We have no need to excuse the esthetic's "prescientific" character, for the fundamental elements of the scene never change. To posit such a change, as progressivists naively do, is in effect to posit the existence within the course of human history of change of as great a magnitude as that in which our species originated. Progressivist gradualism is in reality a mask for a catastrophic anthropology that re-creates a new human species at the beginning of each historical era—an anthropology it shares with superficially so different pessimistic cyclical theories like that of Spengler.

We must be careful to distinguish between the fundamental *categories* of culture and its fundamental *institutions*. The scene of representation itself founds only one institution, that of language. The existence of esthetic contemplation does not require that of an esthetic institution (art), for the appetitive desire-object suffices to stimulate it. The institutional status of the system of exchange is, at first glance, more problematic. The original scene involves the establishment of no *institutions* of exchange; for this to be the case, the desire-object would have to be specified (say as a bison captured by a band of hunters) so that an institutional form of division could be defined. But, in effect, the problem vanishes if we refrain from fetishizing the notion of "institution" and examine the nature of the act of exchange, both in the original scene and in general.

For "exchange" can never be defined wholly in terms of a scene of representation. It is only in today's consumer society that such a conceptualization could ever be conceived. The exchange-system in the broadest sense may be said to include the totality of social interactions made possible by the existence of the scene of representation. But as a definition this would be too broad, since it would include the exchange of, for example, linguistic signs as well as of the material goods by which we would normally expect to define the notion of exchange. Yet although this definition is overbroad, any narrowing of it is in fact a subtraction and defines an institution only in a negative sense. Thus if we isolate the linguistic moment as alone fixed in significant memory—this is the consequence of our nonspecification of the desire-object—we define an institution of language, but only negatively one of exchange proper, as being the totality of the necessary nonlinguistic interactions that take place in the original event.

The evolution of human societies gives rise to a great variety of socioeconomic institutions. But the noncompleteness of exchange as such holds even for these institutions, even including the bourgeois market in which, for the first time, material exchange acquires an institutional framework independent of the wider sphere of social relations. This should not surprise us. For exchange, interaction, is not a purely cultural activity. Through it, individuals and groups acquire material goods that fill appetitive as well as cultural needs. Society as a whole may be looked on as an exchange process with nature, and the cultural exchange-system can only function so long as it retains an opening beyond the cultural to those human needs supplied by nature. There is no autonomous "scene of exchange" cut off from reality, even if the contemporary market in certain goods sometimes approximates such autonomy. Socioeconomic institutions serve primarily to protect the central scene of representation, which is also that of nonconflictive mutual presence, from the external and potentially disruptive factor of appetitive need.[1] The essential openness or nonautonomy of these institutions, in contrast with the formally defined autonomy of the scene of representation, is already prefigured in the original event.

THE SECONDARY HYPOTHESIS: RITUAL AND THE SACRED

The primary or minimal hypothesis has produced only one formally defined institution—that of language. Esthetic contemplation is established, but not art. Could not then the sacred be conceived as being in this regard like the esthetic, already present in the original scene of representation, but in the absence of its institutional framework, that is, ritual? But it is necessary to avoid drawing facile analogies between the fundamental categories of culture. If the sacred were altogether analogous to the esthetic, it would simply be identical with it. This "analogy" may, however, serve to suggest a point of departure. The source of the sacred in the original event is the *significance* of the designated object. In the event itself, this significance, as opposed to the *signification* of the designating sign, is not institutionalized. The sign suffices to defer the appropriation of the object and thus to avert conflict. Significance is here not a human

institution but a feature of the object-world to be reacted to. In this
perspective, a deliberate repetition of the event would be inconceivable; it is the sign that would be repeated on the reappearance of a
significant object, such as could only occur in a similar collective
context (else the object would not be significant). We shall then define
the origin of ritual as the first repetition, not merely of the sign, but
of the event. In such a repetition, the originally significant object is
sacralized, that is, comes to be considered sacred.

But a definition is not yet a hypothesis. The question thus arises
as to what criteria to use in formulating an appropriate hypothesis
of the origin of ritual and the sacred. We may assume that the
secondary hypothesis must obey the same criterion of minimality
as the first. This suggests that we should situate the origin of the
sacred at the first—involuntary—recurrence of the original event,
on which occasion the original sign of designation will itself be—
voluntarily—repeated. But this apparently simple formulation is not
without its difficulties.

For one may object in principle to the minimality of this secondary
hypothesis. If the advantage of the original hypothesis lies in its
rigorous limitation to the minimal originary conditions for the scene
of representation, any such rigor is lost in a secondary hypothesis
that no longer finds its justification in this scene. For why should
ritual rather than, say, art or sociopolitical organization appear precisely at this second moment? How do we know what is second and
what third? Or if we answer this objection by claiming to deduce
the secondary position of the sacred from the originary hypothesis
itself, then we make the sacred a necessary consequence of this
hypothesis, which contradicts our previous exclusion of the sacred
from its minimality.

Our only way out of this dilemma is a *distinguo* that meets both
these objections at the same time. We must show that the sacred is
a necessary yet separable consequence of the original hypothesis. In this
case, the necessity is a feature, not of the scene of representation *as
such*—for this indeed would contradict our minimal hypothesis—
but of its originary, minimal *context*. Separability would follow from
the fact that this context, in contrast with the scene as such, does
in fact evolve. But in order to make such a claim, we must give a
more rigorous definition of the context of the scene of representation
at any given time.

In constructing this definition, we would do better to look to the
end rather than the beginning. It is, after all, only in our own time
that human societies have begun to do without the sacred. Today's

exchange-system has become at least conceivably capable of taking over the function, formerly carried out by religious institutions, of protecting the social order against the dangers of desire. This suggests that it is the absence of any such system in the original event that necessitates the introduction of the sacred, or, inversely, that the nascent element of desire produces effects outside the original scene itself that can only be controlled through this introduction.

In the original event, the desire of the participants was at least partially satisfied through the division of the object; and the same result may be presumed to obtain in recurrences of the event in which the sign and its attendant deferral are repeated. But significant memory retains not merely the deferring function of the sign but also its referent, lacking which we could not indeed speak of a sign. Desire for the referent will thus tend to arise outside the original context. The appetite satiated in that context will recur as desire that cannot be satisfied by the object itself but only by its renewed presence on the public scene of representation. The remembered significance of the object on this scene makes its reintroduction— or, rather, its *reproduction*—on the scene an object of desire. The original event will thus not simply recur but be reproduced. This outcome is, indeed, intuitively obvious, given the referential nature of the sign. The sign is created on the scene of representation, but it refers to an object in the world outside, so that the reproduction of the sign on the scene entails the reproduction of a worldly event. For this not to be the case, the world of desire-objects would have to be drawn as a whole into the scene of representation. But this cannot occur at the beginning but only at the end of the process of humanization begun in the original event.

The sign, reproduced on the scene of representation, suffices to effect the deferral of appropriation of the designated desire-object and thereby to avoid conflict. *But the reproduction of the event as a whole takes place not on the scene of representation but in the real world.* It is this reproduction that we call ritual, and the status of the object in it, sacred.

We immediately observe that this hypothesis is minimal, for it presupposes only the reproduction of the original event. The reproduction of the *sign* cannot itself suffice; for if it did, the scene of representation would have no independent status, and the sacred would, in effect, become part of the originary hypothesis itself.[2] It remains only to justify our definition of the terms "ritual" and "sacred" by demonstrating their compatibility—or, more precisely, their continuity—with our historical understanding.

In *The Origin of Language*, we made much of the distinction between our "formal" theory of representation and the "institutional"
theory of Girard, which took, not the emission of a gestural sign,
but the contemplation of the body of the emissary victim as the first
act of representation. As we have remarked above, this distinction
was no doubt adequate for the elaboration of a theory of language,
but it failed to meet the criterion, essential to the discussion of
culture, of rigorously distinguishing between the significant and the
sacred. In the present discussion, the "institutional" reproduction of
the original event has itself become the object of an independent
secondary hypothesis. As distinct from the reproduction of a sign,
the collective reproduction of a significant event takes place in a
world not representational but real, inhabited not by tokens of the
same sign but by independently existing things.

Whereas the repeated sign is economical of time and effort and
is transparent to its object—qualities that we merely allude to as
requiring no demonstration—worldly events require time and effort
and are significant in themselves, that is, without *signifying* anything
else. These, indeed, are the qualities we normally associate with
ritual, including most particularly the "meaninglessness" we tend to
attribute to it—the pejorative sense of the term reflecting our modern
impatience with cultural institutions other than systems of representation *stricto sensu*.

Our notion of the sacred is even simpler to justify. It suffices to
note that an object becomes sacred when it is the essential central
element of a ritual. Sacrality, as we well realize today in our capacity
as heirs of Judeo-Christian iconoclasm or deritualization, is a paradoxical status that can never be justified or even made plausible
through logicoscientific discourse. (This is very different from attempting to explain the origin of the sacred in logicoscientific discourse.) For, on the one hand, the sacred object is a worldly object,
and on the other, it is conceived as belonging to a world apart, as
functioning upon "another scene" which is not, however, simply
that of representation but that of real presence.

The necessity of reproducing a temporal event rather than a quasi-
atemporal sign is the source of this paradoxicality, which makes
explicit the implicit paradox of desire. For the sacred object must
be in reality what the desire-object is only imagined to be: both the
central object of a real public scene and an indefinitely reproducible
significance. The worldly reality of the sacred object, as opposed to
the purely "scenic" representative one of the sign, is its ineluctably
problematic feature. The transcendentality of the sacred that is a

virtually linear function of the evolutionary level of a culture by no means casts doubt on the validity of this assertion; on the contrary, even the term "otherworldly" serves to confirm it. For the banishment of sacred objects or beings to a transcendental other world is only a more extreme form of the real-world separation of the sacred from the profane that is rigorously practiced in primitive societies and that made so profound an impression on Durkheim and his school. Otherworldly sacred things are not "ideal"; they are real *somewhere else*. As the expansion of the system of exchange turns all worldly objects into profanely manipulable entities, the sacred acquires another world, invisible and yet more real than this one. The specific nature of this departure of the sacred and the concomitant rise of nonritual morality will constitute the fundamental determinant of cultural evolution.

The foregoing should suffice to establish the crucial distinction between the sacred and the significant. Some doubt may nevertheless arise, now that the reality of the institutional, ritually sacred object has been evoked, as to whether the signifying objects of the scene of representation are not equally real—whether, in a word, we have not merely done away with the theological in order better to defend the metaphysical. For signs too are real and material, and Plato's Ideas (or Saussure's *signifiés*) are as paradoxical as any sacred object. But our hypothesis is not indeed vulnerable to such doubts, for it does not depend on the ideality of the sign but simply on its accessibility and easy reproducibility. Not only our original hypothetical "aborted gesture" but all linguistic signs are characterized by the facility with which they may be generated by the individual. This facility is of course only relatively greater than that of reproducing the desire-object itself; it is still a worldly quality. But this great though relative difference leads to the creation of different types of human relations. The imagined sign is not the sign itself, but the ease of production of the latter makes it virtually always producible when it is imagined, whereas the rarity of objects capable of generating an appetitive interest sufficient to bring about the original event makes the distance between desiring imagination and reproduction a genuine barrier to the realization of such desire. The scene of representation, even as imagined, requires a physical substrate (that is, the neurons of the brain) and occupies time; but this scene nevertheless maintains itself as an "atemporal" structure because, in the normal course of things, its operation is reversible, costing so little time and energy to maintain that these need never hinder its functioning.[3]

One might wish to claim for the sake of argument that, insofar as signs are material entities, the act of producing them is a kind of "minimal ritual." In this perspective, the elaboration of sentence-forms permitting the construction of original (and thus nonritual) utterances might be explained as the result of the joining together of a series of preexisting ritual elements. But if we give up the originary distinction between the scene of representation and the scene of ritual, then we must renounce not only the minimality of our theory of representation (which is, in effect, to deny the theory's claim to serve as the foundation of an anthropology) but the very notion of minimality and, with it, of scientific anthropological discourse. For the minimality of our theory reflects that of the hypothesized event. If we assimilate the representation of the desire-object by a sign to the repetition of the event in which this object appears, then we forgo any possibility of understanding human representation (except perhaps as a Skinnerian set of conditioned "associations"). But as soon as we admit this distinction, then we must admit the anteriority of representation, since the deliberate repetition of an event is possible only as the result of an internal representation of it. (If the repetition is not deliberate, there is no point in speaking of ritual.) In a nutshell, representation can occur within a single first event, whereas reproduction requires a second.

THE ETHICAL

We have delayed until now the discussion of the ethical as a distinct category of the original event in consideration of the intimate relation between the ethical and the sacred. The whole of this analysis of culture is nonetheless founded on the presupposition that this relation is a secondary one—that secular culture may replace sacred culture in its central ethical function because the link between representation and ethics is anterior to the sacred.

The ethical in the broadest sense includes the entire domain of human interaction. In this sense, every significant phenomenon has its ethical dimension. It is, however, possible to give a more rigorous definition of the ethical from the standpoint of the originary hypothesis. The moment of the gesture of designation is the moment of formation of a human community, defined by the mutual presence of its members. We may then define ethical acts as those that are specifically intended to preserve this communal presence. In the light of this definition, the original aborted gesture does not qualify as an ethical act. It is motivated by the common fear of violence, that is, of the breakdown of the heretofore existing cooperation among the members of the group. But it cannot have for its aim the preservation of the community, for the simple reason that the community does not yet exist. This is not a mere matter of definition. The fear of violence is common but not communal; its only motivation in each individual is self-preservation. Conversely, once the community exists in the mutual presence brought about by the sign, no particular act need be performed to preserve it. The first act to which we might attribute an ethical motivation is, rather, the distribution of the desire-object. But this motivation is, in fact, ambiguous; the care taken to preserve mutual presence cannot be attributed to interest in this presence itself as a *collective* value because each individual, in maintaining the presence, maintains at the same time his own safety. The origin of the exchange-system requires no reflection on its communal value.

The absence of explicitly ethical motivations from the originary event is, in effect, a direct consequence of the minimality of the hypothesis. The minimal human institution being the scene of representation, the event that creates it can give rise to no explicitly ethical consideration because on the scene of representation no ethical problems exist. The scene regulates interaction by deferring it, not by reflecting on it. The ethic of representation as such is merely implicit, and why indeed should it become explicit if representation suffices to prevent potential conflict? And this consequence carries through even to the distribution that concludes the hypothetical event. The mutual presence inaugurated by the designating gesture is maintained beyond the termination of that gesture and the resumption of appropriative activity, but this presence remains dependent on the originally designated object. This is sufficient to establish the scene of representation but not that of worldly human interaction.

The ethical thus becomes an explicit category only at the moment of the secondary hypothesis, when the originary event becomes the object of (ritual) repetition. Here communal presence becomes the motivation for the reproduction of this event. It may appear odd that we find the origin of the ethical in the "meaningless" ritual reproduction of acts that were originally independently motivated. But we must not equate the ethical with the categorical imperative. We should, rather, take an evolutionary view of ethics, ending but not beginning with the perfect reciprocity of the mature Judeo-Christian system. The first ethical acts are then, not surprisingly, the least free. But we should not let the unfreedom of ritual hide its ethical content. The communal effort to repeat the act that gave birth to the community may be motivated by a sum of individual selfish desires, but each specific act of each individual is nevertheless mediated by a concept of the community as a whole—a "concept" that at this stage is no more than an image that demands reproduction. Which is to say that the "irrationally" constrained nature of ritual reflects, not the absence of an ethical conception, but merely the limitations of such a conception. The ethical act, whether or not constrained by a concrete model, must first and foremost be guaranteed to contribute to the construction of the community. In the primitive case, this guarantee attaches to only a single act: the original event, repeated as ritual.

At this point we encounter what appears to be a serious objection to our relegation of ritual and the sacred to the second stage of cultural originarity. For if the ethical element of culture is from the beginning realized only in ritual, how can we speak of an eventual elimination of the sacred from the domain of our analysis? How, following our own concept of originarity, can the ethical become independent of the sacred? And why should the progress of the ethical be associated with the decline of the sacred rather than the contrary? What indeed has been gained by splitting the originary hypothesis in two in order to isolate a scene of representation independent of ethics? For ethics is, after all, at the very heart of culture. One can maintain little respect for those who exalt the autonomy of systems of representation while gleefully affecting to observe the dissolution of the human Subject.

We have deliberately posed these questions in terms that the critical reader may find naive. Epistemologically speaking, they have for the most part already been answered, but it is worth taking a new look at the scene of representation from an ethical standpoint. For we have never doubted the primacy of the ethical, and the purpose of the present examination of culture is to clarify it and, it is hoped, to reinforce it.

The most important consideration to keep in mind, here and throughout our exposition, is that the different categories of culture relate differently to institutions and should not be treated as incarnate in them. Language, the direct heir of the original scene of representation, is institutional in its very nature, and whatever the future of human society, it would be inconceivable without an institutionalized language. This is not, however, the case for the ethical. The evolution of religion, particularly that encompassed within the Judeo-Christian tradition, has itself shown that as the ethical becomes conceptualized, it continually enters into opposition with institutions that express less advanced ethical conceptions. The evolution of religions is a continual deritualization, a rejection of institutionalized acts in favor of acts motivated by an internalized ethos such as that expounded in the Gospels.

It is important to understand, however, why the revelation of the purely human ethic of "love thy neighbor as thyself" could not lead to the simple abolition of ritual. Ethical conceptions as we define them do not exist merely as representations. They must correspond to a possible practical means for preserving the human community, which is always the primary ethical goal—as opposed, in particular, to the often contrary dictates of moral precepts. The end of the Judeo-Christian evolution occurred precisely when the Judaic ethical tradition was transformed by the early Christians into a universal abstract morality. It is our contention that the subsequent "regression" to an institutionalized Christianity was not in fact a regression at all but a new stage in the evolution of the ethical, in which the worldly realizations of this ideal morality became an explicit ethical—that is, social—goal. And we further contend that modern consumer society, far from a monstrous materialist aberration, is the highest level yet attained of this very same realization. We shall not here attempt a rigorous demonstration of these contentions. We make use of them in order to make the following point: On the highest level of ethical evolution, the entire society would function according to the morality of universal reciprocity announced in the Gospels, so that the very notion of ethical *institutions* would be unthinkable. This is the "realm of freedom" conceived by the German Idealist philosophers, whose extrapolations from the social conditions of their own day, like those of their socialist and communist heirs, unfortunately lacked any concrete insight into this realm's conceivable institutional base.

The original ethical institution, as defined in the secondary hypothesis, is the most constraining because it permits the smallest possible range of ethical acts. Only one past act having qualified as ethical, the first ritual can only repeat it. The overall trend toward the deinstitutionalization of ethics, which passes through stages in which the multiplication of "ethical" (that is, ritual) acts leads to the expansion of ritual institutions, is a generally accepted feature of human history. But there still remains to be answered the question, more pertinent to our theory, of the contribution to this evolution of the ethical made by the scene of representation as defined in the originary hypothesis. The reader will not be surprised to learn that we claim for it the determining role.

The original scene of representation has ethical *consequences* without a specifically ethical aim. This is, in fact, the only possible hypothesis that explains the future evolution of the ethical. For were an ethical aim present from the beginning, as it is in ritual, the consequences, foreseen in advance, would furnish no material for a new synthesis. Were the scene of representation ritual from the beginning—and this is, as we have just shown, the only way it could conceivably be ethical—it could not evolve but only degenerate, as ritual always does, through banalization and the consequent loss of significance of its effects. Ritual cannot itself create new conceptions of the ethical or indeed of anything else, for it conveys no new information and indeed only loses through repetition the cognitive value it originally derived from the ethical conception that inspired it. New "information"—that is, a newly formalized content—can only be produced upon a scene of representation that remains in essence devoid of ethical preconceptions. The scene of representation, in a word, is a scene of truth, and truth, although not an ethical value per se, is the source of all ethical progress. It is thus no accident that Girard's "institutional" hypothesis, which begins with ritual and treats representation as ancillary to it, cannot explain ethical evolution save through divine intervention.

But our contemporary experience shows us that the relation of the scene of representation to the preservation of the community is not limited to the accumulation of information and to the elaboration of new ethical concepts. Today, human interactions are mediated by increasingly elaborate systems of representation the elements of which include, as Jean Baudrillard has astutely observed, the "product signs" of the consumer society.[4] It is precisely in these systems that we observe the progress of the ethical in modern society. As against the abstract moral reciprocity of the "golden rule" and the Gospels, the interactional structure of modern society, although imperfect and lacking in an adequate theory of its own accomplishments, not only provides a relatively high level of basic welfare for all but allows vast opportunities for individual creativity and self-realization. These values belong to an open ethical system as opposed to the closed one of abstract morality. The capacity of the exchange-system to absorb and to convert into socially functional praxis the desires of its members may be measured not only negatively, by the degree to which it rids itself of ritual constraints, but positively, by the extent to which each individual's career within the system permits the full utilization of what we may call his or her "creative potential," a potential that is exercised primarily on the scene of representation.

From this perspective, the scene may be seen as from the beginning the locus of such creativity. For the sign is not merely a means of deferral but, as the term *différance* makes clear, the instrument of an act of cognition that is never collective but, in each case, individual. The community thereby preserved is not a faceless communality but a group of distinct possessors of their own private model of the public scene of representation. The ethical contribution of representation is thus a historical movement toward a reciprocity which morality can only understand in abstract or, more properly, in figural terms, but the ethical reality of which evolves through a continual increase in the complexity of its mediations. We refer to the "figural" terms of morality because, in its highest expressions ("love thy neighbor as thyself"), it can only refer to social relations by means of the figure of intimate relations. "Love" is an inadequate formulation of an ethic because it offers at best an abstract model of social interaction. It is the exchange-system, as rendered significant through systems of representation, that must carry the burden of offering concrete models for the relations that are the real substance of ethics. And it is not unfair to remark that none of the theoreticians that share the fashionable contempt for the values of contemporary society—as though this contempt released them from the culpability of their membership in it—can create even the most skeletal model of an authentic ethic. One wonders why no one since Marx has even attempted to work out with any rigor the basic structures of such a model. Might it be that the so profoundly despised "bourgeois" society has proved itself more intelligent than the intellectuals? that social theory is paying with irrelevance for its arrogant disrespect for social reality?

"CULTURE" AND THE ORIGIN OF ESTHETIC INSTITUTIONS

The closing remarks of the preceding section should not be taken to imply that, the present-day exchange-system having solved or being on the point of solving the fundamental ethical problems of the human community, the examination of its antecedents in traditional cultural forms is at best of antiquarian interest. Were this the case, this work would never have been written. It is rather our conviction that "culture" in the narrow sense is the most problematic element of modern society up to the present day and that the understanding of this element holds the key to the successful ethical functioning of the exchange-system in the future. Human science, which must be, as we have attempted to show, a radically originary science, is in this view a necessary element of contemporary culture the importance of which will continue to grow in the future. The "Copernican revolution" we are attempting to promote in the social sciences reflects the necessary transformation of these sciences from marginal to centrally significant pursuits. The desultory, empirical character they possess in their present-day state is a reflection of their past but not their future role. In a word, the only possible culture of the future must be founded on a genuinely scientific anthropology. The study of culture is itself a fundamental and urgently required element of culture.

But what then is the relationship between "culture" and human society in general? Why, if the exchange-system can indeed absorb and make functional our desiring imagination, do we still have need of cultural objects? These questions can only be answered rigorously in the framework of the originary hypothesis, which we must now apply to the formation of specifically "cultural"—that is, esthetic— institutions.

There can be little doubt that the various forms of secular art derive originally from ritual. Yet, as we have seen, the esthetic contemplation of the desire-object is a necessary element of representation that precedes the sacralization of this object in ritual. Ritual does not invent the esthetic, only its institutional form. Thus the emergence of art as an institution independent of ritual is preceded by the emergence within ritual of objects and activities that we may already qualify as esthetic.

Our minimal definition of a ritual act was the repetition of the original event—that is, the formation of the scene of representation. Now although a *sign* is repeatable by definition, an *event* is only repeatable "within limits." The formalization of ritual will consist in the definition of these limits, by which the reproduced event will be judged as in conformity or not with the sacred original. This judgment may involve extrinsic and unpredictable criteria, dependent, for example, on the success or failure of other communal enterprises; students of primitive religion are well familiar with the "ritual logic" that governs such judgments. But what interests us here is not the ultimate form of the ritual but its original model. In reproducing the original event, the participants are acting in accordance with their remembered images of that event; they are performing an act of *esthetic mimesis*. We are justified in using the term "esthetic" because this act is not the mere imitation of the behavior, appropriative or not, of another, but the reproduction on the public scene of representation of an image of past experience.

We have derived the sacred nature of the ritual act from the necessity of a representation that is at the same time a real, worldly act. But by the same token, this act presents itself to public condemnation as the *figure* of a remembered act. This contemplation remains combined with participation; we have no need to posit pure spectators of the ritual scene. But the acts of the group as perceptible by its members provoke the same oscillation between perceived image and imaginary projection by which we have characterized the esthetic in the original event. This mutual observation promotes at the same time a direct behavioral mimesis that creates the familiar rhythmic order of ritual. Even to say "at the same time" is insufficient, however, for esthetic and behavioral mimesis are inextricable. To reproduce the image of presence is to imitate the others present—to imitate not a sign but a real act that becomes thereby defined to the group as sacred.

The genesis of the sacred, from this perspective, is a hypostasis or fetishization of the esthetic. For the process of sacralization as here described is the "recuperation" by the community of what was in the first place an esthetic image. The sacred as such is *no longer* esthetic; its acts and materials are not images but realities. But the "as such" of the sacred, its *being*, can never be objectively established. The sacred is such only to believers or, in our scene, to participants. The objective observer sees only the figures of what Malraux called the *musée imaginaire*, a frontierless world of esthetic objects from which all sacrality has been bleached out. And, in any case, the ritual reproduction of the sacred must inevitably pass through an esthetic stage where the being of past rituals is re-created as an image to be imitated.

We have thus far refrained from making any specific mention of the appetitive object that stands in the center of ritual. This was done in accordance with the minimality of our hypothesis, in order to demonstrate the generally esthetic nature of ritual figuration. Only thus may ritual without an appetitive center be made conceivable. For it suffices that the central desire-object of the original event be *figured*, and nothing in our hypothesis requires that this figure be itself appetitive. The central object of ritual is a figure like any other ritual element. But the analysis of ritual as figuration requires an examination of the specific problems posed by this object. We have not yet provided a description of the category of ritual figuration. It is, in fact, only after this description has been completed that we may abstract in good conscience from the appetitive center. But it is worth observing how much may be described without specific reference to this center: everything, indeed, except the transcendental notion of originarity from which will derive the self-consciousness and eventual deritualization of ritual, its "fall" into myth and fiction.

For the central object, unlike the other elements of the originary event, cannot simply be *repeated;* it must be *substituted for.* Whatever may be the case for these other elements, the appetitive nature of the object makes this substitution a radical necessity.[5] But the extreme attractiveness that provoked the noninstinctual deferral of the original event can only be a quality of rare, not to say exceptional, desire-objects, such as could not in principle be readily reproduced.[6]

At this point in our exposition we must be particularly careful to avoid substituting for reasoning the presentation of intuitively plausible "scenarios." Rather than attempt to speculate on the possible forms that might have been taken by originary ritual substitution, we only posit awareness of the figurality of the substituted object, that is, of its nonidentity with its originary model. This suffices to explain the historicity of the sacred, the reference to an originary model *in illo tempore* that characterizes its every manifestation. The substituted real object is sacred only to the extent that it shares the reality of—"incarnates"—the original object. Historicity is no doubt present in the whole of ritual, but in the central object it is grounded in the objectal nature, the thingness, of the object. For not only can, for example, an original gesture be repeated more or less identically, but its conative nature makes the performer's image of the earlier gesture more subject to the influence of his present performance than can be the case with a reproduced object. What is crucial about the object is its radical otherness with respect both to the individual members of the group and to their everyday appropriative activities. The figurality of the substituted object is the most external, most visible figurality, as well as the one that determines the success of the entire process. The nature of the ritual act makes the substituted object the center of a contemplation that is at the same time a deferral of all appropriative activity. Unlike the other elements of ritual, this contemplation is radically nonparticipatory or, in the terms of our definition, wholly esthetic.

It would not be difficult to find empirical motivations for the specific manifestations of figurality with which we are all familiar, in particular for tropes or "figures," which term is only a further confirmation of their visual, iconic rather than linguistic origin. This temptation must be resisted, however, lest we fall into the familiar mythical (and anthropological) procedure of offering "natural" explanations for man's cultural creations. Our defense against this danger is to cling to the minimality of our hypothesis, to situate our explanation as far as possible within the bounds of our original and, following it, our reproduced scene of representation.

Within this scene, the figural, however it may manifest itself, is in the first place a *functional* category: the substituted object, and *a fortiori* the other ritual elements, function in the same way as did their originals. Functionality is the only absolute criterion of figurality. In the hypothetical context, this is a mere tautology, although theories of rhetoric, which do not in general refer to such a context, have spent themselves in intricate but sterile systems of unmotivated categories as a result of the ignorance of this fact.[7] The crucial problem of a theory of the figure is rather that of deriving the fundamental figural categories from our hypothesis alone. Differentiated figural categories can arise only as the product of differentiated guarantees of the success—and thereby of the "authenticity"—of the reproduction of the original event.

Now an appetitive attractiveness identical with that of the original desire-object is certainly one such guarantee. We say "certainly" because, at the very least, reproduction of the originary event centered on such an object must lead to the same degree of appetitive satisfaction that made the event successful in the first place. Here there is no need to refer to ethical considerations as part of the guarantee of the reproduced event, even if such considerations may have been paramount in motivating the reproduction. If the desire to reproduce the communal presence of the original event leads not only to the reproduction of this presence but to that of the appetitive satisfaction as well, ritual becomes a most unproblematic activity.

But were this the case, then there would be no point in speaking of figurality at all, or even of historicity. The ritual community would become and remain a utopia. It may be objected that we are abstracting from the tendency of the desiring imagination to seek ever greater satisfactions, or simply to recall past satisfactions as always more complete than objectively similar present ones, so that an impossible inflation of appetitive pleasure would be required to maintain such a utopia. But this objection, founded on an empirical psychology of desire incompatible with the minimality of the hypothesis, is altogether beside the point, because we are here referring not to objective but to *functional* identity. We thus have no need to refer at this point to a psychology of desire that would in any case only confirm our thesis that a more narrowly defined concept of figurality is necessary. Rather than being the source of the historicity of the sacred, these Faustian or nostalgic tendencies of desire are better seen as derivatives of it—as dependent, in other words, not on the scene of representation alone but on that of the secondary hypothesis as well.

Let us suppose, then, that an object of equal appetitive attractiveness is not available for the ritual reproduction of the original event. As we have just seen, this supposition involves no real loss of generality. We may even make the stronger statement that it is implied by the very existence of the secondary hypothesis. For the mere reproduction of the original scene centered on an object of equal appetitive satisfaction would not require the construction of a secondary hypothesis. It is, after all, the need to reproduce the *ethical*, not the *appetitive*, element of the original event that we have made the basis for the secondary hypothesis. The secondary supposition that we have introduced into our original hypothetical model is precisely that the creation of the scene of representation makes it no longer possible for the protohuman community to endure without the reproduction of the communal presence inaugurated in the original event. The supplementary content of this assertion with respect to the originary hypothesis concerns the desire generated by the scene of representation in its relationship with the precultural system of appetitive distribution existing within the society. What we have in fact affirmed is the inadequacy of this system to satisfy the newly generated desire. (Within this inadequacy is contained the possibility of the violent crises that Girard has postulated as the cause of the originary event.) Even if (as we have no reason to suppose) the ritual utopia described once existed, it must eventually have come to an end, for it exists no more. Thus a narrower category of figurality must have come into being. We may call this category "essential figurality," since the guarantee provided by the figure must replace at least in part the appetitive satisfaction given by the original object.

It is within the category of essential figurality that the familiar differentiation of figures takes place. The figural object can resemble its original only through the possession of common perceptible attributes, which there is no a priori reason to classify into categories. But as soon as we consider the specific problems of reproducing different kinds of attributes, a dichotomy appears between being and action, between the stable qualities of the object and its temporal modifications. For to the extent that a reproduction of the object must be *fabricated*, the problem of imitating its stable visual appearance may be dealt with in advance, whereas that of imitating actions requires direct human participation in the course of the action itself. Thus if, in accordance with our secondary hypothesis, the necessity of such fabrication is assumed, the figural will become dichotomized into the domains of the *iconic*, where the (two- or three-dimensional) appearance of the object is reproduced, and the *dramatic*, in which a human or animal plays its role in the original event. And we do in fact observe the universal existence in ritual of both elements, either separately or, in what would appear the most primitive case, combined (for example, in masked or costumed human performers).

Thus we need not posit the existence in man of an "esthetic impulse" or "creative urge." The determining factor of ritual fabrication is the same as that of ritual itself: the communal need, generated by the introduction of the scene of representation and of the desiring imagination that reproduces it in each individual, for the nonconflictive, deferring presence of the original event. The fabrication of a substitute ritual object in the absence of a (presumably rare) object of equal appetitive value with the original presupposes only that the ritual function of the substituted object was enhanced by an esthetically observable similarity to its original, independently of its appetitive qualities, which would in any case only come into play later on. Once an imaginary scene of representation exists, the only new assumption required to explain the existence of the various forms of esthetic mimesis is the communal (and, eventually, the private) functionality—not, in the first place, of these forms (this would be circular) but of the scene itself. The first ritual "artworks" may have involved found objects, perhaps nonconsumed but visible relics of the original (for example, tusks or antlers). Dramatic figuration, which is ultimately of greater cultural significance than iconic, requires no artifacts at all, merely the awareness that the central desire-object in ritual is a role that must be played.

The birth of the various esthetic domains—music, dance, the figurative arts, drama, and so forth—in ritual is not yet their establishment as independent artistic institutions. These later-appearing institutions may thus justly be said to be derivatives of ritual. But what is less often noted is the dependency of ritual, not, to be sure, on art, but on the esthetic. Nor is it possible to object that this

dependency is merely a product of an overly broad or abstract definition of esthetic contemplation. Certainly, the nonparticipant views
ritual as a fundamentally esthetic phenomenon, from the masks and
fetishes of the *musée imaginaire* to the biblical legends recited in syn-
agogues and churches. The esthete will explain this as the result of
an evolution *toward* the esthetic as a higher or "freer" form than the
sacred, but this affirmation, although true on the level of cultural
institutions, is irrelevant to the explanation of how the elements *we*
view as esthetic actually function in ritual. It is inelegant and misleading to posit the existence of an esthetic faculty, or even of a
religious faculty. The only "faculty" required is that of representation, for the origin of which we have provided a maximally plausible hypothesis. The sacred, to be sure, is not equivalent to the
esthetic, but it is *more*, not *less*, than the esthetic.

It is in adding to esthetic representation the ultimately indefensible requirement of reality that the sacred is less free than the
esthetic proper. The point is not that the ritual participant is less
sensitive than we to the beauty of his dance or of his mask, but that
he cannot distinguish, as we can, between this beauty and the real
presence of the original event he is imitating. And this not because
of the confusions of the "primitive mind" but because he has not
yet acquired a conception of the community—an ethic—independent of the communal presence realized in the ritually reproduced
event. As we shall maintain throughout, the independent variable
of historical evolution is not the economic, nor the technical, nor
indeed the esthetic, but the ethical. The only meaningful sense of
the word "progress" is as ethical progress; and it is this sense that
in fact prevails when we speak of the progress from the constraint
of ritual to the freedom of art.

3

Anthropology and the
Logic of Representation

The purpose of this chapter is to demonstrate the limited, regional nature of formal models of representation with respect to their anthropological basis. We shall argue that such models, be they mathematical, logical, or, more generally, philosophical, cannot avoid triviality without introducing an element of incompleteness that can only be recuperated by reference to the anthropological basis they have sought to eliminate.

The limits of nonanthropological "logics of representation" become particularly visible at a time when models of artificial intelligence are not merely being theorized about but are actually being constructed. For, once the possibility of mechanically manipulating already-existing representations has been accepted, the nature of (human or mechanical) intelligence must be defined more sharply with regard to what occurs prior to this manipulation, that is, the creation of the representations themselves. Given the metaphysical bias of contemporary science, it is not surprising that discussion of this subject has never to our knowledge taken an anthropological perspective. The fact that man is the only creature to have created systems of representation, including those used in computers, cannot be given its proper due so long as the existence of representation is treated as a nonproblematic analogue of precultural coding systems. Without a theory to explain the origin of representation the only time it actually occurred, it is impossible even to define what it would mean for a form of artificial intelligence to originate its own representations rather than have them written or stamped in by independently intelligent beings.[1]

Discussions of the artificial-intelligence problem[2] are confined within the same empirical-mystical dichotomy as are the theories of language origin that lack an evenemential hypothesis; if machines are substituted for prehumans, the arguments are in fact the same. On the one hand, the defenders of artificial intelligence claim that any function of human intelligence can be duplicated by machine—that, in other words, there is only a *relative* difference that can gradually be eliminated. On the other, their opponents affirm, on the basis of one feature or another, the absolute difference of human intelligence: humans alone can fall in love, or dream, or what have you. But we can avoid this sterile dichotomy, as we avoided it in the problem of language origin. What is important is to understand the specificity of the scene of representation; whether or not we are able or even want to duplicate it electronically is an altogether secondary matter. Human representation is dependent on appetite and inextricably bound up with desire. At present, computers manipulate signs the significance of which is determined by human appetites and desires; for them even to begin to duplicate human intelligence—defined as the totality of our sign-creating and -using abilities—they would have to possess analogous appetites and acquire analogous desires. So long as computer designers do not deal with these questions, there is no hope or danger that their products will duplicate human intelligence, however skillful they become in solving the problems of sign-manipulation that we feed into them.

WHOLLY FORMALIZED SYSTEMS OF REPRESENTATION— MATHEMATICS

It is obvious from our previous discussion that the traditional view of representation as an essentially gratuitous formal doubling of reality is inadequate. It will however be useful to begin our discussion of "logics of representation" with this traditional model. For it is the simplest, even if it achieves this simplicity at the expense of the completeness that alone could permit an understanding of its genesis. The strength of the traditional model, which permits the construction of the elaborate systems of modern logic and mathematics, is that it corresponds to a mature, fully autonomous stage of formal representation that has liberated itself from its anthropological antecedents.

In wholly formalized systems of representation, the real-world referents of signs are virtual and indefinitely deferred. Thus the sign has not even an imaginary referent (or "signified"). Signs may be created and manipulated at will; the interest of these systems lies in the rigor of the rules by which these manipulations are governed, rules that need not correspond with those implicit in the use of signs in ordinary language or even in arithmetic, although such correspondence is usually the ultimate goal of formal constructions. Here the scene of representation appears altogether detached from any anthropological considerations; it may in fact be generated electronically. In the place of the (representational) deferral/(appetitive) satisfaction dichotomy of the original event, we find the wholly formal temporality of the program that runs until it ends, at which point normally some problem is solved, some question answered, although telic intent is not a necessity of the process.

So long as formal systems represent nothing in particular but constitute autonomous models the application of which to reality remains wholly virtual, they are altogether unproblematic. As such, their elements are not really representations at all, but abstract objects; at the limit their very connection with human representation could be forgotten. But this formal freedom is in fact illusory; it can be maintained only at the sacrifice of the real value and interest of such systems, which is, after all, representational. However one may formally guarantee the deferral of their application to an object-world, the structures of such application inevitably reappear within the formal systems themselves as soon as they reach the level of complexity that alone makes them of interest. That such structures can appear even where we least expect them is the lesson, traumatic indeed when first expounded, of Gödel's famous proof of the incompleteness of arithmetic.[3]

Gödel's discovery is not without significance for the anthropological theory of representation. The work of Russell had already revealed that no logical system that purported to make true statements about an object-world could be freed from paradoxes—Russell's own system of logical types being only a deferral of these paradoxes to an indefinitely higher level.[4] What Gödel proved was essentially that systems with a countably infinite number of members could be made to represent themselves so as to produce statements intuitively true and yet unprovable by means of whatever axioms were used to formalize the system.[5]

The effect of this proof was profoundly felt by logicians and those concerned with mathematical foundations, far less so by those occupied with the more concrete problems of the theory of numbers, not to speak of the rest of mathematics. It has, however, been commonplace ever since to claim that since Gödel proved that the system of common arithmetic contained "unprovable truths," the various unproved conjectures in number theory may be of similar nature. Such claims (whether or not they are true, which I doubt) reflect the ultimate impasse of the formalistic mentality, which, because it must altogether discount the "naive" intuition that tells us that ordinary mathematical statements are quite unlike the artificial ones of Gödel's system, cannot even attempt to formalize this intuition within its system. Yet the formalistic mentality, unlike the empiricist mentality of the social sciences, cannot be rejected, for the anthropological theory of representation has nothing to put in its place. We are thus left with a pair of alternatives, both of which confirm our main point concerning the ultimate dependency of formal systems of representation on their anthropological basis. If the formalistic mentality is not inevitable, and arithmetic can in fact be purged of its autorepresentative element, this can only be done by introducing into the formalism itself a notion homologous to representation. Or if, as is only prudent, we accept the necessity of this mentality, we are obliged to accept as definitive the possibility that any infinite formal system is a system of representation, even if it only represents itself, and more particularly, even if this representational element does not in fact play a role in the functional manipulations of the system. For if the only use of arithmetic were to construct Gödel numbers, it would never have been invented.

We attain here the limits of formalism's ability to understand (or formalize) itself. There are no more formal, more mechanically manipulable criteria for deciding what it means to transform or map one set of symbols into another, to what extent this is a "natural" act analogous to the manipulation of physical realities, and to what extent it is bound by cultural constraints unformalizable in the system. Arithmetic is significant to us because the statements we construct from it are almost everywhere demonstrable; yet we cannot formalize the difference between these practical constructions and such perverse metaconstructions as Gödel numbers. This impasse of formalism reflects the human and nonautonomous nature of sign-manipulation even in the abstract domain of mathematics. It therefore incites us to examine representation from a more concretely human perspective, in the hope of achieving therein the autonomous theory of representation that has been shown to be impossible within the domain of pure formalism.

LOGIC

As soon as we leave the domain of pure formalism for that of representation proper, we encounter not merely incompleteness but paradox. For the "truth" of mathematical statements is only their consistency with the axioms of the system, so that their maximal degree of self-representation is a reference to this consistency—which is not, however, equivalent to our intuitive notion of truth. A mathematical statement may be true (according to the logic of representation) and yet undemonstrable within its axiomatic system, but it can be paradoxical, both true and false, only in the trivial case where the system itself is self-contradictory.[6]

But in logical as opposed to mathematical systems, all propositions refer to an object-world wherein their truth is presumed to be capable of verification. This is made explicit by Tarski's definition of the truth of a statement as its content's "being the case": "X" is true if X; "It is raining" is true if it is raining. The possibility of removing the quotation marks is an essential element of a logical system. But this possibility begs the question of the constitution of the object-world prior to the logical system itself, and thereby becomes the source of paradox. When the logician says "P" (that is, asserts the truth of "P"), he implies the prior existence of an object-world wherein P is the case—that is, where statements made (such as "P") do not modify "what is the case" with regard to such statements. If saying "it is raining" made the rain stop, the logical formalization of such statements would be impossible. But once the set of statements themselves is allowed as a potential object-world for the system, such paradoxes or failures of formalization become inevitable, for statements can no longer be prevented from affecting "what is the case." Simple examples of self-reference like "This sentence is false" can no doubt be eliminated from formal systems, but any such elimination, even through restrictions on "logical types," is only *ad hoc* and necessarily incomplete.

Paradox is an inevitable by-product of representation. But whether logicians recognize this fact, as many do, or prefer to deny it—in reality, to "defer" it—they cannot explain paradox as anything but a parasitic growth on representation. Like Gödel's unprovable truth, paradoxes are perverse. Logicians are more troubled than mathematicians by this perversity, situated as they are a step closer to the representational reality it reflects, but they can give it no meaning, no real function in their systems, and can only wish to exclude it.

From a metalogical standpoint—in effect, an anthropological one—this attitude, unlike the mathematicians' stoic resignation to the incompleteness of their domain, involves a real alienation, a self-blindness that is itself perverse. For unlike the vast majority of mathematicians, logicians spend an inordinate proportion of their time dealing with paradoxes. A glance at a philosophical journal will confirm that paradox is indeed a thriving business, one whose disappearance through a definitive formal solution would certainly diminish the attractiveness of logic as a field of research. Paradox is for logic an inexhaustible source of the sacrificial. But logic can explain neither the historical connection between the repeated beneficial expulsions of paradox from logical systems and similarly constituted ritual expulsions, nor the situation of both expulsions within a scene of representation. This explanation can be found only in anthropological theory of representation.

The logical paradoxes of self-reference are unavoidable outgrowths of a most important property of (declarative) statements: their capacity to refer to other such statements, as well as to states of affairs in an object-world. In *The Origin of Language* (chap. 4) we derived the declarative sentence from a negative reply to the imperative of another: "(Bring) the hammer!" is answered by "The hammer is not here." Because it is the preceding imperative that furnishes the topic or theme of the declarative (here, the hammer), it may be said that the declarative statement is metalinguistic in origin, a linguistic substitute for the action demanded by the imperative. More precisely, the declarative substitutes a predicate for a desired act of presentification. This derivation indicates that the logical proposition is in its origin not a gratuitous affirmation about "what is the case," but a reply to an expression of worldly desire that constitutes at the same time a deferral of this desire. The motivation for telling the truth about "what is the case" is that the desire of the locutee cannot be satisfied immediately; he must accept the truth because the object of his desire is presently unavailable. Thus the exchange that generates the declarative proposition is dependent on the presence or absence of a referential desire-object, not in an object-world, but within the scene of representation, a scene not originally constituted by the locutor of the proposition but by the desiring other. And the origin of the scene of representation in general, and of the desire expressed in it, have been explained by our hypothesis.

The foregoing remarks suggest a relationship between logic in the narrow sense (and, by extension, all "regional" sciences) and our theory of representation. Passing over methodological detail, in the terminology of *The Origin of Language*, logic is the general study of declarative predication for arbitrary topic. The propositions P_i that form the elements of propositional logic are presented as simply given. But in the light of our hypothesis, the proposition or declarative is not an elementary form; as we have just observed, its topic is determined by a prior desire or, more generally, a prior significance. Thus, aside from their formal problems of internal completeness, logics are necessarily incomplete with respect to the explanation of the existence of the propositional form which they take as their basis. This incompleteness may be defined as "regionality," a term that in our theory does not depend on the metaphysical ontic/ontological dichotomy of phenomenology. The regionality of logic is nonetheless of a different sort from that of the natural sciences (or ". . . logies"). These sciences are sets of propositions about a predetermined set of significant topics. Their separation is a result of the different techniques necessary to deal with these topics rather than of any inherent property of representation. This fact is evident from the very existence of logic, which is the science of the proposition-in-general. In this sense, logic is less regional than the empirical sciences. But because its formality shuts it off from the possibility of explaining its fundamental assumptions, logic is *more* regional than the social or even the physical sciences in its inability to explain the possibility of its assertions. For even the physicist can at least assert abstractly that the formulation of propositions (for example, those of physics) is an inherent possibility of matter, and the biologist or the sociologist can make this claim much more concretely.

But it is anthropology as a theory of representation that can alone claim to be complete. For its predications on the topic of the origin of representation explain the origin both of predication and of "topics," that is, referents of signs. Our theory is "regional" in the sense that it can deal only with certain aspects of empirical reality—aspects that, in Jean Piaget's "circle of the sciences," may be said to be predetermined by biological and ultimately by physical reality.[7] But this regionality is of only metaphysical interest, for it is ontological rather than epistemological. Only in the eyes of the divinity is physics prior to biology and biology to anthropology; insofar as the sciences are human creations, it is generative anthropology alone that explains their origin by proposing an originary hypothesis for the scene of representation upon which all propositional knowledge is situated. And as we pointed out in *The Origin of Language*, the origin of representation is at the same time the origin of our theory. Representation is from the very beginning an explanation of itself; the gesture designating the first significant object designates at the same time a hypothetical source of signification, and of the scene on which it manifests itself. By the same token, each ritual (and, eventually, mythical-discursive) repetition of the original event is a further explanation of it, a step in an evolution that is simultaneously and, indeed, equivalently ethical and representation-theoretical. The advantage of our theory over ritual and mythical as well as earlier theoretical explanations is that it thematizes what was earlier implicit by formulating its hypotheses as minimal predicates on the topic of representation, conceived not as a logical but as an anthropological phenomenon.

It is a consequence of the epistemological completeness of our anthropology that it contains neither paradoxes nor references to forms of knowledge constituted in regions to which it has no access. Because it traces the evolution of the foundation of knowledge, all knowledge may be subsumed under it. It is thus essentially open-ended and nonformal, although it is by no means incompatible with formalism, for the limitations of which, as of all regional forms of representation, it provides an explanation.

METAPHYSICS

It emerges from the foregoing discussion that the notion of a "logic of representation" is, strictly speaking, self-contradictory. There is no way for logic, in the sense of an axiomatic system of formal manipulations, to become complete and still remain logic. This follows directly from the fact that the proposition, which is the fundamental or atomic element of logic, is not, anthropologically speaking, an elementary form. Our claim, which metaphysicians must find unacceptable, is that the term "anthropological" involves no loss of generality, that any theory or logic of representation that purports to be complete must be wholly dependent on the human experience of representation, which is, with the extremely marginal exception of a few experimental animals, the only one. If this claim appears radical even today, that is a sign of the power of the metaphysical faith in discourse, inherited from the Greeks, that is the founding principle of the entire philosophical enterprise.

The intuitive justification of the logic of representation is roughly the following: Representation—in particular, language—is not merely an empirical anthropological fact. Like mathematics, it is subject to objective ideal laws independent of the particular conditions of its genesis, as well as of the structural limitations, in competence as well as performance, of natural languages. Therefore, not merely the logical manipulation of abstract propositions but signification in general must be subject to general laws and reducible to a more or less rigorously formalizable system. There are variously broad and restrictive versions of this constitutive claim. Hegel's *Logic* presents no doubt the broadest; in his idealist system, the very structures of reality are constituted by autonomously generated representations, the logical order of which he proposes to trace. The *Logic* is Hegel's most aberrant work precisely because its premises are furthest from their anthropological basis; it is perhaps the most radical demonstration *a contrario* of the incompleteness of philosophy. Its radicality is quixotic, but it has the virtue of making explicit the underlying project of philosophy since Plato, which is precisely the elaboration of a logic of representation as a means for understanding the universe, or at least man's place in it.

Plato's doctrine of Ideas, seen from the perspective of its Socratic source, is a hypostasis—or, in our terms, a *topicalization*—of significant predicates. The Socratic *elenchos*, as illustrated in the early dialogues, is a procedure for demonstrating the necessity and at the same time the general impossibility of such a topicalization, which can in fact be accomplished only on the basis of a general ethical conception such as Plato was later to formulate. The dictatorial features of the *Republic* that so offend a modern philosopher like Karl Popper,[8] whose own ethic demands that thought remain radically predicative (that is, nominalistic), reflect the presumptuousness of all constructive philosophy. An abstract ethic founded on Ideas can be imposed only from above; this is a problem of all utopias. Socratic dialogue demonstrated the implicitness of the deritualized classical ethic: of a man who claims, "This action is good" (or beautiful, or courageous), one asks, "What is the Good (or Beauty, or Courage)?" The predicate per se—that is, without a topical reality—is thus shown to be essentially arbitrary, a verbalistic substitute for ritual. The first act of philosophy as such, as distinct from Parmenides' direct application to reality of the truth-falsity dichotomy of the proposition (thereby creating a two-valued logic of representation), is to assert, albeit negatively, the necessity for understanding predicates as topics. It is precisely this act that Hegel carries to its radical *reductio ad absurdum*. Philosophy can never be a complete theory of representation; a rigorous theory of the manipulation of "ideas" is

only possible as a consequence of the renouncement of any consideration of topics. This is already the case in Aristotle's logic. The
shift in modern logic from predicates to propositions merely eliminates the vestigial substantiality of Aristotle's system. E p:p ⊃ q is
more compatible with formal rigor than "Some a is b" because, as
predicates, a and b exist only in relation to a topic. This becomes
evident when one attempts to formalize the copulative "is"; this can
be done only by a formula like "Some X's that are a are also b."

The utopian formulation "logic of representation" is thus seen to
cover the whole of philosophy, both at its most excessive and in its
most restrictive (that is, in modern logical positivism). The inherent
inadequacy of this notion indeed provides a more specific criterion
for defining the limits of philosophical thought than the popular
equation philosophy = metaphysics, which is the end result of a
century of attempts at postmetaphysical thought. This equation is
quite explicit in Marx, who of course did not claim to be a philosopher; its most influential modern source is Heidegger, who stopped
short of the radical nihilism of Derrida in affirming the possibility
of a premetaphysical and hence of a postmetaphysical philosophy.
(We should, however, note the absence in Derrida's work of any
challenge to Heidegger's thesis that pre-Socratic philosophy was not
yet metaphysics.)

Our own definition of metaphysics is broader than that of the
logic of representation: thought is metaphysical when it denies the
anthropological historicity of the scene of representation, whether
it accepts (nominalism) or denies (realism) that of the representations
that appear on it. Metaphysics is philosophy only when it claims to
be complete, to expound the logic that governs its own assertions.
This criterion allows us to answer the troublesome question of whether
logicians are truly philosophers, and also provides an explanation of
the diverse historical displacements of the fuzzy boundary between
philosophy and the various sciences that at one time or another have
broken off from it. Logicians are philosophers to the extent that their
work pretends to exclusive jurisdiction over the domain of representation. The logical positivists accomplished this by defining the
domain of representation to exclude all "meaningless" statements:
thus the idea of "God" requires no explanation whatever.[9] "Ordinary
language" philosophers are less restrictive in defining the domain of
logical jurisdiction; and rare today is the logician, however mathematical his tastes, who never ventures into the metaphysical domain
of "ideas."[10] The science/philosophy boundary, here as in the other
domains of "natural philosophy" subsequently annexed by science,

is to be drawn at the point where formal models take the place of ontologies. The withdrawal of this boundary into the province of logic is a sign of the exhaustion of analytic philosophy that parallels Derrida's self-deconstruction of metaphysics. In a society that generates an implicit ethic only graspable hypothetically and a posteriori, it is increasingly difficult to remain a believer in the power of the *logos*.

SPECULATIVE ANTHROPOLOGY

Logic proper is the least anthropological variety of the logic of representation. At the opposite end of the philosophical spectrum, we find the genre of speculative historical anthropology, the origin of which may be traced back at least to Vico, and which categorizes the evolution of human society by a series of dominant species of representation. Comte's tripartite division (theological, metaphysical, positive) is the classic example. Among the Neo-Kantians, this evolutionary logic is replaced by a relativistic cyclic scheme, but history is still the history of representation. It will be useful to distinguish our own anthropological dialectic of representation from these schemes.

Hegel's system, in which the logic of representation is prior to its incarnation in human history, remains the *reductio ad absurdum* of all these "logics." In Comte's system, the passage from, for example, "theological" to "metaphysical" forms of representation constitutes in fact a passage from one conception of the universe to another, that is, from one "idea" to another. What appear at first glance as forms of representation are in fact contents, and the superiority of the higher forms is merely the superiority of their content. Dilthey, whose respect for historical specificity could not tolerate Comte's naive equation of form with content, could only turn to the nonevolutionary irrationalism of the *Weltanschauung* where ideational contents acquire a secondary "form" of their own that does not affect the essential permanence of the fundamental representational institutions. Dilthey's system exposes the fatal weakness of Comte's, its failure to capture the cultural unity of historical periods. For Comte could explain the temporal density of historical evolution only through a combination of a purely "positive" notion of natural-scientific progress with a static sociology of knowledge wherein each level of representation corresponded to a particular level of social organization. Dilthey had to reject the evolutionary element of this scheme in order to eliminate the Enlightenment skepticism that reduced pre-positive social thought to ruling-class ideology.

What is lacking in such schemes as Comte's, what makes them metaphysical logics rather than anthropological theories of representation, is their insufficiently radical conception of the anthropological originarity of the scene of representation. Comte's "forms" are merely categories of content because the general form of representation—the scene itself—is always assumed a priori. What Hegel presents as a necessity of the self-revelation of the *Weltgeist* remains unjustified in speculative anthropology. The high point of this anthropology is not, indeed, to be found in the progressivist theories of Comte or Spencer, but in the ambiguously antisocial theory of Rousseau, who, in his second *Discourse*, comes closer to a satisfactory theory of the origin of language than any other thinker before the present time.

Rousseau is deeply aware that the origin of representation is the origin of the ethical, and thus of the human as such, the "cultural" as opposed to the "natural." What prevents him from constructing a dialectic of representational form and retains him in the *toujours déjà* that makes him so inviting a target for "deconstruction" is that he sees cultural presence as merely a supplement to natural instincts that becomes perversely a deferral of them. The *cri de la nature* becomes language through an augmentation of its force that is then perverted from its original function to become an instrument of enslavement. In fact, representation is *in the first place* a deferral of natural appetites, a response to their excess rather than to their insufficiency. Rousseau's anthropology, although it ostensibly rejects the logocentrism of the logic of representation, is nonetheless limited by its failure to grasp the strict dependency of all ideas, including those of the "heart," on the originary collective scene. Rousseau's attempt to ground moral values in a natural ethic cannot avoid recuperation by metaphysical logocentrism, for there is no morality outside the *logos*.

Yet it is worth noting that this recuperation can be accomplished, as it is in Derrida's *De la grammatologie*, only at the price of undermining the entire edifice of logocentrism. So long as philosophers still believed in philosophy, Rousseau remained an anthropologist; he can only be assimilated to philosophy now that it no longer matters whether the *logos* is to be found in the *Weltgeist* or in the *cri du coeur*. Rousseau's second *Discourse* constitutes philosophy's most radical attempt to liberate its anthropology from the logic of representation, just as Hegel's *Logic* is its most radical attempt to liberate its logic of representation from anthropology.

RADICAL ANTHROPOLOGY AND THE
LOGIC OF REPRESENTATION

It should already be clear from the exposition of our theory why it does not share the weaknesses of logics of representation. Logics, paradoxes aside, are formal models of predication; they cannot be applied to the selection of topics, nor *a fortiori* to the general explanation of the origin of representation. What we have here called "logics of representation" are not all logics in the traditional sense. Our justification for the term is that philosophy has from the beginning been constituted by a faith in the essential completeness of an order of representations. However modest his epistemology, Socrates' questions call forth Plato's answers as the only way of pursuing a dialogue that takes predicates as its topics. The Cartesian *cogito*, in rejecting the collective claims of significance in favor of the "clear and distinct" individual scene of representation, turns philosophy toward the epistemological examination of the scene itself as prior to the ideas that appear on it. This movement reaches its limits, as we have seen, in Rousseau's unsatisfactory attempt to constitute the public scene of representation. But the fact that philosophy, rather than ending with the *philosophes*, instead began its modern career in earnest, shows that the ideal of a logic of representation, far from being refuted by eighteenth-century epistemology, had never truly been challenged. German idealist philosophy was created to answer the challenge of Hume's apparently radical demonstration of the incompatibility of representations in general with any kind of logic. Kant showed that Hume was a "logician" after all. The only way to refute the logic of representation is to explain simultaneously the origin of the scene of representation and of its topical content.

This can be accomplished only by a hypothesis of real evenemential origin wherein both the scene and its content are shown to arise from precultural elements. By referring all elements of representation back to this original scene, our theory empties our present experience of these elements of its mystery and exposes the necessary incompleteness of philosophical introspection. There can be no logic of representation because representation is from the outset integrated into a newly created anthropological reality from which even the most flexible philosophical *logos* is an abstraction. But to refute the claims of philosophy it is not sufficient merely to allege the existence of this human reality; it is necessary to demonstrate the dependency of its evolution on factors not intrinsic to the scene of representation itself. For our generative theory of representation to become the foundation of a successful anthropology, it must create a model of cultural evolution irreducible to the old logics. This project is not new; it is at least as old as Marx. But neither Marx nor any of the social scientists that have followed him have succeeded in integrating into their anthropologies the elements that in our theory are articulated from the very beginning in the originary scene. These elements are (1) representation as the originary criterion of the human, (2) the ethical problem of deferring socially destructive conflict, and (3) the material or economic problem of increasing appetitive satisfaction. Their articulation as the foundation of human science will be discussed in the following chapter.

4

The Theory of Representation
as a Fundamental
Anthropology

As we stressed in *The Origin of Language* with respect to linguistics, it is not our intention to substitute necessarily speculative hypotheses for empirical research. Our hope is, of course, that our theories will inspire such research, if only in the Popperian hope of refuting them. But our major concern has been to explain the origin and evolution of representation, not because it constitutes in some sense an "infrastructure" determining the course of cultural evolution in general, but because this evolution alone can be self-reflective and therefore complete, explaining the emergence of all cultural structures, including that of its own explanation. For the sake of this epistemological completeness, we have avoided all analysis of specific situations that would distract from it. In our work on language, this was relatively unproblematic, for the most rigorous part of the book dealt with a hypothetical genesis of syntactical forms, a genesis for which no fossil record exists or is likely to be established. The question of culture is a historical one, however, and it is therefore incumbent on our theory to demonstrate its viability as a basis for explaining historical phenomena.

It is first of all necessary to articulate the categories discussed in the preceding chapters as copresent in the original event. This articulation will provide a model of social causality of greater explanatory interest than the infrastructure/superstructure theories that renew on an empirical terrain the philosophical conflicts between naturalism and idealism.

73

Appetitive interest precedes the scene of representation, and this interest creates the potential conflict around the appetitive object; furthermore, we have postulated that appetitive satisfaction must be greater as a result of this scene than if it had not taken place (that is, if the potential conflict had not been prevented). This implies that, if we consider the event as a whole merely from the perspective of appetite, we may abstract from the act of representation entirely and simply remark that hominization does not contradict the general rule of the animal kingdom that animals act to maximize appetitive satisfaction. This might be called the "principle of cultural materialism," to borrow a term from Marvin Harris, whose work we shall discuss below. The importance of retaining primary appetitive motivation in the original scene is not a mere matter of scientific elegance. For the original scene is not merely a convenient explanatory fiction *for us;* it is by definition the first cultural experience of its participants, which is to say, the first communal experience remembered as such, reenacted and "explained" in every succeeding cultural act. To violate the principle of cultural materialism at this point would be to violate it at every point of our analysis; if our model begins with such a violation, it will retain throughout a principle of nonmaterial causality.

But the principle of cultural materialism is independent of the original scene of representation—independent, in fact, of representation in any sense. That Harris's theory makes representation the hallmark of humanity without being able to explain it or even define it is the clearest sign of its inadequacy (see below, p. 88). In the originary event, appetitive satisfaction is increased, but only because conflict is eliminated, or in any case reduced. We may thus extrapolate from the original event a "principle of cultural conflict-avoidance": cultures will tend to avoid conflict that interferes with appetitive satisfaction. In affirming this principle, we do not diverge from Girard, nor from Durkheim, whose tradition he follows. But many are the social scientists, and many more the humanists, who see human culture as essentially a means either of increasing material production or of creating ideas or artworks. All will agree that every culture has means for preserving order; but it does not suffice to treat these as peripheral regulatory features. They are at the very heart of culture and are more immediately relevant to its specific creations than the more general need to increase appetitive satisfaction. Does this mean that we have abandoned the primacy of the "principle of cultural materialism"? Not at all. Without this principle, we could not explain why conflicts arise in the first place. The point of the second principle may be stated probabilistically thus: in the long run, culture will act to increase appetitive satisfaction, but in the short run, it will act to avoid conflict through temporary deferral of this satisfaction.

Needless to say, this principle deals with intentions that do not necessarily succeed. One might, however, wish in the *very* long run to abstract from the possibility of unsuccess, and thus from the long-term essentiality of the second principle, on the grounds of the Darwinian principle of selection. But it is precisely this cultural-Darwinist evolution that the short run makes impossible. If society has not always evolved linearly in the direction of the "greatest good for the greatest number," this is because conflict-avoiding mechanisms often act to defer new satisfactions even before they can be sought. These mechanisms, even in animal societies, are hardly innocent. They inevitably involve the creation of hierarchies with differential access to desirable goods. Such differential access may even be assumed in the original event, since the prehuman group, like all groups of higher animals, must have been internally differentiated.

The notion of "natural democracy" is utopian. Because natural endowments cannot be equal, an ethic is necessary to ensure equality; and it cannot be assumed of the original—that is, the weakest—ethic that it should entirely abolish natural differences, whether or not supported by animal dominance patterns. The second principle permits the analysis of a theoretical problem inaccessible to the principle of cultural materialism alone: every society and, indeed, every culturally significant act may be seen as, on the one hand, serving to maximize material satisfaction for the society as a whole and, on the other, as serving to maintain the hegemony of a dominant faction or class over those it dominates. In the first ("structural") perspective, the social order is viewed as a synchronic whole that functionalizes the differences that appear in it; in the second ("dialectical") perspective, these differences are *ipso facto* vulnerable to ethical criticism. All social order involves some degree of differentiation, and this must have been true from the outset. Yet once differentiation exists, it may be claimed that the order is only a front for exploitation. Our second principle affirms that the short-run gradient is in the direction of order rather than appetitive satisfaction of any kind, even for the leaders. The abandonment of order in a mad rush to satisfy appetites is a true breakdown of culture.

The two principles of causality we have introduced do not exhaust our analysis of the original event. If the avoidance of conflict is closer to the center of culture than the satisfaction of appetite, at the very center of culture is the scene of representation. All higher animals have an instinctual "culture" that prevents conflict, but only man accomplishes this avoidance through representation. The causal effect of representation occurs, so to speak, in the "maximally short run," that is, during the time of communal presence in which appetitive satisfaction is not merely regulated but deferred. We place this expression in quotes because the "run" it refers to is not merely relatively shorter than the others. For the duration of an act of representation is not that of a simple process; the act possesses its own intentional temporality. The duration of a representation is not only that of deferral but of a scene that fills this deferral both *de facto* and *de jure*.

The time of representation is also the time of consciousness, of the necessary reproduction of the entire scene in the imagination of each participant. Thus we may affirm as a third principle that, in the maximally short run, situations of potential conflict are resolved through representation, whether or not they take place on a central public scene. For not only is any appetitive situation one of potential conflict, but at virtually every moment of our lives, even during sleep, we are aware of representation in some form. This "run" is thus a more or less continuous series. Throughout our conscious lives we may be said to be engaged in the attempt to reduce conflict and ultimately to gain appetitive satisfaction through representation. The continuity of representational consciousness is a product of what we shall later call "cultural universality," a development that stands at the end rather than the beginning of the process of hominization. But it is through its conflict-avoiding function on the originary scene of representation that consciousness first arose, and its later evolution has not modified this basic function. Consciousness is not normally thought of in this perspective; but it suffices to note that even the most aggressive imaginations take place on an internal scene protected from the view of potentially hostile offended parties. Aggression imagined is aggression deferred, if only long enough to carry it out more effectively in practice.

There is, no doubt, a qualitative difference among states of consciousness; (day)dreaming is different from representing to oneself an immediate future action, or from solving a mathematical problem, or from listening to a symphony. But in all these there is an ethical element. This is not an empirical but an a priori statement, a deduction from our originary hypothesis. But our hypothesis explains the existence of consciousness, whereas empirical anthropologists do not consider the origin of consciousness to be any of their business. Whether material existence determines consciousness, as Marx would have it, or whether it is more prudently referred to as merely a "probabilistically causal" factor, material existence certainly is of little value in explaining why consciousness exists. But material causality is inadequate even to explain the existence of a social order, the often extreme differentiations of which are only exceptionally attributable directly to the power exercised by the dominant group.[1]

With regard to the origin of consciousness, no one is more gradualistic than the Marxists, who view all of culture as evolving from the manufacture of tools and the cooperative effort of labor. The ethical element is not lacking in the Marxist conception; but because it is defined gradualistically, that is, non-evenementially, it never becomes thematic. An ethical community arises without at any moment becoming aware of itself; cooperation in practical tasks "produces" language and consciousness, as though there were scarcely anything to explain. Rousseau was far more honest in admitting his inability to determine the origin of language. It does not suffice merely to recount a general course of events that gradually evolves into representation. The only functional temporality in such explanations is that of the explanation itself; after one has read long enough, when the *explicandum* arrives one is expected to be satisfied that it has been "explained."

The articulation of our three principles of causality permits us to understand the ambiguities of the notion of "culture." For just as life is built on a physical substratum that is absolutely determinative of its existence (and thus primarily causal) but, by the same token, incapable of offering an explanation of its nature, so is culture in the narrow sense built on a material-appetitive base that can provide no explanation of it. This simple analogy explains the failure of attempts to explain the "superstructure" by "infrastructure," the most notorious of which is doubtless Lenin's reflection-theory of consciousness. The central institutions of culture, in this perspective, are the institutions of representation, and of these, language is the most fundamental because it is derived directly from the original scene of representation. More peripheral are those institutions that have conflict-avoidance as their direct purpose; and most peripheral are the appetite-satisfying institutions. Thus the order is: representational or "cultural," political, economic. This is the order of cultural centrality, of distance from the material substratum; the order of material causality is the inverse. In the original event, which serves us as a model for all culturally significant events, the two orders are combined in a way that we may represent schematically as follows:

(1) appetitive ⟶ (2) ethical ⟶ (3) representational ⟶ (4) ethical ⟶ (5) appetitive.

An appetitive situation produces (ethical) conflict; it is resolved by the creation, and in the future by the reproduction, of the scene of representation. The result of this scene is the avoidance of conflict and finally the amelioration of the original appetitive situation. The first chain of causality (1–3) is "natural," and essentially unconscious; the second chain (3–5) is conscious and "cultural." This model is rather different from the conception that speaks of a superstructure having a reactive effect on an infrastructure. In fact the entire human contribution to the "infrastructure" was conceived in the "super-structure." For it does not suffice to speak of an institutional super-structure of art, religion, and so forth, to which are opposed economic relations rooted in the infrastructural forces of production. There is a representational element in nearly every economic act, and cer-tainly in those acts that produce functional innovations (or reproduce those accidentally discovered). No doubt in the study of the insti-tutions of a complex society, one is tempted to dispense with the inner structure of acts. But unless one realizes that the relations between institutions and the relations between the elements of any culturally significant act follow the same model of causality, one may be led to assume that the appropriate practical representations are generated by practice, and that the role of sacred or secular ethical institutions in promoting or reinforcing these representations is purely derivative and can therefore be ignored. Ritual law and even secular morality may then be seen merely as cynical tools with which the ruling class controls the exploited. The implication of such analyses, which is rarely stated, is that in uncovering the connection between ethical rules and the differential structure of the society that employs them, one has demystified them, presumably to the advantage of a classless morality no doubt realizable only in the future, but appli-cable as a standard to every social structure.

Here we touch on the question of the tasks of a concrete, historical anthropology. This contrasts with the general avoidance of the his-torical in *The Origin of Language*, where the concluding chapter, "A Perspective on Modernity," presented a so-to-speak posthistorical view made possible by the decline of dominant cultural discourse and the rise of a "dialogic" consumer society founded on a universalized exchange-system. Before attempting to constitute a historical anthropology it is useful to explain why such a constitution was not necessary in a work in which, on the basis of a hypothesis concerning the origin of language, we were able to develop at least the outline of a view of modernity and its culture.

The most significant difference between language and other cultural institutions lies in its essentially nonhistorical nature. Language has a prehistory which we may attempt to reconstruct, but in essence it has no history. This is by no means to trivialize the findings of historical linguistics. But these findings are themselves not chiefly of a historical interest; the changes of language are significant not in themselves but because of what they tell us about the transhistoric phenomenon of language change. The knowledge that the most backward peoples known to us have languages essentially similar to our own and just as complex reduces historical linguistic change to the cyclic reshuffling of alternate structures under the pressure of a dynamic governed by the need to maintain language's dramatic, scenic function. Language is eternally in a state of disequilibrium due to the opposition between its functions of *significance* and *signification*. In attaining the "maturity" that we have defined to correspond with the possession of the declarative sentence—a structure that is the basic utterance pattern in all known languages—language becomes a system of significations with the capacity of unlimited reference while retaining its original function of designating the significant. The disequilibrium that is productive of linguistic change on every level, from the phonetic to the lexical and syntactic, is a necessary consequence of the fact that signification depends on the repetition of the same elements, whereas significance, in the absence of a significant object, is reinforced by originality. Hence the elements most highly charged with significance will come to be abused and eventually worn down to banality, only to be replaced by a new set of emphatic forms. This process involves no long-term change in the "universals" of language, which we may well consider with Chomsky to have become a part of our genetic patrimony. If, indeed, this is the case, then the contrast between a prehistoric stage, in which the evolution of language provided selective pressure for the evolutionary changes in the brain observed by paleontologists, and a historic stage, in which language change had no such effects, would provide biological justification for our distinction between elementary and mature language.[2]

Language, as the central cultural institution, the only one indispensable to the preservation within the mind of each human being of the original scene of representation, would thus evolve only so long as the brain using it evolved. This is emphatically untrue of cultural institutions. On the contrary, it is an undisputed fact that the possession of a brain capable of learning mature language—the brain possessed by all normal humans—is sufficient for the adaptation to any specific culture. The child of a Papuan headhunter can be raised as a member of the most advanced society on earth; his difficulties, if any, will be cultural, not biological. Culture in general has evolved significantly and irreversibly without essential genetic change. This is indeed the innovation most commonly associated with cultural evolution. Although historically irreversible, such evolution is from a genetic standpoint completely reversible; the conquest of one cultural group by another need not result in extermination but may end in assimilation. But it remains legitimate to ask what kinds of cultural forms were associated with prehistory in the sense in which we have defined it with respect to language. In other words, what were the limitations of human culture during the period in which language, and with it the human brain, were evolving toward their mature state? Is it possible to construct a plausible hypothetical definition of mature—that is, historical—culture as opposed to its prehistoric forms? This question, which we did not need to ask in *The Origin of Language*, becomes crucial in a more general discussion of culture. It will be dealt with in the second part of this volume.

THE HARRIS-SAHLINS CONTROVERSY— A PARADIGM OF ANTHROPOLOGICAL CAUSALITY

As the preceding discussion shows, we have included "cultural materialism" as the most fundamental—but not the most specific—principle of anthropological causality. In doing so we pay homage to the work of Marvin Harris, whose anthropological works are models of lucidity and polemic verve. Harris's doctrine or "research strategy" of cultural materialism is a salutary development that clears the great insights of Marx both of Marx's own Hegelianism and of the Leninist dogmatism of his followers. Harris's work is exemplary within modern social science. Yet it does not transcend the fundamental limitations of social science, a fact which makes it vulnerable to attacks on the part of other social scientists, partisans of other schemes of causality. We shall here discuss briefly the polemic between Harris and his most outspoken and visible critic, the University of Michigan anthropologist Marshall Sahlins, who himself was formerly a "cultural materialist" in practice if not in name, but who, as Harris explains, has let himself be seduced by French structuralist thought into a stance Harris today qualifies as "obscurantist." Our analysis of this polemic will aid us in elucidating the problems of anthropological causality from the standpoint of our theory of representation. It will also serve here as a paradigm of our critique of the social sciences, a subject we hope to take up some day in greater detail. Our discussion focuses particularly on two specific problems treated by Harris, on the first of which he has been rigorously opposed by Sahlins. These are (1) Aztec cannibalism and (2) the Hindu-Buddhist interdiction on slaughtering cattle in India.

Before entering into the specifics of the debate, we should note the particularity of its subject matter, which is not atypical of that of Harris's analyses. Subjects like Aztec cannibalism are both curiosities and test cases for Harris's theory; if he can explain such bizarre, apparently functionless culture traits by the principle of cultural materialism, then surely he can account for the main run of cultural development, the economic rationality of which is at least plausible on the surface. And, indeed, along with collections of curiosities like *Cows, Pigs, Wars and Witches*,[3] Harris has also developed in *Cannibals and Kings*[4] (from which the Aztec example is taken), and in summary form in the largely polemical *Cultural Materialism*,[5] an overall picture of social evolution based on the cultural-materialist causal factors of demographic pressure and technological progress.

It is not unfair to remark that Harris's analysis, in offering evidence for economic rationality as a sufficient explanation of the specific customs he studies, takes for granted the adaptations of the representational superstructure and the ethical-social order to this infrastructural rationality; nor that his general outline of cultural evolution neglects not only the problems of structural and superstructural adaptation but the more fundamental question of how humanity and its culture ever got started on its evolutionary path. Sahlins has not neglected the first of these points in his critique, although, in conformity with structuralist agnosticism, he has nothing there or elsewhere to say about the second. For Sahlins, Harris's materialist explanations are "devoid of social content. Once we characterize meaningful human practices in these ideological terms, we shall have to give up all anthropology, because in the translation everything cultural has been allowed to escape."[6] Harris's defense against this aspect of Sahlins's critique, as found in *Cultural Mate-*

rialism, is that concern with the "emics" (internal thought-categories) of cultures, while no doubt of interest in its own right, must be secondary to the understanding of the "etic" (objectively determinable) situation. Accusing Sahlins of "[constricting] anthropology to the emic and mental aspects of Aztec sacrifice," he continues, "We should certainly try to understand why people think they behave the way they do, but we cannot stop at that understanding. It is imperative that we reserve the right not to believe their explanations. . . . A ruling class that says it is eating some people for the welfare of all is not telling the whole story."[7]

This polemical answer on the Aztec question is a less significant reply than the theoretical point, made earlier in the book, of defining cultural materialism as a *probabilistic* research strategy based on "the principle of infrastructural determinism . . . that provides a *set of priorities* for the formulation and testing of theories and hypotheses about the causes of sociocultural phenomena. Cultural materialists give *highest priority* to the effort to formulate and test theories in which infrastructural variables are the primary cultural factors"[8] (emphasis ours). The lack of concern with superstructural factors results from the success in formulating a causal hypothesis based on infrastructural factors. But, as we saw above, cultural causality is a more complex matter. Harris's causal hypotheses may be perfectly legitimate in themselves, but they fail to provide the slightest understanding of the human social order either in specific cases or in general. The existence of human society and its fundamental institutions is simply taken for granted, and hypotheses are formulated to explain certain of its features as adaptations to infrastructural conditions. This is a case in point of how the absence of an originary hypothesis makes proper respect for the specificity of the cultural— of the human—virtually impossible. As we shall see, however, this is even more the case with Sahlins, who lacks the egalitarian moral principles that Harris retains (albeit without theoretical justification) from the Marxist tradition.

Let us now turn to the specifics of the debate, begun in the pages of the *New York Review of Books*, over Harris's explanation of Aztec cannibalism (derived from a controversial article by Michael Harner[9]) as a compensation for the lack of large edible fauna in the Aztec ecosystem. Harris provides, largely on the basis of Harner's research, data that show the Aztec's average daily intake of animal protein to have been extremely low compared even with that in modern India. Therefore, so his argument goes, "the uniquely severe depletion of animal protein resources made it uniquely difficult for the Aztec ruling class to prohibit the consumption of human flesh. . . . Cannibalism therefore remained for the Aztecs an irresistible sacrament, and their state-sponsored ecclesiastical system tipped over to favor an increase rather than a decrease in the ritual butchering of captives and the redistribution of human flesh."[10] To this argument, Sahlins replies in two ways: by attempting to refute the "economic cogency" of the protein hypothesis, and by providing a lengthy description of the Aztec sacrificial system in its own terms, noting that "the logic of Aztec sacrifice conforms to that in the classic texts of French sociology on the subject."[11] It is characteristic of his article as a whole that this latter "emic" argument is given first and with far more detail and fervor, the other being reduced to an afterthought. One quotation will capture the rather disconcerting lyric tone:

> Rolled down the western steps of the temple, in a descent that paralleled the course of the sun and the Aztec metaphor of birth, the body was received and shared by the owners of the dead. The cycle between sacrificer and god was thus closed by the mediation of the victim. . . . In the last moment, victims, gods and communicants became one. The consumption of human flesh was thus deifying, not degrading. Precisely by conceiving sacrifice as an extension of the physiological functions of digestion, Harner and Harris abandon the possibility of understanding it, either as a ritual or as a necessity."[12]

Thus Sahlins's chief criticism of Harris is not that his hypothesis is false but that it fails to provide "understanding" of the "meaning" of Aztec sacrifice. To this, Harris replies that the "meaning" is in the minds of the eaters but not the eaten, that this "communion" was "the highest form of exploitation."[13]

Our purpose in describing this controversy is not to take sides; but it is difficult to avoid concluding that Harris displays both the more powerful method and the more acceptable moral attitude, and that method and attitude are not independent. The Aztec case is a test of the ethical value of causal systems because the unusual brutality of the known facts makes us impatient of the sacrificers' descriptions. This is true even if we reject, along with the Harner-Harris thesis, the very contention that the victims were eaten. Sahlins does not do this, although he decries the efficiency that Harris attributes to the slaughtering process. His only attempt to explain the enormity of the sacrifices is to blame "hubris" for providing positive feedback to the system—and this in a brief afterthought to his lengthy "emic" descriptions. A provocative work by W. Arens,

The Man-Eating Myth,[14] attempts to cast doubt on the evidence, all second-hand, for Aztec cannibalism. If this doubt is justified—and it cannot simply be dismissed, however apparently convincing that evidence—then Harris is definitely wrong, but the mystery of the large-scale human sacrifices remains unsolved. Sahlins's argument would remain virtually untouched. But that is not a recommendation. In Popperian terms, his thesis is unfalsifiable, for he "explains" the system in terms of its own mythology, whereas Harris has, at the very least, proposed a testable hypothesis.

And because this hypothesis proposes a (materialist) causal system, it is, so to speak, entitled to the egalitarian morality that has generally accompanied that system. But that this moral attitude is not theoretically justified but taken for granted—that, in other words, it never acquires the status of a socially integrated *ethic*—is a consequence of the inadequacy of this causal system. What, indeed, is the connection between material-appetitive causality and egalitarian morality? The latter is not, after all, a mere consequence of the former; one might just as well suppose an essentially biological causal principle to justify the social-Darwinist morality of "survival of the fittest." Egalitarian materialism is a reaction to the conditions of the modern exchange-system, which in the course of the industrial revolution of the eighteenth and nineteenth centuries appeared to be moving in the direction of a wholesale transformation of (to use Hannah Arendt's terms[15]) artisanal, differentiated "work" into undifferentiated "labor." The role of this model in Marx requires no commentary. It is evidently far closer to the realities of the period than that of social Darwinism, which could be termed an ideology rather than a sociological theory precisely to the extent that its ethic determines its model of causality rather than the reverse.

But whereas Marx could allude directly to nineteenth-century reality in formulating his ethical judgments, which may be said to have thereby acquired at least a semblance of scientific status, this is no longer the case today. The inadequacy of cultural-materialist causality as an anthropological foundation is reflected in the abstractness of its ethic, which, in particular, can no longer serve as an adequate model for the understanding of the contemporary exchange-system. Marx's revolutionary egalitarianism was an extrapolation—unjustified, as it turned out—from the industrial conditions of his day; Harris's is nothing more than a moral principle. This is a crucial point in our critique of cultural materialism. We do not mean to suggest that this moral principle itself is somehow a "product" of the industrial era. Egalitarianism (albeit of a less specifically material sort) has always been an essential feature of Judeo-Christian morality, not to speak of the ethic of typical hunter-gatherer societies.[16] But only in Marx does it become a plausible ethic for modern society and is it provided with an at least apparent justification through a principle of causality. It is an important feature of modern society that its ethic is implicit and controversial—that statements of it, even when (as is certainly not the case in Marx) they refer only to the present, are projective and therefore ideological in content if not in intent. Harris's version of the materialist ethic is also ideological, but only in the weak sense of condemning the "exploitation" he is forced to see virtually everywhere in the contemporary world.

Let us now turn briefly to a second, contrasting example of the cultural-materialist method: the problem of the "sacred cow" in India. Harris has dealt with this problem in a number of publications, from "The Cultural Ecology of India's Sacred Cattle"[17] to the recent *Cultural Materialism*. His basic argument is very simple: refuting those who emphasize the irrationality of the Hindu ban on slaughter of cattle, supposedly the result of an exaggerated respect for arbitrary religious laws, Harris demonstrates that the practice is in fact economically adaptive. The cows give milk and dung and provide traction for plows in the planting season. Most interesting is his specific explanation for the ritual taboo, which parallels with a difference the Jewish-Moslem ban on pork. In the hungry winter months, the Indian peasant might well be tempted to slaughter his cow for food, and thereby irreparably impair his economic viability. The ritual taboo serves to reinforce a possibly vacillating willpower. Similarly, the Jews and Moslems ban pork, in Harris's view, because, although it is ecologically unsound and potentially economically disastrous to raise pigs in a desert climate, their flesh is tasty and individuals might therefore be tempted to try. The difference is that pigs, having no economic function other than meat production, are banned altogether, whereas the Indian cows are revered for their other services.

Harris's position on this issue, as on the others, has been severely attacked as well as hotly (and in our eyes, convincingly) defended. We shall not take up these specific polemics here, but rather quote a passage from the concluding portion of Sahlins's *New York Review* article, which points out the central weakness in cultural-materialist causality while demonstrating its author's own misunderstanding of the crucial problem involved. Our interest in this passage, and in Sahlins's article in general, is not to point out his peculiar failings but to pinpoint the blind spot he shares with Harris, and, indeed, with contemporary social science in general.

Mr. Harris makes a considerable point of the tough-mindedness and scientism of his anthropology. But his theory is really no more deterministic than it is cultural. When he discusses the points in history when population endangers resources, a symptomatic ambiguity appears regarding what kinds of adaptation societies make to such demographic crises. . . . Harris does not indicate any theoretical curiosity about [intensification of production, stabilization of population], or other radically different adaptive strategies. For societies with internally opposed interests, as between antagonistic social classes, he does not make it clear whether it is some part or the whole of society that adapts effectively. In India, the lower classes are served by the preservation of sacred cows. Among the Aztecs, the upper classes benefit from the cult of human sacrifice. But when each of a regional set of warring communities kills its female infants, it is the set as a whole that stands to gain. The problem is not merely that the explanations are ad hoc. It is that in all these conditions, any given material rationality will be from some other social viewpoint, irrational.

The issue disappears for Harris because he considers "the population" to be a *quantity* rather than a *society*, consisting of organisms with biological requirements rather than people with cultural interests. . . . "Materialism" becomes a kind of academic parlor-game. . . . Any sort of economic value that can plausibly be suggested for any cultural practice scores points—regardless of whether the same custom entails economic penalties or irrationalities in some other sector of the social order.[18]

There is no doubt that this critique points out the central weakness of cultural materialism: its failure to define the relation between what we have called the appetitive and the ethical elements of social causality. How, indeed, do the economic benefits reaped by one class or another contribute to the stabilization of the social order, which is to say, the prevention of conflict between its constitutive classes or other subgroups? Although Harris's statistics on the Aztecs and on Indian agriculture are population-wide, the benefits conferred by human sacrifice or the sacredness of cattle are not. How can he claim to have given an economic justification for these practices without entering into the structure of the totality within which he selects the constituents (Aztec rulers, Indian peasants) that justify his theories?

We shall attempt shortly to suggest a methodology for dealing with such questions, one that is compatible with Harris's conclusions if not with his notion of anthropological causality. But first we should remark on the fuzziness, even the incoherence, of Sahlins's attack.

Sahlins accuses Harris, on the one hand, of confusing benefits for one sector of society with benefits for the whole, thereby strongly implying that the general welfare should be our criterion, and, on the other, of treating the whole as an undifferentiated "population" when he attempts to measure the general welfare by statistical methods. Sahlins's attack on the "determinism" he accuses Harris of falsely claiming to have demonstrated is wholly negative, meriting Harris's qualification of "obscurantist." While appearing to admit the accuracy of Harris's economics, he rejects the explanations based on them because "any given material rationality will be from some other standpoint, irrational." But not only is this no refutation of the claim that *those who benefit* are indeed acting on "material rationality," it implies that the demonstration of such rationality is simply irrelevant to the explanation of human acts. The theoretical nihilism of this view may be made clear by a thought experiment. Let us suppose a tribe is divided into Groups A and B. Both groups follow an apparently irrational ritual practice. Harris then demonstrates that this practice is in fact economically beneficial to group A while being detrimental to group B. Sahlins replies that this analysis, even if accurate, *is of no use in explaining the ritual* because from "some other" standpoint (that is, that of B) the practice is in fact irrational. But now let us suppose that texts recited during the ritual speak of the "communion" between members of A and members of B at a moment when the former are receiving large quantities of tribute from the latter. *Now* Sahlins has his explanation!

This thought experiment does more than point up the weakness of Sahlins's criticism; it illustrates the central feature of both the Aztec and Indian examples we have discussed, as well as a good many others. This feature is ritual, the sacred, and more generally, representation. For it is curious that in so many of the puzzles solved by Harris, and in virtually every one the setting for which involves a society more complex than the tribe, the source of the puzzle is a rite. Nor is tribal society truly an exception, for the warfare he describes as population-controlling is itself a highly ritualized phenomenon. At the tribal level every public activity is essentially ritual, whereas in more complex societies, and particularly in state societies, the sacred ritual sector may be contrasted with an institutionalized secular sector that includes such activities as war as well as the central operations of the production and exchange-systems.

The crux of such puzzles as Aztec sacrifice, Hindu cow-worship, or the Judeo-Moslem pork taboo is located in the interface between the sacred and the profane, the ritual and the economic. The fas-

cination of Harris's solutions for the nonspecialist is not simply a
function of their explicative merit; it is above all the product of our
recognition in ourselves of traces of ritual mentality. For even without practicing these rites, by our acceptance of the commonsense
understanding of them as engaged in for religious reasons, we ac-
quiesce to the power of the sacred. The sacred cow fascinates us not
because we wonder what use it may have but because its apparent
counterutility seems to us a demonstration, both nostalgic and ir-
ritating, of the continued hold of sacred irrationality over others.[19]
Thus Harris's demystifying, desacralizing explanations have an effect far greater than would be warranted by similar accomplishments
in less sensitive areas. This is indeed what makes Harris a "popular"
anthropologist; his explanation of ritual as disguised commerce is
itself commercial.

Ritual, in short, is Harris's stock in trade; yet, to our knowledge,
neither he nor any other member of his school has ever devoted a
single page to the discussion of the sacred-ritual phenomenon as in
itself a universal human trait. The words "religion," "ritual," "sacred" (except in "sacred cow") do not even appear in the indexes of
Cannibals and Kings or *Cultural Materialism*. Even the Marxian figure
(of Hegelian origin) of the "inverted world" of religion—familiar to
the American left through the homelier "pie in the sky"—is absent.
For Harris, the sacred is purely epiphenomenal. Sometimes (for
example, with the Aztecs) a mask for upper-class voracity, at other
times (for example, the Indian case) a beneficial supplement to lower-
class economic wisdom, it has no specific socioeconomic function,
merely a mediating, facilitating, "superstructural" one of no intrinsic
interest to cultural materialists.

But we have a term for such mediating institutions: we call them
systems of representation. In our anthropology, man is not distinguished
from the animals by his propensity to economic activity but by his
use of representation. How, indeed, does Harris distinguish man
from the beasts? In defending his discipline against the sociobiologists, he affirms: ". . . sociobiologists overlook or minimize the genetic trait that by their own criteria ought to be emphasized above
all others. That trait is language. Only human language has semantic
universality—the ability to communicate about infinite classes of
events regardless of when and where they occur."[20] And a few lines
later, he reaffirms: "Indeed the emergence of semantic universality
constitutes an evolutionary novelty whose significance is at least as
great as the appearance of the first strands of DNA." We could not
agree more with the thrust of these statements, although the term

"semantic universality" is not altogether appropriate, implying as it does that animal "languages" differ only semantically from ours.[21] But language, as Harris has earlier explained, "cannot be viewed as an exclusively infrastructural, structural, or superstructural component."[22] As we have seen, within limits the same may be said for the sacred. Yet far from comparing the appearance of ritual with that of DNA, Harris has not a word to say on the subject, and this in a book most of the concrete examples of which are explanations of ritual practices.

We are now ready to grasp the inadequacy not only of cultural materialism but of positive anthropology in general, that of Sahlins as well as—and more than—that of Harris. In a word, *it has no coherent theory of representation.* For Harris, representation is the essence of man, but it has no place in his system. He devotes much of his energy to explaining representations away, but not to explaining either why they exist in the first place or why they so fascinate him and his readers. For Sahlins, following the disembodied version of Durkheim's great but insufficient intuition current in postwar French anthropology, representation is a value in itself, explicable only in its own terms. This view is only on the surface more consistent than that of Harris; for if the latter has an insufficient principle of causality, Sahlins has none at all. Far from respecting the central principle of Durkheim that sacred representation is the crucially human means of preserving *social* coherence, Sahlins finds the only explanation for ritual in its coherence *tout court.*[23] As for its material benefits, whether proven or not, they are denied a priori any reality; what is gained in one sector is lost in another. Sahlins and Harris thus occupy symmetric positions with regard to the ritual-economic interface. Harris, aware that the connection exists, insists on its radically determined nature even when his own demonstrations (as in the Aztec case) are scarcely indubitable; Sahlins, even in the face of evidence, refuses to admit the existence of any significant connection. Thus Harris is only partly right, but Sahlins is guaranteed of being wrong.

But to borrow an aphorism that Harris quotes with deserved approval, "purely negative criticism does not kill a research program."[24] If we would criticize current positive anthropology and social science, then we must be prepared to present social scientists with the outline of our own "research program."

Implicit in the idea of science is the notion that not only its results but its method are objectively reproducible. Science is wholly democratic; there are greater scientists and lesser ones, but no scientist can claim to be able to do science in a way no one else can. The application of these statements to the physical and natural sciences is incontestable, all but tautological. The question we should like to raise here is how they apply to the social sciences, and, in this case, to anthropology. It is our contention that research programs based on positive—that is, concretely falsifiable—hypotheses are indispensable in the social sciences. Harris is to be praised for his lucid presentation of his own program, which has no parallel in the anthropological literature. As we have observed, this program is based on a probabilistic principle of material causality that seeks the explanation for social phenomena on the infrastructural level of productive and reproductive conditions before proceeding to the higher (that is, structural and superstructural) levels. The results of research along these lines will permit the prediction or "retrodiction" (= explanation) of social phenomena. We can have no quarrel with this.

But it is equally our contention that such programs are necessarily insufficient to explain or to predict the most significant anthropological realities, which are not "phenomena" in the strict sense, nor "structures," but rather *ethical systems*, cultures in the broad sense of the term. Because we too inhabit such systems, we cannot expect to find on the phenomenal surface the means for explaining the basic features either of others or of our own. As we showed in *The Origin of Language*, only a generative perspective based on an originary hypothesis can truly explain representation. If we did not present a research program for linguistics, that is because, as we have observed, linguistics is in its essence ahistorical and combinatorial: nothing really "happens" in the history of a mature language.[25] In the present case, the originary hypothesis, presented as rigorously as possible, may well become the core of a genuine research program. For any cultural system may be studied in the light of our hypothesis. But the hypothesis is not a principle of causality, but a *model*. It does not help us in a search for the correlations or probabilistic causes that link phenomena, but in the analysis of these phenomena in terms of their prehistorical antecedents. The principles of causality we have referred to are not meant to suggest an improvement or refinement of Harris's principle but an entirely different perspective.

From the perspective of linear causality between external phenomena (or "etic behavior," as Harris calls it), Harris's probabilistic system is, in fact, perfectly plausible. Quite evidently, the material basis of culture offers fewer degrees of freedom than the representations or even the exchange-systems we construct upon them: there would be no point in constructing such systems otherwise. But, expressed in this fashion, cultural materialism reveals itself to be very nearly tautological. The fact that such principles as Harris's have been hotly contested demonstrates that the social sciences are still far from having cleansed themselves of ritual elements—of the kind of thinking that asserts what Freud called "the omnipotence of thought." But the sort of unrigorous thinking of which Sahlins's critique is an example expresses nonetheless an intuition of the inadequacy of such principles to explain, not the rationale of some particular custom, nor the overall progression of social systems from tribe to state, but the very *existence* of ethical systems, of cultures, both in general and in particular.[26]

It was the necessity of constructing a "research program" for the understanding of contemporary society that led us to approach the question of culture or, more precisely, to attempt to understand our culture in the broad sense (= ethical system) by examining culture in the restricted sense. The confusion of these terms is no accident. Thus we emphatically valorize the preanthropological intuition that makes culture—in particular, the esthetic institutions of art and religion—the obvious primary focus of the study of societies other than our own. It is certainly no accident that these institutions are the most directly accessible to our understanding; the intentionally esthetic is meant to be contemplated. The difficulty is, rather, that anthropology as a science was founded precisely in opposition to the study of culture in this sense, and that it consequently regards with not undeserved suspicion the sort of cultural analyses that limit themselves to artworks and neglect the material and organizational elements of the societies within which they were created. It is therefore necessary to respond in advance to the accusations of idealism that might otherwise be lodged against our program. This response will serve more generally as an exposition of a method which we claim to be maximally scientific.

The five-place causal chain of p. 78, with representation at its center, applies not merely to culture but to all conscious human activities, even the most "infrastructural." No study of any culture can, however, take into consideration more than a very limited number of such chains. The question for designers of research programs is therefore not simply the definition of principles of causality but the choice of significant phenomena. And we would claim that this choice is ultimately dictated by a perception of what is relevant to an understanding of our own society and to its future. We deliberately use the word "relevant" here in order to exorcise its powers of attraction and repulsion. "Relevant" is a modern synonym for "significant," to which are attached all the danger and fascination of the sacralization that is from the beginning a potentiality of the significant. Our notion of relevance is not confined to what is interesting or to superficial appearances; it is the expression, as must be at the outset all conceptions of the significant, of a wager, in a very nearly Pascalian sense, on the future of society as the locus of virtual presence. The original impetus for the social sciences, not to speak of philosophy or of religion, was not a disinterested curiosity about the past but a desire to grasp the invariants of the human in the hope of understanding the future of a changing society. It requires no argument to show that this is as true of Rousseau as of Durkheim, of Comte as of Weber, and most eminently true of Marx. (It is also, incidentally, clearly true of Harris and Sahlins; one need only read the last chapter of *Cannibals and Kings*, or the whole of *The Rise of Anthropological Theory*, or *Cultural Materialism*, or Sahlins's *Culture and Practical Reason* to see that contemporary society and its future are always the horizon of their analyses.)

We are not speaking of "inspiration," or of "ultimate aims" of merely topical importance. All theories of society, all works of social science, whether or not explicitly oriented to specific or general practical application, are only really testable in the context of the more or less immediate future. Insofar as culture is an ever-productive, worldwide phenomenon, it is the present state of world culture that defines the limitations of our current theories and the future that puts them to the test—that makes them in Popper's sense "refutable." Where Popper is lacking is not (as Harris claims[27]) in his doctrine of "refutability" but in his failure to distinguish between natural and human science. The hypotheses of human science may no doubt be measured, like those of natural science, by their success in predicting or explaining specific well-defined phenomena. But this sort of measure, however much it may appear to correspond to the ideal of the social sciences, distorts the scale of values with which human science operates. The "future" of physical or even biological reality is at most a minute accretion upon the present; but the future of society is not only a far more uncertain state but the projected result of every social act. Every anthropological theory of sufficient generality is essentially a theory of the future, because future society is the only radically unknown society by which the theory may be tested. And even the most specific and limited statement depends for its significance, if not its factual truth, on such a general conception.

What we are suggesting is that the notion of "relevance" is not merely the external impetus for the formulation of anthropological theory but its only objective measure. This emphatically does not mean that the past thereby loses its interest—*au contraire*. For because world culture (and to a lesser extent all national and regional cultures and traditions) is cumulative, every study of the past is a study of the origin of the institutions of the present and the future. And such a study can formulate significant hypotheses only to the extent that it permits us to test whether the originary structures it posits are confirmed by the evolution of the present version of these institutions. A historical study, for example, of the earliest states is a part of human science only if it contains causal hypotheses, and what is ultimately testable about these hypotheses is the limits they place on any possible future state structure. This *ultimate* testability is not their immediate test, as would be the case if relevance were interpreted in a superficially radical fashion. Hypotheses must first be tested against the given facts. But the causal links are always ambiguous, to the extent that our ability to determine invariant factors is limited by our historical experience. Only the future can disambiguate our choice of invariants; social like biological evolution provides its own "survival of the fittest." In the case of general anthropological theories, ultimate testability alone is possible. Such theories, in hypothesizing the origin of man, place a wager on his future. Historical data confer plausibility on such theories only to the extent that they indicate trends that will maintain themselves in the future.

Our research program is, then, a wager on the central social importance of representation, not only in the ethical but in the economic domain. Culture as the set of significant public representations is the focus of our interest because it is precisely these that are most sensitive to the ever-increasing unification of the ethical and economic spheres.[28] The study of cultural phenomena does not of course provide direct knowledge of these spheres. But such knowledge acquires theoretical significance only upon its integration into a model of society as a whole. Because the production and "consumption" of cultural objects is illustrative of the causal schema derived from the hypothetical original event, it must be at the center of any such model.

This proposition can scarcely be contested on its own terms; but some may be tempted to dismiss it with the observation that the "center" of society becomes, with the decline of ritual, increasingly unimportant, and that modern societies dispense altogether with a center in the sense of a well-defined set of public representations. But it is precisely this condition of modern society that both permits and renders indispensable the carrying out of our program. This is not to belittle economic problems like energy crises or the ethical ones posed by the existence of the means of self-annihilation, nor to imply that esthetic culture can in some sense solve these problems. But the study of such problems, however much they may preoccupy us, cannot furnish us with an understanding of our society as an integrated whole. The promotion of each to the rank of essential problem of modernity reflects a partial view of human society that has its counterpart in general anthropology—for example, Harris's cultural materialist doctrine of infrastructural causality, or Girard's "institutional" theory which makes deferral of violence the essential factor. In each case, the activities of the society itself are conceived as epiphenomenal with respect to the extrasocial factors on which they depend (energy or deferral of violence), which thereby become secularized versions of the transcendent. The attribution of significance to these problems is certainly indispensable to the conduct of contemporary society; but they cannot provide us with a model of it any more than the equivalent elements (that is, the appetitive and the violence-deferring) would have sufficed to describe the original event.

The recent surge of interest in demography attempts to translate the ethical problem of social organization into a quantitative model of population pressure on resources—whence Harris's inclusion of human reproduction in his basic set of material constraints (the "infrastructure"). The neo-Malthusian perspective makes population the independent variable in cultural evolution. In any form of social organization, population will tend to increase to the limit of economic capacity, thus leading to reorganization in the direction of greater intensity of production, which requires concomitantly a greater energy input per capita. This argument is developed for agricultural societies in Ester Boserup's highly influential and persuasive little book *The Conditions of Agricultural Growth* (London: George Allen and Unwin, 1965). Boserup shows that technological progress is not an independent variable, because it always entails an increased labor input that can be enforced only by population pressure. Necessity is thus the mother of invention.

Materialists do not seem to have noticed that this is in direct contradiction with Marxist theory, which makes social evolution dependent on the creation of a surplus such as could never exist in the neo-Malthusian view. Demographic determinism is, as an anthropology, vastly inferior to Marxism, which recognizes as essential the problematic of differential powers and rewards in society. And, surely, population increase is determined by the desire for social benefits rather than the other way around. One need only cite as an example the extraordinary demographic stability attributed to paleolithic populations. Demographers' attempts to demonstrate that sedentarism (generally speaking, agriculture) involves an irreversible transformation of this stability into a maximization of population often lead to the most tiresome and unconvincing arguments.[29] The determination of the correlations of fertility with any number of other variables does not make it any less true that a woman's fertility is determined first and foremost by her and her husband in conformity with social and economic pressures. Ethical conceptions are not mere ideologies that reflect an alienated perception of economic realities. These conceptions express the degree of man's understanding of himself possible in the societies in which they were created; and without the evolution of this understanding, no evolution of socioeconomic organization would have been possible.

Man is not above material constraints, but he did not become human, as the materialists imagine, simply in struggling against them. Humanity was forged rather by the need to overcome the conflicts involved in living and acting together to transcend material constraints. The origin of representation, which defines the human, was not "practical" but ethical. And the material problems of man have been mediated by the ethical ever since. Even if we accept the pessimistic conclusions of the neo-Malthusians concerning the material base of modern society, we must never forget that the difficulties we face in an energy crisis are, in the first place, problems of social organization. Above all, now that we possess the material means to annihilate all human life, we are forced to recognize that our most urgent and essential problem is ethical, not material.

To the extent that models of ethical organization are desirable, indeed, indispensable, a generative theory of representation is the only adequate anthropology. It is the lack of adequate explanatory models that makes all other anthropologies incapable of properly evaluating the extraordinary achievement of modern society, which they either implicitly or explicitly denounce or, even worse, glorify from the narrow standpoint of its privileged members. These theories reflect rather than adequately explain the mutual resentment of privileged and underprivileged that is so apparent a feature of our society. That—as shall shortly be apparent—we are indeed able to situate this resentment within our model instead of simply ignoring or condemning it should already suffice to demonstrate the greater power of our theory.

Our claim of superiority for the anthropological model founded on the theory of representation is not "value-free." On the contrary, it depends on an implicit valorization that we shall now attempt to clarify. What we are wagering on is the continued evolution of human society on the basis of its highest achieved evolutionary level, that is, the society of today. Expressed in this manner, our wager may appear unobjectionable, but a moment's reflection on the competing anthropological theories will show that they disagree most dramatically with it. For we insist on the central significance of representation, not from the idealist perspective that considers ideas more real than things, but from a faith in the proven human capacity to make use of its ideas to solve the problems posed by things. Thus we prefer to see modern society not as poised on the brink of disaster but as the source of the best available model of the society of the future, provided this model is constructed according to the general anthropology that follows from our hypothesis.

That the archetype of the human community has as its center the scene of representation is of course only a hypothesis, however plausible. That representation occupies this central position in modern society is perhaps a controversial proposition, but one which, if properly understood, is far from arbitrary. The creation of high-speed electronic data-processing may well be the most significant social development of the last generation, the effects of which on the production-system can only continue to grow and ramify. That acts of consumption have themselves become acts of representation, as Jean Baudrillard has asserted, is an arguably accurate description of the "consumer society," in which consumer goods constitute an elaborate semantic system; our own qualifications of this assertion in *The Origin of Language* do not attempt to refute its fundamental thesis. But most striking of all is the importance of cultural phenomena in a society whose critics never cease to condemn its materialism. The commercial vulgarity of the majority of the esthetic creations of our society should not blind us to their indisputably cultural nature.

Modern society, whatever its failings, is the product of an accelerating series of triumphs of the scene of representation over man's material and ethical problems. This fact is in itself no proof that all present and future obstacles will be amenable to similar triumphs.

And surely there is a place in human science for the positive study of such obstacles and of the concrete options available for dealing with them. A general anthropology cannot provide solutions to an economic crisis or a population explosion; it can at best help us to understand the social institutions within which any proposed solutions will have to be implemented. But the chief task of human science is to provide a holistic model of human society and its evolution. While it attempts to save itself from future annihilation, our society continues to function on a day-to-day basis. As we have already pointed out, the ethic of this society is only implicit, and differs greatly from the more or less traditional moral principles that are at the heart of all current social ideologies. The necessity that human science seeks to render this ethic explicit rather than devote itself exclusively to the formulation of analyses of and solutions to specific social problems cannot be decided on purely logical grounds. Our choice of the first alternative is based on our conviction that our society can and should become conscious of its ethic.

Ethical conceptions have occupied a central position in the systems of representations of all premodern societies, albeit in an esthetic (ritual or secular) rather than a theoretical form. Today, only theory can elaborate such a conception, and theory is therefore called upon to situate itself at the center of our culture. Human science must become, in this hypothesis, the "high culture" of our age. But this can be accomplished only if it accepts the burden of considering its own culture with high seriousness.

FROM THEORETICAL TO POSITIVE ANTHROPOLOGY

In our preceding discussion of the originary event and its immediate consequences, we were careful to maintain the minimality of our model. In this section, while presenting some speculations on this matter, we shall attempt to justify our minimalist, deductive theory of representation as a necessary foundation for a positive—that is, empirical—anthropology, in contrast with the gradualist methodology of traditional social science.

Studies of primate behavior on the one hand and paleontological discoveries on the other have produced a large body of knowledge relevant to the life of early man.[30] It is generally assumed, for example, that he lived in bands of twenty to fifty individuals, and that the hunting of large animals, a task requiring cooperation, communication, and the use of weapons, was the primary stimulus to the hominization of apes that already walked on two legs as a result of their forced descent from the trees. This being the case, it is reasonable to assume that the central object of the originary event was a large animal, brought to bay by primitive hunting methods (which usually involved stampeding over cliffs or into swamps rather than direct combat). This supposition would provide a plausible explanation for the sacrificial, alimentary nature of most major rituals down to the time of classical civilization (that is, before the Buddhist and Christian "reformations") as well as help to explain the predominance of large game animals in paleolithic art. The connection between the origin of representation and ritual with the presumably male-oriented occupation of the hunt would also help to explain the cultural subordination of women that persists to this day, although the greater male potential for violence requiring deferral through representation is no doubt already a sufficient explanation for male cultural supremacy.

Many further suppositions could be made along these lines that would be of use in constructing models of primitive human (and prehuman) social forms. But those given will suffice to illustrate our main point, which is that our theory of representation, as opposed to the positive anthropology that can subsequently be built upon it, must scrupulously avoid including any such suppositions in its fundamental hypothesis. We have explained this earlier by the principle of minimality or parsimony (Occam's razor); but in the context of positive social science a new formulation of this principle is required. For we are not now speaking of the necessity of deriving the same result (that is, representation) from the fewest postulated data (the minimal hypothesis), but rather of dealing with representations as they exist in a minimal—that is, deductive—manner as opposed to an inductive or "positive" manner. To the extent that we presuppose an originary event, this event must have occurred to real men faced with a real object; our choice to ignore the specificity of this object is a methodological decision of a higher level than the choice between possible versions of an already abstract originary hypothesis.

Our choice of a minimal hypothesis represents in fact a maximal use of what we have called the logic of representation. There is thus an apparent justification for classifying our theory as a *philosophical* anthropology. We must reject this designation, but this rejection does not involve a claim that we are merely redefining positive anthropology on a more rigorous basis. Our claim is a more ambitious one: that the "philosophical" element in our theory makes it stronger than any possible positive theory, and that this superior strength implies as a corollary that positive human science on the model of the natural sciences is intrinsically inadequate to its subject matter. More specifically, whatever its success in codifying and predicting human behavior, positive anthropology is constitutionally incapable of constructing an adequate theory of representation, whereas our theory can without difficulty integrate within itself the results of positive anthropology. It suffices for this that we ignore the relationship between the phenomena it describes and the originary scene of representation—that we set this relationship, so to speak, equal to zero.

The minimal hypothesis is distinguished in principle from any positive hypothesis by the absence of any specific characterization of the central desire-object, and by the corollary absence of a preliminary "scenario." Such a scenario could no doubt be supplied. We could describe a hunting scene in which the band of hunters, armed with primitive weapons, face each other around the body of their victim. But the link between such a scene, however plausibly engendered, and the originary act of representation must always be conjectural. No set of circumstances can be constructed from which representation may be simply *deduced*. Thus the details of any originary scenario can never be justified. At best such a scenario can be of heuristic value, a means of persuading skeptics of the reasonableness of the theory that follows; but there is always a danger that such a persuasive model is nothing more than a myth of origin in a modern guise. The minimal hypothesis does not suffer from this weakness because it is constructed by working backward from its necessary result—that is, the act of representation—rather than forward from a conjectured prehuman state.

Positive hypotheses too may be conceived as a posteriori explanations for a known result; but this fact is belied by their actual construction, in which narrative plausibility is presented in the guise of causality. No doubt this is generally an adequate procedure for formulating the in principle testable hypotheses of the social sciences. But the origin of representation differs from the normal social-science explicandum in two related points. First and most obviously, our hypotheses on this subject are not testable. Even the experiment of King Psammetichus related by Herodotus (2.2) and recalled by Condillac[31] would not be conclusive, for the human brain is no longer that of the first creators of language. But what is more, a causal hypothesis is not only radically untestable, it is *unformulable*. The notion of causality can be applied statistically or concretely, but it is illegitimate to use it to bridge the gap between a general context and a specific event. If previous discussions of the origin of language, or of representation in general, have been rendered all but worthless by what we have called "gradualism," the refusal to recognize the necessarily evenemential nature of this origin, that is because causal hypotheses cannot derive an event from a general situation. No doubt the *probability* of an event could be so derived, but that probability would be meaningless in a situation where it suffices that the event occur once.[32]

Thus the philosophers have not simply been deluded in refusing to countenance positive theories of the origin of representation. What we have called the "logic of representation" has as its sole valid object the inference from the fact of representation itself back to the minimal-hypothetical situation. In that restricted sense, any formulation of this hypothesis is "philosophical." One may even see the formulation of this and, presumably, other minimal hypotheses as the sole legitimate domain for the exercise of philosophy—that is, if we conceive of philosophy as something other than formal logic, which is a "logic of representation" from which the problematic aspect of the form-content relation has been removed. The origin of representation poses a unique problem to human science that must be dealt with by means of a unique methodology that integrates the fundamental intuition of philosophy. That our theory is not itself philosophical needs no further argument here; the fact that modern continental philosophy has reached the impasse of Derridean self-deconstruction is sufficient proof that it has been unable to solve its fundamental problem and can only demonstrate that a solution in its own terms is inconceivable. That the theory of representation can go further than philosophy was already demonstrated in *The Origin of Language*, although the less rigorous, more positive formulation of our hypothesis may have overstated the differences.

One further caveat is necessary concerning the relation of the originary hypothesis to positive anthropology. Nothing in this section implies that the origin of representation is in some sense unknowable or paradoxical, that representation is something "always already" existing, as our Derrideans are fond of saying. Were this really the case, there would be in fact no problem, for the gradualists would be right. Indeed, their coexistence with the philosophers, although they generally ignore each other's work, is based on a secret communality in the *peur sacrée* of the original event. Our hypothesis, on the contrary, posits its existence, not as the probabilistic result of a prior situation, but *because representation exists*. The nonconstructibility of the event is no proof of its nonexistence. It is precisely the opposite that is the case. It is because the origin of representation is an event that it is nonconstructible, just as any other historical occurrence is nonconstructible through positive hypotheses.

The problem of the first historical event is one of formalization, not of logical possibility. That we have succeeded in formalizing it is not, however, something to be taken lightly; for as we shall attempt to show in what follows, the whole sequence of human culture has taken the unformalizability or, more broadly, the nonconceptualizability of this originary event as the underlying guarantee of its fictions. This event is the prototype of all esthetic subject matter, both ritual and artistic, as well as the "always already" a priori given of philosophy. But once its formalization has become "unthinkable" rather than simply unthought, it becomes itself a theme of thought, a problem the solution to which is inevitable. Thus we cannot take credit for a theoretical event on a par with the event our hypothesis describes. Generative anthropology is the product of the entire history of culture up to the present. The end of culture; the beginning of human science.

PART II

The Origin of Culture

We have hypothesized in the preceding chapter that the original ritual was an esthetic reproduction of the original event. This reproduction is the prototype of all cultural phenomena, which all ultimately derive from it. We must now attempt to construct this derivation as a hypothetical historical sequence, just as in *The Origin of Language* we proposed a hypothetical construction of the fundamental forms of language. The vastly richer domain of culture makes such construction both more difficult and more essential. For if we can do little to language, the fate of culture is in our hands.

The first question to be asked is that of the "elementary forms" of culture that would correspond to the elementary forms—ostensive and imperative—of language. "Ostensive" language is the most primitive form of language proper, consisting of locutions uttered (by sound or gesture) only in the presence of their (significant) referent. Ostensive language could possess no grammar to speak of. In the second, "imperative" stage of language, where the utterance of a word could serve to make its referent appear (that is, through the agency of the locutee), we find protogrammatical structures such as noun-adjective governance, person, tense, and negation. Only in mature language, defined as containing declarative sentences, can these and other structures be fully grammaticalized; other sentence-types like the interrogative or the subjunctive are derivatives of the declarative. The elementary linguistic forms continue to exist in declarative language, but no empirical evidence is available for the immature stages of linguistic evolution, our reconstruction of which is wholly hypothetical.

Chapter 6 of *The Origin of Language* hypothesized about the sort of cultural forms that would be associated with the elementary forms

103

of language. The inadequacy of that discussion for our present purposes may be largely attributed to the marginal, very nearly epilogic status of the forms of discourse in the scheme of that work, but there is a substantive difficulty as well. The hypothesis of *The Origin of Language*, in contrast with that developed here, placed ritual and language on an equal footing as derivatives of the original event. Thus when the time came to discuss the forms of discourse, which are, indeed—although this was not brought out as such—*cultural* forms, their content could be derived, in keeping with this originally instituted symmetry, only from ritual, as if ritual had evolved independently of language and yet "included" it in some undefined way.[1]

Our present discussion no longer attributes a primary status to ritual, which is subordinated to the broader category of the cultural—that is, the institutional-esthetic. The question of the sacred is not eliminated by this subordination; it must be faced head-on. But by subordinating the sacred to the esthetic (which we postulated as an element of the original event and not merely of its reproduction), we are able to deal with ritual and secular-esthetic acts within the same evolutionary framework. Thus the "esthetics" defined by the stages of linguistic evolution may be seen to define in their turn the stages, not merely of discourse, conceived as a secular derivative of ritual, but of ritual—and of culture—itself.

If we consider linguistic form as an indication of the degree of esthetic evolution, without taking any position as to a possible causal relationship between it and the rest of culture, we may define two "elementary" esthetics corresponding to the two elementary linguistic forms. We will thus call these the "ostensive" and "imperative" esthetics.[2] The esthetic moment of the original event as well as its institutionalization in the ritual reproduction of this event already exemplifies the ostensive esthetic; the imperative esthetic will be discussed below.

5

The Elementary Forms
of Culture

OSTENSIVE CULTURE

In ostensive language, the word, although retained in significant memory and always capable of being imagined, is uttered only in the presence of its referent. This usage in the context of virtual but not actual communal presence—that is, in a context not "cultural" in the strong sense employed here—is of considerable practical value as a warning or, more generally, a catalyst of appropriative action. This "acultural" or private usage does not concern us directly; we mention it only in order to help clarify the difference between the cultural and acultural contexts. In the acultural context, it is the utterance itself that establishes presence between locutor and locutee, the state of receptivity-in-principle of the latter to the words of the former being what we have defined as virtual presence. The cultural context may be defined as that in which communal presence is already established from the beginning. Here the scene of representation does not function for practical ends, that is, those determined by appetite and objectal desire; the scene is itself the focus of the desire of each member of the community. In this context, the utterance is not, as in the acultural case, the origin of the public scene but rather the consummation that confirms the success of the reinstitution of this scene. This utterance confirms, in particular, the presence of the new referent that "esthetically" reproduces its original.

An ostensive culture may be defined as one in which signs are realized only in the presence of their referents. The reproduced referent is not itself a sign; it does not refer to its original but replaces it. The sign uttered by the participants confirms this replacement as adequate. But in the communal cultural context, the appearance of the new referent is not merely a contingent occasion for the emission of the sign but a necessary element of the reproduced scene. The impulsion for this reproduction is ethical in nature; the referential object is a necessary mediator of the self-reproduction of the community on the periphery of the scene of representation. What we may call this object's ostensive sacrality is the perception of this necessity by the participants. As the referent of the sign in the acultural context of virtual presence, the object cannot be spoken of as sacred; but in the communal context, its presence has the same degree of necessity as the sign that designates it. Sacrality exists, no doubt, only in the minds of the participants, but this does not prevent its essential traits from being rigorously determined by the ethical situation in which the sacred object functions.

What is precluded in ostensive culture is any form of representation of the sacred object in its absence, as well as the conflation of the representation with its object that representation *in absentia* makes possible. The sacred object thus retains at this stage its absolute difference from its worshipers—absolute because defined by the originary opposition between appetite and its object. The eater, in other words, has no occasion to "identify" with the eaten. No doubt a strictly appetitive relation no longer obtains; the necessity that characterizes the sacrality of the object is ethical, not appetitive. But this ethical necessity has not yet determined, as it will at later stages, a breakdown of the original appetitive difference. For the referent of the sign, even if it is, for the duration of the ritual, contemplated "in itself" rather than coveted as an appetitive object, is still identifiable with its original only by means of esthetic criteria of functional resemblance that reduce without eliminating their original appetitive basis.

The specifically esthetic component of ostensive culture may still be identified with the "dramatic," as in *The Origin of Language*, provided we make clear that "dramatic" discourse at this level does not correspond to what will later become dialogue—that is, the interactions of the participants—but to the designation of the scene from without—that is, the unspoken *mise en scène* symbolized on occasion by the written characters of the program or the playbill. One can find scenes of the designation of the victim within classical drama and its modern derivatives. But this designation, an element of what we have called the "form of content" of the drama, is secondary with respect to the dramatic (that is, scenic) form itself.[1] For the dramatic scene generally includes not merely the central object but other peripheral figures, and it is precisely this mediating scenic presence that would be unthinkable in an ostensive culture.

From the outset, ritual involves its participants in playing a role in a public scene that is, as we have taken pains to define it, reproduced rather than simply allowed to come about. But in ostensive culture, this reproduction must be entirely dependent on the presence of the central object that can alone be designated, that is, *signified*. The scene, in other words, can be interpreted by its participants only as that of the designation of this object. Or if the term "interpretation" is thought overly subjective, we may say that only the act of designation can be *reflected upon*, as opposed to being simply reproduced in an unreflecting intuition of necessity. The designative, signifying element alone makes of the rite a cultural activity, and for this reason it is seen as central even by modern observers. Even for one who knows that the essence of ritual is the peaceful collaboration of the participants, it is natural to begin a description of a rite with its central object. But the modern observer can immediately see the primacy of the act of signification as opposed to the signified object, whereas the participants in an ostensive culture, for whom emission of the sign is wholly dependent on the presence of its referent, must invert this relation of dependency.

This preliminary exposition permits us to begin to clarify the ambiguous role of mimesis in cultural forms. For at the most elementary cultural stage the structure of this ambiguity is most clearly visible. On the one hand, the designated object is an "imitation" of its original; on the other, the participants in the act of designation "imitate" their original act. But it immediately follows from the definition of an ostensive esthetic that, in the first case, imitation must be wholly independent of the public scene of representation, whereas in the second, it is, if not wholly, centrally dependent on it. For the central feature of ritual repetition is the reproduction of the sign, that is, an act of representation. The central object, on the contrary, cannot be *represented* at all in the absence of its original model; its esthetic adequacy can only be ascertained after the fact, not created.

The contrast between these two varieties of mimesis highlights the formal frame that is the essential determinant, the sine qua non, of all cultural phenomena. The sign is not "imitated," or "reproduced" in the ordinary sense of the term; it is *repeated* as an act the performance of which presents no difficulty, an act, as is commonly said, "transparent" to its signification. Whatever else the ritual participant may do, he expresses the essential identity of the central object in the present performance with that of all preceding performances, and ultimately with its original model. This identity is formal, not esthetic. For although the resemblance of the new to the original object is esthetic, the sign does not express resemblance but identity. This formal identity is alone essential. But it is not yet experienced as such; for the object must be available to provoke the sign. In an ostensive culture, the mimesis by which an object may be reproduced is still purely passive. At the higher levels, when the mimetic reproduction of the central content of the cultural act becomes a significant occupation, it is easy to overlook the element of formal equivalence expressed by the ceremony enacted around the mimetic object. At the ostensive stage, it is still this formal designative element that predominates. Here art is fully subordinate to ritual. In so saying, however, we imply a definition of these terms that cannot without further refinement be made to hold for all cultural stages, particularly if we wish to consider the possibility of a purely secular—that is, nonritual—art.

The esthetic of ostensive culture implies a basic ethical order that allows us to define within limits the socioeconomic organization of an "ostensive" society. The ethical conception of the community at this stage being limited to the ritual situation, the existence of laws or interdictions is not yet possible.[2] The sort of exchange-system that can be supported by such an ethic is limited to the distribution of the central object as described in Part I. At this point, there is no loss of generality in assuming this original object to be in fact an item of food, or, more particularly, a large game-animal; for our definition of ostensive culture does not limit it to a single rite, merely to a single basic type of rite. Thus we may assume that such rituals will develop around the distribution of any potentially conflict-inspiring items in the community, replacing prehuman dominance mechanisms as the essential means of keeping the peace.

There is, however, another variety of ritual that constitutes an elaboration of the basic form within the limits of ostensive culture: the apotropaic or avoidance ritual. For if the community defines itself ethically in the ritual designation of an appetitive object, the same self-definition may be expected to be used as a defense against dangerous objects. Both sorts of objects may in fact be spoken of as "appetitive," in the sense that both affect the material (precultural) needs of the members of the community, either positively or negatively. The only true asymmetry is in the area of distribution, for the allocation to each member of a portion of the offending object would not produce the direct appetitive satisfaction of a portion of a desirable one. This presents no problem if we assume the ethical existence of the community to be established and reinforced by positive, distributory ritual, which we suppose to be primary at this stage.[3]

Just as the ostensive utterance form is still used in mature languages (in expressions like "Fire!" "Man overboard!" "Ouch!"), so ostensive cultural forms are not simply displaced by more advanced ones. This is particularly true in the conservative domain of ritual. For although ritual, like language, evolves into higher forms, this evolution is considerably less dramatic than that of language. The cognitive domain of the latter can indeed increase without limit, making the elementary, precognitive linguistic forms appear mere survivals less important than in fact they are (imagine a language— or this sentence—without an imperative). Ritual, on the contrary, remains bound to its original ethical function, and as the ethic of modern society becomes indefinitely complex, secular discourse alone can attempt to cope with it, there being no central scene of representation for ritual participants to gather round. But of the rituals that survive today, the most elementary fare perhaps the best, because their ethical intentions, more modest than those of the higher rituals, risk less being disappointed. Any ritual occasioned *ad hoc* by a contingent cause is essentially an ostensive ritual, even if its linguistic content is not strictly limited to the ostensive. This category includes quotidian social gestures like greetings, excuses, responses to "dangerous" events like sneezes, as well as the more elaborate rites generally classed under the rubric of superstition. These all fall into the category of "small-group" rather than general communal rituals, the latter being hard put to survive in the modern world. Although the details are unknowable, the main line of the derivation of such rituals from the communal form is not difficult to trace. To the extent that an event is significant, that is, potentially conflictive, a ritual usage arises to prevent conflict, and its forms are adapted to small groups just as those of language are.[4] Such rituals are "ostensive" because they are performed in the presence of a contingent significant object and serve to enhance the coherence of the group that might otherwise be disturbed by it. "Hello" in effect announces the speaker as a potential perturbing element; the replying, sym-

metric "Hello" turns this autodesignation into the common designation of a mutual presence. Answering "God bless you" to a sneeze
reestablishes group cohesion after a "violent" act.

In none of these or similar cases is the *linguistic* content of the
ritual act simply designative. What is said is generally derived from
an imperative expression requesting the divinity to confer blessings
upon an injured party, requesting to be excused for an inadvertent
violent act, and so forth. Yet these imperatives have retained a merely
ostensive function; they have become formulas, often shorn of the
grammatical marks of the imperative ("hello," "good-bye," "sorry,"
"thanks"). Evidently the efficacy of these rituals was at some point
enhanced by the "exchange-value" of the imperatives employed in
them. Rather than merely designating the problem, the verbal element attempts to offer a compensatory solution: blessings, good
wishes, excuses. The tendency of this imperative element to decay
is nevertheless a sign of the essentially ostensive context of the ritual.
No doubt such decays, followed by renewals, occurred on an indefinite number of occasions. Today, for example, there is a tendency
to replace the meaningless "Good-bye" with the more significant
imperative "Have a nice day!" Some object to this as "insincere";
the ritual leave-taking context appears to them inappropriate for such
wishes. What this teaches us is that the imperative forms are, in
effect, naturalizing, deritualizing. Thus, when one is genuinely afraid
that the other will be offended, or genuinely desirous of showing
appreciation, the linguistic formulae are expanded, grammaticalized,
and spoken as true sentences ("I'm really sorry," "Please forgive
me," "I really want to thank you very much"). That these are clichés
is a secondary matter, for the passage from significant expression to
cliché remains encompassed within the realm of language, not ritual.
The act of saying good-bye may be deritualized in its linguistic
content, but its ritual character reasserts itself, not because "Have
a nice day!" becomes a cliché but because it is being used in the
context of a social ritual.

The apparent difficulty of these familiar examples stems from the
fact that, precisely because of their ritual nature, they do not involve
ordinary linguistic usage. The use of a linguistic ostensive is *not* a
ritual: crying "Fire!" or even "Ouch!" is making practical use of
language to call the attention of one's interlocutor(s) to something
significant. Saying "God bless you!" to a sneeze is not. An ostensive
ritual is not a ritual use of the ostensive, but the re-creation of the
scene of representation around a significant object not created or
recalled for the purpose, but found contingently and designated *by
the ritual* as equivalent to its previous objects. Thus such rituals serve

to define real-world situations as falling within previously established categories. That ostensive rituals alone are found in quotidian circumstances follows directly from this fact; even in a society little given to large-scale rites, these remain functional because they define the ethic of small-group relations. Their verbal content should not be analyzed in itself but as a function of such definition.

If we consider terms of greeting, for example, we frequently find interrogatives like "How do you do?" or "How are you?" as well as optatives like "Good morning!" or "Greetings!" That the interrogatives are not really concerned with seeking information is obvious from the fact that, even when they are not shortened to "Howdy" or "Hiya," they tend to elicit symmetrical responses, that at best include an "answer" as a preliminary element ("I'm fine, how are you?"). The disequilibrium between question-answer asymmetry and symmetrical repetition cannot be explained on linguistic grounds, even by invoking the category of banalization. But it can be explained quite easily on *ethical* grounds. The point of the question is to elicit a response. The symmetry of the *content* of this response is secondary with respect to the symmetry of its existence as such. (It is not "form" that is opposed to content; ethical function is a more general category than linguistic form.) Thus verbal symmetry lags behind ethical symmetry.

But why must this symmetry be created through words? Why, in other terms, must a conversation be started? Because the common act of speech is precisely what establishes between the parties a scene of representation, not as a locus for the exchange of information but—just as in the original ritual—as the locus around which the solidarity of the group is established. Quotidian small-group rituals most often serve to define the very existence of such groups. In the case of greetings, there is an urgent need to define the new group peripherally to the scene of representation; the content of the scene must remain undefined because no specific content could be counted on in the general case. Here the linguistic content is in greater disequilibrium with the ethical symmetry of the group than is the case, for example, in leave-taking from a group already established and now facing dissolution. The sneeze, by which one member of a group distinguishes himself temporarily, is closer to large-group rituals in nature. In each case the ethic of the ostensive ritual requires that mutual presence be established or reinforced only around a contingent public scene of representation.

As a final point, we should note the relationship of such rites to the category of the sacred. Even in "ostensive culture," we may, after all, assume the presence of rituals such as greeting; in what sense are or are not such rituals sacred? A society where the sacred mediates the existence of contingent subgroups will evoke a sacred being on greeting. But the linguistic content can never be the determining factor. The contentless nature of the greeting ritual demonstrates that, without specific content, sacrality is a meaningless concept. Even a sneeze, or a broken mirror, may be spoken of as sacred *to a degree*. But, in effect, this degree can be measured operationally at the ostensive level only by the intensity or importance of the ritual it determines.

The conclusion we must draw is this: the only truly desacralized rituals are those, like greeting and leave-taking, that have no stable central object.[5] The use of ostensive rituals with central objects cannot be defended rationally; it corresponds to a survival of sacrality, a "superstition." Because most such survivals are in the process of extinction in modern society, our conclusion is not a mere artifact of our definitions. And, indeed, the decline of such rituals, like the decline of the sacred in general, can be traced to the loss of their ethical functions. The ritual creation of arbitrary *ad hoc* "communities" to stand against symbolically perturbing objects like sneezes is no longer functional. In contrast, the creation and dissolution of *ad hoc* communities of acquaintances remains important in itself. The ethic of such small groups is not affected by desacralization on the level of the community as a whole. Any concrete motivation for ritualized interaction tends either to be rationalized or to lose its motivating force; but the mere coming into and out of contact is not subject to such calculations of rationality.

IMPERATIVE CULTURE

Ostensive culture could add no new forms to those already described under the rubrics of the originary hypothesis and its immediate secondary outgrowth, ritual. The notion of imperative culture provides a greater challenge, for this is the mediating category between the original ostensive forms and the mature forms associated with the declarative sentence.

The linguistic aspect of the transition from the ostensive to the imperative stage of culture has already been described at length in *The Origin of Language*. The question may arise whether the broader perspective of the present work is compatible with the independent status therein accorded to linguistic evolution. Would not ritual, for example, offer a locus more appropriate, because more intense, for such innovation? But this question is based on an insufficiently rigorous understanding of the originary hypothesis. It is language, coeval with the scene of representation and not dependent on any reproduction of its preconditions, that stands at the very center of culture. Any innovation in the fundamental object-relation of ritual would be *in the first place* an innovation in language, in the intentional relationship between the sign and its (ritual) object. Thus the question of whether or not linguistic innovation first took place within ritual is a secondary one. And even as such, we should still answer it in the negative. It is not at moments of greatest but of least significance that innovations become possible. The significance of the ostensive object is not merely an esthetic one, it is appetitive as well. In ritual, a whole distributive apparatus is established to serve this appetitive function, and there is nothing an imperative sign could do to satisfy it. As we shall see, the development of imperative ritual must involve no small reorganization of the structure of ostensive ritual. It is in the independent, secular use of language, at a lower level of significance than ritual, that the transition from ostensive to imperative must have taken place. Thus we have no need to revise on this point the exposition of *The Origin of Language*.

The ostensive becomes an imperative when it is pronounced in the absence of its object, with the desire of making appear in reality the object that is already associated with the word in the imagination. This usage of the word, once understood by another, leads him to supply the missing object, thus establishing the performative element characteristic of the imperative form. The period of deferral during which the production and reception of the ostensive sign took the place of appetitive action now becomes extended into a period of awaiting the performance that alone will "complete" or fulfill the imperative. Thus the symmetry among the speakers of the ostensive is replaced by a radical asymmetry. But, as in the Hegelian master-slave dialectic, it is from the performative element of the imperative that objective grammatical structure will develop. Analysis of the performance precedes the analysis of the utterance.[6]

The imperative esthetic is independent of the presence of its object. If our derivation is correct, this esthetic was indeed the source of the imperative form, because the use of the sign in the absence of its referent could only have been motivated by its "esthetic," presentifying value. That is, the imagined sign gives way to the real (uttered) sign because the contemplation of the latter is more effective in making its referent appear (esthetically) present. But the most characteristic use of the imperative esthetic is in the visual arts, where figures representing the referent are created on the basis of its remembered image. Esthetic mimesis can here create objects, and not merely "performances" as in the ostensive case. Although we have rejected the hypothesis that the origin of the imperative as such—that is, as a linguistic phenomenon—took place in a ritual context, we must assume a ritual origin for esthetic figuration. For, as we have already seen, figuration is from the first a necessary element of the reproduction of the central object of ritual. The possibility of substituting a created image for the real original would thus have an obvious motivation, although not yet a sufficient explanation. For this substitution would not immediately modify the ostensive character of the ritual; on the contrary, its very point would be to preserve this character in the absence of an appropriately substitutable central object. The long-term consequences of such substitution would, however, be the restructuring of the ritual and of the culture associated with it. For the esthetic substitution of an image for its object would profoundly modify the ethic of the ritual.

The asymmetry of the linguistic imperative contains an implicit ethic, but one that is purely situational and reversible. The passage from language to ritual fixes this ethic in an ethical conception, the structure of which we shall now examine. In the first place, the substitution of a figure—image or mask—for the central object implies that the real referent of the figure is not only absent but *essentially* absent. This is the beginning of religion in the sense of the worship of transcendental beings. The status of the referent must remain ambiguous in an imperative culture wherein no statements can be made concerning it. Its absence may be essential, but no transcendental abode has been imagined for it. It simply exists elsewhere, and this existence guarantees the solidarity of the community around its image which, in the course of the ritual, will by the very nature of ritual participation become functionally identical with its original. For it is the community whose power to defer its own violence through representation is incarnated in the central object. The central figure is not a mere copy that takes or holds the place of the original. We are justified in calling such a ritual "imperative" because the representation of the central object is an appeal to that object to manifest itself in the representation. But this implies a more complex relationship between participants and center than was the case in ostensive culture.

The figural representation cannot be conceived as a mere *pis aller*, a substitute for an unfindable original. Because the figure can never be identified with the original, it can be substituted for it only if the latter is conceived no longer as a sacred *object* existing only in its manifestations but as a sacred *being* that exists above and beyond the concrete manifestations it may take on. The "signified" of the word/gesture of designation has thus become partly independent of its referent. This independence is not merely formal; the imperative is effective only insofar as it is *addressed to* this "signified," summoning it to be present. Thus the sacred being in imperative ritual possesses, in the eyes of the participants, an *intentional* ability to manifest itself or not.

The asymmetry of the imperative is a step in the direction of establishing symmetry between the sacred being and its worshipers—in a word, of *humanizing* the sacred. The animal images and masks that we may associate with the imperative level of culture are in fact signs of a growing anthropomorphism. This is the beginning of a development of profound ethical consequences. The notion of an anthropomorphic divinity is a precondition of the eventual spiritualization of religion in the Judeo-Christian (and Hindu-Buddhist) traditions. The ethical conception of the community depends no longer on the mere *ad hoc* appearance of the sacred being but on the will of a being whose judgment whether or not to manifest itself in the rite reflects the real cohesion of the community. This judgment can already at this stage express itself in the form of interdictions and prescriptions, although the notion of "justice" can be conceived only at the level of mature language.

In order to understand the motivation for this evolution, we must examine the asymmetrical ethical structure of the imperative. It is too easy to view this asymmetry as the expression of an unambiguous authority-relation between the speaker and the designated performer of the deed. For the asymmetry between word and act may equally well be interpreted to the advantage of the latter; an imperative may be an order, but it may equally well be a supplication. It is evidently in this manner that we must interpret the typical religious use of the imperative in prayer (not itself an imperative ritual in the sense used here: see below, p. 119), although the existence of shamans with the power to command magical forces shows that the hierarchy between man and divinity long remains ambiguous. It is therefore better to avoid the question of hierarchy altogether and to consider only the word-deed asymmetry that is constitutive of the imperative.

This asymmetry is, in fact, pregnant with a richer symmetry than the superficial one of the ostensive. For the equality of all participants in the ostensive is made possible only by the absolute differentiation of the central object that serves as its referent. This differentiation can be conceived only on appetitive grounds. In the imperative, however, there is no absolutely differentiated object. The real referent is absent, and in its place is a relation between men. The disappearance of the real referent in imperative ritual may well give the appearance of creating a more rather than less absolute difference between this object and the participants. But the transcendental existence of the sacred being is in fact wholly defined by and dependent on the representation that replaces it, whereas the real central object of ostensive ritual belonged to a world irreducible to representation. Nor should we be too hasty to speak of an increased "alienation" on the part of the participants. Their ethical conception of the human community is far closer to maturity than that of ostensive culture. For the alienation of the group's cohesion in a signified being gives it a permanent—and permanently representable—status, unlike the contingent one of the ostensive object.

Substitution of a representation for the central object of ritual implies, not the simple abandonment of the distribution of appetitive satisfaction, but its reorganization. The real source of appetitive satisfaction is no longer the sacred object/being itself but a representative of it. The representation of this being by, say, an animal need not take place in the same ritual as the figured substitution described above. The figural rite may be, for example, a prelude to the hunt that precedes the ritual feast. The deferral made possible by imperative ritual remains limited by a horizon of concrete appetitive satisfaction. The absence of the divine being whose presence is to guarantee the success of the rite, and who can manifest himself functionally only as incarnated in his figural representative, may be maintained for the duration of the rite, but the rite is not complete in itself. The "manifestation" of the being in the rite must be understood as preliminary to the concrete manifestation of an appetitively satisfying representation of this being. The ethic of imperative culture holds the community together in the absence of material satisfaction, but always with an eye to increasing it. The purely spiritual values of communal solidarity belong to a higher ethical level.

The sacred being that imperative ritual centered on could only be the signified of an appetitive object. Students of paleolithic cave paintings have attempted to reconstruct the animal cults in which the paintings must have functioned.[7] What has been lacking in such discussions has been an appreciation of the ethical nature of these rituals, the "magical" value of which is usually simply assumed. A rite centered on an image of a game animal, whether or not animated by a human participant, is a preparation, both psychological and physical, for the hunting of the animal represented. This preparation reflects the ethic of a community no longer at the most primitive stage of its development. Whatever the details of the practices surrounding them, the paintings provide confirmatory evidence of an imperative culture. Most remarkable is the care expended on these images. Their realism demonstrates the detailed specificity of the absent beings around which the rites of these hunters must have been centered. It does not, however, imply a merely naturalistic relationship to these objects. The link between real animal and painting is the remembered image; but this very image that we take for granted was no doubt the sign of divinity for this society of hunters. For the persistence of this image in the memory and the desire to represent it publicly are, at the stage we are now describing, the sign of the liberation of the signified from its concrete original.

Several particularities of the cave images may be interpreted in the light of our analysis of imperative culture. That only large game-animals are portrayed, and the largest the most frequently, is fully in keeping with our hypothesis. Only large animals would present appropriate centers for the originary event and for similar events, because of both the necessarily collective nature of the hunt and the extreme potential for appetitive satisfaction offered by the prey. The fact that animals are often shown pierced by spears should be attributed not to wishful thinking but to remembered images of earlier hunts; that the point of the image-centered rite is to reproduce the same results goes without saying. The virtual absence of human images from the earlier caves is explained by the fact that it is the central ritual element that is sacralized, not the participants.

But that there is already at this stage an incipient identification between participant and victim is illustrated in a famous image from Lascaux that shows a buffalo wounded by a spear and, next to it, an apparently supine ithyphallic man with a birdlike head and an erect staff bearing the figure of a bird. The man has often been called a "shaman," and the bird his emblem. What would appear to be portrayed here is a ritual mimesis by the man of the animal's death. The human would be the center of an imperative ritual in which he substitutes for the animal, or more precisely, for the sacred being that would incarnate itself in the animal. The association of bird with buffalo remains unexplained, but this is a complexity that should not obscure the essential association, which is that between man and beast of prey. The trance of the man and the death of the animal are on the same plane because they are both ritual centers, one figural, one alimentary.

The earliest known artworks were probably produced at the stage of imperative culture. The existence of statuettes of apparently pregnant women ("Venuses") shows that figuration was not limited to the hunt and implies that ritual in such cultures had already attained a certain level of complexity. These men had apparently reached the level of modern *homo sapiens*, their brains having attained full evolutionary development. Thus they would have presumably been capable of speaking a mature language, and we have no reason to believe that they did not. Ritual being more conservative than language, there is no necessary incompatibility in their artwork reflecting an imperative level of ritual. On the contrary, it would only serve to confirm our hypothesis that language evolves prior to and independently of ritual.

About the sort of economic system possible in an imperative culture it is more difficult to speculate. Before imagining hierarchies communicating through unilateral imperatives, we should take note of the fact that all known hunting societies are relatively egalitarian. The imperative corresponded rather to the organization of work than to the birth of social hierarchies. The creation of ritually functional esthetic images must have corresponded to a progress in technology. If, as is often assumed, the stages of linguistic and technological development are strictly parallel, the ostensive would correspond to "found" tools and weapons shaped on an *ad hoc* basis, whereas the imperative stage would give rise to standardized tool- and weapon-making techniques. To pronounce the word in order to obtain its referent would then correspond to the act of seeking out appropriate materials and making whatever article was necessary. In the area of stone toolmaking, where alone there is a full archaeological record, the transition from ostensive to imperative culture might be reflected in the passage from the simple pebble tools and choppers associated with the earliest protohuman forms to the flaked hand-axes and other tools that first appeared over three hundred thousand years ago and which (with the exception of the axes) are still used by stone-age people today for a variety of uses. Such toolmaking requires not only a supply of appropriate stone (generally flint or obsidian) but, in particular, a precise image of what the final result is to be. This mental image may, of course, have been aided by the presence of real models, but the intellectual operation remains the same.

Imperative rituals are not an important part of modern culture. The idea that the ritual production and manipulation of an image will have an effect on its referent can only be thought of today as a superstition. There is, no doubt, a rational aspect to the "imperative" use of images. Teaching situations, rehearsals, and war games make use of simulated objects; the display of an unflattering picture of the enemy to soldiers before a battle might be said to approximate the psychological effect of imperative rituals. But, precisely, these usages are worldly, not ritual. The specifically ritual element of a social usage is that in which the repetition of an act otherwise inexplicable fixes the situation within a preestablished ethical category. The irrationality of ritual, its overtly (and, however mechanically performed, always consciously) conventional nature, is incompatible with rational, goal-seeking activity.[8] Imperative ritual has thus been relegated to voodoo and the calling up of the dead in seances.

There is one familiar ritual use of the imperative that should be clarified here: this is *prayer*. The existence of a fully transcendental divinity to whom the prayer may be addressed, individually or collectively, cannot be a feature of imperative culture *stricto sensu*. Prayer makes essential use of the imperative; the divinity is requested to provide the supplicant with some object or favorable state of affairs. But it is this absolute distinction between the divine being and the requested object that makes us reject the notion that prayer falls under the category of imperative ritual. It is not the naming—that is, the representing—of the object that is to make it appear; rather, the omnipotent divinity is expected to give consideration to the request. The imperative is thus used here as in normal conversation; only the addressee is of a different nature.

The relation with the sacred being that we have described as manifested in imperative ritual is one in which the representation of this being has for its aim making the being itself appear. This is the essence of the imperative as a linguistic form as well. The word "produces" its referent, the performer of the act being in effect only an instrument of the linguistic form. A transitional form between imperative ritual and mature religious prayer may be found in the evocation of spirits that are only then asked to perform specific deeds. Aladdin in rubbing the lamp is engaging in a true imperative ritual, independently of the wishes he will ask the genie to fulfill. To the extent that modern prayer, particularly to mediating figures like saints or angels, still retains an evocative element, it is a form of imperative ritual; but requests made to an immortal transcendental god can scarcely be placed in this category.

A significant development that we must associate with imperative culture is the formulation of laws and interdictions. Such laws would perpetuate virtual cultural presence (and not merely virtual linguistic presence) beyond the limits of specific ritual acts and thus prepare the way for the total humanization and acculturation of mature (declarative) culture. The content of these laws would refer rather to specific significant objects and acts than to general categories of acts, not to speak of internal attitudes. It is by such laws that certain objects would be designated as sacred and their use limited to the ritual context.

The formulation of laws is not a mere mechanical consequence of the existence of imperative language. The fact that objects could now be represented in their absence implies that their restriction to the domain of communal ritual—a restriction enforced in ostensive culture by the fear of the violence that would erupt upon an individual's appropriation of these objects, the same fear that had motivated the originary event—could not itself be thematically represented. And the same would hold true of positive prescriptions with regard to appropriate acts to perform when confronted with ritually significant objects.

In the case of laws, the period of awaiting associated with the imperative is extended to infinity, although periodically reinforced by their ritual reenactment. Laws always apply; their retention by the individual is the formation of a "superego" in which the voice of the community as expressed in ritual remains virtually present to the individual on a permanent basis. This virtual presence is not, however, equivalent to the fully acculturated state we associate with mature culture, for it is activated only in specific, problematic cases. Nor can imperative laws be ascribed, as they are in mature culture, to a real or legendary law giver, independent of the ritual context of periodic reenactment and speaking with the voice of a divinity whose concerns are explicitly ethical. It is only with the advent of the declarative sentence that the entirety of human activities can be placed within the cultural orbit where they are accounted for explicitly in the society's ethical conception.

Declarative ("Mature") Culture

The transition from imperative to declarative language is of a significance second only to the origin of language itself. This transition takes place when the locutee of an imperative, finding the requested performance impossible, describes the requested object as absent rather than presents it to his interlocutor.[9] The origin of the declarative is thus the moment at which language can express an objective truth rather than simply indicate the presence of a significant object or the desired presence of one that is absent. This truth is expressed in opposition to the desire expressed by the preceding imperative. The declarative describes the absence of an object the significance of which was established by the imperative, whose expression of this significance was supposed to make the object appear. The a priori significance of the subject, "topic," or "theme" of the declarative sentence remains a general feature of this form in mature language.

The declarative, upon which mature language is founded, is also the basis for grammatical form, that is, the division of utterances into parts of speech and their different morphologies and interrelationships. If, as we are assuming here, the emergence of mature language corresponds to the final stage in the genetic evolution of the human brain, then the cultural level that corresponds to this emergence would be created by modern *homo sapiens* more or less genetically capable of participating in our own culture. Hence "declarative culture" is open to further evolution in a way that lower cultural levels were not. It is this very openness that makes this transition so difficult to define in cultural terms, for all of the diverse historical forms of culture, even the most primitive, are demonstrably well past the transitional point.

Declarative culture would be the first stage to possess narrative, in which the hearer shows a "disinterested" concern for events that, having already occurred, cannot directly affect him. Only at this stage could the esthetic contemplation of a representation be altogether separated from an appetitive relationship with its referent. This emergence of the esthetic from its precultural appetitive basis is not, however, the moment of the separation of secular art from ritual, which will occur only much later, in hierarchically differentiated society. The creation of the means of liberation of culture from its appetitive base must long precede the separation of the cultural itself into separate sacred and secular domains.

The transition from imperative to declarative language, with the concomitant transformation of the ethical conceptions of the communities involved, may be considered to have brought about the first fully human society. It is at this point that we may situate the creation of *institutions*, elements of social organization independent both of the external contingencies that had determined the cultural acts of ostensive culture and of the desiring imagination that became significant at the imperative stage. Now the community becomes fully conscious of its cultural existence. That earlier ritual activities could only have been of an *ad hoc* nature does not mean that previously man lived in a vacuum; the space between cultural activities was filled with precultural forms inherited from the animal past. The drama of the originary scene must have existed and cannot be explained away by dilution over time; but this drama could not have filled the lives of its participants. Language itself at the elementary level was probably a relatively rare occurrence. Only with the advent of the declarative could the world in general become a subject of conversation.

The foregoing genetic scheme integrates the gradualism of positive anthropology within the framework of our evenemential hypothesis. The passage from imperative to declarative language and culture, unlike the origin of language, cannot be construed as instantaneous, although its association with cranial development and other features of human physical evolution makes it certain that it occurred only once.[10] The birth of declarative language would not have heralded from the outset a fully "declarative" culture. It is in this sense, and not in reference to the origin of language itself, that the question of origins is a false, mythical problem. The "always already" of deferral and supplementation has its place here, not at the very beginning of human culture. It is mature, declarative language and culture that can only emerge from more primitive linguistic and cultural forms as if it had "always already" existed. Mythical indeed are the theories of origin that suppose that the human sprang up fully formed from the head or hands of a deity.

We thus find a place in our evolutionary scheme for Lévy-Bruhl's category of the "savage mind," a notion fallen into a disrepute that has never been rigorously justified.[11] If modern stone-age tribes are indeed the most primitive humans now existing, the affirmation of the similarity of their thought processes to ours remains an act of faith so long as no models are available for the description of truly primitive states. It was linguistic studies that laid the foundation for Lévi-Strauss's reassessment of *la pensée sauvage* by demonstrating the essential structural similarity of all known natural languages. But, as we pointed out in *The Origin of Language*, modern linguistics has refused to propose hypotheses concerning the origin of the mature, declarative phase of language; and without such hypotheses we can form no notion of its antecedent immaturity. Lévy-Buhl's *âme primitive* here finds its appropriate, prehistoric, referent.

The Question of Culture

It is only at the declarative stage that we can begin to treat the main theme of this work: the question of culture. For only at this stage can the institutions of culture be said to come into existence, organized around the central scene of representation. Outside of the formal institution of language, and confined within the limits of the culturally peripheral, objectively constrained economic institutions that provide satisfaction for appetitive needs, lies the intermediate zone that we speak of as cultural in the narrow sense. The most primitive mature culture was, we may assume, wholly ritual or sacred. But it is a direct consequence of our hypothesis that the difference between such a culture and our own largely deritualized one is secondary in comparison with that between the earliest mature culture and its immature antecedents. The question of deritualization thus placed in its proper perspective, we may confront the central question of culture at its earliest stage, before its component institutions have begun to differentiate themselves.

As we have observed, from the very beginning the central function of cultural institutions is *ethical;* they function to promote the cohesion of the community at whatever level of complexity it may operate. This use of the term "function" should not incur the accusation of "functionalism." Our entire hypothetical edifice has rather been constructed in order to avoid having to explain social institutions a posteriori according to the functions they are seen to perform. Only originary hypotheses may truly be said to explain the existence of institutions. But if these hypotheses are rigorously formulated, they attribute to the institutions in question an original central function. Subsequent history may modify the importance of this function and may generate others. But these modifications must be continuous if, indeed, the institution is to be identified as the same. Examples abound of customs or articles of clothing that have become "meaningless," but these are always minor elements that should by no means provide the basic model for cultural evolution. Clothing covers our nakedness and keeps us warm, whether or not we have buttons on our sleeves.

The question of culture is not resolved for all that; even alluding to its ethical function provides only the first step in explaining its historical existence. But we must be permitted to take this first step; to refuse to do so is to renounce the problem entirely, or to solve it in a purely verbal fashion by positing "cultural" or "esthetic" needs.

It is perhaps a measure of the difficulty of this question that the intellectual world still tolerates in the domain of culture the sort of *vertu dormitive* that has long disappeared from the discourse of the natural sciences.

To claim that, because culture possesses in its origin an ethical function, it must retain this central function throughout its history is not to add a supplementary hypothesis to that originally proposed. The original cultural act as such—that is, as apart from language, the minimal use of the scene of representation—has been hypothesized as caused by a common desire to reproduce the original event. To call the basis for this desire "ethical" is to say too little; this desire is *the* original ethical impulse, and the communal presence surrounding the central object, the original ethical conception of the nascent human community. The difficulty is not in these original definitions but in defining the ethical independently of the cultural at the stage of mature culture, in order that the attribution of an ethical function to culture might not be a mere tautology.

But to search for objective definitions of such concepts is to fall into the original philosophical pitfall—the presumption that worldly judgments are founded on conceptual truth, that to adjectives like "good" or "ethical" there corresponds *a fortiori* an Idea of "the good" or "the ethical." The originary hypothesis avoids this trap, as it does that of functionalism, which substitutes behaviorism for idealism. The ethical in our formulation *is* the cultural. But we must justify this equation to the extent that cultural phenomena do not generally present themselves as ethical; our idea of the ethical involves a thematic reflection on the cohesion of the community that is not a primordial or necessary element of cultural events. Culture is, in Hegelian terms, alienated from its ethical essence, and, indeed, its diversionary element may be seen as functioning precisely to distract its participants from this essence. This should not, however, be taken to imply, as it did for Hegel, that the cultural as such—that is, the religious and the esthetic—were ultimately to be weighed and found wanting on the basis of this cognitive inadequacy.

The first ritual act was motivated by a collective desire for cohesion, which is to say, for the avoidance of conflict over appetitive objects. This negative determination of communal cohesion permitted us to introduce the notion of the "ethical conception" of the community, as manifested in the original ritual situation of mutual presence surrounding the central appetitive object. But at the mature level of culture, the notion of an "ethical conception" realized face-to-face in ritual cannot be maintained unmodified. Once the declarative sentence becomes possible, the ethical reality of the community can no longer be limited to the specific instance of ritual presence, or even to the prescriptions and interdictions that were formulated at the imperative stage. The organization of the community has reached the point at which it can no longer be fully expressed by any single cultural activity. Thus the notion of "ethical conception" must be refined to permit us to grasp specifically which aspects of communal organization are given a place in its cultural forms, and at what degree of conceptualization.

Examination of our own culture makes it obvious that cultural content cannot be determined a priori, that it contains a large discretionary element within which esthetic creativity can operate. A screenwriter attempting to convince a producer that Hollywood "needs" a film about intergalactic warfare or the life story of a man with some rare disease is seeking to turn this discretionary element to his advantage; the public will determine its "needs," but only after the film has been shot. It might seem that this aspect of culture is a product of the modern exchange-system and that the cultural content of traditional societies is well-defined. Certainly that was what the German Romantics thought about Homeric Greece, which, for a modern anthropologist, is hardly an example of primitive society. But a glance at any collection of myths—for example, those collected in the *Mythologiques* of Lévi-Strauss—will show that no object or activity of a society is so trivial that a myth cannot be invented to explain it. This does not mean, however, that *every* object or activity is in fact so included. And even if it were, the corpus of myths and, more generally, of culturally significant representations of any given society is an artificial construct of the anthropologist not likely to be possessed as a whole by any individual member of that society.

We shall employ the term "cultural universality" to denote the absence in mature culture of any well-defined limits, such that every element of social life that can be identified may be included within it. This potential universality of mature culture could not have been shared by cultures at predeclarative levels; it cannot be conceived of in the absence of narration, which is a specifically declarative mode of discourse. In primitive mature cultures, the basic form of narrative is mythological and presumably retains a demonstrable connection with ritual. But we should not so fetishize the category of the sacred that we fail to recognize what is, at the very least, a considerable latitude in the handling of its components.

It is thus appropriate to associate cultural universality with mature culture from the very outset. But this universality by no means implies the sort of cheerful technical and organizational progress described by the paleontologists. The potentiality for any element of human existence to become the content of a cultural act is not a sign of universal harmony but of its opposite. That even the most trivial matter may become a cultural content means that even the most trivial matter is a potential source of disequilibrium, of conflict. We will understand the ethical function of culture—and the ethical *tout court*—once we realize that culture is primarily not a celebration of order but a response to disorder. And here the word "culture" may be used in its broadest sense, as equivalent to the human community as a whole.

Why can we not offer a positive definition of the cohesion brought about by the original ritual, instead of defining it, negatively, as "conflict avoidance"? Because any positive formulation would reflect rather than reveal the utopian nature of the ethic of original presence. Here again we must not too quickly dismiss the lessons of philosophy. Presence as an absolute coincidence of sign with referent, as a moment of absolute peace and communion in transcended and annulled desire, is a myth created not, indeed, in the originary event, which had no such self-reflexive ambitions, but in its first ritual and ethical reproduction. Because the scene of representation solved the problem of averting conflict over appropriation of the central object, its reproduction made it appear as the model of a world without conflict, a momentary golden age. "Made it appear," but not thematically. Cultural representation is never purely formal; it is the formal that serves as its utopia. Culture reproduces the scene; on the scene the formal designation of the central content attempts to recapture the "original" utopia and in the process manages to reproduce, not this utopia itself, since it never existed, but the deferral of conflict that was all it achieved in the first place. Not utopia, but culture.

The "cultural question" may thus be stated as follows: if representation is not in itself an irrational activity incapable of the thematic expression of truth, why then does there exist a set of representations called "culture" that can express whatever truth they possess only through fictions, which is to say, through *lies?* The proverbial visitor from Sirius might well ask us this question. Science, mathematics, even history he can comprehend as rational attempts to create models of reality—but religion? poetry? Our preliminary answer to this question can now be given: representation as such is rational because it reproduces the worldly on an unworldly scene, creates an unreal model that does not disturb its real referent. Culture is irrational because it presents this act of representation that defers the real as a worldly act of adequation between man and reality.

It is of greatest importance that, although philosophers and theologians see this adequation as a moment of divine bliss, the creators of cultural fictions, including religious fiction, always portray it as the moment, instantaneous or extended, of the resolution of a preceding conflict. What the originary representation accomplished for an instant, cultural representation makes "eternal." And in so doing, it gives an *ethical* value to man's difference from—and deferred appropriation of—the central object. Where the original gesture merely designated this object, its ritual reproduction designates it as the source of the conflict that led to its destruction, and of the satisfaction that ensued from the resolution of the conflict. The cohesion of the group exists only with reference to the central object that is experienced as the source both of the lack of cohesion that preceded and of the cohesion that followed. The ethical conception of the group is defined *by* and *against* the central object, "by" and "against" being our analysis of what for the participants was a single concept.

We may reply in advance to those who may accuse us of utopian blindness in our own depiction of the originary event. The argument is this: we reveal culture to be utopian in that it represents the original scene of representation as a definitive resolution of social disequilibrium. But, at the same time as we deny this cultural utopia, we create an essentially equivalent utopia by attributing to this original act the rational qualities of formal representation, while reserving the irrational for its ritual repetition.

This is a model of the sort of deconstructionist arguments that have been raised against *The Origin of Language*. It can, indeed, be answered, although not to the satisfaction of its proponents, for it is essentially nihilistic. We have motivated our decision between the moments of originary and ritual representation, but this motivation, being based on another difference, that is, another decision, can in its turn be deconstructed. This new difference is quite simply that between logical and fictional discourse—the difference that disturbed our Sirian.

We all realize that designing a rocket to the moon and writing a science-fiction novel about moon flights involve different uses of representation, but this difference might, after all, be only relative. Our construction is based on the assumption that it is not. What we suppose in the originary event is not a conceptualization of the designated object but a minimal designation of it. Rather than being somehow "more advanced." than its ritual reproduction, this first designation is in fact more primitive. The act of representation is, at this stage, infinitely ambiguous, and hence susceptible of taking on the utopian role assigned to it by ritual; all we can definitively say about it is that *it designates its referent*. The formalization of representation, and its extraction as a rational core from its various cultural accretions, is possible only because this designation was originally independent of these accretions, which in fact affirm this very independence as the guarantee of their utopia. We claim that culture can only ethicize representation because there was something there to ethicize, something that continued to exist alongside cultural representation: language. But nihilists have no faith in language. One recalls Lewis Carroll's turtle and his passion for infinite regression.

6

The Evolution of Ethical
Conceptions

THE INTERPRETATION OF ETHICAL CONCEPTIONS

In the original event, social dis-
equilibrium leads to the act of representation that in turn brings
about increased appetitive satisfaction. In a second moment of crisis,
however instigated, the reproduction of the situation that obtained
in the originary event makes of this reproduced event, with the scene
of representation at its center, a means of eliminating potential social
conflict. Thus, although for us the fundamental cause of such conflict
lies not in any particular object but in the potential of protohuman
appetites to exceed the capacity of animal (that is, nonrepresenta-
tional) conflict-prevention mechanisms, in the eyes of the members
of the group the central object is an *essential* source of conflict. The
act of representation, which arose, in our hypothesis, as an *ad hoc*
means for deferring conflict, has acquired for its participants an
absolute, eternal value, apparently ending social disequilibrium once
and for all; yet were this really true, the ritual would not have to
be repeated. Because representation creates a desiring imagination
that exacerbates animal appetites, the prehuman equilibrium cannot
be restored after the originary event. Culture is from the outset a
sign of this lost equilibrium, which its always temporary resolutions
of conflict render ever more precarious, thereby pushing human
society toward the cultural universality we associate with the mature,
declarative phase of cultural evolution.

129

The ethical element of culture is thus the correction of one disequilibrium by means of another. Potential conflict within the group
can be deferred only by designating the sacred object as the source
of conflict as well as of its resolution. The anthropologizing tendency
of the imperative stage operates to cast the sacred object in the role
of a transgressor of the laws by which the community is regulated,
albeit one whose transgression leads to a higher order than that which
had previously obtained. At the imperative level, however, this transformation could not be complete. To distinguish between the sacred
being and the esthetic and/or appetitive objects that represent it in
ritual is to attribute to it the same permanence that the scene of
representation had bestowed on the individual imagination; but this
being can only demonstrate its existence in imperative culture as
incarnated within the ritual performance. And the appetitive satisfaction that demonstrates the beneficial effects of the scene of representation, and of the "transgression" that motivated it, can be
temporarily deferred, but not eliminated. A ritual in which the
sacred being is represented esthetically by a created representation,
or by a masked or costumed actor imitating its transgressive role,
cannot be complete in itself. The purely esthetic representative is
not sufficient to satisfy the awaiting set up by the imperative ritual;
only an appetitive object that can be distributed to the participants
can furnish such satisfaction. Thus the "esthetic" rite can only be
conceived as preliminary to a distributive one. The success of the
imperative ritual is demonstrated in the fulfillment of the awaited
appetitive satisfaction.

But this does not mean that we should understand such rites, for
example, as were associated with the cave paintings as mere rehearsals for the hunt. This sort of interpretation appeals to anthropologists because it allows them to view the ritual as possessing (1)
a rational utilitarian core—psychological preparation for and re-
hearsal of an activity involving delicate coordination among the members of the group—and (2) an irrational "sacred" element that for *us*
is transparently superfluous but which incarnates for the individual
participants the needs of the group as a whole, needs which they
could not be made to feel in any other way. We may recall the
reasoning found in Harris: the sacred helps the individual Hindu to
obey a long-term rationality that he would otherwise be likely to
abandon in favor of short-term satisfaction. In this perspective, the
sacred is truly a deus ex machina that descends from the clouds with
the solution to otherwise intractable practical problems. But the
appearance of this aid, both supernatural and superfluous, cannot

thus be taken for granted. Its ethical-conceptual content must be taken at face value and its practical utility assessed in consequence. The sacred is not, after all, always practical; it will always sacrifice economic efficiency for ethical cohesion.

If, indeed, the unity of the group is to be affirmed, this can be done only by recalling the *ethical* danger that the sacred being represents for the group. There is, of course, real physical danger in a "being" that incarnates itself in a large animal. But this becomes effective in a ritual context only if it is assimilated to a potential for ethical disorder. To the separation between ritual and fulfillment would then correspond an ethical division of labor between sacred being and real (edible) representative. The being makes the law and must be appeased; his representative transgresses the law and must be eliminated. What is asked of the sacred being is that he manifest himself in a potential victim. But once this manifestation has been accomplished—we refer here to the results of the hunt rather than to the hunt itself, which could scarcely have been a ritual—the fulfillment of the imperative could only return the participants to the same fundamental situation as in the original (ostensive) ritual. The difference between sacred being and real representative would vanish; the distributed victim would *be* the sacred being, both source of disorder and bringer of peaceful satisfaction. The notion of *sacrifice*, in which victim and divinity remain permanently distinguishable, is conceivable only in mature culture. The imperative permits significant objects to be spoken of in their absence, but only to the extent that their presence is awaited as the result of the utterance. Transcendental beings can be conceived of only in the declarative mode.

Imperative or any other form of ritual is practical to the extent that its ethical structures are functional. The hunt requires the cooperation of the group against a common victim; just as hunting may well have led to the originary cultural event, the reproduction of this event can benefit the organization of the hunters. The irrational element of a ritual is constituted by the excess of its ethical structures over the needs of practical reality, which becomes assimilated to the *social* reality of the group. It is important to note that we can speak of "irrationality" only because ritual indeed possesses a conceptual content.[1] This content is not yet thematic, as is the case in theoretical discourse. In order to make it thematic, so that it can take on a truth-value and be judged as to its rationality, it must be *interpreted*. The process of interpretation is not an artificial activity of latter-day social scientists; it is inherent in ritual itself, as the emergence of etiological myth demonstrates. Interpretation consists of making explicit the ethical conception that is expressed nonthematically in the ritual. Specifically, if the concrete performance of the rite is taken to represent the formation of the community that performs it, the central, explicitly representational element may be interpreted as a causal statement concerning the origin of the human community in general. Every ritual would then express a "theory" of the origin of culture.

Several aspects of this procedure must be clarified.

1. Ritual represents the formation, not the preservation, of the community. It can aid in this preservation only by reproducing the formation, that is, the passage from "nature" through conflict to cultural order. This is not an empirical observation (although this passage is universally displayed in large-scale rituals); it is merely a restatement of our secondary hypothesis.

2. The central act of representation is, at any cultural level, a derivative of the original act of designation. This is an act of signification that is never "meaningless." But particularly in immature culture—and, on a different level, in mature culture as well—this act is not an explicit expression of the ethical conception we derive from it. What justifies this derivation is the continuity of our present understanding of elementary linguistic acts with their hypothesized origin. We can attribute propositional meanings to such utterances today because we possess declarative language. Hence in the same way, we are justified in attributing meanings to elementary linguistic acts even when they took place before the existence of mature language. This principle of representational continuity is a tacit principle of all anthropology, one almost too obvious to mention, save that it can be given a rigorous formulation only in terms, not of representation in general, but of *language*. The continuity of linguistic form is the connecting thread of human history.

3. Once this linguistic continuity is established, it can be observed that our interpretation of, for example, an ostensive or an imperative linguistic act at the center of ritual is in essence no different from the sort of interpretation that we naturally make of any elementary linguistic act. In real-life situations, we indeed react to these speech acts in an "elementary" fashion, by turning our attention to the object of an ostensive or by performing the act requested by an imperative. But at the same time, we have no difficulty in interpreting such speech-acts in their context as cognitively—if not practically—equivalent to propositional statements.[2] It is more effective to cry "Fire!" than to affirm "There is a fire here that must

be brought to your attention," but in the context of normal usage such interpretation poses no problem. The designative act at the center of the first ritual may be similarly interpreted, except that it designates its referent not only as worthy of the attention of the group but as the *raison d'être* of its formation. The ritual use of the sign that conveys no information commemorates the original act of designation through which the group transformed itself into a community, its members communicating with each other through representation and deferring appropriative activity.

4. The irrational element of ritual is thus interpreted as the commemoration of a rational act of representation. The fact of this commemoration establishes the act as expressing not a contingent but a necessary causal dependence of the existence of the group on the content of the central linguistic act. The reasoning behind this is simple. The repeated act must have originally communicated significant information to the group. The re-creation of the act in its original circumstances conveys no new information within the group, but functions to demonstrate that the group's existence as a community depends on its designation of the original significant object. In this manner, the formal core of ritual is interpreted as the ethical conception of the community.

Thus the original cultural act and those derived from it, which is to say, the whole of the cultural sphere, may be said to express an ethical conception that is, at the same time, a theory of the origin of the human community in the first act of representation. For what we called an "ethical conception" is in effect a synchronic projection of a diachronic "theory." To say that the community originated in a given manner is not necessarily to claim that the present community is structured according to the conditions obtaining at its origin. But ritual implicitly makes this equation. In interpreting it as the expression of an ethical conception valid in the present, we must therefore at the same time interpret its commemorative element as referring to the origin of the community of its celebrants.

Ritual has no means for differentiating between present and past conditions. It evolves, to be sure, but cannot take this evolution into account. The evolution of its ethical conception is thus concomitant, and in fact identical, with that of its theory of origin. We must avoid the temptation to view this evolution as combining ethical progress with a falling away from an original truth concerning the origin. On the contrary, the movement toward an ethic both freer and more inclusive that leads eventually to the cultural universality of the declarative stage—not to speak for the moment of subsequent cultural evolution—is at the same time a movement toward a more, not a less, adequate theory of origin. The original theory—that the existence of the community depends upon its designation of the central object as both potential cause of conflict and source of the increased appetitive satisfaction that follows its distribution—is the bearer of a very limited, indeed a minimal, truth about the origin of humanity. And it is minimal not because it fails to identify the circumstances of the originary event, in which respect the first humans had obvious advantages over those who must reconstruct this event hypothetically, but because it has so little to say about *what this event was the origin of*.

This point is of general validity for human science. The conceptual content of any generative theory, whether thematic or interpreted, will always be affected by discoveries concerning its object, just as theories of the origin of life were profoundly modified by the discovery of the genetic code. But, in contrast with knowledge about cosmological or biological structures, increased knowledge about human institutions is the product, more or less direct, of the evolution of these same institutions. "More or less," according to the degree to which these institutions are self-reflective, include their own "metainstitutions"; there is no human institution altogether lacking in representation of its own activity. In the case of the origin of the human as such, which is also the origin of representation, any knowledge we gain contributes at the same time to the evolution of human culture as a whole. But this evolution is not merely cumulative. It corresponds to a gradual deritualization or secularization of cultural institutions, as well as to the increasing integration of desire into the rational exchange-system, an integration that makes desire ever more comprehensible and, potentially at least, controllable. The originary hypothesis must be understood as a new step in the evolution of human culture as well as of an understanding of the origin of this culture; only in a highly deritualized society that has already begun to understand ritual from without is the formulation of such a hypothesis conceivable. The original "theoreticians" who created the first ritual could hardly have conceived of man as destined to accomplish this ultimate act of deritualization.

The original community can understand itself in ritual only as united by and against a sacred object. This is an understanding of man as the creator of representation, but it is at the same time an ethical understanding. And it is our contention that the ultimate basis of our own understanding of the human, like that of the first men, is through an ethical conception. If human science can now replace esthetic culture as the privileged locus of the expression of such conceptions, this determines a new stage in cultural evolution, one marked by the thematization of the ethical as its central locus. This is, in effect, to make the ethical the "independent variable" in the causal chain of history. Cultural materialism is surely right in taking material constraints as the ultimate limiting factors. But it errs in concluding that these constraints are the *determinant* factors. The very existence of culture belies this claim. Man might in fact be uniquely defined precisely as the creature for which the constraints of intraspecific interaction are more restrictive than those imposed by its physical environment. It is thus not prideful rejection of our material nature that obliges us to reject the anthropological claims of cultural materialism, but respect for the specific subject matter of anthropology.

SACRIFICE AND THE ANTHROPOMORPHIC DIVINITY

It is only at the mature stage of culture that the practice and concept of sacrifice can evolve. Here we encounter the complex of events proposed by René Girard in *La violence et le sacré* as the origin of the human.

In our discussion of Girard's theory at the beginning of Part I, we emphasized the difficulties it presents as an originary model, the most obvious of which are the total abandonment of the original appetitive center of the crisis[3] and the lack of any act of representation by which the sacralization of the victim might be accomplished. But although these points cast doubt upon Girard's hypothesis as a theory of origin, they do not prevent its consideration within the framework of our theory as a description of the passage from immature to mature culture. The value of this description qua evenemential hypothesis is less important than the presence within it of certain essential categories the origin of which we are, in any case, obliged to explain. For if Girard's anthropological researches have demonstrated one thing, it is the quasi-universality both of sacrifice and of the "emissary" or scapegoat mechanism in all known societies.

The weaknesses of Girard's originary hypothesis are mitigated if we take into account that the "human" is, after all, something of a matter of definition. The first men, in our definition, would have been far from *homo sapiens;* their invention of a representational gesture could scarcely have permitted them to leap over what were perhaps several million years of genetic evolution. In contrast, the

sort of men who could become involved in mimetic rivalry to the
utter neglect of appetitive objects, who could select a member of
their own group both to blame for the original crisis and to thank
for its peaceful conclusion, could only have been full-fledged *homo
sapiens*—that is, in our hypothesis, participants in a mature culture.[4]
It remains, however, important to explain how participants in such
a culture might have developed the sacrificial and scapegoat mechanisms Girard describes.

We have already assumed at the imperative stage a quasi-sacrificial
ritual complex, in which esthetic representation of the sacred being
in the first (imperative) rite was followed by the distribution of a
real (and edible) representative in the second, presumably as a result
of a successful hunt. This second rite could not be called sacrificial,
because its fulfillment of the imperative would annul the difference
between sacred being and appetitive object that had originally given
rise to it. In imperative culture, once the sacred being presents itself
in the form of a concrete object, it can no longer be distinguished
from this object.

In contrast, in declarative culture the sacred being can exist independently of the ritual, as the subject of affirmations and eventually of narratives (that is, myths). Following the evolution of
linguistic form, we may assume that the first affirmations concerning
sacred beings were negative—"negative theology" thus preceding
the positive. The transcendent status accorded such beings is that
of inaccessibility, of being elsewhere, just as the first declarative
sentences affirmed the inaccessibility of the objects their speakers
had been requested to produce. In such circumstances, the appetitively satisfying representatives of the sacred being would not lose
their status as mere earthly incarnations. Conversely, the sacred
being itself, as an anthropomorphic "subject," could be expected to
display toward this appetitive satisfaction an anthropomorphic attitude: if the ritual participants gain satisfaction from eating the
product of their hunt, then the good graces of the divinity that
permitted the hunt to be successful may be interpreted as motivated
by the desire for a similar satisfaction. What this "desire" in fact
expresses is the awareness on the part of the participants that peaceful
distribution is possible only through the—at least partial—renouncement of *their own* desire. The hunger attributed to the sacred
being is an inverted and sublimated version of their own. Whence
the practice of "feeding" the divinity with sacrifices, the major part
of which is of course reserved for the human participants in the
feast. One recalls that, in Homeric feasts, the gods are content with

the smoke of cooking fat, while the meat, less spiritual but more nourishing, is distributed among the faithful in portions appropriate to their standing in the "equal feast" (δαίτη ἔιση).

This explanation of the origin of sacrifice lacks the radically ethical character of Girard's scapegoat scene, where it is a human member of the original group that is sacrificed, and where the appetitive element is altogether absent. For Girard, human sacrifice is primordial, animal sacrifice a more civilized substitute. For us, human sacrifice and scapegoating can only be seen as more radical and thus more evolved versions of the original ritual, in which appetitive satisfaction played an essential part. We would consider, for example, the sacrifice of captives in warfare as a secondary development of animal sacrifice, whereas for Girard, sacrifice of nonmembers of the community would constitute an attenuation of the original scapegoat mechanism. Girard supports his position with interpretations of mythical and sacred texts. We shall now attempt to demonstrate that these materials in fact permit of counterinterpretations that lend support to our hypothesis.

We will take as our primary reference the Bible, not least because we share Girard's view of the ethical exemplarity of the Judeo-Christian tradition. Girard's works offer a number of examples taken from the Old Testament concerning what he interprets as the transition from human to animal sacrifice; the "human sacrifice" of the New Testament he conceives of as the final revelation of the emissary mechanism, after which effective sacrifice is no longer possible.

1. One essential biblical text, mentioned only in passing by Girard,[5] concerns the rite from which the very name "scapegoat" is derived: the description of the atonement ritual in Leviticus 16.[6] This ritual involves no human sacrifice nor any suggestion of derivation from it; on the contrary, it displays clear signs of derivation from traditional animal sacrifices of the sort described elsewhere in the Pentateuch. Comparison with the "guilt offering" described in Leviticus 5:14–6:7 and 7:1–10 is particularly pertinent, for the latter may be interpreted as a form transitional between the more traditional type (exemplified in the "peace offering" described in Leviticus 3:1–17 and 7:11–21) and the extreme represented by the "scapegoat." The point of comparison lies in the distributive element of the rite— the eating of the flesh of the sacrificed animal. It will be seen that the ethical intensity of the sacrifice, the degree to which it serves as an expiation for transgressions against communal laws, is inversely proportional to the degree of appetitive satisfaction obtained by the participants. This is in full accord with our hypothesis and provides

a model of the reflective radicalization of the ethical in mature culture. The validity of this model is not affected by the fact that these
rites were in no sense "primitive" and in fact could only have been
practiced in this fashion when the Hebrews had attained a state
structure.

We may begin with the "peace offering." Here the sacrificed
animal is eaten by the person(s) offering it, save that the fat and
blood as well as the liver and kidneys (which contain a large proportion of blood) are burnt on the altar. As in Homeric sacrifice,
"All fat is the lord's" (3:17).[7] In the "guilt offering," which is made
in order to atone for specific transgressions, after offering the fat
etc. to God, the animal is eaten, but only by the priests, not by the
atoning sinner, who must forgo the appetitive benefits of his sacrifice
for the sake of its moral benefits. Finally, the day-of-atonement ritual
offers two further degrees of sacrifice. Two goats and a ram are
offered by the people, and a bull and a ram by Aaron, the high
priest. The bull and one of the goats chosen by lot are offered as a
"sin offering"; after their fat is burned on the altar, the bodies are
taken to be burned outside the camp. The rams are then burned on
the altar. Thus none of the flesh of these animals is consumed,
although their burning must be understood, in the light of the lesser
rites, as an aborted form of food preparation. It is the remaining
goat that is the "scapegoat." After the high priest has laid the sins
and transgressions of the people of Israel on his head, he is sent into
the desert "for Azazel."

This series of rites offers a paradigm of sacrificial procedures in
which the ethical and appetitive elements are inversely related. They
lend themselves to the interpretation that the growth of explicit
ethical consciousness involves a progressive renouncement of appetitive satisfaction and, in the most extreme case, moral identification with the victim. The goat that is roasted but not eaten is still
treated as if it were food; the goat set free is, in contrast, made to
bear an explicitly verbal "message": the sins of the people are not
only placed on his head, they are "confessed" over him by the high
priest (16:21).[8] The conclusion implied by this analysis is that ethical
evolution proceeds concomitantly with the humanization of the victim rather than in the inverse direction, as would be required by
Girard's theory.

2. Our second biblical example is Isaac's blessing of Jacob, who
had disguised himself as Esau by placing animal skins on his hands
and neck (Genesis 27:16). In *La violence et le sacré*, Girard, in a brilliant

feat of comparative anthropology, associates this scene with Odysseus's escape from the Cyclops hidden under the belly of a ram. But in both cases, the human "victim" is presented as a substitute for the animal rather than the other way around. The Homeric example leaves no doubt as to what was the normal and what the abnormal form of sacrifice. Nor do the Cyclops's human sacrifices illustrate an earlier, more primitive form from which animal sacrifice is derived. The Cyclops represents for Homer an uncivilized state, not because he has not yet substituted animals for men, but because he inverts the principles of civilization in treating animals like men and men like animals. This is a sign of chaos, not of genetic precedence. The Cyclops's barbarism is no more a reflection of an earlier stage of human development than his one eye reflects a more primitive stage than our two.

If sacrificial animals were indeed substituted for men, the men would not wear animal costumes as they do in so many rites, and as Jacob apparently does in Genesis. The original of a man in animal garb is the animal, not the man, and the direction of this evolution is precisely that predicted by our hypothesis. The humanization of sacrifice, with the concomitant identification between sacrificer and victim, passes through a point at which human sacrifice, more terrible and therefore more potent than the traditional form, becomes a real possibility.

The Genesis text, more allusive than the Homeric, admits of a similar interpretation. Jacob or "Israel" substitutes himself for Esau ("Edom") in a blessing—the positive, not the negative moment of sacrifice. Humanization is here unencumbered with the paradox of human bloodshed. Israel inherits the paternal blessing and birthright because he represents a higher stage of humanity than his elder, more primitive brother. For Esau, the blessing must be mediated through (his father's) appetitive satisfaction; Jacob uses only his (or his mother's) wits. Isaac is, like the Cyclops, a figure of prehumanized ritual, but the Hebrew projection is historical, not fantastic. The Cyclops treats men like sacrificial animals; Isaac thinks merely to bless his son through the mediation of animal sacrifice, when his blessing is in fact given to unmediated humanity. That Jacob, not Esau, understands the supremacy of ethical over appetitive considerations is shown unambiguously in the elder's sale of his birthright for a "mess of pottage" to assuage his hunger.

3. We come now to the most celebrated of all biblical texts concerning sacrifice: Abraham's abortive sacrifice of Isaac in Genesis

22. Here the text would appear to support Girard's interpretation; the animal victim is, after all, presented explicitly as a substitution for the human.

But myths cannot always be read so directly. It is curious that Girard, who decisively rejects Lévi-Strauss's preference of myth to ritual, prefers to interpret the Genesis text as a biblical myth of sacrifice and to ignore the specific rituals described in Leviticus. The latter may reflect a stage no longer "primitive," but in view of the nearly identical time of composition of the two texts, one may express precisely the same doubts concerning the passage in Genesis. Certainly the moral of the story is rather that human sacrifice is not a primitive form but the highest act of faith, which thenceforth informs the traditional act of animal sacrifice. Indeed, animal sacrifice is depicted in the legend as preexistent. Isaac asks his father (22:7), "Where is the lamb for a burnt offering?" No doubt it is not easy to dismiss the connection with the "consecration of the firstborn" mentioned in Exodus 13:2 and elsewhere. But even if we accept as factual the accusations of sacrifice of the firstborn leveled at such evildoers as Ahab (1 Kings 16:34) and Ahaz (2 Kings 16:3), according to what is described in the latter verse as one of "the abominable practices of the nations whom the Lord drove out before the people of Israel," there is nothing particularly "primitive" about such rites, which are associated, in the only concrete cases cited, with established states.

As a pastoral rite, as it is presumed to have occurred,[9] the sacrifice of the human firstborn could have been practiced only by analogy with animal sacrifice rather than the inverse. Human and animal firstborn are mentioned together on every occasion such consecration or sacrifice is referred to in the Pentateuch (Exodus 13:2, 22:28 ff., 34:19 ff., Leviticus 27:26–27, Numbers 3:13, 8:17–18, 18:15). The "redemption of the firstborn" is no proof of original human sacrifice; it more plausibly indicates an extension of the domain of the sacred from animal to human. And the same must be said for the story of Abraham and Isaac, at least if we take its ethical content seriously rather than seek in it the allegory of a real historical development. The story gives a higher meaning to all subsequent animal sacrifice, now conceived as a substitution for the immolation of what one holds dearest. This is a stage of the abolition of animal sacrifice rather than of its establishment; its ethical content has reached the point at which sacrifice has become a sign of devotion to a divinity who is no longer a sublimation of man's object-desires but of his solidarity with his fellows.

Girard's reading of myths as the disguised accounts of "lynchings" may be contested in the same fashion. His analyses of two myths treated by Lévi-Strauss[10] will serve as illustrations. In each case, a culture hero's murder, more or less thinly disguised, is presented as the origin of the fundamental traits of the culture. Girard's analyses constitute an incisive contestation of Lévi-Strauss's formalism, which reduces mythical violence to the creation of discontinuity among discrete cultural elements through the "radical elimination of certain fractions of the content." Violence for Lévi-Strauss is a space-clearing operation devoid of moral significance. But the question of the correspondence between the myth as thus interpreted and the originary event or mechanism of human culture is not decidable by this or by any analysis of a mythical text. We need not contest a word of Girard's interpretation in demonstrating this point, as will be made clear from the following.

In the first place, the variety of these and other myths, if we are to take their specific details as elements of actual murder-scenes (in the examples mentioned, one hero is taken to the bottom of the sea, disguising a drowning; the other leaps from a cliff to avoid pursuit and flies away, an action that Girard assimilates to the familiar execution procedure of collectively forcing the victim to leap from a precipice without actually pushing him off), can only be attributed to a fairly recent local origin. Not only does this effectively exclude the possibility of a unitary origin of human culture, but it limits the time of reference of each specific myth to a state at which a mature state of language and culture already existed. Such myths may possibly be interpreted as depicting the fundamental mechanism of hominization, but they certainly cannot be seen to describe an *event* of hominization. This already suffices, without further argument, to situate Girard's hypothesis in the mature stage of culture.

Second, let us assume with Girard that these myths depict actual "lynchings." It is then obvious that these lynchings, which could only have occurred within established cultures, did not in fact produce *ex nihilo* the cultural benefits mythically attributed to them. For example, in the Ojibway myth, the submergence of the hero-victim "produces" the five clans of the tribe and their totems; in the Tikopia myth, the leap of Tikarau leaves behind four basic vegetable foods. Evidently neither clans nor foods were likely to have appeared in the culture as the result of a single event, "lynching" or not. The question then arises—regardless of whether or not the lynching is historical—why the origin of these cultural categories is attributed to it. A defender of Girard's position might well answer that these categories simply stand for the cultural order as a whole. Because all such categories originate in sacrificial "decisions" resulting from lynchings, the myth conflates a number of separate events (perhaps all carried out according to the same procedure). The mechanism, not a specific occasion, is commemorated as the source of each culture's chief structural elements. But this argument begs the question. The real origin of such things as clans and vegetable foods, even in the "structural" sense of categories of thought, cannot reasonably be said to be commemorated in the myth. Etiological myths of this type are too fanciful and, at the same time (as the *Mythologiques* demonstrate), too dependent on narrative *topoi* to be in any sense factual accounts of cultural origins. The same need not be true of the lynchings. But the event-status of these is undefinable. Their specificity is culture-dependent, yet they cannot be associated with any specific moment in their culture's history. Our question thus remains unanswered.

Let us return for a moment to Lévi-Strauss's formalistic explanation of such myths as describing the elimination of one element, after which the others become categorically distinguishable from each other. This explanation has, at least, the virtue of explaining the myth as myth—that is, as narrative discourse, as an attempt, not to commemorate an event, but to tell a story that is to render plausible the existence of cultural categories. Nevertheless, the explanation is inadequate, not only because it ignores the element of human violence but because it fails to demonstrate why in fact the passage from elimination to categorization is narratively plausible. This suggests that we should understand the description of this passage in myth not as an account of an actual originary event but as a narrative element whose plausibility is derived from real experience.

The scapegoating mechanism is real, and its disguises more or less transparent. But it is the effect, not the cause, of the anthropomorphization of the sacred that becomes operative in mature culture. Myths are narrative explanations, "theories" of rituals. And if we cannot reconstruct with certitude the rituals from the myths, it is altogether chimerical to attempt to reconstruct on their basis the *events* commemorated by the rituals. It is at once apparent that, whether or not these myths describe real murders, they follow the fundamental pattern of ritual: crisis, representation of the central element, distribution. This is particularly apparent in the Tikopia myth, where the distribution is of foods rather than, as in the Ojibway myth, of clan memberships—although clans are almost universally associated with food items ("totems") that would presumably be distributed at the ritual feast following the ceremony. The crisis-element of ritual corresponds mythically to a state of indistinction among clans or, in the Tikopia myth, between gods and men. The athletic contests referred to are transparent transpositions of conflict that are frequently incorporated into ritual. And in the climactic narrative sequence we find the moment of the "lynching" or "elim-ination." If we regard this sequence not as a distorted description of worldly events but as an etiological account of a ritual sacrifice, its narrative plausibility is evident. The "eliminated" hero is an anthropomorphic representative of the ritual victim.

On the most obvious level, that of narrative plausibility, the victim is humanized because, as representative of the sacred being, he has become a narrative—or, in linguistic terms, a declarative—*subject*. The declarative primordially describes absence. In narrative terms, the sacred being is the subject of this absence; that is, he has made himself absent. The motivation for his departure justifies the ritual process of designation, which has since the beginning implied the exclusion of its (victimary) object from the community that, in effect, defines itself against it. Narration relativizes this originally absolute ethical opposition into a relation between anthropomorphic beings in which the divinity is motivated by the same desires as his believers.

Narrative humanization is the expression of ethical humanization. The attribution to the sacred being of narrative subjectivity reflects this acquisition of ethical responsibility. The use of the declarative and of narrative discourse in ritual reflects the consciousness of an ethical paradox only implicit at the origin of culture, the practical or "pragmatic" counterpart of the ineluctable formal paradox of self-reference. The sacred being/victim is both guilty of transgression and creator of order; he is both responsible for the community and wholly subordinate to its will. The difference of the community from the significant appetitive object at the origin of representation becomes the source of ethical paradox when this "absolute" differ-ence, originally guaranteed by man's appetites, is shown to be more an ethical than an appetitive necessity.

The myths under discussion—and, indeed, all myths—were cre-ated to justify this founding difference. From one difference come all the others; that is the theory of Lévi-Strauss, who errs only in reducing the cultural to the formal at the expense of the ethical. Girard grasps the ethical element of myth; but instead of seeing in it the revelation of a higher ethical understanding of ritual, he pro-jects it onto the event to which the myth ultimately refers and from

which the ritual was derived. The attribution of human characteristics to a ritual victim is not proof that the victim was "originally"
a man. On the contrary, it is a sign of awareness that the originally
obvious and a priori difference between community and victim has
now become problematic—that it must now be justified on the purely
human grounds of transgression and punishment. This is not, to be
sure, the end of ethical evolution, but it is the decisive step, just as
the creation of the declarative sentence was the decisive step in the
evolution of language. Once the central object of ritual has become
a guilty victim of punishment, we are not far from the radical identification with the victim that is the distinguishing characteristic of
the Judeo-Christian tradition.

The crucial question concerning the original victim is cognitive
rather than concrete. The first victim might perhaps have been a
man, if we assume he could have provided sufficient appetitive satisfaction. But a society that had no way of distinguishing between
a human and an animal as the central object of the original event
might just as well have killed and eaten an animal. The ethical value
of the anthropomorphizing of the victim in ritual and myth lies in
the discovery, not of the factual nature of the original event or
mechanism, but of its ethical implications for mature culture. The
original "crime" of culture is not intraspecific murder—which other
species commit as well on occasion—but the uniquely human act of
representation, which defers appetitive action and creates difference.
It is this difference that gives rise to the ethical laws that define and
forbid murder as well as to the desire that motivates it.

Thus we need not claim that the lynchings Girard has shown to
be hidden in Lévi-Strauss's myths did not occur, nor that they did
not occur in the rituals from which the myths arose. Our point is
that the lynchings described in the myths are no proof of the humanity of the victims. Tikarau is not himself eaten; he is not therefore
a part of the distributive moment of the ritual. As the source of the
elements of the feast, he has come to represent the imaginary sacred
being in opposition to the sacrificial victim. But that he was originally
of edible—that is, animal—nature is implied by the fact that only
vegetable foods are mentioned among his gifts to the tribe; one would
assume that meat as well was consumed at the sacrificial feast.

Rather than as a model of the originary event, we should view
the emissary mechanism as a paradigm of cultural universality. Girard's theory, like Chomsky's, poses as originary the structure that
marks the end of the protohuman and the beginning of mature humanity. The emissary mechanism, like the declarative sentence, absorbs within it and reinterprets the elementary forms that preceded

it. Girard's textual studies, like Chomsky's sentential analyses, are unimpeachable within the framework of the texts and sentences themselves. But they cannot illuminate the pretextual and presentential origins either of language or of culture as a whole.[11]

Cultural universality means, in effect, finding an explanation for everything that goes wrong. The declarative sentence is, in its origin, an instrument for thematizing unsatisfactory situations; but these thematizations become culturally functional explanations only when an ethical justification—that is, a transgression—can be found for them. Only at this point does the ethical conception of the community become universal. This universality is not a static state, and would not be even if every element of human experience were included within the corpus of cultural texts. It is rather a *systematic* state, provided with a complete set of homeostatic mechanisms for returning the group to normality after minor or major disturbances. Cultural continuity has filled in all the gaps left by the most primitive ethical conception, wherein the community existed only in the act of repetition of the original event. Even the imperative level of culture could have had no mechanism for associating real or supposed transgressions of its interdictions with communal crises. The imperative can only understand performance, which is in fact presupposed by it. Nonperformance is incomprehensible because unsayable; its punishment could be carried out only at the periphery, not at the center, of the communal scene of representation.

The emissary mechanism is indispensable to mature culture, both as a solution of last resort in crises and as a model for interpreting all cultural phenomena. Older rituals come to be explained by myths that embody this mechanism; minor crises are blamed on malevolent acts, even if the evildoer is never identified and punished. Rites of passage come into being that prevent crises before they begin, often by ritually "punishing," through privation and/or mutilation, the newborn child or newly initiated adult for his or her "crime" in disturbing the previously obtaining social order. Higher levels of cultural development lead to the desacralization of the emissary mechanism, although not to its elimination, as recent history has shown and continues to show.

The Evolution of Mature Culture

There is a vast distance between the first mature culture and modern society, but we should consider this distance as secondary with respect to that between mature and elementary cultures, a distance that is in turn secondary with respect to the fundamental difference created by the original event between the human and the nonhuman. Because the ethical universality of mature language and culture is found in all human societies, the worldwide dispersion of man must have taken place after this level was attained. We must therefore attribute to the systematic nature of mature culture man's adaptation to virtually every earthly habitat, as well as his elimination, presumably by force, of the earlier protohuman forms. The problem of reconciling the diversity of protohuman remains with the uniformity of the human species today may perhaps be solved by positing a well-defined period of origin, during which the first men— that is, the descendants of the users of the original sign—were able to expand to a variety of habitats, only to be reduced to a single line when *homo sapiens*, having evolved a mature culture, was able to eliminate his "immature" protohuman competitors. The rest of the story, largely if not entirely found in the archaeological and historical record, is that of the evolution of increasingly complex societies. It is already clear from the preceding discussion that this evolution, although bound by the material constraints that define at every point the limits of each culture's exchange-system, is primarily an ethical one.

From what standpoint, then, may we speak of history as a progression toward "higher" or "more advanced" ethical conceptions? This question does not arise at the earliest stages of culture, during which man undergoes the not merely cultural but genetic process of hominization. Cultural universality is the mode of our existence as a species; we have no choice but to treat it as the *telos* of the preceding evolution. The Rousseauean "state of nature" is not merely irreversibly lost; it is a state of another species. It corresponds in our hypothesis roughly to the period, possibly of some one or two million years' duration, between the original event and the emergence of mature culture. The early humans of this period, incapable of the higher forms of representation, were, if not more peace-loving, at least not so potentially violent as their descendants; yet it is difficult for us to long for a utopia inhabited by men not yet evolved into *homo sapiens* and speaking a language without declarative sentences. The evolution of mature culture is another story. There still exist today groups of men whose culture has progressed little since paleolithic times. These men are genetically identical to us, and in principle we could initiate our children into their cultures. There are of course material reasons for not doing this; but it is still valid to inquire into the ethical reasons. Ethnological humility should not be exaggerated. It is a paltry tribute to human creativity to measure our superiority to stone-age tribes only in technical and military terms, without mentioning the cultural achievements of Western society. But if these achievements are not merely ornamental, they must be in some sense the products of a higher ethic.

The heart of culture is the deferral of violence through representation. At first this is necessary only in isolated crisis-situations; at the level of mature culture, it has spread to the totality of human interactions. How then do cultures continue to evolve? In some cases, of course, they do not. Those that are represented by the myths compiled by Lévi-Strauss have remained static, and their myths reflect this state by undergoing, like the structures of language, continual transformations without ever reaching a higher level of integration of their content.

Because social evolution takes place in a universe of competing societies, it may be explained on the basis of the Darwinian "null-hypothesis" of the survival of the fittest. The competitive process forces us to judge societies by economic and, above all, military criteria, for these are the chief modes of competition among societies. Traditional historiography, the protagonists of which are states and empires (pre-state societies being left to prehistory and anthropology), concerns itself directly with this competition and takes from it its criteria of significance. At a higher level of generality, social evolution may be studied in terms of economic and military organization. Here the course of history takes on a higher degree of continuity, the progress of technique and organization being in the long run largely independent of the specific societies that make use of them. The ever more rapid diffusion of successful methods and, conversely, the breakup of overextended political systems accelerate social evolution as well as increasing its uniformity. Thus today, in a world of well over a hundred nation-states, there is really only one fundamental system of economic and military organization—although the secondary difference between "capitalist" and "socialist" systems remains of enormous political importance.

The history of individual states is tragic and chaotic. These societies attain their creative limits and decline for a variety of reasons, to be replaced either by essentially similar competitors or, more catastrophically, by more successful social systems. Economic history, to which the military is perhaps too easily subordinated, is more continuous, but it too has its moments of regression, most notably in the "fall of the Roman Empire," the replacement of ancient civilization by the stagnation of the early Middle Ages. The end of antiquity is the most problematic of historical phenomena and the most scandalous crux for economic historians. How, indeed, could a "higher" system decay from within and be replaced by a "lower"? Internal explanations are enlightening, but never conclusive. Ultimately one must return to the level of political history to observe that Rome finally succumbed to more primitive competitors because it lacked competition on its own level. Surveying the political diversity of the world today, we do well to inquire why classical civilization could so easily become attached—as it turned out, suicidally—to a single political system whose universality stifled the process of social evolution.

Yet it is striking that on the ethical level a certain continuity of evolution may be restored between antiquity and the modern era. Whatever else may be said about the Middle Ages, the ethical superiority of Christianity to ancient religion is difficult to deny. This is perhaps truer in theory than in practice, but the very permanence of the "theory"—that is, Christian doctrine—throughout the vagaries of worldly action demonstrates that an ethic grounded on a transcendental moral conception constitutes a higher form than the traditional ethics of antiquity, if only in its increased capacity for survival. Millennia of hypocrisy have not killed the Judeo-Christian ethic, but rather strengthened its hold over social reality to the point that its transcendental guarantees have become all but unnecessary. The radical economic superiority of modern over ancient society suggests that this ethic has not simply "reflected," but in fact provided the basis for, a higher level of material development.

Thus the paradox of the "regressive" transition from antiquity to the Middle Ages disappears if, as we have hypothesized, ethical evolution is the most fundamental, most nearly continuous factor in social evolution. For it is the chief contention of this work that the ethical is ultimately more constraining than the economic, that it is, in a word, the true infrastructure.

One obvious counterexample suggests itself: the passage from the relative equality of hunting societies to the extreme inequalities associated with the accumulation of economic surplus in agricultural societies. All-powerful kings and powerless slaves make the early states of Mesopotamia and Egypt appear far less just and humane by modern standards than the more primitive hunting-gathering cultures. Rousseau's "state of nature" may be pure myth, but his idyllic picture of primitive society—the *société commencée* described in Part II of the second *Discourse*—in comparison with the inequities of property ownership in sedentary agricultural society has not been disconfirmed by more recent ethnological research. In proposing an explanation for this development on ethical—and not merely economic or demographic—grounds, we will be able to clarify our criteria of ethical and thereby of cultural progress.

Let us first recall the disequilibrium that led to the creation of ritual on the basis of the original scene of representation. The original event was the result of the saturation of prehuman—that is, genetic—means for controlling conflicting appetites directed at the same object. The creation of a scene of representation solved this problem but generated in its place another that led to the ritual reproduction of the original event and thence to the whole panoply of "irrational" cultural phenomena that have grown up alongside the scene of representation. This problem, in a word, is that of *desire*. By creating in each individual a desiring imagination, representation became a factor of disunity as well as of unity. Because the scene of representation generated desire but could not control it, other less rational means had to evolve. Ritual is regressive in comparison with the formal efficiency of language, but this very efficiency had made language incapable of meeting the additional demands on its ethical function. Linguistic deferral cannot be arbitrarily increased; more powerful means were therefore necessary, even if deficient in information-bearing capacity.

We suggest that the "regressive" evolution from hunting to agricultural societies reflected a similar ethical deficiency in primitive equality. In both cases, the increase of individual desire led to a systemic disequilibrium that brought about the institution of arbitrary differences: in the first case, that between sacred and profane objects; in the second, that between possessors and nonpossessors of the agricultural surplus. The perspective reflected in this analysis is likely to strike cultural materialists, Marxists, and, indeed, liberal economists as perverse—without satisfying, we might add, the proponents of the various forms of structural or synchronic anthropology. Once we have conceded the claims of individual desire, why not admit that we are simply referring to good old *homo oeconomicus?* Man inaugurated ritual—and with it, presumably, an expanded exchange-system—in order to control his material desires; and certainly the transition from hunting to agriculture, to the extent that it did not depend on purely Malthusian considerations, was the product of a series of economically motivated decisions to increase production.[12] After an indeterminate period of helping nature along with a little selective sowing, some Rousseauean Adam committed the original sin of claiming *ceci est à moi!* Where is the ethical in all this?

Ethical conceptions, and the category of the ethical in general, are not simply synonymous with the structures of social organization. They necessarily involve another element, which is the *control of individual desire.* This was as true at the originary moment of ritual as on the day of publication of *Civilization and Its Discontents.* Desire always takes as its object the significant, or at least the potentially significant. The desiring individual does not merely want to enjoy whatever appetitive satisfaction may be gained from the object; his desire is mediated by the public scene of representation. To desire is to desire to possess the difference conferred on the object by this scene—in a word, to be different.

In an essentially egalitarian society, desire must be kept within narrow limits. The ethic of such a society can permit only marginal differences involving no major contrasts in material wealth. This ethic may appear attractive to our own moral views, but it is founded on absence of opportunity rather than on its renouncement. As soon as the material opportunity arises for the creation of an even temporary surplus of foodstuffs and other goods over and above the needs of immediate consumption, this egalitarian system will break down, for the real differences in ability as well as ambition among the members of the group had hitherto largely been repressed rather than employed in the service of the community. Once the economic base makes it possible, competition for prestige or social dominance will break out. This is not because early agricultural man behaves like *homo oeconomicus* but, on the contrary, because his acquisition of an excess of appetitive goods over his own immediate needs or possibilities of consumption becomes a means for obtaining supplementary significance in the eyes of the community. We need not even consider in this model the differential effect of energy, intelligence, or ambition, for once economic activity becomes individualized, the variance of circumstances will be sufficient. That human variance does exist is, however, beyond dispute.

THE "BIG-MAN" AND THE ORIGIN OF SOCIAL DIFFERENTIATION

The competition for socially recognized significance does not simply dissolve the old egalitarian order. It can only take place within the old system, and in particular, through its mechanism of ritual redistribution. Marshall Sahlins's *Stone Age Economics*[13] is of great use on this subject, although Sahlins has no particular theoretical interest in the ritual, cultural, or ethical focus of what he persuasively presents as a model of the origin of social differentiation. This model is based on the potlatchlike feasts held by certain Melanesian societies under the auspices of self-appointed "big-men." These individuals, more energetic and ambitious than their fellows, and above all, more able through family ties and charisma to persuade relatives and associates to collaborate in the work of preparation, amass over a period of time a food surplus that is consumed in a communal feast to which the whole village is invited. Sahlins points out that these big-men are so anxious to perform this distributive function that they generally consume less for their own purposes than the less ambitious villagers.[14] The similarity of this behavior to displays of "conspicuous consumption" in modern society makes explanation appear unnecessary; certainly anyone who enjoys giving parties can understand the psychology of the big-man. But no doubt we can understand the psychology of the egalitarian hunter as well. What is of interest is to understand the passage from one to the other as a model of ethical evolution.

The accumulation of a material surplus is dependent on the existence of a suitable material base, such as only agriculture or sedentary fishing (as in the Pacific Northwest) can provide. But before we cite this phenomenon as evidence that material conditions "produce" the surplus, we should examine the causality of our model more closely. If we assume that the survival of the social group must always be its own primary concern, then the development of techniques that promote this survival is not in itself a revolutionary phenomenon. This implies that agriculture and husbandry originated not dramatically but gradually among hunting societies that found themselves in marginal habitats—for example, where game was becoming scarce relative to population. The basic techniques of primitive sedentary societies are already known to hunting populations, just as the more advanced agricultural techniques are already available at least *en puissance* to primitive agriculturalists.

This element of Ester Boserup's thesis, which is independent of her "population-push" theory of economic development, is her most revolutionary point.[15] It does away with the paleontologically and technocratically inspired notion that the evolution of society is in essence an evolution of technique. Technique must evolve, of course, but its evolution is at every step discouraged by the neglected fact that more advanced techniques, be they of flintworking or of plowing, inevitably and, one might almost say, by definition demand an increased output of labor at least in the initial stage of tooling up. And in preindustrial society, there is essentially nothing but this "initial stage"; as Boserup shows, each successive level of intensified cultivation requires greater marginal labor input per unit produced. No doubt, in some cases, particularly in our era, when backward agricultural societies are in contact with modern medical services as well as with an individualistic culture that erodes traditional models of conduct and specifically of population limitation (for example, via deliberate or "neglectful" infanticide), demographic pressure may provide the major incentive. But the big-man model described by Sahlins has a far more general anthropological relevancy. Here we see that, on an individual level, intensification of production, accomplished by the simple means of working harder, is caused neither by technical innovation nor by Malthusian necessity, nor indeed by a "Marxian" desire to appropriate the surplus. Big-men work harder and eat less in order to acquire differential social significance. More precisely, they seek a unique, privileged status in ritual distribution comparable to and, no doubt, associated with that of the central sacred being as source of communal appetitive satisfaction.

An examination of the myths of these societies would no doubt demonstrate that a transformation in ethical conception has taken place or is in the process of doing so.[16] The old egalitarian ethic is being or has been replaced by an ethic that specifically recognizes the differentiated role of the big-man. But the ritual behavior is itself sufficient confirmation of this supposition. The ritual feasts are, like all ritual occurrences, socially necessary events; if they are not given, the community will be plunged into a state of crisis. Partly arbitrary as the self-selection process may be—comparable, say, to that of ecclesiastical dignitaries in traditional state-societies—the big-man is not a mere conspicuous consumer or party-giver but an indispensable and central figure. The differential ethic thus created is more advanced than the primitive, egalitarian one in permitting the increased employment of individual desire for the community's benefit. How indeed could any morality condemn the "altruism" of these energetic, self-denying individuals? Yet their activity quite obviously permits the transition from the equality of the hunter to the radical inequalities of "oriental despotism." The big-man is already a charismatic leader; it only remains for war, famine, or some other disequilibrating pressure to turn him into a tyrant. But that this has not everywhere taken place is no more surprising than the fact that groups of primitive hunters still survive in isolated areas.

The big-man phenomenon is transitional only in the long term; it possesses its own equilibrium and an ethical conception that expresses it.

The big-man example permits us a privileged insight into the relationship between material and ethical evolution. If we accept this example as canonical, both the Marxist and the Malthusian models, as well as the Marxist-Malthusian model proposed by cultural materialism, are proved inadequate.[17] Nor does the Parsonian status criterion familiar to American sociologists stand the test any better. Only an ethical model offers an adequate explanation, albeit one that is still in need of further elaboration.

It will be of use to first dispose of the arguments of what, echoing the Marxists, we might call "idealist" sociology. Our dialogue has thus far been concentrated on the side of the materialists because their greater awareness of constraints makes them more rigorous than their opposite numbers. "Vulgar materialism" can demonstrate genuine quantitative correlations, for, even if it underestimates the human, it at least respects material reality; vulgar idealism can only glorify the conclusions of common sense. And despite the unmistakable resemblance between explanations based on status-seeking and those that may be derived from our model of ethical evolution, these explanations remain *ad hoc* and a posteriori because they are not grounded in a rigorous theory—or, for the most part, in any theory at all—of desire, let alone a genetic theory of the human.

Even the most status-conscious sociologist or anthropologist cannot fail to note that men require food or that armies require weapons. Status cannot pretend to stand alone, as appetitive need can, as the unique motive of social action. Thus idealist social thought is reduced to a more or less openly avowed eclecticism that expresses itself in lists of "motivating factors" irreducible to any common denominator. What we consider to be the chief virtue of our theory in this regard is that it avoids from the outset the material/ideal dichotomy by situating the origin of the representational within the appetitive existence of our species. Prestige or status is thus made dependent on representation without thereby becoming magically detached from its ultimate appetitive base. By giving primacy to the internal over the external relations of the social group, we do no more than show respect to the central, specifically *cultural* features of all culture. Such analysis is neither slavishly emic nor arrogantly etic; *à la rigueur* it is an etic analysis that constitutes itself through a dialectic oriented by emic elements. Thus we neither explain social structures as homologous to the structures of cultural products (like Lévi-Strauss's myths) nor focus on "material culture" to the neglect of what the very participants in such a culture recognize without contest as essential: its cultural—and for simple societies, ritual—center.

The sociological, and not merely anthropological, interest of Sahlins's big-man example may now be given a clearer focus. This is a primitive and, so to speak, originary example of a phenomenon of far more general importance than the birth of *homo oeconomicus:* the integration or cooptation of individual desire by the exchange-system. We have already expressed in *The Origin of Language* the idea that modern society is most essentially defined by the generalization of this integration to include, not, to be sure, the totality of all desires (a notion as paradoxical as the "set of all sets"), but the quasi-totality of each individual's productive life. It is the universalization of the concept of the individual career that defines modernity, of which such phenomena as the consumer society are corollaries.[18]

In the societies described by Sahlins, only the big-man can be said to have a "career" in this sense, one that is no longer comparable to the differential functions available in primitive egalitarian society, although it must have evolved out of them. The shaman, the war chief, or the clan chief of primitive society exercises a distinct role and receives that role's accompanying ritual honors. Such roles, aside from their communal usefulness, are also outlets for individual desire; shamans in particular are nearly always volunteers, whatever the tests they must pass in order to be accepted as such by the community. What makes the big-man different is the essentially economic nature of his functions. This personage attains communal significance by monopolizing the exchange-system function of distribution—by converting it, at least at periodic intervals, into a personal *re*distribution. Thus his cultural centrality is founded on economic centrality rather than, as is the case with the shaman and even the chief, on economic marginality.

We have reproached Sahlins for not having given sufficient emphasis to the ritual nature of the big-man's role, but it is easy to explain this omission. In the light of modern society, the ritual aspect appears secondary; it appears, in fact, as a mere legitimizing mask for the role's economic functions. Sahlins is a less consistent materialist than Harris, but they share an economist perspective that reflects the fundamental and often overt opposition between ritual and economic means for integrating individual desire into the social order. What is most lacking in this perspective is not respect for ritual as such, which would be merely fetishistic, but an appreciation of the ethical problems that had to be solved before ritual could be reduced to ornamental status and eventually eliminated altogether from the economic sphere. This insensitivity reflects a familiar blindness toward the Judeo-Christian component of Western culture. Belittling our own ethical achievements is, in fact, possible only as a result of them, but it does not make for good anthropology.

The institution of the big-man is a step in the direction of hierarchy and tyranny; yet it continues the humanization of the sacred that we have observed at work in the evolution toward cultural maturity. To worship a man in place of a transcendental being, as was done in all the ancient empires from the Egyptian to the Roman, strikes us as the ultimate folly, just as the symmetrical phenomenon of human sacrifice appears to us as the extreme of inhumanity (a parallel that further confirms our derivation of human from animal sacrifice). But these extremes constitute a framework not merely for economic progress—the increased extraction of "surplus labor" and its material results—but for ethical progress as well.

We must not confuse ethics with morality; the proper attitude toward history should be not moral but ethical. Moral condemnations of past societies and their rulers form an essential element of the Judeo-Christian tradition; indeed, the historical books of the Old Testament contain little else. But this foundation story of Western moral thought remained useful only so long as the formulation of the moral, as accomplished in Christianity and in postsacrificial Judaism—not to speak of similar formulations in Buddhism and Islam—had not yet been achieved. It does us little good today to condemn ancient tyranny or slavery as evil. The contrast between an absolute morality of reciprocity and an ethic that is by definition holistic should not be neglected, but to make this contrast an excuse for the neglect or disparagement of the ethical is to reject science for sentiment. The ease with which this is done by an "etic" anthropologist like Harris, whose moral condemnations of exploitation and inequality are innocent of any constitutive theory of morality, is a telling demonstration that adherence to behavioral criteria is no guarantee of the respect for reality that is the highest value of empirical science.

Before we condemn as monstrous the worship of pharaohs and emperors, we should reflect that neither the egalitarian morality nor the indefinitely differentiated ethical structure of modern Western society could have arisen without it. The equality of hunting societies is qualitatively different from that to which we aspire, and no direct passage from one to the other is conceivable. Equality is not, in the real world, a supreme value, as the nineteenth-century founders of utopian colonies like New Lanarck and Icaria soon learned. As Fourier in his fantastic manner had the insight to realize, individuals do not merely have different interests; they want to *be* different. Contrary to the Rousseauean myth, this is as true of Australian aborigines as it is of us; the proof of it is not some ethologically inspired sociobiological imperative but the elaborate nature of the ritual life of these people, who spend a considerable proportion of their lives organizing networks of ritually consecrated reciprocal exchanges destined to substitute representational differences for imagined real ones whose attempted inauguration would cast these societies into suicidally violent conflicts. From this ritualized equality to our own deritualized differentiation, the path passes unavoidably through the extreme inequalities of the ancient empires.

In condemning this evolution, anthropologists, through their impatience at "nonempirical" thought, have unwittingly enslaved themselves to a romantically naive misreading of Rousseau.[19] They would do better to reread Rousseau and then go on to read Hegel, whose anthropological deficiencies they share far more than they realize and whose dialectical theory of social evolution they condemn on the grounds that it was all really an ill-disguised apology for the Prussian monarchy. Hegel had little understanding of primitive society, but his historical model "none is free"——➤"one is free"——➤ "all are free" makes a good deal more sense as a description of the passage from the primitive state through despotism to democracy than the "fall of man" notions implicit in Harris's discussion of the subject.[20] The concept of freedom that idealist thinkers from Kant to Sartre use as a fairly reliable intuitive substitute for an anthropological constitution of the ethical at least guides Hegel past the stumbling block of social inequality upon which anthropologists continue to flounder.

If the concept of freedom has any meaning, it cannot be understood from an account of roles in a social structure, for, in such an account, all roles being determined a priori by the model, no individual role possesses any more freedom than any other. Freedom must rather be understood as the possibility of realizing one's desire within the social structure—it being kept in mind that desire is always desire for significance. From the standpoint of the modern observer, the big-man is the *least* free member of his community: he works the hardest for the least material satisfaction. His "freedom" lies in the realization of his desire for significance, which coincides with the production of an economic surplus at specified times. We see from this example that the communal significance of the surplus is not continuously measurable as a simple quantity of wealth, that is, as an economic value, but is derived from the act of ritual distribution performed upon it.

Only in a market economy, such as has only really existed in modern times, can economic value become a quantity detached from any ethical function. In earlier societies, the economic surplus acquires significance only through its use in cultural—and in the simplest societies, purely ritual—activities. This fact evidently affects the conditions under which the surplus is acquired, as well as perceived by its acquirers. The simple equation of the surplus with the cultural is possible only from the vantage point of modern society as narrowly understood by modern social science. Our perspective shows itself to be more faithful not only to each culture's own vision of itself (its "ethical conception") but to our own esthetic appreciation of cultural activities and objects. This appreciation is, as Kant well knew, involuntary and objective. (We reject, however, his contention that it is "without a concept.") Commonsense admiration for the artifacts of past cultures is far wiser than quantification of them in economic terms.

This is not to deny the significance of the economization of culture, either in the developed form taken today or in its origin in phenomena like that described by Sahlins. But that culture can never, today or in the future, be wholly or essentially reduced to economic terms is demonstrated by the fact that its origins antedate the production of an economic surplus. This surplus is associated not with the birth of culture but with that of "freedom," which is, as we have defined it, the integration of individual desire, as opposed to its transcendence, into communally significant activities. It is the very quantitative nature of the surplus that makes this integration possible. For, however the quantity is perceived, its accumulation can only be accomplished through a time-consuming, individually motivated praxis. The deferral characteristic of representation, which is carried over into technique as the teleological representation of its purpose, is here raised to a higher level. For deferral is not merely considerably prolonged; its prolongation has a new, differential motivation. There emerges here a new, praxial definition of the individual's place in society.

Representation, and most notably, ritual, was from the beginning a "surplus" with respect to appetitive activity.[21] Man's ability to create an economic surplus is a corollary of his originary creation of a representational surplus. The appetitive is primordial, but the economic is secondary to the cultural. The fact that both the ap-

petitive and the economic are "material" fails to justify a materialist—
that is, economist—theory of human society. On the contrary, we
are led to question the material nature of the economic surplus itself.

But if the cultural dominates the economic, if representation already constitutes a surplus, why then is the constitution of a *material*
surplus the condition of ethical progress? The very word "surplus"
implies something other than merely increasing appetitive satisfaction, which as such moves within a very limited range. The satisfactions provided by the big-man's feast are appetitively based, but
their importance to the community cannot be measured by appetite
alone any more than can that of our own festive ceremonies. We are
thus led to consider the differential relationship between the consumption of the surplus and its production. This analysis will help
prepare us for our later examination of the relation between the
producer- and the consumer-role in relation to the artworks of high
culture.

The big-man (and his dependents) produce; the entire community
consumes. Their consumption no doubt satisfies their appetite; above
all it satisfies their desire. But relation between their desire and its
satisfaction is not of the same character as that of the big-man, who
has forgone even normal appetitive satisfactions for the sake of the
significance to be gained through his praxis. This dichotomy between
producer and consumer has its roots in the original event.

1. In the original scene of representation, the members of the
community, in designating the object, at the same time imaginarily
prolong their act of designation into the originally intended act of
appropriation. But this imaginary act aims at the possession, no
longer merely of an object of appetitive satisfaction, but of the unique
significant referent of the designating gestures of the entire community. This desire, absolute and unfulfillable, is the model of what
we may call "producer's desire."

2. The scene of representation terminated, each member of the
community acts to appropriate his own portion of the object. Now
the appetitive goal is subsumed within a desire for participation along
with the others in the significance that has just been conferred on
the object. We may call this "consumer's satisfaction." The unattainable desire for the whole is compensated for by participation in
a collective appropriation where each receives an equivalent share.
Although the portions of all the members of the group could not
have been exactly equal, and may well have been influenced by the
preexistent primate hierarchy obtaining within the group, the creation of the scene of representation and of "producer's desire" for

the whole so devalorizes this hierarchical differentiation that nothing is lost by neglecting it. For could the preexistent hierarchy have sufficed to permit the peaceful distribution of the object, the scene of representation need never have arisen.

Producer's desire evolves in mature society into the desire to replace the collectively conceived divinity as the origin of communal distribution. That this desire does not in fact aim at the consumption of the object is corroborated by the big-man example; but this example is not necessary to our argument. Not only is there too much for any individual to consume; the object consumed in isolation would cease to be communally significant. In the original scene, desire is pure paradox: appropriation of the central object is precisely what is prevented by the significance accorded it in the scene itself. But the elaboration of ritual permits the gradual resolution of this paradox. The individual who plays the central role of the sacred being in the imperative ritual previous to the hunt may well imagine himself in possession of—or possessed by—the desire-object whose form he assumes. This possession, realized figuratively by his position in the rite, is clearly distinguished from consumption; it has meaning only insofar as it is preliminary to redistribution. Producer's desire is here still paradoxical; were the object truly available, its distribution would not be accomplished by any single individual. But because the imperative makes desire formulable in the absence of its object, it permits this desire to adapt itself to communal reality. Possession by an individual as such is chimerical; possession as preliminary to redistribution is the realization of a communally significant representation.

In mature culture the distribution function, although under the control of a sacred being, is, in asymmetric rituals like clan or "totem" feasts, presided over by an individual family head or clan chief. This act would appear fully to realize producer's desire, no longer figuratively but concretely. But what is realized in the ritual is not truly the fulfillment of the individual desire of the distributor. For the realization is merely an acting out; the distributor has never really possessed in the first place the objects he distributes. He plays the part of the sacred being who is believed to delegate him to carry out the distribution, but he cannot in any real sense substitute himself for this being.

The big-man has already taken a major step beyond the ritual leaders of egalitarian society toward the divinization that will be the lot of the ancient monarchs. This step, which is the first concrete realization of producer's desire, is effectuated through *praxis* and *deferral of use.* In order truly to dominate the act of distribution, the leader must turn it into an act of *re*distribution. Here the originally unpossessable object is possessed in reality, or rather it is implicated in the process of production. Praxis becomes a means not merely of representing but of replicating the central source of general appetitive satisfaction, of re-creating it as a surplus *outside* the communal distribution-system of (egalitarian) society, a surplus that is then introduced into this society through the redistributive act of an individual. At the moment of this introduction, at least, the producer's desire for central significance may be said to be fulfilled.

This fulfillment remains dependent on the capacity of the goods produced to satisfy the ritual consumers. If no one ate his food, the big-man's efforts would be for naught. The continuity of consumer satisfaction has maintained the appetitive center of ritual. That this continuity is, nevertheless, not permanent is shown both by the subsequent development of ritual away from distribution (for example, the Hebrew atonement rite) and by that of consumption away from appetitive objects (for example, to luxury goods). We must specify the parameters of the consumer's relation to desire, lest consumption appear, to quote Jean Baudrillard's description of its modern form, as merely a "mirror of production."[22]

All desire is desire for significance. Producer's desire aims at its unique possession and, in its most radical sense, can never be fulfilled. Even the deified pharaoh cannot hope to be more than a partial and temporary focus of the desires of his subjects. In contrast, as consumers, all can be satisfied, if only in a mediate fashion, through participation in and identification with the central desire-object. Consumer's satisfaction arises posterior to the pacification of the community in the original event and may be considered as in principle solidary with the communal order. In a universalized (mature) culture, our assumption that the ethical is more constraining than the material implies that the most significant feature of even a private desire is its potential for conflict with this order. This last point absolves us from establishing mediations between every desire, however "natural" (food, shelter, safety), and the communal scene of representation. For it suffices to note that a crisis in the community virtually abolishes consumer's satisfaction. Conversely, the possibility of acting to obtain such satisfaction demonstrates a noncrucial relationship to the community. The producer's praxis must be *integrated into* the community; the consumer's behavior takes its existence for granted and, by so doing, contributes to its survival.[23] For, by definition, objects of consumption, if not actually social artifacts, possess at the very least a well-defined social value.

The material nature of the original productive praxis and, more generally, the contrast between the "conservative" appetitive *object* of this praxis and the radical nature of the praxis itself may now be explained. Consumption is not always material, but it is largely so because its object is taken from what the community already has to offer, a set of possibilities that must in any case include the material necessities of existence. Yet once the occasion arises in which it can be *functionally* distinguished from production—that is, in the big-man case that we have taken as paradigmatic of the emergence of social differentiation—its material basis may always be shown in hindsight to be contingent with respect to its ethical or cultural basis.

At earlier stages, producer's desire was afforded at best imaginary satisfactions; the real satisfactions of desire were at the level of consumption, to which the primitive egalitarian social order cannot fail to reduce it. However one may desire to possess the significant object in its entirety, one must always content oneself with a specific portion of insignificant differential value. It is only when a differentiated individual producer arises that his fellows are—as yet only on widely spaced occasions—reduced to the role of mere consumers. When, in other words, all produce and consume more or less equally, producer's desire is experienced merely as an excess or "supplement" to consumption. It is only when the consumer becomes distinguished from the producer that the two relations to the desire for centrality give rise to differentiated forms of social activity. This coincides with the production and redistribution of a surplus that is *structurally* outside the subsistence needs of its consumers. The status of the food distributed at the big-man's feast does not depend on the immediate caloric needs of the feasters.[24] The latter, because they are eating "surplus" food, cannot be said in terms of their own culture to *need* the food at all. What their satisfaction really depends on is the ritual function of the foods produced: the blankets used in the famous Kwakiutl potlatch feasts do not differ in essence from the food as objects of consumption.

The contingency of the appetitive has important consequences for the subsequent evolution of ritual. In immature society, ritual feasts may not have been indispensable to alimentation, but their occurrence coincided with the most critical moments in collective nourishment—those that were potential sources of generalized conflict. In mature egalitarian cultures, cultural universality gives *all* appetitive activity a ritual basis. It is unimportant whether the food consumed in ritual feasts actually fulfills a biologically essential function—whether, in other words, enough is eaten outside such feasts to permit the survival of the population. Ritual eating is not discontinuous from nonritual eating; distribution of appetitive satisfaction in the ritual context is central to the culture, and this context cannot be understood by its participants independently of such distribution.[25] But this is no longer the case when the ritual life of a culture comes to depend on the redistribution of a surplus. Whether the latter takes the form of food or of blankets, its supplementary nature is a structural fact and hence is potentially subject to conceptualization. Ritual is no longer essentially tied to appetitive satisfaction; the consumer's satisfaction it provides becomes independent of its appetitive base.

7

The Esthetic Element in Culture

The distinction between secular esthetic culture and sacred ritual is secondary to the more fundamental distinction between formal-linguistic and esthetic-cultural representation. Primitive societies are innocent of any difference between the sacred and the esthetic, and only in modern society has this difference taken on the character of institutional dichotomy.

Yet all is not so simple. The esthetic, although originally lacking in any specific institutional basis, is, unlike ritual, a component of the original scene of representation. It is therefore never wholly subordinate to ritual. Linguistic representation is not itself esthetic, but the desiring imagination is from the beginning productive of esthetic images, and the contemplation even of ritually consecrated objects involves a private esthetic activity that can never be wholly subsumed within the communal character of the ritual. Far from the esthetic being a subcategory of the ritual, ritual is rather an attempt to reaffirm in esthetic form the communal basis of individual desire. There is no sharp dividing line between ritual and art, not because art developed out of ritual (for one would still have to explain why ritual contains a potentially independent esthetic element), but because ritual is from the outset esthetic. And the esthetic is never entirely confined within ritual. It is neither content nor form that is problematic in the emergence of secular esthetic culture, but the conditions that warranted the separation of art from ritual.

The most obvious difference between ritual and art lies in the different relationships they promote between participants and non-participants. Curiously enough, this form of the bipartite division between "sacred" and "profane" is truly absolute only in art. No one can witness a rite without to some extent participating in it (whence the embarrassment of, for example, a non-Catholic attending a mass, or even inspecting the interior of a cathedral). In contrast, creative participation in an artwork of any kind is limited to a well-defined set of one or more persons who act for the sake of a group, not necessarily well-defined, of nonparticipants. It is not without significance that there is no simple word that describes these latter persons or their actions: spectators, audience, readership all specify the channel of relationship to the work rather than the nature of the relationship as such.[1] It is indeed characteristic of the whole esthetic vocabulary that it is pieced together from terms relevant to the specific arts. The conscience of the esthetic and of its general subcategories is very late and reflects the beginning of the modern cultural crisis. Yet there are few intuitions surer than that on which we found the general notion of the esthetic. Could it be that what we face here is less a cognitive impossibility than a general disinclination, an unexpressed taboo of the sort Freud would call a repression, that prevents premodern culture from reflecting on the unity of the cultural universe for fear that the conditions of its universality will be recognized as bearing a contingent and anthropological rather than an a priori and "ideal" relation to its human participants? Art proves to be more sacred than the sacred itself, the nature of its sacrality being more truly enshrouded in the mystery of the ineffable.

If we take the preceding statement of the performer/public relation as a provisional definition of secular art, without concerning ourselves for the moment with the formal problems of such a definition—which pointedly neglects the more obvious, if less operational, opposition between sacred and profane as normally defined—we see immediately why primitive egalitarian societies could not know the radical separation that has become our criterion of art. For no social difference in these societies is sufficient to warrant such a separation. Certainly, specialized "artists" must have existed even in very early societies. The cave paintings and bone carvings of Pleistocene man were surely the work of talented specialists. But the caves were not museums, and the artist's work was not destined for mere contemplation. Once the paintings became centers of ritual action, the conditions of their composition were irrelevant, as is still the case for ritual objects today. This follows from the indissolubility of the link between ritual and the distribution system: ritual participation was not merely a spiritual but a physical necessity.

Beside ritual in mature culture we find myth, which, to the extent that it is or becomes detached from ritual, is unrelated to direct appetitive satisfaction. The participation of the community in myth is intellectual rather than physical, yet not appropriately designated as "artistic." Myth is an instrument of cultural universality; its public finds in the mythical narrative an explanation for its ritual and pararitual acts. The events described in myth are originary hypotheses that maintain their narrative coherence through the presence on the imaginary scene of anthropomorphic agents[2]—a presence that derives at least formally, and in the oldest myths concretely, from that of the sacred being in ritual.

But the origin of this ritual presence is itself esthetic. The central object is not simply represented but made an object of esthetic contemplation. If we separate out this moment of contemplation from the rest, it will appear unchanged from ritual through myth to modern art. We should therefore not overemphasize the passivity of the public of myth. The participatory element is deferred in myth but not eliminated. In egalitarian society, the myth is not the property of the teller, nor is the listener's relation to its protagonist that to be found in secular narration. Even if its telling takes place outside of a strictly ritual context—and its detachment from this context can never be complete—it is at least retrospectively associated with the performance of the activity whose origin it describes. Thus the interest of the hearers of myth is not merely that inspired by the human-in-general; it derives from the ethical value—the elimination of potential social conflict—attributed by the myth to what would otherwise appear as arbitrary and thus potentially divisive practices.

The myth consecrates and therefore justifies the internally differential practices of the community. These differences are not essentially hierarchical; on the contrary, the function of myth, and of the cultural universality it expresses, is to integrate them into the egalitarian communal structure by attributing their differential aspect to a transgression—punished or transcendentally rewarded—on the part of a mythical being. It would be a mistake to see in this process a rearguard action against an irreversible tendency toward differentiation. Egalitarian societies are stable, even if their myths evolve with changing circumstances. For the differences they contain produce insufficient positive feedback to counteract the negative feedback of myth and ritual. As the big-man example shows, social differentiation becomes structural only when it can reproduce among the members of the group the absolute difference between sacred center and profane periphery. And it is this differentiation, in reducing the peripheral participants not simply to deferral of action but to the passivity of mere consumption, that prepares the way for the radical artist/public—or "producer"/"consumer"—dichotomy characteristic of secular esthetic culture.

For the consumer of the big-man's feast is satisfying desires the appetitive concreteness of which is by no means their most fundamental or most durable aspect. Just as relatively little is required to transform the altruistic big-man into a chief, and from a chief into a tyrant, the consumers of his feast may easily be transformed into dependent workers to whom is redistributed only a fraction of the product of their own labor, or, in somewhat different circumstances, spectators of a self-contained spectacle that distributes only imaginary—and no longer even imaginarily appetitive—satisfactions. The institutional separation of producer from consumer with the concomitant emergence of the producer's praxis—to which the nonpraxial but all the more onerous economic activities of the "consumers" may eventually become subordinated—is the fundamental structural determinant of the countless variants of hierarchical social structure.

Ritual deferral had always depended upon esthetic contemplation of its central object, as well as on the mimetic activity (dances, song) of the peripheral participants. The expulsion of the latter outside the realm of the representation itself, or alternatively, the addition of a tertiary class of nonparticipant spectators, converts the rite into a secular esthetic phenomenon. The parallel between the central producer status of the artist and that of the ritual big-man clearly suggest that it was the latter who served as the model for the former, that the consumer role of the artistic public is derived from that of these first true consumers.

The esthetic—as art—and the ethical—as morality—have both outlasted their undifferentiated union in ritual because their roots in the original event make them more fundamental than ritual. The superior vitality of the esthetic over the ritual is an indubitable part of our experience of past cultures. Whether or not we understand the ritual uses to which they were put or, more pertinently, the ethical conceptions they incarnate, we include without difficulty the esthetic artifacts of these cultures in the *musée imaginaire* of our own.

Anesthetic religious objects do exist, in the form of relics or other objects deemed to possess sacred "powers." These powers may be real (for example, hallucinogenic plants) or founded on a cultural memory (for example, the purported remains of a saint). Such objects are substantive, not representational, although the esthetizing tendency of ritual is likely to lead to their being decorated or framed in some way. But as soon as ritual objects become representations, regardless of their substantivity, they are understood as such, by their believers as well as ourselves, *independently of their ritual function.* This holds as true for material as for formal representations. An idol is just as much an esthetic object as a sacred text is a linguistic object.

In the original event, the esthetic contemplation of the central object qua referent of the sign is indistinguishable from the deferral of appropriation. The reality of the object is, for the duration of this deferral, reduced to a mere support of its appearance on the scene of representation, which guarantees the images of appropriation generated by each individual's desires. In imperative ritual, when esthetic representations are substituted for the sacred object, scenic appearance functions detached from its real support. There is now no longer any question of real appropriation of the object, although appropriation may be carried out symbolically. The deferral accomplished by the esthetic object is no longer the deferral of a specific appropriative act; it is constitutive rather of ritual than of practical action. Within ritual, a variety of attitudes toward the esthetic object are nonetheless possible, ranging from esthetic contemplation per se to participation with it in, for example, an acting-out of a forthcoming hunt. The existence of both figural and dramatic possibilities in what we should probably call the late imperative culture of Magdalenian Europe is substantiated by the existence, on the one hand, of the animal paintings and sculptures, and on the other, of represented figures like the "sorcerers" and "bison-man" of Trois-Frères (Ariège), whose ritual function as substitutes for the desired (and presumably sacred) game animal finds parallels in numerous rites of present-day primitive hunters.

We have already referred to the possible ritual functions of these paintings in our section on imperative culture. But although such references are unavoidably speculative, we need not for all that refuse credence to our *esthetic* intuition. Certainly the paintings were the object of lengthy contemplation by the artists who created them, and certainly they were produced as objects for the esthetic contemplation of others. Whether, as seems most likely, these designated others were the other members of the hunting band, or whether they were merely ideal beings—a hypothesis that cannot simply be dismissed—if the paintings attract our contemplation today, we have every reason to suppose that they attracted that of their first spectators. "Esthetic value" is no criterion of an advanced state of culture.

The significance of the represented content is sufficient to inspire, as these paintings show, a sophisticated artistic vision, albeit of animal rather than man, desire-object rather than self.[3] The same could not be said of discursive—that is, literary—forms, which provide a far more accurate measure of the ethical level of a culture. (See Part III, chap. 8.) But our point here is that these artistic images can function in a primitive ritual context in much the same way as they would in a modern museum. It is thus not the museum but the ritual context that must be understood as the original occasion for an esthetic contemplation that we would be hard pressed to prove less sophisticated than our own.

Contemplation is not a sufficient guarantee of esthetic achievement; under the constraints of the ritual context, even the crudest image could be contemplated in the place of a sacred object. Unless we can make more specific the nature of esthetic reception within ritual itself, the whole question of esthetic value will forever remain a mystery. For, like any other cultural phenomenon, if this one is not explained at its origin, it can never be explained later. The cave paintings, by removing our illusions about the primitive nature of primitive art, force us to take up the question of esthetic value at a point well before the notion of secular or artistic culture could have had any meaning.

The question of esthetic value cannot occur to us without having been at least operationally present in the artists. Their finished work implies a conscientious critical or judgmental examination of the aptness of a lengthy series of more approximate images, including both those executed during the apprenticeship of the artist and those obtained at the preliminary stages of production of the individual works.[4] Many images must have been rejected as not (yet) good enough. In rejecting them, the artist acts as the agent of his community; his criteria are those of a communal esthetic judgment. The approved images are presumably felt to be better likenesses of their original and/or more formally perfect in themselves, that is, as Gestalts. The spectators of these images must have demanded these qualities as a guarantee for their desiring imagination; this follows from our supposition that their contemplation was essentially no different from ours. This guarantee of desirability presumably appeared to the members of the community as a form of possession of the referent. Yet what is most notable in this possession is its purely visual character. Painting, as opposed to statuary, does not provide a palpable model of its referent, and its location on cave walls makes even temporary physical possession by an individual at most highly symbolic.

This point may be taken one crucial step further. In the case at hand, it is evidently not the mere presence of the image but its *esthetic form* that makes it effective. But the formal quality or coherence of the image is precisely what demonstrates its unpossessability by the spectator: its formal otherness. The ritual object is in this case anything but under the control of the participants; once painted, it stands against them as an inaccessible guarantee of their desire—a desire that can no more be satisfied by the appropriation of a real animal than the desire we feel before a portrait could be satisfied by "possession" of its subject.

Thus there can be no direct application of the esthetically generated desire to the practical activity of the hunt, or to any practical activity. But this only confirms what we have known all along. Ritual, and culture generally, is not a simple instrument of appetitive goals; it is not economic but ethical. Making the painting of a bison more beautiful is not a simple means of intensifying the desire for bison hunting. Indeed, on the plane of practical activity, its function may well have been just the opposite: to console the hunters, in the event of failure, with the certitude that no appetitive satisfaction could in any case have fulfilled their desire. But the function of this "consolation" need not be given so narrow a basis. The painting is a demonstration not of an individual but of a *collective* intuition of the essential otherness of its sacred object, an intuition that possesses a unifying force. One does not contemplate an image of this object *faute de mieux;* its otherness, its status as an object of pure desire, is essential. For in this context "otherness" is simply another word for "transcendence." The unity of the group is affirmed in the face of such an image not through the deferral occasioned by the originary fear of conflict but in a qualitatively different and more durable manner.

Thus our conclusion concerning the ritual function of the cave paintings, which in its generality may be extended to all esthetic elements of ritual, is that it is precisely their esthetic value that makes them instruments of communal solidarity. The difference between these sophisticated representations of the sacred object and the cruder images presented by masked or disguised actors reflects the different types of participation (and not *degrees* of participation) to which they contribute. In the case of the actors, it is their performance of dances and gestures that provides the chief component of the esthetic satisfaction, as opposed to the static image provided by the paintings.

The study of the cave paintings, produced millennia before the founding of the first hierarchically differentiated societies, allows us

to understand the function of esthetic value within ritual at a relatively primitive and perhaps predeclarative stage of cultural evolution. This understanding may appear to be founded on the
anachronistic attribution to primitive people of modern esthetic sensibilities. That the works of these people clearly demonstrate to the
unbiased observer the existence of such sensibilities is an argument
not so much met as avoided, for theoreticians of ritual have no
mechanism for dealing with it. But the anomalous nature of the cave
paintings in the light of our knowledge of the art of present-day
hunting cultures may well be an illusion of perspective. Our ethnological reverence for these latter cultures should not blind us to
their relatively backward nature, which contrasts with what was no
doubt an advanced and "progressive" society twenty thousand years
ago. A contemporary society economically (and ethically) equivalent
to ancient Athens would produce no Parthenons.

Our high estimate of the esthetic value of these paintings compels
us, as lesser achievements could not, to face the question of the
esthetic nature of ritual objects. The exotic mythology of the *musée
imaginaire* must give way to the realization—in reality a far greater
tribute to man—that all the essential structures of artistic creation
and appreciation were already present in prehistoric ritual. There
is not only no intrinsic opposition between the beautiful and the
sacred, but the beautiful existed within the sacred in the same terms
as after its emancipation. This does not imply the subordination of
esthetic values to ritual ones; quite the reverse. To the extent that
the esthetic element we have noted from the outset in ritual is indeed
artistic, that the ritual esthetic already differs in no essential manner
from the secular, it is rather ritual that risks appearing as a detachable
frame for art. If this is not altogether the case, it is because the ritual
frame can be detached only after another has been put in its place.
The explicit ethical function of ritual, realized in the general participation of the community, must be replaced by an *implicit* ethical
function for art to become the basis of a secular culture. Thus the
form of esthetic contemplation does not change, but its content
changes, as do, in more or less subtle ways, the means of formalizing
this content, of making it "esthetic."

We may sum up the thrust of the foregoing in a perhaps surprising
statement: the evolution from ritual to art, from sacred to secular
culture, involves not an esthetic transformation but an ethical one.
Thus the understanding of culture, its origin, its now virtually complete desacralization, and its future, does not require us to find some
mysterious justification for "esthetic pleasure," which could then be

added to other ingredients of culture—historical awareness, philosophical reflection, "high seriousness"—to make a more or less palatable eclectic stew. The meeting place of the diverse elements of culture is the ethical—the formulation of explicit or implicit ethical conceptions. The esthetic problems of nonritual content and formalization are not inconsiderable, but they do not require the creation of an *ad hoc* esthetic.

RESENTMENT AND THE EMERGENCE OF SECULAR CULTURE

It is the establishment of social differentiation that motivates the emergence of a secular esthetic. But we should bear in mind that egalitarian and hierarchical societies are *types* in the Weberian sense and that any number of intermediate or transitional forms may exist. Social differentiation in egalitarian societies is never altogether absent, nor is any hierarchy altogether irreversible. Our discussion of the emergence of secular culture must remain on a general level; we are dealing with forests, not trees.

We have given the category of *participation* the decisive role in separating secular art from ritual. But, as the cave-painting example shows, the (ritual) participant/(artistic) spectator distinction is independent of the phenomenon of esthetic contemplation. Nor is it useful to consider the ritual function of the paintings as exceptional in view of the limited nature of the participation they inspire. For the most participatory elements of ritual, such as dance and song, appear to us as governed by a critical esthetic sense. Even the central moment of sacrifice may possess esthetic value—for example, in the ritual antecedents of the modern bullfight. Each of those engaged in such collective activities is not only the spectator of the others but a perceiver and judge of his own movements. The esthetic value of ritual activity must have undergone considerable evolution with the emergence of individual specialization within primitive egalitarian society. When dancers or musicians specialize in their functions, their talent and pride in their work must produce superior results to those of an undifferentiated group such as the first ritual participants must have been. But for esthetic judgment to evolve, it must have been present from the outset. The emergence of a secular esthetic was the result neither of specialization nor of the evolution of esthetic judgment, but of a transformed ethical conception that affected, not the esthetic relation to and judgment of the ritual object, but the insertion of this judgment into the ritual context.

The tendency toward "estheticization" is not in itself deritualizing or secularizing, for it cannot come into conflict with its ritual context. Secular culture is not "more esthetic" than ritual culture, as the popular arts of all periods well demonstrate. The highest esthetic values are fully compatible with ritual in all the arts save those of language. In other words, the ethical contribution of estheticization—its liberation of the individual imagination—cannot by itself transcend the ethical limits of ritual. Any esthetic experience, albeit not any literary experience, can be integrated into ritual, just as modern art, music, and architecture (but not modern literature) are in fact so integrated today. The fact that this integration cannot save ritual culture from decline merely confirms our thesis that the secular/ritual opposition is located elsewhere than in the esthetic domain.

Social differentiation is the breakdown of the effective reciprocity among the members of the group. The egalitarian band can tolerate artists, musicians, shamans, and even certain kinds of chiefs because these individuals are firsts among equals whose realization of producer's desire is never absolutely superior to that of their fellows. But with the emergence of big-men or their equivalent, this is no longer the case. Reciprocity is destroyed when one produces and others consume—the "producer" being defined, as in the motion-picture industry, not as he who does the work but as he who oversees it and (re)distributes its product. This does not imply a breakdown of solidarity within the community. Such an implication would in fact be a contradiction in terms, given that nonreciprocity manifests itself precisely in a ritual context, that is, within the very institution that functions to reinforce communal solidarity. Nor does esthetic secularization imply the deritualization of ritual; it is rather the development of parallel esthetic forms outside ritual. What we must now investigate is how these forms help deal with the breakdown in reciprocity.

We must first determine in what sense this breakdown, which is in its beginnings confined to the specific set of interactions related to the preparation of the big-man's feast, is in fact a problem. In our own eyes, although the big-man case may not be particularly shocking, nonreciprocal relations are, generally speaking, morally offensive. Nonreciprocal relationships may be perfectly ethical, and consecrated as such in ritual, but they are not moral. This intuition is the fundamental source of the Jewish contribution to Western culture.

But it is equally the source of the Greek contribution. For secular art, like ritually based—and yet deritualizing, if not deliberately secularizing—morality, is a response to the rise of nonreciprocity. The problematic feature of nonreciprocity is revealed by our theory of desire. For it is one thing when all producer's desires remain equally unsatisfied, and another when this unsatisfaction is no longer equal. There now exists a socially designated praxis leading to the satisfaction of desire. But the inability or even the disinclination to engage in this praxis, which requires, among other things, a great deal of hard work, does not imply the absence of the producer's desire it satisfies. On the contrary, the emergence of real models of satisfaction can only serve to exacerbate this desire. Yet it has a far more significant effect. For instead of merely continuing to desire in vain a central position in the community, the victim of nonreciprocity comes to desire as well the ousting of the actual holder of this position. This second element of desire may contribute to various praxial alternatives: one may seek to overthrow a leader, to take his place, or one may seek merely to emulate him. But it is not these praxial implementations, which can never be those of the majority, that interest us here; they are relevant to the study of politics but only indirectly so to the study of culture. We are concerned rather with the fact that the social inferior's desire, whether or not it eventually gives rise to a praxis, constitutes a source of impotent frustration.

We might think to call this desire "envy," but Nietzsche gave it the more specific name of *ressentiment*. *The Genealogy of Morals* (chap. 1) expresses a profound if unfortunately partial insight into the cultural productivity of this phenomenon. For Nietzsche, *ressentiment* (which we shall henceforth call simply "resentment") is the source of only one of the two revolutionary cultural developments of antiquity—Judeo-Christian morality. The author of *The Birth of Tragedy* failed to realize that the Greek artforms he so admired had their root in the very same phenomenon.

There is no doubt that resentment often finds refuge in moralistic prudery and hypocritical denunciations of those whose real accomplishments one envies. The artist's own resentment, so visible in the bohemia of Nietzsche's time or in the attitudes of an "antibourgeois" like Flaubert, is transcended in his art, whereas the moralizer creates nothing. But this should only make us all the more respectful of a moral tradition that insists on the right of all to reciprocal relations. It is Nietzsche's solution—to live as "artists"—that is otherworldly and subjective, whereas the resentment that expresses itself in moral terms leads to real social and political change. The cultural productivity of resentment is far more universal than Nietzsche would have us believe—ironically enough, for he could scarcely have failed to be aware of the degree to which it motivated his own work.

Resentment may be defined as the scandal of the peripheral self at the centrality of the other which transforms the equality of the original scene of representation into an absolute polarity of significance. It differs from mere envy in being directed not at contingent but at communally significant and hence ethically necessary differences. It is thus a necessary evil. But its necessity makes it, at the same time, an instrument of a new form of solidarity that is no longer bound by the concrete ethical limitations of ritual. This solidarity is expressed in secular esthetic and theoretical culture, that is, in art and philosophy, and, ultimately, in the sciences, where it appears purified of all contact with its origins in desire. In contrast with abstract morality, which poses as a norm the reciprocity that has become an ethical impossibility, art renounces normativity in order to realize this reciprocity in the purely imaginary relationship between the spectator and a fictional universe. Within this relationship, resentment is demystified and abolished. The artist, whether individualized or anonymous, acts as the regnant divinity of the fictional universe, the spectator's temporary subordination to whom is untroubled by resentment because it is purely transcendental, lacking in any element of worldly rivalry. (The worldly success of the artist is a source of a resentment less easily transcended; this is, indeed, a constitutional problem of art in bourgeois society.)

The esthetic transcendence of desire is not an invention of secular art. But although the experience of the esthetic object may be essentially identical in ritual and in secular art, in the secular context the desire attached to the object is no longer transcendentally utopian producer's desire but resentment directed at the nonreciprocity of the ethical system. Here it is no longer sufficient for the formal otherness of the image to reinforce the solidarity of the community, all of whose members are equal in being unable to possess it. In an egalitarian community, the possession of the central ritual object by another individual would be incompatible with the communal ethic; in a hierarchical society, this possession corresponds to a real, socially consecrated distinction. Here the otherness of the esthetic object is no longer that of a transcendental desire-object that can be possessed only by the community as a whole. Hence esthetic contemplation creates no ritual solidarity to tide the group over the period of deferral of appetitive satisfaction and to render the quest for this satisfaction more effective. Instead, esthetic otherness must now guarantee the imaginary existence of a fictive universe wherein the inaccessibility of the object is the same for all. ʻSuch a universe is not even in imagination a community in which the spectator can participate together with his fellows, but a fictive world in which the individual spectator can imagine himself, secure in his awareness that the desiring imagination of his fellow spectators is no less unrealizable than his own.

The emergence of secular esthetic culture, although involving an essential structural change, does not require a radical transformation of the ritual esthetic that preceded it, any more than the emergence of nonreciprocal socioeconomic relations in such phenomena as that of the big-man need take place as a revolutionary event in egalitarian society. The ritual and the secular, egalitarian rivalry and hierarchical resentment, are poles rather than incompatible essences. That no radical change is necessary in the esthetic object in order to convert it from ritual to secular usage is clear from our experience of the cave paintings. In contemplating them as art, we experience the same formal otherness as their original contemplators. But we gain thereby no solidarity with our fellows, not to speak of improved cooperation in hunting the worldly referent of the image. The image is not ours, for we do not share in advance the desire that inspired it; but our contemplation itself generates a desire to exist in the fictive universe inhabited by such powerful and majestic creatures. No doubt this contemplation gives no specific solace to the resentments generated by the modern world; but it provides an escape from them. None of our contemporaries possesses these beasts more than we; no one can outdo us in our temporary submission to the vision of their creator. Our imaginary prolongation of the lines of force makes us identify with the beasts themselves, and the imaginary fulfillment of our desire for their power leaves us eternally unsatisfied, but in a failure that, unlike our worldly failures, we share with all our fellows.

PART III

The Birth of High Culture

8

The Emergence of High-
Cultural Discourse

Viewed from the perspective of
modern Western culture, the period that stretches from the first
hierarchically differentiated societies to the end of classical antiquity
yields its finest fruit in the contributions of two peoples: the Greeks
and the Jews.

For there are two central lessons to be learned from the passage
from equality to differentiation: the primacy of the ethical and the
autonomy of the cultural. One may wonder why, if the cultural
domain is that of the expression of ethical conceptions, these two
lessons could be so easily separated—why, indeed, their union in
modern Western society remains even today incomplete. Deritualization having led, on the one hand, to a secular culture, and, on
the other, to a social structure that is bound by moral rules but
whose ethical conception is increasingly open, the question posed
to culture is that of its capacity to express such a conception.

Neither the Greeks nor the Jews could have formulated such a
question, a fact which suggests that neither the ethical nor the cultural can radically absorb or eliminate the other. Their development
into centers of social self-consciousness is not the mere emergence
of two separate but hitherto undifferentiated elements of egalitarian
culture. The latter is immanently normative: its rituals and the myths
that branch out from them toward every significant cultural element
maintain a tight link between norm and reality, one altogether strange
to our society and in the very unfreedom of which ethnologists seek
to liberate themselves from the "original sin" of failing, as we all
must, to live up to the transcendental norms of the Judeo-Christian

tradition. Ritual, as a concrete enactment of an ethical conception, realizes the norm it expresses; myth, more flexible, is in primitive societies forever occupied in justifying a posteriori everyday practices as rituals. Present practices are thus made dependent on a sacred being's past transgressions, but these, unlike Adam's, transmit no moral impurity to future generations.

The separation between the ethical and cultural-esthetic elements produced transcendentally normative cultures of two different sorts. The ethical element, no longer embedded in the concrete details of ritual that connected it directly to the system of distribution, becomes a *moral* norm that conceptualizes an ideal state of communal relations against which real relations are to be judged, including, in the exemplarily radical case of the Hebrew prophets, those of the entire social universe. But the esthetic element, once detached from the distribution system, transforms itself into a transcendental norm of a different sort. Although morality may be said to conceptualize an ideal community, its precepts are abstract and universal. In contrast, the works of secular art attempt to create such a community concretely, without recourse to abstract moral concepts, in their audience.

THE CULTURAL FUNCTION OF DISCOURSE

Greek culture included all the arts. For Hegel, as for Winckelmann, it was in sculpture that the Greek esthetic was most perfectly expressed, not in the more "spiritual" mode of literary discourse, which, along with music, was best adapted to the infinite aspirations of what he called the "Romantic"—that is, Christian—era. No doubt there is a grain of truth in this comparison. Classical literature does not exploit the capacity of discourse to express its subject's consciousness of the paradox of his own difference—a consciousness that can be expressed only in a limited and artificial manner in the plastic arts (for example, in Escher's drawings). But however perfect its sculpture and however naive its discourse, it is the latter that truly distinguishes Greek culture from all those that preceded it, as well, indeed, as from all that followed. No culture has ever had such faith in the power of discourse; and from this faith came the logical discourse of science and mathematics, as well as the major literary genres.

Literature, unlike the other arts, is generally incompatible with the ritual context. And conversely, whereas ritual forms of the other arts could be transported unchanged into a secular context, ritual discourse is not so adaptable. Ambiguous forms exist on the borderline between myth and secular narrative; but even such forms are experienced as ambiguous, not as simply indifferent to their sacred or profane status. This greater sensitivity to context is at first glance attributable to the richer semantic content of linguistic as opposed to plastic or musical representation: language must define the sacred or profane nature of its referent, whereas the other arts need only present images. But this facile explanation fails to take into account the special cultural status of language that is a consequence of its preritual origin. Language discriminates thematically between sacred and profane because, unlike all other forms of representation, it was not subordinated from the beginning to the sacred. The esthetic experience of a painting involves no radical decision as to its sacred or profane status. Its content may, of course, make this clear; but there is no way of distinguishing between "sacred" and "profane" *experiences* of the painting.[1] The "profane" experience is merely a ritual moment in a new context. This is not so in the case of language. Discourse may have originated in a ritual context, but its basis in language is independent of ritual. Whereas ritual—and, originally, the nonlinguistic art forms contained within it—poses its object as sacred—that is, as inaccessible outside the ritual context— language claims for its object only *significance*, the status of being worthy of the attention of one's interlocutor. This claim is, in effect, truly minimal, for it is contained in the very act of linguistic designation, as, so to speak, its performative component.

Because linguistic representation originally posits significance rather than sacrality, the presence of the sacred must be *marked* in ritual discourse. At the ostensive and imperative stages, this mark may simply take the form of the naming of the sacred object/being, at first by designation, later, in its absence, by evocation. Already at the imperative stage, the sacred name may be supplemented by epithets that emphasize its transcendental nature ("all-powerful," "immortal") and/or its role as source of worldly—that is, appetitive— benefits ("bountiful").[2] The introduction of discursive myth at the level of mature culture provides an etiology of such epithets in their application to the concrete details of social life. Here the mark of the sacred becomes elaborated into a causal principle that no longer requires a ritual context to remain productive. Myths may be not only narrated but created, or at least modified, in nonritual settings; their function is precisely to bring the totality of profane activities into contact with the ritual center of the community. So long as this function is maintained, myth cannot lead to the formation of a secular literature. Because the mark of the sacred is a function internal to the mythic discourse, rather than its external context, as in the plastic arts, its disappearance must correspond to structural changes in the narrative.

It is tempting to associate the passage from egalitarian to differentiated society with the transition within myth from divine to human protagonists—from gods to "heroes." But, in reality, the difference between gods and heroes is all but impossible to establish so long as they perform the same functions. The really significant difference occurs when the hero becomes a center of interest in himself and not a mere functionary of the community. Here we pass from myth to secular legend, for, instead of attributing the categories of reality to a sacred origin, the narration promotes our identification with the hero's human—and resentful—desires, an identification by means of which we are purged of our own worldly resentment.

These features of etiology and identification can coexist within myth when a human hero takes the place of a god as protagonist. But this latter form should rather be seen as transitional than as expressing the ethical conception of an established hierarchical society. Myth does not disappear in differentiated communities; nor is it useful to speculate on precisely what forms myth takes once secular forms begin to emerge. Because mythic and secular narrative perform different functions, although both may be combined in a given text, the texts of a given culture will display the relative importance of the two elements, and thereby the relative importance of ritual and secular means of resolving conflict. But the evolution of culture is most significantly revealed not in transitional mixtures but in unified ethical conceptions. It is therefore no surprise that the two most radical configurations hold for us a particular interest. In one, the sacred narrative wholly dominates the secular; in the other, the secular wholly integrates the sacred. These two cases are precisely those of the Jews and the Greeks.

THE EARLIEST CULTURAL TEXTS

Before taking up these extreme cases, we should cast a passing glance on the less radical forms of ancient cultures. The old Mideastern empires, particularly Egypt and Babylon, have left us representative samples of their cultural texts.

Egyptian secular narrative is of a minor nature, with no admixture of mythical elements; its ritual literature, from what we possess of it, is fragmentary and procedural rather than narrative. The lack of integration between ritual and secular forms seems to have foreclosed the development of a major literary culture of either kind. The stability of "hydraulic" rule[3] keeps secular resentment within well-defined limits. Ritual culture is intense but highly individualized; rivalry is rather deferred to the "other world" than subsumed in solidarity. Thus individualism is expressed in ritual formulas for individual use, not in mythic epics. The afterlife compensates for the relative immobility of the secular world, with which it is never confused.

The *Story of Sinuhe*, dating from about 2000 B.C., is generally considered the masterpiece of Egyptian literature.[4] It is a simple tale of the adventures of a former companion of the pharaoh, forced to flee Egypt during the time of troubles that preceded the succession of the new pharaoh. Sinuhe, after wandering through the Near East, becomes the chief of a Bedouin tribe; in his old age, impelled by nostalgia, he returns to Egypt, where he is rewarded by the pharaoh with the title of Friend of the first rank and permitted to construct—to his enormous satisfaction—his own pyramid. It was presumably on the walls of this pyramid that his story, written in the first person as if by a man already dead, was first recorded.

The most significant feature of this "masterpiece" is its illustration of a minimal state of literature. The unquestionable centrality of the pharaoh reduces the possibilities of significant individuality to the margins and interstices of Egyptian society. The foreign adventures of Sinuhe are conceivable only as the result of an interregnum that eclipses for a moment the pharaonic power. Lefebvre accepts Sinuhe's own explanation for his departure for Egypt: a loyal follower of the new legitimate pharaoh Seostris, he feared for his life when a rival prince became—unsuccessfully, as it turned out—a pretender to the throne. But the logic of events implies a simpler explanation. Sinuhe was forced into exile because he had, in fact, supported Seostris's rival.

The text is obscure on this point, but it would appear quite hospitable to our interpretation. To quote [translating from Lefebvre's French]: "The Friends of the palace sent to the West to inform the son of the king [Seostris] of what had taken place at court [that is, his father Amenemhat's death]. . . . But the royal children . . . had also been sent for, and an appeal was made to one of them. Finding myself present, I heard his voice. . . . My heart was troubled. . . . I went off to seek a hiding place . . ." (Lefebvre, pp. 6–7; R 19–28). The "voice" Sinuhe hears is that of Seostris's rival. If his heart is troubled, this trouble may well have been provoked by Seostris's victory in the war of succession. Professions of loyalty to "the perfect god Seostris" (R 13) prove nothing in a text written many years later during the latter's reign. The confusion of the text is most easily explained by the impossibility of telling the simple truth. The inconceivability of the slightest expression of disloyalty to a reigning monarch is not the least significant constraint on this literary work.

This momentary conversion of resentment into praxis is punished by a lifetime of exile. The most moving moment of the story occurs when, after being permitted to return to Egypt, he is received by the pharaoh *en famille* and treated with affectionate familiarity. The fulfillment of the hero's dream is the gracious gesture of the god-king in granting his subject a few moments of human reciprocity. The reader is touched by Sinuhe's joy; the hero's career provides us with a model of expiation and redemption of the minimally resentful subject. But this is only marginally a literary text, not because it is autobiography rather than fiction, but because it is so marginally subversive of ritually established significance.

Such nonproblematic acceptance of central authority expresses itself more readily in monumental sculpture than in literature. Egyptian moral reflection gave rise to a considerable "wisdom" literature that was presumably the direct source of Hebrew books like Proverbs and the Wisdom of Solomon. But these lists of moral-ethical aphorisms reflect none of the radical criticism of the Hebrew prophets, for whom morality provided an absolute standard from which no ethical structures were exempted. There were no Egyptian prophets to challenge the legitimacy of a pharaoh's rule on moral grounds. The hydraulic basis of this rule was no doubt too patent an ethical justification.[5]

Mesopotamia, unlike Egypt, produced an epic literature, best known from the *Creation Epic* (*Enuma Elish*) and the *Epic of Gilgamesh*, which date back to Sumerian origins. In the first case the mythical, in the second the secular element predominates: we seem to stand at the watershed between the Hebrew and Greek ways. In the *Creation Epic*, communal solidarity is justified through a cosmic etiology leading to the legitimation of the third-generation god Marduk, who, like Zeus, is a bringer of a cultural order imposed on the natural forces incarnate in the creator-gods. This mediation between a particular social order and the order of the universe-in-general (which, although expressed in cosmic terms, has its origins in human cultural universality) will be altogether eliminated from the Hebrew creation account, which owes to the Babylonian so many of its details.

The story of Gilgamesh, the earliest known text to hold for us a genuine literary value, expresses a far more problematic relationship to social authority than was ever found in Egypt. Gilgamesh's ultimate reluctant acceptance of his mortal status is, in effect, a constitutive myth of literature, just as the narrative that culminates in it marks the emergence of literature from myth. Gilgamesh's acceptance of mortality and eventual death makes the narrative itself, rather than the communal presence of ritual, the locus of the sacrifice of the hero's desire for centrality. This sacrificial theme is traditionally explained by critics as reflecting the fear of death that is supposedly a defining characteristic of our species. But the analysis of the preceding section permits us to understand that Gilgamesh's unsuccessful search for immortality reflects not the audience's fear of death but its resentment; the hearer finds solace in the knowledge that all men are equal in the face of death. The medieval *danse macabre* too, but more transparently, had resentment as its source.

That the *Gilgamesh Epic*, and "tragic" secular literature in general, includes within it a sacrificial moment may be more clearly understood if we compare this hero's final resignation to mortality with the transcendental conclusion of the Tikarau myth referred to above (Part II, chap. 6). The transformation of Tikarau's leap off the cliff into a supernatural flight rather than a natural fall to his death reflects the community's unwillingness to admit to a collective ritual murder, the memory of which is thus preserved in distorted form. The ritual victim was killed, but the mythical one must escape, because only thus can he remain a transcendental source of cultural benefits to the community. Here cultural universality requires deification. But in concrete—that is, ritual—terms, what this means is that the deified hero becomes the figural supplier of the goods for the communal feast, which are eaten in his honor, or, in other words, *sacrificed* to him. Sacrifice is, here as elsewhere, depicted as nourishing the gods because the communal feast under their auspices serves to reinforce their transcendental peacekeeping role. The members of an egalitarian community can share equally in the sacrifice only if the hero of their myth is imagined as divinely surviving his ordeal. The myth combats appropriative rivalry, not resentment; it functions by founding the equality of all on their submission to a transcendental being.

The result of the *Gilgamesh Epic* is precisely the opposite. In this

archetype of the emergence of secular literature from myth, Gilgamesh is, rather, a god who becomes transformed into a mortal.[6]
Any feasting that may have gone on under his auspices must now
find another divine patron. But Gilgamesh's demotion to mortal
status could occur only if the resentment that motivated it had become a greater threat to communal solidarity than the appropriative
rivalry formerly controlled by the ritual held in his honor. Gilgamesh
is "sacrificed" to this resentment.

Our Judeo-Christian heritage, which opposed a unique transcendental God to fictional and mythical heroes alike, makes us insensitive to the critical difference in extradiscursive status between a
god and a literary protagonist. Tikarau exists for the community of
his believers outside of the myth that merely justifies his transcendent
ritual status. Gilgamesh exists only in the text. Yet the "sacrifice"
of his fictive extratextual existence is, like any sacrifice, not merely
a loss. The text has now become the unique source of imaginary
identification with its hero. It is as if a god, as a result of freely
entering into a narrative, became so anthropomorphic that he acquired the trait of mortality and could never again emerge from it.
Yet in this transformation from a ritual to a textual figure, the central
hero does not lose his immortality; he merely passes from one form
of immortality—that is, of imaginary permanence—to another.

For the secular hero, although confined to a text, is just as permanent a cultural reality as a god.[7] Literary heroes are indeed far
more resilient than gods, whose imaginary existence depends on a
community of belief. The gods of Homer survive, like his mortal
heroes, only as literary characters. And as a literary character, the
mortal hero has over the god the advantage of superior anthropomorphism. Because his life is confined to the text, the desires we
share with him remain confined to the imaginary universe we construct around the text and do not impinge on our worldly lives. The
Gilgamesh Epic, in illustrating the transition from mythical to secular
narrative, allows us to situate Babylonian culture very near the bor-
der between the ethical conceptions expressed in both types. Individual resentment that can be consoled only through the private
satisfactions of the text is taking the place of the communal spirit of
the ritual feast. The *Creation Epic*, in contrast, demonstrates the
movement within ritual toward ethical universality if not toward
abstract morality. Sumerian-Babylonian society, less stable and more
agonistic than the Egyptian, displays as triumph the ethical superiority that Egypt in its isolation took more or less for granted. Its
still-despotic social order contains the seeds of both Greek secularism
and Hebrew moralism.

Our use of the term "culture" might be said to imply a bias toward the Greek rather than the Jewish sources of our Western heritage. For however scrupulously the cultural is traced back to the ritual, culture is a classical, not a Hebraic, or even a Judeo-Christian, conception. Jewish literary culture is not only not secular, it is very nearly anesthetic, being limited to compilation of biblical commentaries that deliberately distort the narrativity of the biblical text in order to extract from its every letter a lesson in morality. Nor is there a way to define a pure state of "Christian culture" abstracted from its classical elements. The Renaissance gives clear proof of the dependence of Western culture on classical forms.

But this bias is in fact illusory. Having taken pains to demonstrate that man's original self-consciousness is cultural, we preclude the possibility of a symmetrically opposed perspective. Jews and Greeks contribute to the same whole. Our interest in Greek forms would be merely antiquarian or, worse, estheticist and antimoralistic in the Nietzschean sense, had these forms not become, in Western society, privileged vehicles for ethical conceptions the source of which is not classical at all.

For our concern with culture, ancient or contemporary, is not merely "esthetic." Our purpose is not to promote the superior enjoyment of the arts but to define our place within contemporary society through our explanation of its culture. The "end of culture" is precisely this understanding, which is no less cultural for being theoretical, just as Plato is no less a cultural figure than Sophocles. And the contemporary vantage point from which this understanding becomes possible is determined precisely by the dissolution of the old constitutive opposition between the "Greek" and "Jewish" elements of culture.

The moral imperative is a cultural scandal, for it possesses no content and suffers no independent elaboration into a set of cultural objects. Iconoclasm is its fundamental relation to the esthetic, and, in the long term, the art of the Christian West is a historical realization, not a denial, of the iconoclasm of its Hebrew origins. Confronted with this uncompromising abstractness, all idols eventually lose their power. Yet our examination of these idols implies no inconsistency. It is not through perversion of its spirit that Western cultural reflection has maintained its gaze fixed on its Greek more than its Hebrew ancestry. The moral imperative may be our greatest cultural force, and its formulation our greatest achievement, but in its purity it cannot be realized as a positive ethic. In the concrete social context, only esthetic culture permits us to construct an imaginary universe of reciprocal relations. It is through the estheticization of social interaction that modern society offers the only possible path to the realization of the moral imperative. The incomparable energetic cost, in labor and raw materials, of our consumer society is the result neither of Malthusian nor of Marxist inevitability. It is, rather, the price of a still very imperfect realization of reciprocity, which can be realized without ritual constraint only in a society not of universal similarity but of universal difference. The "end" of esthetic culture is thus its spreading outside the confines of the specifically artistic context to encompass the entire universe of social interaction. That this interaction can be truly moral only if it is first esthetic, that we must find our neighbor "beautiful" before we can love him—this is a conclusion which, here yet unproved, may at least serve to defer our doubts about the cultural significance of Judeo-Christian morality. For to the extent that it is true, culture has in modern society been transformed into an esthetic basis for the realization of the moral imperative of reciprocity in social relations.

9

Jewish Culture:
Narrative Monotheism

As we observed in the preceding chapter, the motive force for moral as well as artistic evolution beyond egalitarian ritual culture is resentment. In secular culture, resentment is esthetically satisfied through the "sacrifice" of a fictive content within the work, a content generally associated with a mortal protagonist. This process is not, as we shall see, without cognitive value, but it can never uncover its own origin in nonreciprocity as such, rather than in a hubristic or criminal excess of it.

Unlike the Greeks, the Jews were less concerned to purge resentment than to extract from it its originary kernel of reciprocity. This is a gradual development in which the prophets play the most visible role and which, with the radical Christian separation between morality and ethics, enters into conflict with the Jewish ethical and communal tradition. The original motivation for this development, unique in the Western world at least, would appear to be the endemic political and military weakness of an imperfectly united group of tribes, each ready to see in the leadership of a rival the explanation for their common failure. This attitude was reinforced by the defeat and the Babylonian captivity, but it must have had its roots in the period of the kingdom, and no doubt before.

Hebrew "culture" is limited essentially to a single collection of sacred books, but we would be wrong to dismiss the narrative element of this culture simply because it expresses itself in a sacred context. The Hebrew Bible is no mere liturgy, nor is it a mythical epic like the Babylonian *Enuma Elish*. What it exemplifies is not the simple elimination of the secular by the sacred but its integration

189

within it in the most radical sense, not as mere esthetic content but as history. Mythical, legendary, and historical elements all find their place in a sacred narrative that establishes between them no generic distinction. The recorded acts of men are given the same significance as those of purely legendary and originally mythical origin. This significance is an explicitly ethical one; but it is an ethic presented throughout in a moral perspective that becomes, as the story progresses, increasingly independent of the ethical reality to which it is applied.[1] What is unique about the Jews is less their discovery of morality—which is at least implicit in any cultural expression of resentment—than their application of it to the history within which this discovery arose. Only thus could its principles be tested against the reality from which they emerged.

Although it is possible to read the Bible as literature—as the widespread use of the term as a university course-title suggests—it never presents itself as such. Fictions are used very sparingly. Only the Song of Songs and short Megilloth like Job and Esther exploit literary techniques on a fairly large scale, and only the first of these can be read as a piece of secular literature. The Bible, like myth, purports to be true, not fictional, but unlike myth, its characters, even the most fabulous, are all human save one. The narrative, despite the stylistic beauty that distinguishes it from anonymously told myth, makes few concessions to literary effects. Individuals die, but their death is not "tragic" and is certainly not intended to produce catharsis. Like the *Gilgamesh Epic*, Genesis presents the transition from immortal to mortal protagonists, but rather than inaugurating a secular literature, it marks the permanent subordination of the secular to a transcendental moral principle. The separation within Babylonian literature between sacred and secular epic, between divine creation and human reality, and thus between an esthetic based on desire and an esthetic based on resentment, is definitively abolished. The fall of Adam into mortality that accomplished this abolition is thus the most significant episode in the Bible.

THE CREATION AND THE FALL

Gilgamesh's mortality is the locus of identification of public resentment, a relocation of public sacrifice within the text. It is this "endotextuality" of sacrifice, which precludes ritual participation, that makes this epic the archetypal literary work. Adam's fall is not a sacrifice to resentment but a punishment of it. There is no secular-literary satisfaction to be gained from the esthetic contemplation of this episode. Adam's role is etiological, like that of Tikarau in the Tikopia myth; yet the communal "benefit" brought on by his sin is death, which is thereby assimilated to the ethical order, while the expulsion of the protagonist is effected neither by divinization nor by ritual murder but by the establishment of human equality in the face of a purely transcendental difference.

The story of Adam is thus neither myth nor literature. This is an etiological narrative that explicitly sets resentment rather than any ritually derived phenomenon at the origin of culture. The transcendental moral order here deals directly with worldly desire, without mediation through a system of ritual satisfaction. The insight of this narrative into the relations between simple desire and resentment, and of both with sexual difference and the fear of death, provides an implicit theory of the origin of culture the lessons of which are still far from fully learned. We also learn from it the immense cultural productivity of monotheism as a means for converting resentment into morality, that is, of maintaining the idea of reciprocity in the face of contrary ethical necessity. There is little in the Jewish contribution to Western culture that cannot be found, in germ at least, in this episode.

In mythical epics like the *Enuma Elish* or Hesiod's *Theogony*, the creation of man, which is, after all, the *raison d'être* of the preliminary cosmology, appears as a somewhat embarrassing secondary phenomenon, almost forgotten in the all but interminable series of births and battles by means of which the various gods—some actually worshiped, others invented to serve as precultural precursors and anticultural antagonists—are organized into a pantheon.[2] The status of man in these epics is uncertain because he is neither an object of worship nor an object of consumption but the subject of both activities. His coexistence with the immortal objects of worship and providers of the feast could be justified only by the establishment between man and god of a symmetry that only the full moralization of resentment could inspire. The battles of the gods leave no place for this symmetry, for they reflect a priority of ritual over secular questions, a subordination of resentment to desire.

Whence the significance of Hebrew monotheism. Even if we choose to see in the plural name (Elohim) given to God in the first version of the creation story the sign of a former plurality, these "gods" all acting in unison have lost the function of plurality in polytheistic pantheons—the ritual organization of the union of separate subsections of the community. The gods of the various Hebrew tribes have lost all interest in their separate constituencies because the differential god/man opposition has become uniquely urgent. Whether it be a product of the founding of David's kingdom or of its disintegration, this opposition becomes a sacred model of necessary difference that is at least arguably unimprovable.[3]

Singular or plural, God creates man not out of an arbitrary caprice but "in our image, after our likeness" (Genesis 1:26). Man is indispensable as an identical copy of God who is nevertheless absolutely inferior to him. Mortality is implicit in this account, for man is told to "be fruitful and multiply"—reproduction always implying the death of individuals. And in this version, unlike the second, he may eat of "every tree with seed in its fruit" (1:29). This abstract primary symmetry between God and man reflects the abstraction of pure resentment: man's inferiority simply reflects his ontological dependence. Appetitive satisfaction is the immediate reward for this dependence, independently of the specifics of any sacrificial system. The relation of man to the sacred is the pure difference between the sign and its referent, just as it was in the original event; but since man *is* the sign, cultural universality is established a priori. This account demonstrates both the inevitability of resentment and its lack of content. Whatever man does, he will be identical with God and yet never be him. All the ethical functions of myth are concentrated in this brief passage, which celebrates, in effect, the discovery of monotheism: the concerted action of "the gods" (Elohim) resolves *ab ovo* all cultural problems.

But because the Bible does not end at this very point, we must assume that this resolution was insufficient. For monotheism does not abolish in one stroke the moral problem of social differentiation, any more than the discovery of representation abolished the problem of conflict-avoidance in the original human community. To be an image of God is to be above law. Whence the necessity for the second, "Yahwist," account of the creation, wherein man's identity with God becomes subject to restriction. Here monotheism is no longer a resolution of the contradictions of polytheism but a practical form of the sacred. Yet the text cannot state this nor present it within a narrative sequence; the two accounts must be juxtaposed. The necessity for this juxtaposition, and hence for the narrative inconsistency that it entails, is of no small significance, for it demonstrates the limits of biblical narrative as the vehicle of a coherent anthropology.

The passage from the Elohist to the Yahwist account of the creation of man is essentially homologous to our hypothetical description of the passage from the original scene of (ostensive) representation to the stage of ritual. In the first stage, the sign is sufficient to prevent conflict and provide appetitive satisfaction: in the second stage, a worldly representative of the sacred—which can only then be said to exist as such—becomes the object of an interdiction. In our account of the original event, this transition is motivated by the imaginary persistence of desire that attaches to the sign. In the biblical narrative, however, no such motivation is possible: the absolute difference between sign and referent, man and God, makes not only this persistence but the desire itself inconceivable. The only "desire" present in the Elohist text is that of God himself for a human double: but this "desire," which is the mirror image of human resentment, cannot be regarded as falling under a theory of desire. It is rather an incomprehensible act of will or, in other terms, an appetite of God, who is, in effect, a purely natural, not a cultural being.

From an anthropological rather than a theological standpoint, the Elohist creation-account pictures man too as a natural being, the last created and the master of the others but requiring no cultural mediation between himself and his appetites. This "man" is indistinguishably singular and plural, male and female; lacking individuality, he lacks the desire that cultural individuality inspires. This cultureless anthropology is founded on an oversimplified assimilation of resentment to desire, as though the establishment of a single absolute difference purged the real world of difference. The account solves, as we have said, all the cultural problems of mythology proper, but it solves them too well. Yet this "solution" cannot be merely dismissed, that is, eliminated from the text. For it describes the necessarily unique creation of difference that is the birth of humanity. A more rigorously anthropological description would have to do without God altogether; and such a possibility is open only to those whose secular social order can provide unaided a satisfactory outlet for resentment.

The Yahwist creation-story must be read after the Elohist; for only thus can its portrait of a "jealous God" be founded, albeit inconsistently from a narrative point of view, on the absolute, natural difference of the first version. Here the creation of man precedes that of his nourishment, which is not merely naturally but culturally subordinated to him. The creation of Eve from Adam's rib follows the same pattern.[4] After Adam's naming of the birds and animals, he still requires a "helpmate," who is constructed of "bones from my bones and flesh from my flesh" (2:23). This is an account of the genesis of the most fundamental of cultural, not of natural, differences. Its contradiction with the non-"sexist" Elohist account thus lies only on the narrative surface. The cultural anteriority of food over sexuality is here founded on the insufficiency of animals as "helpmates" for man, which is to say, on the tendency of desire to move from nonhuman to anthropomorphic objects—the very same tendency that we saw at work in the humanization of the sacred.

The most significant difference of this second account is the interdiction that *precedes* the creation of the animals and of woman. The sacred is here given an earthly locus, and its recognition made a precondition for man's cultural, desiring existence. The penalty for eating the fruit is death; but it is never stated, as most readers seem to think, that man was otherwise immortal. Death is not *created* by the interdiction but *assimilated to it.* The point of the text is to give death a cultural significance, just as, in the *Gilgamesh Epic*, the point of the hero's mortality was not to reflect a universal human fear of death but to sacrifice immortality to the audience's resentment. Thus what matters is not that Adam will die but that he will conceive his death as a punishment; this is emphasized by God's words, "*in that day* that you eat of it you shall die" (2:17). Adam will in fact survive his fall by several hundred years; but his punishment dates from "that day." This is scarcely how the punishment of death would be described to a hitherto immortal being.

The possibility of death's serving as a punishment reflects the breakdown of the absolute man/God distinction of the Elohist creation. In that account, there was never any question of man's being immortal. Here, however, there is found the revelatory passage of 3:22, where God expresses the fear that man, now that he has become "like one of us, knowing good and evil," might eat of the tree of life and "live for ever." Now the tree of life had already been mentioned as occupying the middle of the garden (2:9), but its existence was never made known to Adam. His eating of *this* fruit would be a free act, not the mere disobedience of an interdiction, and by exercising this freedom he would become the true equal of God. God's fear that Adam would thus become immortal is final proof that he never was immortal in the first place. But this denied possibility of immortality, by which the sacred reasserts its difference, constitutes the moral catharsis of a resentment that, by attacking sacred difference itself, attains the folly of desiring attributes that can qualify only representations. Gilgamesh's loss of the herb of immortality produces the same effect on the reader, but in a context where no moral values are involved. Gilgamesh's loss makes the becoming-sacrificial of the mythical hero more poignant; we identify more strongly with his desire and thus gain all the more benefit from its sacrifice. In the biblical story, this literary effect is subordinated to a moral principle. Gilgamesh's acquisition of immortality would change nothing in the structure of his universe, whereas Adam's would destroy the human relevance of the narrative that has only just begun. God's "jealousy" here is a mirror image of human resentment, but it serves to maintain the coherence of a narration that is no mere fiction but a history of the world.

The temptation scene that precedes the expulsion is not without reason the best known episode of the Bible. It illustrates better than any other the power of the biblical narrative to convert resentment into a source of moral understanding; indeed, this conversion is precisely its theme. This text has resisted reduction to anthropological theory because the moral productivity of resentment has never heretofore been recognized. Thus Adam's sin has been (mis)-interpreted as the *felix culpa* of desire for knowledge or as a perverse longing for "forbidden fruit"; Eve's role has been decried by feminists but pointed to gleefully by misogynists. Readers submit themselves to this text more than to any other because the effort to understand it would do more violence to their own desire than any other.[5] Not merely is the fruit of the tree desirable only because it is forbidden, but the knowledge derived from it is precisely that which derives from the violation of the interdiction. The *felix culpa* is nothing but resentment in action. Nor does the serpent's speech to Eve require prior knowledge of anything but resentment. The epistemology of this passage is far more subtle than that of its traditional readings.

1   Now the serpent was more subtle than any other wild creature that the Lord God had made. He said to the woman, "Did God say, 'You shall not eat of any tree of the garden'?"

2   And the woman said to the serpent, "We may eat of the fruit of the trees of the garden;

3   but God said, 'You shall not eat of the fruit of the tree which is in the midst of the garden, neither shall you touch it, lest you die.'"

4   But the serpent said to the woman, "You will not die.

5   For God knows that when you eat of it your eyes will be opened, and you will be like God, knowing good and evil."

6   So when the woman saw that the tree was good for food, and that it was a delight to the eyes, and that the tree was to be desired to make one wise, she took of its fruit and ate; and she also gave some to her husband, and he ate.

7 Then the eyes of both were opened, and they knew that they were
naked; and they sewed fig leaves together and made themselves aprons.

8   And they heard the sound of the Lord God walking in the garden
in the cool of the day, and the man and his wife hid themselves from
the presence of the Lord God among the trees of the garden.

9 But the Lord God called to the man, and said to him, "Where are
you?"

10 And he said, "I heard the sound of thee in the garden, and I was
afraid, because I was naked; and I hid myself."

11 He said, "Who told you that you were naked? Have you eaten of the
tree of which I commanded you not to eat?"

12 The man said, "The woman whom thou gavest to be with me, she
gave me fruit of the tree, and I ate."

13 Then the Lord God said to the woman, "What is this that you have
done?" The woman said, "The serpent beguiled me, and I ate."
[Genesis 3:1–13]

1. The serpent is already included within the cultural context
determined by the original interdiction of 2:16–17. Serpents being
both dangerous and unappetizing, his place in this ideal culture is
questionable, and the etiological element of the story (3:14: "upon
your belly you shall go") explains this; but this element is of secondary importance. What is primary is that although the serpent's
cultural role, like the woman's, depends on the original interdiction,
he, unlike her, is not subject to this interdiction. Thus we need not
assimilate him to Satan or even describe his action as "temptation."
Rather, his question to Eve (3:1) should be ascribed to his resentment
at being excluded from the interdiction and thereby from human
status. His question implies that he does not know the specific nature
of the interdiction, or even that he has no prior knowledge that such
an interdiction exists. By obtaining knowledge of it, he will assimilate
himself to the human. It may be relevant to note that the serpent
was sacred in Egypt and may therefore be expressing the resentment
of the animal-gods excluded from worship under Hebrew monotheism. At the very least, the serpent resents his relegation to an
inferior level of culture as a result of the dissimilation of human
from animal that resulted from the creation of man's "helpmate."

2. The serpent does not ask merely if something is forbidden; he
asks if *everything* is forbidden. We should take his question at face
value rather than assume malicious intent and thereby depart from
a minimal interpretation of the text that makes the fewest extratextual
assumptions. To the serpent, who lives in a "state of nature," in-

terdiction that constrains appetite appears as an utter denial of it. Culture is thus presented in the worst possible light, in a kind of *reductio ad absurdum* that nevertheless requires on the serpent's part no hypocrisy, only ignorance.

3. Eve's answer (3:2–3) specifies the forbidden object and the penalty of death. Her knowledge of it comes presumably from Adam, not from God, for she was created after the interdiction. Yet her answer confirms the distance between her and the serpent, who remains excluded from its domain and to whom it is transmitted merely as a piece of information.

4. The serpent's reply (3:4–5) is the key statement of the episode, the "temptation" itself. It consists of two parts: (1) a denial of the punishment and (2) a statement of the benefits to be gained by the act. The first statement is a perfect example of the epistemology of resentment. The serpent merely denies the terms of the interdiction; he requires for this no additional knowledge and thus no intention to mislead. In effect, his statement is true! Eve will not die for several hundred years, whereas the implication of God's statement is that death would be instantaneous—in fact, that the fruit is poisonous. There is, strictly speaking, nothing in the biblical narrative to indicate that death was hastened by eating the fruit. The serpent's denial is that of the freethinker who scoffs at the irrationality of sacred prohibitions.

But this is not the whole story. The couple are indeed punished, even if not by immediate death. Their suffering is mediated by further divine commands, but it is derivable from the act of disobedience; in the "knowledge of good and evil" which they acquire lies the germ of the conflict between morality and ethics that is implicit in differentiated as opposed to egalitarian society. This will be indicated in the text by the conditions of the expulsion, which transfers them from an (egalitarian) hunter-gatherer economy to a (differentiated) agricultural one (3:19: "in the sweat of your face you shall eat bread"). The serpent tells the truth, but his truth is the ethical equivalent of a lie.

The serpent's second statement (3:5) is, in contrast, unambiguously true; in fact it is true a priori. To disobey the interdiction is in itself to acquire the knowledge of good and evil, which is to say, knowledge of the ethical value of the interdiction. And in the terms of the text, this is indeed to be "like gods," in a situation where one must create one's own laws—as demonstrated by the couple's covering their nakedness after the act. The serpent's claim that "God knows" this puts his deductions squarely to the account of resentment. This is not simply to say that God imposed the interdiction to prevent men from becoming "like Gods," but that he imposed it precisely in order to permit them to do so, on the condition that they disobey it. The sacred difference is attacked by the serpent but at the same time justified and understood. This understanding can do the serpent himself no good, for *he* cannot become like a god. All he can do is ruin the structure of differences that excludes him. Nothing that the serpent says, it must be noted, could not have been deduced by Adam or Eve. But as the beneficiaries of the cultural system, they would have no motivation to do so.

5. Now serpents do not talk, and animals do not experience resentment; a human author was obliged to put himself in the serpent's place. Its outsider's position was occupied in fact by a man; it is cultural difference that is here presented as the resentment of the natural against the cultural. The culturally disadvantaged sees himself in a "state of nature," while being impatient with his superiors for not realizing their potential for being like gods. The attribution of this role to an animal is essential because human society is portrayed at this point as egalitarian. Resentment is endemic only to differentiated society. The figure of the serpent in this regard is indeed Satanic, and however we may explain his evil intentions, there is no doubt that in the narrative he plays the villain's role. The necessity of this role constitutes a limitation of the biblical narrative. The "original sin" is that of man, not beast; but because the understanding that motivated this sin is already sinful, it must be presented as coming from without. The epistemology of the text is founded on resentment and therefore cannot grasp the origin of resentment itself. This is a limitation not only of the Old Testament but of the New as well; it defines the boundary of Judeo-Christian culture in general. Nietzsche's analysis of resentment, incomplete as it may be, has this great truth to its credit.

6. Eve's reaction is not to the serpent but to the tree, which strikes her in the first place as appetitively desirable and only secondarily as "to be desired to make one wise" ("desirable for the knowledge it could give" in the Jerusalem version). Here the serpent's radical message is, so to speak, vulgarized; the motivation of the woman's act is confused, as, indeed, all worldly desire is confused. The serpent had the lucidity of the outsider; the woman acts as a subordinate figure within culture who has only a mechanical understanding of its categories. In her mind, if not in the serpent's, one might surmise that the undefined "knowledge" is somehow physically present in

the fruit. Eve does not exemplify resentment but mere openness to desire which makes her give the serpent's words more credibility than God's.

7. The man's role is the most obscure of all in the text. It was once common to speak of Eve's "seduction" and to bewail the deleterious influence of woman; today what is denounced is the "sexism" of the narrative. Yet there is nothing to suggest seduction. The woman having eaten, the man accepts the fruit from her hand with no indicated motive. If the text implies anything, it is that the dominance of man over woman at this point is without content. Man was created first, but upon the creation of woman "they became one flesh" (2:24); it is only in God's malediction that Eve is subordinated to Adam who "shall rule over you" (3:16). Adam's abstract primacy makes him even less aware of the significance of his act than Eve; as the primary beneficiary of culture, he abides in it as in a perfectly innocent, "natural" state. Eve is influenced by the serpent, but formulates her own desire and commits an independent act; Adam neither desires nor acts but only consumes.

No clearer indication could be given of the epistemological role of resentment, the absence of which in the man is also the absence of all reflection and, consequently, of defense against evil. Eve is not inferior in any concrete sense; she is merely secondary with respect to the interdiction and is to that extent irresponsible. But Adam is not even irresponsible; he makes no judgment whatever. Lacking in desire, he acts vicariously through the desire of his wife. The interdiction was given to him to obey, but its effect was to make him altogether passive, as though it were somehow absorbed into his being without ever acquiring a moral reality. Because he would never himself have thought to eat the fruit, he cannot think to refuse it. Adam's unreflective passivity, as much as Eve's confused desire and the serpent's lucid resentment, illustrates the impossibility of a culture innocent of resentment's imaginary abolition of difference. For the privileged possessor of this difference cannot defend it against those deprived of it, unaware as he is that there is anything to defend.

8. The couple's act of covering their nakedness reflects their new-found knowledge of "good and evil." Without awaiting a sacred interdiction from above, they take on the regulation of sexual desire. A passage previous to their sin, in stating that "they were both naked, and were not ashamed" (2:25), had referred implicitly to sexual difference as a potential source of desire. The text of 3:7 says nothing specific about sexuality; but the concealment of the appearance of

an unchanged reality can only be in order to reduce its input to the desiring imagination. Having been led by desire to disobey an interdiction, they now construct their own interdiction as a bulwark against desire.

The possibility—and the danger—of sexual desire appears only after disobedience. Two types of desire—as opposed to mere appetite—are thus distinguished by the situation of their object within or without the human community. Object-desire is generated by the sacred interdiction; sexual desire arises contemporaneously with the ethical consciousness that seeks to control it. Yet there is no mention of desire in the text, only of shame. Nakedness is shameful per se and must be hidden from others. Interdiction is thus presented as the *source* of sexual desire, just as in the previous case of the sacred object. Hence shame at nakedness could not arise from desire but only from *appetite that is now recognized as a potential source of desire* and therefore of potential conflict. Sexual desire is presented here, in full accord with our hypothesis, not as an originary outgrowth of sexual appetite but as a secondary cultural formation by analogy with object-desire. For culture could only be founded upon an external desire-object.

So long as the original interdiction was obeyed, appetite, sexual or otherwise, presented no danger. But now that appetite must be controlled, sexual appetite falls under particular suspicion. Precisely because it involves no object-relation to something nonhuman and thus cannot be regulated directly by the sacred, that is, by ritual distribution, it can be controlled only by shame, which is nothing but the internalization of the individual's fear of his sexual difference as a potential object of the other's desire. This is man's first independent ethical discovery. The disobedience of the divine interdiction occasioned no immediate punishment because the knowledge it provided was precisely that of the distance of the sacred from human affairs. But this new knowledge separates its perpetrators from one another, fearful of each other's potential desire.

Such discoveries require that the distance of the divinity be realized on the narrative level. God leaves his charges alone just long enough for them to discover his noninvolvement in their worldly interactions. Hence the naive picture-book image of God "walking in the garden in the cool of the day," the only passage in the entire Bible where God is thus anthropomorphized. Adam and Eve hide from God not because they are ashamed of their deed but because they are naked; they thus repeat in more radical form the mutual suspicion they felt before each other. God is here no more than another mortal, the fear of God no more than the fear of man for man in a world deprived of the guarantee of the sacred. God's retrieval of his sacred role is thus motivated by the purely human reality of the narrative situation. Adam's and Eve's human fear is enough to motivate the reestablishment of sacred difference because only this difference could abrogate the fear.

This reading of the passage, it might be objected, distorts its narrative continuity. God has never ceased to be God; his "walking in the garden" is necessary to motivate his return to the scene from which he needed to be temporarily absent so that the serpent, Eve, and Adam could accomplish the original sin. All this is true, and its truth is an exemplary illustration of the epistemological value of biblical narrative. From the narrative standpoint, God is a "character," and never more than here, when he can leave his newly created humans in order to walk about his property. His acts thus require no specific motivation other than an anthropomorphic pleasure in cool evening breezes; their interpretation as necessary acts of the divine will may be left to the theologians.

But for the anthropologist, the sequence of events must be explained by a radically nonnarrative causality, the principle of which is the human society's relation to the sacred. What permits us to read the text in this way is the fact that the narrative imagination that produced the text is governed by the very same principle of causality. This is true of all sacred tales and in particular of myth. But the difference between the biblical narrative and myth is that here there is no question of explaining, or even of elaborating on, a ritually given—and hence real and concrete—sequence of events. Nor is the narrative determined by the contingently "cathartic" motivations of the secular adventure-story. God's motivations as imagined by man can only be those a man would have in his place; but to imagine oneself in God's place, to imagine "what God would do" in such and such a situation, is already to understand, albeit only implicitly, the secondariness of sacred difference with respect to the needs of humanity.

This implies that God's acts are motivated by the same jealousy of his privilege that men of position display—a jealousy that is the symmetrical inverse of resentment in that it is equally founded on a suspicion of the arbitrary nature of social difference, lacking which the superior would be as secure in his position as the inferior would be respectful of it. It further implies that the acts motivated by this jealousy have no independent source, that they merely mirror step by step the resentment of the human actors. For the moral catharsis of resentment requires that every display of sacred difference be justified by human need.

Nor is this a mere imperative that should, but in reality may not, govern the composition of the text. It is rather a structural necessity of our—of any—reading. If God takes vengeance, then we *must* read his punishment as being for man's good. The entire history of the Jews as told in the Bible bears out this statement, for in the context of the monotheistic narrative, all history is sacred history. The naive reading of the narrative at face value is founded on a theocentric optical illusion. The only difference between claiming that it is man's fear of his fellows that motivates God's reassertion of his sacred priorities and claiming that the cause is rather God's own jealousy of these priorities is that this second reading provides an imaginary catharsis, whereas the first constructs an anthropological model.

We may similarly interpret the series of God's inquiries and the buck-passing answers he receives. Adam's reply underlines the essential inconsistency of God's plan, which is, in anthropological terms, the ultimate instability of a society that includes internal difference. Eve was put with Adam by God; she is not a naturally but a culturally given partner, and her cultural posteriority sufficed, as we have seen, to motivate her crime. And with the same logic, Eve puts the blame on the excluded serpent.

God's malediction on the human couple establishes as social hierarchy between man and wife what had heretofore been only an abstract cultural anteriority. It is of great anthropological interest that the expulsion from paradise is associated with the founding of agricultural society, which is, as we have seen, the origin of social hierarchy, of resentment, and of its moral transcendence. Adam and Eve are expelled from the presence of the unique difference of God into a world of social difference. The very first episode that follows the expulsion, that of Cain and Abel, is the archetypal story of human resentment—the worldly cause of which, we should well note, is not economic but ritual superiority.

THE MONOTHEISTIC NARRATIVE

Our purpose in examining the creation and expulsion scene in some detail has been to understand the workings of resentment as an epistemological force in the biblical narrative. That this narrative has remained a central vehicle of Western moral concepts down to the present day can surprise or dismay us only if we conceive of morality as embodying the essentially contentless notion of universal reciprocity. This is no doubt the Christian ideal proclaimed in the New Testament as the "good news" that fulfills and abolishes the law of the Old. But the very textual, narrative existence of the New Testament belies this ideal, or rather the possibility, not merely of its realization but of its worldly functionality.

What the biblical narrative accomplishes is the incarnation, in the figure of the "jealous" monotheistic God, of an equilibrating reflection of human resentment, just as more primitive divinities constitute similar reflections of human desire. This form of divinity is so inseparable from the narration of the history of his "chosen" people that we may define Judaism as "narrative monotheism." The narrative constitutes a discovery procedure that allows for the integration of worldly interaction into a global moral revelation. Our textual analysis has shown that this discovery procedure is at work even in the wholly imaginary preliminary episodes of Genesis which, derived from myth, are nevertheless no longer constructed as myth. The results of this analysis will now permit us to define more rigorously the difference between biblical narrative based on resentment and mythical narrative based on desire, as well as to understand more clearly the tension between morality and ethics that this new narrative form both reflects and resolves.

The moral notion of the sacred as an "inverted world" passes from Hegel to Feuerbach and Marx, in whom it becomes a purely ethical device devoid of moral value. Durkheim, who grasped the ethical functionality of the sacred but, failing to distinguish between inversion and mere doubling, never understood its moral function, is thus far closer to Marx than is customarily thought. Conservative and radical sociology, the creations of two Jews who renounced Judaism, find themselves united in their blindness to the moral role of the sacred, a role that Judaism was instrumental in creating.

Myth has no moral content, as Plato was well aware; even Plato's own "myths" only convey moral values contingently, as reflections on their narrative reality that lead to the scarcely radical conclusion that one is better off good than evil. For myth remains amoral even when it is detached from any concrete ritual basis; it never transcends the purely ethical level of social organization. This is not because myth is innocent of resentment but because mythical resentment remains episodic and never becomes the fundamental relation between the human and the sacred. The mythical narrative makes use of sacred and semisacred personages in order to explain reality— human reality, but often including the cosmic backdrop of human

experience—in terms of conflicting desires. The chief mythical function of the gods is to fight among themselves, a function in which
they do not differ essentially from the heroic demigods who fight
against earthly opponents and who end their careers as immortals.
The dispositions of social and natural reality are then explained as
the result of these conflicts. The hearer of primitive myth accepts
the absolute otherness of its characters because they stand at the
inaccessible center of his own desires. He identifies with them, however immoral their behavior, because they incarnate the imaginary
freedom of his desire; whatever they do, they do for him, not to
him.

No doubt things are no longer so simple in classical Greek mythology, which is the cultural expression of a society that was anything but devoid of resentment. But because resentment remains a
secondary feature of myth, it never challenges there the moral innocence of the sacred world. When the challenge is posed, sacred
myth is transformed into secular literature, a process already complete in Homer. We shall discuss the cultural implications of this in
the following chapter.

Resentment poses a challenge to sacred difference that tends to
subject it to the moral criterion of reciprocity. But only the biblical
narrative develops this subjection into the foundation of an ethic.
Only the Jews, in other words, were able to do away entirely with
myth. We have already said a few words concerning the possible
social origins of this phenomenon. But it is important to recognize
that these social causes are subordinate to cultural causes. Only
certain social structures could have permitted the Jewish spiritual
experience. But closely similar structures existed in many other societies. The essential difference is not to be found in the precise
quality of social relations but in the fact that these relations came to
inspire a radical reformulation of myth in the context of the history
of this particular society. This history in itself is scarcely noteworthy.
The survival of the Jewish people and their religion is in no sense
a product of their historical uniqueness but in every sense a product
of the existence of the book that recounts it. The existence of the
Bible is by no means a miracle; its writing can be explained in causal
terms. But it is not its causes but the fact of the writing itself that
is of real cultural importance; for the process of writing is a discovery
procedure that led to the formulation of a religious anthropology of
unparalleled moral as well as cognitive significance.

Narrative monotheism does away with the amoral mythic conception of the divinity as providing an imaginary wish-fulfillment

satisfaction of unrealizable ("producer's") desire.[6] Resentment has altogether eliminated the satisfaction to be gained from a god's realization of forbidden desires. The absolute sacred difference between the Hebrew God and man is founded, on the contrary, upon the former's utter *lack* of desire. God's "will," natural and not cultural, is uniquely determined by man's ethical needs. His "jealousy," the inverse reflection of human resentment, may be, as is never the case with men, *absolutely* distinguished from desire. God is jealous of man but never envious of other gods. Thus his establishment of ethical laws, as opposed to that of his mythical counterparts, is never by (desiring) example, but by edict. God himself is above ethical law because he incarnates the principle of morality, not as abstract reciprocity but as *action for the ethical benefit of the community.* Mythical gods may be said to incarnate the ethical reality, in whole or in part, of the communities of their worshipers; the Hebrew God stands outside and sustains the ethical reality of the Jews.

This reality itself, even when it receives God's uncritical encouragement, is not always of the highest moral exemplarity. The story of the conquest of Canaan makes no concessions to the cosmopolitan humanism we find in the *Iliad*, or even in the *Chanson de Roland;* the Hebrews are God's people, and their enemies mere obstacles to foreordained victory. What the story of the conquest illustrates is that, had the story ended there, it could never have become the Bible at all. But the narrative of conquest, integrated within the whole, becomes an element of a sacred history that can survive military defeat, because whatever happens in the future will continue to be interpreted as the effect of a divine will that always has at heart the community's interest. Worldly success will no longer be required; worldly failure is equally a sign of divine election, for it forms merely another chapter in the narrative.

God's punishments began with Adam and reflect at each point man's needs. Yet there is a difference between the imaginary constructions of Genesis and the historical narrative. In the first, God's role expresses anthropological necessity; in the second, it validates the verdict of historical reality. This passivity before historic fact is in fact the height of Old Testament morality, and as such, the guarantee of survival for the Jewish people and their contribution to Western culture. No earlier culture could and did survive political defeat and eventual dispersion. The doctrine that "all that is real is moral" allows for a cultural flexibility before historical experience that is sufficient for survival if not for success. The limits of this flexibility—a subject we must postpone to a later volume—are reflected in the paradox and the scandal of the historical existence of the Jews in the West.

The productivity of narrative monotheism is qualitatively greater than that of myth because it does away with the need for any direct, short-term applicability of the textual content to the satisfaction of desire. This latter mechanism, as soon as it departs from strictly ethical, communal realities, leaves the sacred domain for the secular, and mythology proper for literature. Because the deferral of satisfaction characteristic of all representation is structured in myth by the opposition between the (imaginary) sacred and the (deferred) real, it cannot enter the domain of the imaginary itself without "deferring" at the same time its sacred character. Myth, in a word, cannot be suspenseful without becoming literature. As soon as not the immediate acts but the ultimate fate of the protagonist interests us, these acts lose all real or potential ritual significance and might just as well be attributed to a fictional hero. But in the monotheistic text, a nonliterary "suspension" is possible that integrates and transcends the cultural dissatisfactions of desire that are unassimilable to myth.

For resentment, unlike desire, is constructive of the self; it possesses an internal temporality. It has no positive wish and is therefore invulnerable to wish-fulfillment. The figure of its satisfaction is the simple inversion of present reality, and hence this reality suffices to figure it. The resentful imagination sees in the suspension of satisfaction, in its continual deferral, a confirmation of the eventual conversion of its own peripheral position into a new center. For if the central position on the public scene of representation can now be occupied by one like the self, then the self's position, too, can become central.

The historical suspension contained in the biblical text is perhaps most strikingly exemplified in the forty years' wandering imposed on the Hebrews after the Exodus to purge them of the sins of the generation that had known slavery in Egypt. This final trial is the culmination of a far longer deferral stretching from the covenant with Abraham to the conquest of Canaan. Suspension of satisfaction is a constant feature of the biblical narrative, from the sociopolitical covenant with Abraham to the purely individual testing of Job and the apocalyptic condemnations of the prophets. Divine justice defers reward as a test of faith, which is to say, ethical cohesion. And under the protective authority of divine justice, lack of satisfaction, whether collective or individual, may always be thought of as a means for producing this cohesion. *Qui aime bien, châtie bien.*

Yet this potentially all-encompassing mechanism has its limits, which are ultimately those of Judaism. Deferral, however indefinite, must be followed by ultimate satisfaction. This satisfaction may be delayed *ad infinitum;* but it is figured, albeit negatively, in reality, and its figure can never be forgotten. Most Jews consider the Messiah promised by Deutero-Isaiah to be no more than a metaphysical concept; yet without the awaiting of the Messiah, Judaism loses its religious *raison d'être.* Narrative monotheism requires that the moral authority of God be substantiated by a capacity to enforce his ethical laws through a system of reward and punishment, and the latter cannot be eternal if one is to maintain faith in the possibility of the former. Eternity being a long time, the limits of biblical narrative as formulated in this manner do not become apparent. But a stronger formulation is possible. Biblical narrative is not, indeed, open-ended; at a certain point it exhausts the "divine inspiration" that produced it.

Why, indeed, cannot the narrative continue forever, as it does in myth? Why does narrative monotheism produce a finite book that will henceforth regulate actions and provide an explanatory framework for them, but that can no longer include them? The point of no return is reached when the deferral of communal hopes loses its constructive function to become a fixed a priori that, as such, defines the ethical unity of the Jewish people. The Hebrew Bible thus ends with the destruction of Jerusalem and the promise of return under Cyrus (2 Chronicles 36), even though the books of Ezra and Nehemiah recount later events and in Christian versions are placed after the books of Chronicles. For canonization of the text was achieved only after the return had proved futile and the rebuilt Temple had been destroyed a second time. In Jewish tradition, the two destructions are considered to have taken place on the same day of the year (the 9th of Av). The second is thus assimilated to the first; its effect was to make the first the end of sacred scripture. Henceforth, the promise of return and secular triumph, no longer even a remotely historical possibility (and which would not be fulfilled even in a limited sense for nearly nineteen hundred years), became a stable temporal horizon unrelated to concrete acts, which thereupon lost their historical exemplarity.

At this point, resentment is no longer culturally productive. Post-biblical Jewish culture contributes only commentaries that, however great their ethical interest, never challenge their subordination to the monotheistic narrative. Nor could a secular culture grow up within the awaiting created by this narrative, at least not until the

Jews had fallen under the influence of the surrounding (Christian) secular culture. Jewish iconoclasm rejects fictions as well as myths, for the monotheistic narrative must remain the unique source of catharsis under penalty of loss of cultural identity. The Jews contributed to surrounding cultures but could create none of their own. For no cultural mediation is possible between the sacred history of the Bible and the concrete experience of later ages. The desire of the individual Jew qua Jew could have cultural significance only with respect to the Messianic return. Not until this desire could be visualized from without, as a "culture trait" comparable to other manifestations of ethnological identity, could a Jewish secular literature be created—for example, in the writings of Sholom Aleichem. But such writing, because it cannot reflect the uniqueness of the promise on which Jewish Messianism is founded, can be only of a minor nature.

The survival of Judaism to the end of what we may still call the Christian era is epiphenomenal in the eyes of those—not all of them Christians by any means—for whom the cultural contribution of the Jews is merely preliminary to Christianity or to Western culture in general. Sartre's *Réflexions sur la question juive* expresses this viewpoint more categorically than any Christian theologian. But the scandalous refusal of the Jews to accept Christianity, their stubborn attachment to their "tribal" religion despite innumerable individual conversions and apostasies, is anything but epiphenomenal. It is a sign of the ultimate inadequacy of Christian morality as the underlying basis of Western culture. We shall have more to say on this subject in a future volume. But we must deal at this point with the converse question: why indeed did Judaism remain a tribal religion that only in the radically transformed versions of Christianity and, later, Islam could acquire universal influence?

It would be facile to allege as causes the maintenance of the sacrificial monopoly of the Temple in Jerusalem, or the attachment of the Jews to their Palestinian homeland, as first formulated in the covenant with Abraham. We require a more fundamental cause, one that displays the necessary particularism of the essential cultural contribution of the Jews—that is, narrative monotheism. To make the question more specific: what is there already in the story of the creation and the fall of man that prevents its general applicability to Western society save through the intermediary of Christian reinterpretation? To pose the question in this manner is to begin to interpret the notion of "universal religion" that is so easily taken for granted in studies of the development of Western culture.

As we saw in our examination of the creation story, the first, Elohist, version provides a complete resolution of the problem of worldly resentment. The subordination of man-in-general to a unique creator establishes an absolute difference beside which all worldly differences lose their importance. Yet, as we also saw, this version does not suffice; nor does the second, for it is followed by the fall and expulsion leading eventually to the history of the Hebrew people. The establishment of an absolute sacred difference is only the point of departure for a narrative in which God, at every stage, incarnates the moral force that converts human resentment into ethical order. As this force is personalized, it cannot be conceptually understood but can be recognized only in specific acts of God's will. The Bible is thus, from the very beginning, historical and not universal. Adam may be called the ancestor of all men, but only a particular group of his descendants can be chosen to continue his story. The necessary linearity of narration makes the limitation to a single line inevitable. But narrative monotheism could arise only on the basis of a particular historical sequence, which then, as its *telos*, inspired the preliminary narrative. The linearity of this sequence is presented as morally necessary, even when its material is that of myth rather than history. This will be more easily understood by observing how the Hebrew creation-text is reinterpreted by Christianity—a reinterpretation whose very possibility displays the inherent incapacity of narrative monotheism either to exclude or to become itself a universal religion.

The beginning of the fourth Gospel refuses at the outset the absolute difference upon which the entire edifice of monotheism was founded. "In the beginning was the Word (logos), and the Word was with God, and the Word was God." (We should note in passing the anthropological interest of the primordiality of representation in this passage, which combines the Greek faith in the *logos* with Jewish historicity.) The identity of the Word with God, which is assimilated to the identity of Father and Son, is incompatible with Genesis and an explicit rectification of it. God and his creation are ultimately of the same essence. Jesus is the "last Adam," which is to say that the difference between God and Adam was from the beginning only temporary. Nor is the abolition of this difference a matter for historical awaiting; the awaiting of the "second coming," as opposed to the Jewish wait for the Messiah, is precisely a *secondary* phenomenon. Christ is the Word, he is God, and because he has *already* come, awaiting or deferral is removed from the present to the past and, by the same token, made illusory. The historical, narrative element of monotheism is reduced to the status of a prologue, and as such, dehistoricized. For God was the Word from the beginning. His revelation was misunderstood—John 1:5: "The light shines in the darkness, and the darkness has not overcome it"—and Genesis reflects this misunderstanding rather than the primordial and immutable truth.

This "deconstruction" of the creation story involves numerous secondary reinterpretations: the expulsion from paradise is no longer definitive; Adam's crime is no longer an irreversible act for which all men are punished, but an "original sin," repeated in each man, but always contingently, as Christ's human counterexample demonstrates. Adam's crime had been an etiological explanation of man's lot in differentiated society that permitted a transcendence or sublimation of resentment, now morality has become independent of the monotheistic narrative and applies to each individual independently of communal conditions. The divine justice that operated historically in the community as a whole now grants each individual his deserts in an afterlife divorced from any even imaginary form of collective organization. Christ's history abolishes the historical continuity incarnated in the Hebrew God, the very continuity that makes the Old Testament the story of a particular people, and the religion founded on it an ethnic religion.

That the crux of the incompatibility of narrative monotheism with universality is not the absolute difference of the Jewish God is demonstrated by the success of Islam, which maintains monotheistic difference but abolishes the narrative-historical element. What is indispensable is to destroy the irreversible character of the narrative. Christianity attacks it radically at its origin in absolute difference; Islam is content to replace a narrative monotheism by a lyric one.[7]

The Yahwist story of Adam's creation and expulsion, conceived as the absolute foundation of human history, is already "particular," independently of the specific history of the Jews, because it justifies as morally necessary man's concrete, and hence necessarily particular, worldly existence. The religion it founds is ethnic because concrete ethical laws define the limits of the totality within which the particular worldly existence of individuals is included. Judaism, which unites religion and ethnicity, is a total religion in a way that Christianity and even Islam are not. The latter is content to remain a backdrop to social organization, which is therefore free to take on the superethnic form of the state; Christianity possesses an antiestablishment character that makes the Christian state always something of a contradiction in terms—a contradiction resolvable only by progressive secularization. Judaism cannot be other than ethnic because it can transcend ethical but not political resentment. Politics can enter the monotheistic narrative only as a moral punishment for the failure of ethics.

A test case of the limits of Judaism, both in its worldly aspirations and in its sacred narrative, are the two Books of Maccabees, excluded from the Hebrew canon but accepted by the Roman Catholic Church as part of the Old Testament. It is easy to understand why these books could not have been admitted into the Hebrew scripture even had they both been written in Hebrew, which the second was not (the first, significantly, was written in Hebrew but survives only in a Greek translation). The Maccabees were part of a restoration of temple and sovereignty that ultimately failed. The promise they attempted to realize was not fulfilled by their victories, because these victories led only to new defeats. Thus, although their heroism is remembered by the Jews and celebrated at Hanukkah, their story could not enter the monotheistic narrative, which cannot prolong itself beyond the transformation of the promise of return into a fixed structure of awaiting. In contrast, the Book of Esther, in which the Jews hold a subordinate position and can be saved only by a non-Jewish monarch, was accepted into the canon, albeit as an independent story (*megillah*) rather than as a continuation of the historical narrative. For Esther carries this narrative, illustratively if not historically in the strong sense (a sense no longer available after the fall of the kingdom), into the time of the first Diaspora, for which it presents an exemplary ethic. It is marginally acceptable as a moral tale—and as a demonstration that, henceforth, Jewish history can at best be told in moral tales. It thus represents a limit of the canon. Another very similar tale, the Book of Judith, was not included, for, like Maccabees, it represents the victory of arms rather than persuasion.

It is of particular interest that of these excluded books, 1 Maccabees emphasizes throughout the necessary connection between observance of the Law and the maintenance of national unity (and political power), whereas 2 Maccabees contains the only even apocryphal Jewish affirmation of the doctrines of bodily resurrection and of the afterlife. The first book expresses a doctrine which, shorn of its political optimism, would become the basis for the ethnic survival of the Jews of the Diaspora; the second, a doctrine that was to become an essential component of the universal religions of Christianity and Islam, but the status of which for Jews has always remained marginal and derivative.

Neither of these doctrines is compatible with the pursuit of the monotheistic narrative. The second contradicts its historical character, although this contradiction is not apparent in a context where the martyrdom of the individuals (the "seven brothers") to whom eternal life is promised is redeemed by Jewish victories (over Nicanor). The first sets the Law against contemporary reality as a fixed set of ritual acts rather than as a set of ethical doctrines evolving under the moral impact of God's will. The Law has become the residue of the promise of return, now eternally fixed. This too was not apparent at a time when the Jewish state appeared to be in the process of assuming an equally permanent existence. But the exclusion of the Books of Maccabees from the canon reflects the illusory nature of this permanence, and of the apparent redemption of martyrdom by military triumph. Henceforth their doctrines could apply only to Jews of the Diaspora and to no longer Jewish Christians, for neither of whom the Hebrew Bible could remain an open, living narrative.[8]

THE PROPHETS

Unlike the "prophets" of other ancient religions, to whom we may add oracles, sibyls, and so forth, the Hebrew prophets purveyed an essentially moral message which they wrote or dictated as the word of God. This message takes on various surface forms—threats and imprecations, oracular predictions, prayers, descriptions of visions—but its moral unity throughout the prophetic writings is plain. Prophetic discourse is an extension of the monotheistic narrative—itself traditionally considered to have been dictated by God to his prophet Moses—into a historical future that in some cases actually preceded the time of writing. But, in this extension, the moral element of the narrative is transformed. This transformation is of particular interest to Christianity, where it is seen as forming a transition between the Old and the New Testaments. We have noted that the Christian Bible, unlike the Hebrew, places the prophets at the end of the Old Testament, which thereby ends with Malachi's curse rather than the Chronicler's "go up." This arrangement is possible only from an external, universal rather than ethnic perspective; but the prophetic text's inherent tendency toward religious universality implies precisely the possibility of such a perspective.

Prophetic discourse, like that of the biblical narrative, describes the moral action of God as revealing itself in the history of his chosen people. But by situating this history in the future, the prophet separates the revelation from its worldly realization and thereby endows this revelation with an independent moral force. Prophecy is prediction, but it is also warning; it threatens divine punishment for sin, but, by the same token, it allows the potential victim of this punishment to change his ways before it is visited on him. Thus, irrespective of the future reality of such punishment, prophecy imposes a moral judgment on social reality that can no longer be assimilated to the inscrutable force of God's will. As we have seen from our examination of the creation story, this "will" is anything but arbitrary; it reflects man's ethical needs. But this reflection, even when (as is not always the case) it takes the form of punishment for a violated moral law, fixes between God and man the locus of the essential moral relationship, despite the fact that the content of the law must refer at least implicitly to human interaction. Thus, in the first biblical example of human crime, God tells Cain, "The voice of your brother's blood is crying to me from the ground" (Genesis 4:10). Cain violated moral law only implicitly; no one had told him it was a crime to kill his brother. It is God who must impose moral values on ethical relations.

But prophetic discourse, although presumably spoken at the dictation of God, presents moral law before punishment, and does so, most significantly, in contrast with prevailing ethical relations, even if these are in keeping with the letter of earlier divine precepts. The earliest prophetic text, that of Amos, already pronounces the typical prophetic condemnation of ritual observance in the absence of moral rectitude: "I hate, I despise your feasts . . . and the peace offerings of your fatted beasts I will not look upon. Take away from me the noise of your songs . . . but let justice roll down like waters, and righteousness like an ever-flowing stream" (Amos 5:21—24). No doubt God had always demanded "justice" and "righteousness," but divine morality had hitherto been reflected in concrete ethical precepts. Amos's condemnation *anticipates* God's future action, and can do so only by abstracting from the divine will moral precepts that may be universally applied. Morality still expresses God's will, but it has become independent of any concrete manifestation of it. Whatever God may intend to do, for the moment he does not choose to end the feasts and impose justice; these are merely declared hateful because of the existence of uncorrected social inequities. Prophetic discourse has taken a major step toward the divine noninterventionism of the New Testament, as expressed in the Sermon on the

Mount: "for [God] makes his sun rise on the evil and on the good, and sends rain on the just and on the unjust" (Matthew 5:45).

For Christian theology, this is indeed the sense of Old Testament prophecy. In contrast with the "Pharisaic" insistence on the letter of the already-revealed Law, the prophets exhort man to institute moral relations with his fellows. Morality in the abstract sense is nothing but reciprocity. The rich are immoral "because they sell the righteous for silver, and the needy for a pair of shoes" (Amos 2:6). Amos expresses most clearly the defense of "the widow and the orphan" that will be echoed throughout the prophetic tradition (for example, Jeremiah 7:6).

More problematic from our perspective is a second major prophetic theme, significantly absent from Amos but present in all the major prophets (Isaiah, Jeremiah, Ezekiel): that of apostasy. If God desires justice above ritual worship, then adoration of foreign gods or idols should be at worst an indication of injustice. Yet an insistent attack upon idolatry may be found in the most advanced of all prophetic texts, that of Deutero-Isaiah, so important to the Christian exegesis of the Old Testament (Isaiah 40:18–20, 44:9–20). God's future redemption of his people through the "suffering servant" is founded on the demonstration that his power alone is real, in contrast with that of idols "that will not move" (40:20). Here the problem of human justice, prominent in the original Isaiah, recedes into the background; the merited sufferings of Israel are not those of oppressors of widow and orphan but of men blind to God's law: "Who gave up Jacob to the spoiler, and Israel to the robbers? Was it not the Lord, against whom we have sinned, in whose ways they would not walk, and whose law they would not obey?" (42:24). No doubt these "ways" include an ideal of social justice, but it is here as subordinate to divine will as it was in Genesis. Indeed, the emphasis, even in this passage, is on the "blindness" of the "servant" Israel, not on his iniquity. In the most radical development of this idea, the very notion of merited suffering disappears. In the "suffering servant" episode on which so many New Testament passages are explicitly or implicitly based (Isaiah 52:13–53:12), Israel's sufferings are not merely innocent but sacrificial: "Surely he has borne our griefs and carried our sorrows; yet we esteemed him stricken, smitten by God, and afflicted. But he was wounded for our transgressions, he was bruised for our iniquities" (53:4–5). Here the identity of the speaker is vague; it appears to be the "nations" and "kings" mentioned in 52:15. But it could just as easily be the Jews themselves, whose sins have been borne by the personified collectivity of Israel. The theme of innocent suffering as redemption from sin is inseparable here from that of Israel's election, which depends in turn on the definitive superiority of its God over the "idols" of other peoples.

It is worthwhile to trace back to its roots in the prophetic tradition the "higher morality" of this passage, in which the internal iniquities of Israel lose all importance in the light of the open, agonistic expression of superiority. We need not share Nietzsche's moral nihilism to apply to this passage his analytic principle; for we will not be surprised to find resentment at the root of this as of any other higher cultural phenomenon.

Returning then to Amos, the earliest and simplest of prophetic writings, we encounter another theme prevalent among the prophets, although by nature secondary to their divinely dictated message. Amos's inclusion among the canonical prophets is dependent on the fact that *he is not a prophet*. Thus, in the first of many such confrontations, he replies to Amaziah, priest of the royal sanctuary at Bethel, "I am no prophet, nor a prophet's son, but I am a herdsman and a dresser of a sycamore trees, and the Lord took me from following the flock, and the Lord said to me, 'Go, prophesy to my people Israel'" (Amos 7:14–15).

This ambiguity of the term "prophet" (*nabi*) is not merely a regrettable confusion. In the historical books, companies of "prophets" or holy men are sometimes encountered, and in one passage (1 Kings 22:5–28), when King Ahab inquires about the appropriateness of a military action, "four hundred prophets" tell him to attack, and only one prophet (Micaiah, elsewhere unmentioned) reveals that this is a temptation of a "lying spirit"—a service for which he is placed in prison. Here the one true prophet is opposed to the many false; but there is no criticism of their professional standing, or even of their moral integrity: the "lying spirit" inspires them on God's orders. Yet we already see in this episode a devaluation of prophetic guilds at the expense of the inspired individual, an opposition to which Amos will give an implicit moral sense. Like Moses the shepherd, Amos was personally selected by God to convey his message; the professional prophets are, by implication, not similarly inspired. In Jeremiah (2:8, 5:3, 6:13, 26:7) prophets and priests are always found together as part of a corrupt religious establishment, with nothing to choose between them. Yet Jeremiah, who is, unlike Amos, the son of a priest, is nonetheless counted as a true prophet. No doubt the same word is used because false and true, professional and divinely inspired prophets perform the same function of prophesying. But there is more to it than that. The opposition between the one

true and many false prophets, like that between the one true and
the many false Gods, is affirmed to exist only by the interested
party. Amos and Jeremiah are making an "antiestablishment" claim;
and, as we shall see, the claims made for God himself are not devoid
of this element.

The historical books of the Bible, from Genesis through Kings,
were written and compiled anonymously. Narrative monotheism can
admit of no author; if the Pentateuch is attributed to the hand of
Moses, this is an external tradition never substantiated in the text—
which, as has often been remarked, recounts its purported author's
death. Moses would indeed be the archetypal prophet in that, where
later prophets present their writings as dictated by God, he never
even claims to be writing. In contrast, the prophetic books are written in the first person by well-defined, albeit often little-known
individuals. Their claim to divine inspiration, unlike that of the
Pentateuch, is mediated by the religious experience of their authors.
In their present state, this claim is guaranteed for us by their inclusion in the canonical text—and it is to be remarked that there are
no Apocryphal prophets, no doubtful cases, in contrast with the
authors of "wisdom" literature (Wisdom of Solomon, Ben Sira), for
whom divine inspiration is a virtually nonexistent consideration. But
originally, prophetic writings were not part of a canon; their author
had to guarantee their acceptance on his own.

From a cynical viewpoint, this acceptance would itself be primary
in the prophet's mind and would determine the particular quality
of his writings—in particular, their antiestablishment character. For
in order to demonstrate the authenticity of a new revelation, one
must show how its newness contradicts what went before. This is
the very principle of the continued revelation of the monotheistic
narrative. God's moral revelation consists in the transformation of
the social order through the imposition of new ethical laws. In prophetic revelation, the reactive element becomes dominant; it is no
longer a question of justifying ritual practices (for example, as in
Leviticus) but of criticizing the present in the name of moral principles, the threatened application of which can only be punitive.
The desire for individual recognition would suffice to explain the
social radicalism of the prophet's messages and its coincidence with
their hostility to the prophets of the establishment. But this Vol-
tairean cynicism is not merely in bad taste; it is insensitive to the
epistemology of resentment that it purports to explain.

The prophet, as Amos's case well illustrates, is an individual
exponent of social resentment. Whatever his own economic status—

and the status of similar individuals in modern society is certainly not always, or even most often, that of the underprivileged groups whose interests they defend—the prophet gains individual standing through his expression of the resentment of the victims of the "unjust" wealthy and powerful. His critique of apostasy expresses the jealousy of the Hebrew God, which is itself a mirror of human resentment. But this resentment remains ethically productive only so long as it effectively generates new moral ideas. "Divine inspiration," as a psychological reality for the prophet, is demonstrated by the incisiveness of these ideas that makes them the authentic prolongation of narrative monotheism into a critical reflection on the present. The prophet's desire for recognition in opposition to the established ethical code is conceivable only on the basis of faith in these ideas, lacking which he would have no reason to count on future—perhaps posthumous—vindication. The test of "divine inspiration" can function only if the society is receptive to the continuity of the prophetic message with that of the preexisting narrative. This is an objective test, for the sense of this continuity is not a mere matter of taste. Prophetic resentment is easy to notice, but its continuity with the biblical text would be incomprehensible if the latter too were not based on resentment of a less personal expression.

The prophetic movement cannot continue forever; once moral ideas, like the divine promise of return and triumph, have become fixed structures, prophets can find no new material. Prophetic resentment as a discovery procedure is limited by the essential abstraction of moral as opposed to ethical structures; Ezekiel's visions, particularly the highly detailed one of the restored temple (chaps. 40–58) are the furthest prophecy could go toward ethical reconstruction.

But the progressive nature of the prophetic movement becomes most clearly visible in the text of Deutero-Isaiah that originally posed for us the problem of the epistemological limits of prophetic resentment. This text is the most morally radical of the Old Testament, and whatever the exact chronology, it constitutes the effective end of the prophetic movement. Its inclusion in Isaiah, the first (if not the oldest) prophetic book of the Bible, makes this book a summary of the entire movement, including its Trito-Isaian epilogue in which this movement is reintegrated into a ritual establishment expanded to include the entire world. "All flesh shall come to worship before me, says the Lord" (66:23). The limits of Old Testament prophecy and of its expressed moral values, although their transcendence by Christianity may be historically inevitable, are those of a coherent religious order different from that of Christianity. This most advanced text of the Hebrew Bible permits us a more precise insight than any other into the difference that separates the two Judeo-Christian religions. It is thus an appropriate basis for our concluding assessment of the nature of the Jewish contribution to Western culture.

The "suffering servant" figure has a notable parallel in Job, and the cosmogonic sequence that opens the Deutero-Isaian writings (chap. 40) fulfills the same function as the similar passage in Job 38:39. God must impress both sufferers with his cosmic power, in the absence of any more concrete manifestations of this power in their own lives. The same God that asks, "Where were you when I laid the foundation of the earth?" (Job 38:4) now similarly asks, "Who has measured the waters in the hollow of his hand. . . ?" (Isaiah 40:12). But Job's sufferings were an individual and, indeed, fictional test of faith; those of the Hebrews were real. God's power over the Jews in the second Isaiah's time was challenged by "idols" whose influence reflected less an ineradicable tendency to backsliding than the superior might of the other nations they were presumed to defend.

The second Isaiah is the most universalist of prophets precisely because only a universal providence can justify God's apparent disinterest in his chosen people's worldly success. From this standpoint, Israel's sufferings can no longer be looked upon merely as punishments for her own iniquities. Her sorry place in the international scheme must be given an exemplary role. Here the jealous God abandons a narrow for a broader morality. The limited reciprocity of justice ("an eye for an eye . . .") is replaced by the unlimited reciprocity of sacrifice: however great Israel's sufferings, they reflect in their exemplarity God's plan of universal redemption. Israel will, in this plan, be ultimately rewarded not with military victory, the fruits of which could be only temporary, but with universal spiritual leadership. "Behold, I make him a witness to the peoples, a leader and commander for the peoples. Behold, you shall call nations that you know not, and nations that knew you not shall run to you" (56:4–5).

This is the definitive statement of Israel's role as the "chosen people" in a universe where national supremacy, even if it could be envisioned, would be at most partial and temporary. The Jews' political resentment here creates for them a role impervious to future political upheavals, one that can no longer be falsified by any worldly development short of utter annihilation, and which thereby guarantees their ethnic survival. No afterlife is necessary to insure this survival, which is that of a people, not an individual. It is to be noted that this text, which emphasizes the unity of Israel in its international role rather than its internal divisions into the iniquitous wealthy and the innocent poor, is the work of an individual who, "prophet" or not, was content to subsume his individuality within the preexistent figure of the greatest of the prophets. For the "suffering servant" is no longer the persecuted prophet but the Jewish people as a whole.

The continued moral relevancy of Judaism within Western culture is borne out by the continued persecutions of the Jews, most notably by Christians. Since the beginning, these persecutions have been inspired less by the Jews' presumed role in Christ's death than by their refusal to resign to him their exemplary role. If the New Testament is truly a transcendental interpretation of the Old in general and of the "suffering servant" passage in particular, then it is curious that, with regard to the history of Judeo-Christian relations, it is this Old Testament passage that reinterprets the New: the individual sacrifice of Christ only personifies the sacrificial role of the Jewish people, for the most part at the hands of the Christians themselves. The eradication of the Jewish "remnant" would falsify the Deutero-Isaian prophecy, as its persecutors have always known, but the attempt to carry out this eradication can only begin—and has so far always ended—by confirming it.

This confirmation transcends by far the Jews' own contribution to the persecutions by their refusal to conform to the Christian majority. It calls in question the individualist reinterpretation of the "suffering servant" figure accepted by this majority and guarantees our identification of the conflict between these two interpretations as a central and untranscendable one within traditional and even industrial Western society—the era of "Western culture" in the broadest sense. If today this opposition appears to have all but played itself out in the apocalypse of the Second World War, the same might be said of Western culture itself as a creative enterprise. Which is to say that this passage of the second Isaiah contains a moral crux of the most fundamental cultural implications.

What is the particular attraction of the sacrificial role? To be sure, it offers a guarantee against political setbacks: the worse Israel fares in the international arena, the more it is entitled to hope for ultimate redemption. The history of the Jews under the Roman Empire is sufficient demonstration that those who remained faithful to this interpretation were moved rather to revolt than passivity; moral evolution cannot be accused of inciting the Jews to national masochism. Nor is this the case for Christ, at least for the Christ of the Gospels. Yet the position of the sacrificial victim possesses a power that is incommensurable with either collective or individual psychology.

For René Girard, it is precisely Christ's assumption of this position that demonstrates his exemplarity and even his divinity. This assumption cannot be *desired;* it must be the result of communal persecution provoked by the revelation of the true meaning of the victimary position itself, a revelation that fundamentally endangers sacrificial ritual and the ethic founded on it. In this view, Jesus himself, as well as the religion founded by his disciples, was essentially and primordially devoid of resentment. Resentment is blindness; and liberation from it, which can only take place miraculously, the understanding of the origin of man in the familiar victimage mechanism. Our epistemology being different from Girard's, it is not surprising that this difference is reflected in our interpretations of the Isaian passage and its rereading by Christianity. For us, resentment is the source of moral knowledge just as desire was the source of ethical knowledge. To define Jesus as devoid of resentment may well be consistent with the foundations of Christianity; but that this definition is miraculous is only a demonstration of the ultimate inconsistency of Christianity. Our interest at this point, however, is not in Christianity but in Judaism, and it is precisely on this point that the two religions can be most fundamentally differentiated.

Certainly no reader of the Isaian passage is likely to find it devoid of resentment. But this remains a mere subjective judgment unless we can demonstrate that this sacrificial morality reflects not a diminution but an *increase* of resentment with respect to the more traditional prophetic oracles of doom against the powerful. And this demonstration hinges on the strength of the connection between the irrefutable guarantee of divine favor given in the Isaian passage and the general cultural significance of the position of the sacrificial victim. What is at stake, in other words, is the epistemological productivity of resentment on which we have founded our theory of high culture.

Resentment attacks social difference. And, as we have seen, the first essential social difference was that between the central "producer" and the peripheral "consumers" in the ritual feast. The big-man or his equivalent in other cultures effectively usurped the central position formerly held by the presiding divinity, of whom the ritual feast, whether or not it contained a sacrificial victim, was a material manifestation.

Our epistemology, founded on an originary hypothesis, allows us to abstract from social difference to difference as such, to reduce all significant difference to its original terms as that between the central figure—both divinity and appetitive object—and the community of worshiper/appropriators. This reduction asserts the underlying structural identity between sacrificial victim, divinity, and significance-in-general as forms of centrality. Yet how can it be a product of resentment that seeks only to destroy social difference? The answer is that this reduction still lies within the limits of narrative monotheism, as revealed from the evolution of God's role in the Old Testament.

The God who punished Adam and Eve was acting from "jealousy"; the maker of the covenant with Abraham acted from generosity; the punisher of offenses against widow and orphan acts from a (moral) sense of justice. These are all secular motivations. In contrast, the God who sacrifices the "suffering servant" for the sins of the world would appear to be acting *ritually*. The mirroring of resentment in God was meant to explain ritual; now it seems to have *become* ritual. But to whom, after all, can God be sacrificing? Sacrifice is here no longer a merely ritual act but a *moral* one, a test of the victim's willingness to accept his assigned role: "The Lord has been pleased to crush him with suffering. *If he offers his life in atonement*, he shall see his heirs, he shall have a long life and through him what the Lord wishes will be done" (53:10).[9] Israel must voluntarily accept her sacrificial role "like a lamb that is led to the slaughter-house" (53:7). This acceptance is not the acceptance of suffering, for on this score, Israel has no choice, but the acceptance of a particular interpretation of her suffering, the offering of her life in atonement for the sins of others. It is precisely this interpretation that constitutes the anthropological reduction we are discussing, in which social difference—that between Israel and her more powerful neighbors— is converted into the relation between victim and sacrificer.

In most prophetic discourse, as indeed in the historical books, Israel's sufferings are presented as atonement for her sins, carried out in a strictly dual relation between Israel and God. Yet the political realities of such "atonement" involve precisely the same inferiority of Israel with regard to other, more powerful nations that we find in the "suffering servant" passage. The nations that dominate Israel in reality are presented as instruments of God. In Deutero-Isaiah, however, God himself is shown as carrying out the sacrifice. Political inferiority is transformed not merely into a relation of moral surveillance and punishment but into that between the sacrificer and his chosen victim, a relation in which the other nations play the peripheral role of sacrificial consumers. Thus the absolute transcendental difference between God and man characteristic of monotheism permits the transformation of resentment of political inferiority into a justification of the chosen victim's role as the innocent bearer of the sins of his worldly persecutors. The insight that makes the victim's position the locus of originary difference—thereby effectively subverting the real-world superiority of the more powerful nations—depends on the subordination of this difference to the absolute, a priori difference of God.

The ritual act of sacrifice is thus justified by the voluntary accession of the victim to its central ritual location, by which it places the fulfillment of the producer's desire for centrality above the consumer's quest for appetitive satisfaction, even at the apparent cost of its physical existence. But this central position is not defined by the victim or by its consumers but by God, who has promised the sufferer ultimate satisfaction. He who suffers now "shall see his heirs." What is changed here from earlier prophetic texts is the moral role of suffering, not its ultimate worldly result. The Jews' future triumph remains assured, because the primary difference is not that between victim and persecutor-consumer but that between man and God. God may appear to carry out an act of ritual slaughter, but his victim will survive to prosper in future generations. Israel-as-victim in effect abolishes sacrifice by the very act of offering itself up willingly. For the offer will never be fully accepted. "*He shall divide the spoil with the mighty*, for surrendering himself to death and letting himself be taken for a sinner" (53:12). Israel thus obtains the glory of the victim's central position without suffering the irreversible consequences. Her penalty is only deferral of ultimate satisfaction; and this, indeed, is the very purpose of sacrifice *from the standpoint of its participants*. The moral triumph of the victim is ultimately the sharing of the worldly triumph of the persecutor—a "division of the spoil," not a simple reversal that would put the victim in their place. Thus the ultimate result of resentment is the reestablishment, on an international level, of an egalitarian society; and such a society is indeed possible because the essential, transcendental difference between God and man reduces to unimportance all human and national differences.

What remains to Israel in this ultimate vision is her moral superiority in having willingly occupied the position of the victim. But in this vision, "Israel" will, in effect, become the entire world, for all will be made righteous by her sacrifice. The figure of the servant is one with whom all are permitted to identify. If this vision remains ethnic and particular, it is only because, as we have seen to have been true from the beginning, narrative monotheism is grounded in an ethical reality. It is no coincidence that the continuation of this Deutero-Isaian passage (Trito-Isaiah) begins with an appeal to "foreigners" to accept the Law: "And the foreigners who join themselves to the Lord . . . everyone who keeps the sabbath . . . and holds fast my covenant . . . their burnt offerings will be accepted on my altar; for my house shall be called a house of prayer for all peoples" (56:6–7). Ritual observances are here ethically necessary signs of allegiance to monotheism—necessary because such allegiance requires the acceptance of the continuity of the narrative. But this continuity ensures in advance the failure of Judaism to become a universal religion, as it imposes on converts allegiance to what is, in effect, an ethnic tradition. Only by identifying the sacrificial victim not with an ethical community but with a single individual were the Christians able to create a universal monotheistic religion.

Like secular texts, the biblical narrative accomplishes the sublimation of resentment through its inclusion of differential relations; its distinctive trait is the subordination of all worldly distinctions to the absolute difference between man and God. As a result of this subordination, the Bible, no longer myth, is not literature but sacred history. For the transcendental superiority of God is not merely textual, but continuous with the present. The human personages, real and legendary, are of interest to us not, like literary characters, as individuals who seek mastery over the world of their experiences, but as ancestors whose actions provoked the divine moral reactions that shaped the ethical relations of the Jewish community.

We have called God's will, as manifested in the Bible, moral rather than ethical because it is not bound by the practical constraints of human interaction. The imaginary constitution of this will as the expression of an anthropomorphic deity defined only by formally absolute difference from man is the essential sublimative mechanism of the Bible and the source of its insight into the nature of the resentment that is at the heart of human relations in differentiated society. As we have seen, God's "jealousy" is an inverse reflection of man's resentment. Here we speak of resentment in general rather than any specific manifestation of it; in this sense, resentment is an imaginary rejection of the differential structures of reality. Every manifestation of God's will in the text, even including the creation, reflects a realized or implicit destructive capacity of human resentment. The narrative may be said to "sublimate" this resentment because the acceptation of the absolute difference of God implies the acceptation of the worldly order he has imposed. This acceptation is not an abstract admission. In the monotheistic narrative, every human action and interaction is inhabited by this difference: implicitly, so long as the moral order remains undisturbed; explicitly, by the manifestation of divine punishment as soon as it is violated. There is never any danger in the Bible that conflict with this order will go unpunished, and the suspenseful awaiting of this punishment, which depends in literary works on its essentially contingent character (even when literary convention dictates its eventual manifestation), is not permitted. The reader of the sacred text maintains a permanent moral security, which differs from the security provided by myth in that God's motivations, which merely negate human resentment, are never motivated by arbitrary desires of his own.

The reader can never feel resentment against the characters of the biblical narrative; their desires are subordinated at every point to God's moral will that reflects the ethical needs of the community. This is, indeed, what we meant above by "security." Sublimation takes place here without catharsis, that is, without the sacrifice to resentment of the imaginary satisfaction obtained through identification with the literary protagonist. But this is possible only because the text does not present itself as a fiction. What matters is this fact itself, and not any "mark" of it in the text. The empirical study of narrative always errs in seeking intratextual marks by which to distinguish the categories of texts. Needless to say, such marks can be found—the references to God have no equivalent in literary texts, even those that make great use of divine personages. But these signs would be ineffective were we unable to understand them, and the text makes no self-evident display of the means of this understanding. Our ability to read and understand the monotheistic narrative lies in our cultural continuity with its creators, our susceptibility to the same resentment, and our need to rid ourselves of it. This need is a fundamental consequence of the structural difference between resentment and desire.

Desire is ultimately paradoxical: it invests its object with qualities its possession would negate. Although it is in essence involuntary, provoked by the designation of its object on the public scene of representation, which is then internalized in the imagination, it is not destructive of the self. On the contrary, the self is a reflective object of the imagination that exists primordially as the subject of desire. It is in the presence of self and object on the imaginary scene of representation that the "self" as such comes into existence. In producer's desire, which represents the most radically metaphysical pole of a continuum that becomes, at the other pole, pure appetite, the individual may imagine himself divine, an illusion that is not painful because it is held in the knowledge that no one else has realized it any better than oneself. The very existence of desire is a sign of society's success in maintaining the rivalry of its members in a purely imaginary state. The periodic occupation of the principal ritual positions in egalitarian society by the different members of the group, depending on age or family connections, should be seen in this same positive light: the leader of a ceremony may imagine himself as a god, but the other participants know very well that he is not and that their turn will come to occupy the same position.

The same is no longer true in differentiated society, where the producer's desire of some is, at least temporarily, fulfilled. Here the resentment of the others, like the jealousy of the central figure, is an essentially agonistic sentiment. The resentful imagination is a reaction against real perceptions that are painful in that they show another in the place that the self would like to occupy. Irrealizable desire is faced with the scandal of a humanly realized centrality. It is thus through resentment that the individual comes to feel his essential unfreedom within the social order, or, in other words, that he comes to exist fully as an individual, with the consciousness that his human capacities are not necessarily destined to receive their maximal satisfaction within the community. Lamartine's man, "Borné dans son destin, infini dans ses vœux," is not merely a man of desire but a man of resentment, for he could feel the pain of this contradiction only in a world in which the possibility of a higher destiny is held out to him. And this is as true of kings as of commoners; the existence of differential roles makes even the bearer of the highest uncertain that a still higher does not somehow exist beyond his grasp. If the commoner sees the monarch in the place he would like to occupy, the king sees in his subject's resentment a refusal to accept his occupation of this place. Even those absolute rulers who have been spared the spectacle of their subjects' resentment must have been well able to imagine what they could not see.

The cultural sublimation of resentment is thus experienced by all members of differentiated societies not merely as a prior reality, like the lower forms of culture, but as a felt need. The individual subject becomes aware of himself as anterior to the culture within which he finds himself. Both the major forms of higher culture, the religious-moral and the secular-esthetic, require of their adherents a choice, an act of allegiance that is free in its essence even if it is dictated by social necessity. In the religious sphere, this is what we call faith; and without faith, only primitive religion, that of ritual and myth, is possible.

The text of the Bible contains numerous expressions of voluntary acts of submission to God's will, of which the archetype is Abraham's aborted sacrifice of Isaac. For the believer to whom God has not in fact revealed himself, as he supposedly did to Abraham or to the prophets, faith is a decision to accept the sovereignty of God's moral will over the universe. This faith should, in principle, abolish resentment; but if it did, the Bible itself, which, as we have seen, illustrates at every turn the epistemology of resentment, would never have been written. The author of the scene between Eve and the serpent could not have been innocent of resentment, however effectively it may have been sublimated. The "divine inspiration" of the authors of sacred texts designates the contradiction inherent in a sacred difference that must be imagined a priori but can only be adhered to a posteriori. Only the horror of resentment and the fear of its conversion into a destructive praxis could overcome this contradiction. But this is to say that the form of sublimation carried out within the Judeo-Christian tradition is ultimately vulnerable to the prior reduction or sublimation of resentment by means *internal* to the operations of the social structure. These means are essentially economic, and their creation in modern society is indirectly dependent on the moral system that was supposed to render them superfluous—on that system, but also on another, to which we shall now turn: the system of high secular culture first elaborated in classical Greece.

10

Greece: Secular Esthetic Culture

The Birth of High Secular Culture

The work of Karl Polanyi and his followers has cast doubt on the once unquestioned notion that ancient civilization in general and archaic Greece in particular had already evolved a market economy. It is therefore no longer possible confidently to explain the origins of secular culture as reflecting the emergence of "bourgeois" values in ancient societies. If the society of Aristotle already was beginning to feel the impact of such values,[1] this was certainly not the case in Homer's day.

The specific and even the general characteristics of Greek economic history are far from settled.[2] But our contention is that cultural phenomena reveal more of anthropological value about a given society than economic phenomena. The establishment of chains of causality between different stages of social evolution may be carried out on various levels of specificity. In the short term, where the span of interests of an individual lifetime play a significant role, it is no doubt more feasible to use causal models based on economic or political rather than cultural criteria.[3] In the long term, however, we must be concerned with the most fundamental aspect of social structure, that most resistant to the vicissitudes of economic and military domination; and this aspect is precisely the cultural. It is at this point that the specificity of our methodological choice of the cultural begins to be felt, because it is with the Greeks that the cultural begins to constitute a relatively well defined domain within

227

the larger society. That is, indeed, what we mean by "secular culture": one distinct from the more evidently fundamental ritual regulation of social relations.

We have remarked that the artworks and the sacred or literary texts of a society are very nearly the only effective source of our intuitive grasp of what life in such a society might have been like. It is our contention that this intuition is a privileged path to anthropological truth. But it cannot suffice to point to texts and artworks merely as objects of esthetic satisfaction. In order to claim priority for them over the study of economic and political structures, we must show that they reveal the most fundamental level of social organization. Our conception of culture as the locus of ethical conceptions is unobjectionable for primitive societies, in which all social interactions are mediated by cultural (that is, ritual) forms. Even the early empires subsume all social relations, including the economic, under an overall religious structure, of which the divinity of the monarch is the keystone. It is only with the advent of higher cultures that our claim begins to oppose itself radically to other apparently plausible methodological hypotheses.[4]

This should not be taken to imply that we advocate the subordination of socioeconomic history to literary analysis, nor that we claim to find in such analysis socioeconomic data more concrete than those generally considered by historians. What we propose is, rather, that cultural analysis is not reducible to "literary" analysis, that the anthropological foundations of the very phenomenon of the literary text must be examined before the content of individual texts becomes of interest, and, indeed, that the sort of literary analysis that takes the existence of literature for granted is of use only to others for whom the same is true, that is, to participants in, not students of, culture. The primary cultural significance of Greek and Hebrew texts is in their general form, which, once given, permits the inclusion within them of a wealth of content. The individual genius of literary creators is of secondary importance in comparison with the collective ethic that provides them with their formal means.

No economic history of the Greeks, not even to speak of the Jews, can give any inkling of the immense cultural differences that separate these societies from neighboring, socioeconomically similar ones. "Superstructural" differences, some may say, the result of aleatory secondary factors. Not in the least. These ancient cultural achievements endure because they remain relevant to the realities of modern society, and this continued relevancy would be incomprehensible were it not based on ethical structures that are *ipso facto* of anthropological interest. It is not "estheticism" to insist on the anthropological relevancy of the esthetic experiences that take up so large a portion of man's time and energy. Only those for whom culture is nothing more than an ornamental sign of social status can believe that Greek secular culture is not the most significant element in ancient Greek society; and only those who read the Bible "as literature" can hold equivalent beliefs about the Jews.

The Esthetic Sublimation of Resentment

We have already had occasion to make use of the Aristotelian term *catharsis*, which we shall retain to distinguish the specifically artistic version of sublimation from the general case that also includes that of religion. Yet the notions of purification and purgation that are associated with catharsis provoke images diametrically opposite to that of sublimation; the latter occurs *par en haut*, the former, *par en bas*. "Pity and terror and other such emotions" are not transformed into something higher, but expelled.

Pity and terror are in no sense the equivalent of resentment; their generation in the spectator is, on the contrary, the very mechanism of sublimation that we seek to define. For it is no accident that modern criticism employs the term "identification" to describe the relationship between spectator and protagonist that Aristotle spoke of in terms of pity and terror. Identification is precisely what is problematic in resentment, where we are separated from the other as from a god by an insuperable barrier of social necessity, at the same time as the other's humanity makes him a model for ourselves. In the literary work, the spectator sees himself in the place of the hero, however far above him the latter may stand in his fictional universe, because this place is the center of the scene of representation in which our desire always situates us. Unlike the gods of myth, the inhabitants of the fictional universe are offered up to the community as wholly contained within it. We identify with them by imaginarily espousing their desires, in which resentment in one form or another is always present, but this vicarious resentment is not painful because it is experienced as a form of desire, the inaccessibility of whose object is guaranteed by the formal barrier that separates us from the work. On the contrary, our emotional reaction of "pity and terror" to the sufferings of the hero serves to assuage our own worldly resentment. What we experience in literature is the originary identity, within the scene of representation, of the central figure with the sacrificial victim.

This assimilation to the victim's role makes literary characters impossible to resent even when they incarnate, as in the highest literary forms, the social roles that are central foci of resentment—kings, "tyrants."[5] The sacrificial origins of this assimilation have already been referred to in our discussion of the *Gilgamesh Epic*. What must be firmly rejected is the notion that literary identification is based on "natural" emotions. For Rousseau, "pity" and "terror" were precisely the originary bases of culture. But Rousseau's anthropology can recognize the cultural productivity of resentment only as a negation of man's original cultural bonds. The equality of literary identification, our discovery that kings and heroes are really just people like ourselves, is by no means founded on an instinctive sympathy for other members of our species. We identify with fictional kings and heroes in their sufferings as sacrificial figures provided for us by the author-Subject. And this remains true even of those "heroes" we identify with in the real world through the intermediary of the media of mass communications. It is our fictional, literary identification that is primary, not the human fellow-feeling that supposedly motivates it. Our ambivalent reactions to the misfortunes of the great as recounted in the media exactly parallel our sentiments toward fictive heroes.

Literature is not founded on "human interest." The naive notion that narrative grew up originally from the stories we recount about our everyday activities is the opposite of the truth. The archetypal actor in narrative is a god; his reduction to human status is already an irredeemable fall that remains felt as such by the reader. Thus the passage from myth to fiction of any type is already a decisive victory for resentment. In the *Gilgamesh Epic* we may observe this passage historically. But the modern reader has not gone through this historical experience, and hence, in reading fiction, he has no reason to make even implicitly the comparison with myth. In a world in which ritual sacrifice is no longer meaningful, the privileged locus of the sacrificial is in the trivalent relationship between the reader/ spectator, the literary character, and the implied author whom we shall call, in more formal terms, the "Subject" of the literary work.

The lower cultural forms have all been shown to have an esthetic basis. Because the ritual is ultimately a subcategory of the esthetic, there is no difficulty in understanding how esthetic forms may exist outside of ritual. But the same may be said for the sacrificial as an esthetic—and not specifically ritual—category. The esthetic scene is, from the beginning, the locus of desire. In the lower stages of culture, the figures that occupy it become progressively more anthropomorphic as the totality of the social sphere, as well as the cosmos that surrounds and influences it, is brought within the domain of cultural explanation. Etiological myth already involves "identification" in the sense that rule-guided activities are understood as products of anthropomorphic desires which the hearer can identify with his own. Yet the mythical protagonist is, in essence, immortal and extratextual. The myth is about him but does not constitute him; he is incarnated within it, just as he may be by an actor in ritual. The sacrificial element of myth does not directly involve its divine protagonist, who is rather the provider of the feast. The disparity between ritual sacrifice and its mythical recounting constitutes an epistemological limit of myth and, more broadly, a limit of the sacrificial esthetic of lower cultures. Whether the ritual victim that lies behind the myth is animal or human is secondary; what is essential is that he is never the god himself. Thus when the myth recounts the story of the god—as opposed to his incarnation in the victim—it must disguise killing as transcendence, as the Tikopia myth discussed above illustrates. The universe of desire can go no further than this. For even if human sacrifice already implies a transition toward resentment,[6] the ultimate identity of victim and god can never be established—not because it has been "forgotten" but because it has not yet altogether abandoned its appetitive basis in the original event. And this can be accomplished only in the culture of resentment.

In differentiated society, a man, not a god, occupies the central locus of ritual redistribution. No amount of appetitive satisfaction can compensate for the difference between him and the other members of his society. The mythical identification that had justified the distribution of appetitively oriented activities and protected the ethical structure from the destructive effects of desire is no longer sufficient to guard against the resentment this difference engenders. What must henceforth be sacrificed is not a representative of the divinity who protects the social order against desire, but a representative of this human difference.

Hebrew culture alone makes this representativity unnecessary by generalizing it to the entire social universe. The lateness of the Jews relative to the ancient empires permitted these still-primitive nomadic tribes to pass from a relatively egalitarian stage to a state structure without abandoning the centrality of their transcendent divinity, to whom even the most extreme human social differences could be subordinated. Neither David nor Solomon could ever be in the least a rival of the Hebrew God. The Hebrew ritual sacrifice retained, in its redistributive aspect, something of the spirit of primitive society—in marked contrast with the "modernism" of such Greek religious practices as the Dionysian festivals or the Orphic mysteries.

The primary lesson of the story of Cain and Abel is that sacrifice per se was ineffective in purging the resentment aroused by social difference. (In contrast, the Jewish festivals, whatever their primitive origin, are reinscribed within the sacred history recounted in the Bible, and thus subordinated to the resentment-based culture it maintained.) The first sacrifice mentioned in the Bible leads to invidious comparison and thence to murder. God's rejection of Cain's sacrifice implies that the social superiority of herders to agriculturists could not be purged of its potential for conflict through sacrifice alone. What Cain should have done was to relinquish his central sacrificial role to Abel; for social difference was subordinate to the equality of all men as consumers under the aegis of God as unique "producer." To the extent that the Cain-Abel story portrays a historical reality, it is that of the big-man stage, and its outcome reflects the instability of this stage, the incapacity of its ethical structures—in contrast with those of narrative monotheism—to maintain control over resentment. Had Cain been able to read the preceding chapters of Genesis, he would have known that Abel's flocks were his in the first place only by virtue of God's having created them for the benefit of mankind.

Unlike the Jews, the Greeks did not abolish myth before it evolved into secular narrative. The shift in focus from god to man reflects the similar shift in ritual centrality. The gods remain, and, indeed, are never challenged, but their role becomes subordinate, not in power, but in interest. The task for divine etiology is no longer to explain taboos and customs but to justify the results of human conflict. This transformation is not discontinuous; the new justifications are founded upon the imperatives and interdictions established by the old taboos and customs. But whatever the ritually derived "flaw" that is made to justify the discomfiture of the mortal hero, it is now this discomfiture that is of primary interest. Secular literature, as opposed to biblical narrative, never generates an abstract moral law of reciprocity. Its triumphs are founded on resentment, and their justice is a posteriori. Literature is, by its very nature, in "bad faith," because its sublimation of resentment cannot avoid granting it esthetic satisfaction—even if this is by no means the same as "wish fulfillment."

Unlike myth, the biblical narrative is not fundamentally anonymous. But if the Pentateuch is traditionally attributed to Moses, it is not as creation but as divine dictation; Moses is the archetype of the scribe, not of the author. The text itself says nothing about this role, which would appear to be an extrapolation from Moses' reception of the Ten Commandments. Its significance is to reinforce the self-contained nature of the Torah, the closure of which presages that of the Bible as a whole, and this is done precisely at the expense of its real authors. The increased authorial presence in the later books remains always subordinate to the dictation of God, which is put forth as the fundamental criterion of inclusion. The prophet is never an "author" because he speaks in the name of the divine will; his real originality is manifested through his intuitive interpretation of the moral basis of that will. Thus as the Bible becomes less anonymous, it becomes, at the same time, less like fiction. As God's presence becomes potential rather than actual, its weight only increases; prophecy is presented as God's own prediction of what he intends to do.

The opposite is the case in secular literature. The case of the Homeric poems is archetypal proof of the necessity, whatever empirical evidence there may be to the contrary, of fixing authorial responsibility for the literary text. Even if we firmly believe that the *Iliad* is no more the creation of a single author than the Pentateuch, we cannot read it without positing a fictive Homer as Subject of the fictive text. Similarly, at the other end of the historical spectrum, we attribute a film to an "authorial" director, although many other persons have not merely contributed to it but actually made decisions as to its final form. This is a fundamental characteristic of secular culture that must be explained.

The question of individual authorship does not arise as a result of authorial vanity; the Homeric problem is a sufficient indication of that. It is a structural necessity of the high secular culture for which the Greeks provided the original model. A popular ballad needs no author—but such a ballad is not truly a work of literature. The specificity of the creative Subject is, in fact, a stronger criterion for defining literature and the higher arts in general than esthetic quality, however it may be measured. Neither myth, popular literature, nor the biblical narrative possesses an individualized Subject, and their example proves that the formal comprehension of discourse does not require it.[7] In contrast, the individual Subject stands in symmetric opposition to the individual hearer or reader of the literary work. That such works are always, at least potentially, written texts—again the Homeric example is probative—follows from the essential solitude of the hearer, who stands in a one-to-one relationship with the Subject. The collectivity of spectators at a Greek tragedy is by no means equivalent to a community of ritual participants. It is, in fact, homologous with the democratic assembly: each member of the audience is an individual who makes his own judgment concerning the value of the work being staged. The competitive nature of the Athenian dramatic festivals reflects this fact.

Desire has been a strictly individual, and individualizing, phenomenon from its birth in the original scene of representation. The desires aroused even by the ritual recitation of a myth are "individual" and could not conceivably be otherwise. But the ritual participant, or even the isolated hearer of a myth, although his intuitive grasp of it is based on his own desire, does not remain cut off by this desire from communion with his fellows. Just as in the original event, he recognizes in its object something whose very inaccessibility unites all the individual members of the community.

A similar phenomenon occurs with popular cultural works, which call forth even from the isolated individual a "collective" response that reduces him to the lowest common denominator of his culture. Here, unlike the ritual case, a fully developed resentful individuality is submerged in the collectivity; whence the degraded, regressive nature of popular culture. It is no accident that "popular" refers to a type of culture by means of an ambiguous sociological reference. The "people" is both the community as a whole and its inferior and presumably more numerous strata. Popular literature is the literature of the mass; it is experienced by elites as if they were indistinguishable fractions of the mass. For we are all members of the people in the broad sense, whereas, in the narrow sense, the people includes only those whose low social standing does not arouse resentment and leaves them anonymous with respect to the society as a whole. The resentment of popular literature is collective, not because it must be experienced collectively but because the individual, in experiencing it, separates himself irreconcilably from the resented elite, whose status as an inaccessible desire-object is a source of solidarity between him and the mass for whom it is equally inaccessible. When an ordinary citizen hears a story ridiculing the powerful, he avenges his resentment as a member of the vast collectivity of the powerless. The story will make him feel closer to his equally powerless neighbor, united with him against the powerful victim.

This is not a mere matter of individual psychology. The social difference contested by resentment is understood to be unfavorable to a large class of individuals other than the hearer himself. The Subject of a popular work is essentially collective; an individual author may be said to write as a spokesman for the group. The desired elimination of social difference is imagined as beneficial to a collectivity that includes the individual hearer. Rather than picture himself as taking the place of the fallen tyrant, he is content to savor his vengeance as one of the crowd. The popular imagination thus regresses to the level of egalitarian sacrificial ritual, with its central victimary position occupied by a member of the social elite.

Thus in popular literature—as in popular politics—resentment creates a collective solidarity that mimics the communal solidarity of primitive society. But the primitive spectator's esthetic satisfaction opposes, not mass to elite, but the human community as a whole to the gods whose desires are free of the restrictions they place on his own. The basis of this solidarity is not resentment but fear and awe. There is never any question of even imaginarily eliminating the transcendent superiority of the gods or of taking their place. They are needed to prevent the conflict that might arise from conflicting desires among the members of the group; once the divine interdiction has been established, all members of the community are linked by their common incapacity to carry out their desires. Popular literature in differentiated society creates a solidarity that is both less absolute and more intense. It is not guaranteed by the very ontology of the culture, but it involves positive common interests that may, on occasion, attain political expression. The collective revenge of the mass can satisfy only the individual who is able to see himself as nothing more than a member of it. In politics, "the art of the possible," such limited satisfactions are often the only ones available; but politics is not culture.

High secular culture is the esthetic, as opposed to the sacred, response to the demand of cultural universality that all significant desire be sublimated within the cultural sphere. The high-cultural work reaches the spectator not qua member of the "people" but qua individual; and the spectator's individuality is reflected in the unique authority of the Subject over his fictional world. The mere contemplation of, for example, the tragic downfall of a king is not a sufficient description of the spectator's experience. This contemplation is mediated through the submission of the spectator to the individual will of the Subject, who functions as a "monotheistic" deity within the universe of his creation.

Once literary works exist wherein the imagination of the spectator becomes dependent, not on a collectively imagined reality independent of any specific discursive formulation, but on the discourse itself (even if the subject matter of this discourse exists independently), then the Subject of this discourse becomes the sole guarantee of the coherence of the imaginary universe created in the work. At any point, we may freely permit our imagination to range among various desirable and undesirable outcomes for the characters with whose interests, contradictory or not, we identify, in the knowledge that the outcome is already known to the Subject independently of our desires. This knowledge differs from the collective knowledge of myth, even when, as in nearly all Greek literature, the subject matter is mythical or legendary and presumably familiar to every member of the audience. In the mythic material, the audience's desires are fulfilled by the actions of the characters, whereas in its literary transcription, the fulfillment of these desires is sacrificed to our resentment, not of the literary/mythical heroes themselves, but of the transcendental central position to which all desire tends. The characters, who can no longer inhabit this absolute position, even if they can occupy its worldly equivalent—kingship, tyranny—feel and express the same resentment as their audience. The Subject's knowledge of the outcome of the interaction of these characters, like that of the unique God of the monotheistic narrative, reflects his grasp of the ethical necessity of the fictional universe as a whole, which he maintains in the face of the resentment of his characters. It is our respect for the Subject's transcendent authority—a respect granted a priori but which may be withdrawn if we feel him to be overindulgent toward the desires of his creatures—that permits our desire to exercise its full liberty. This is not necessary in myth, where each element of the story realizes a desire that explains some aspect of social reality. But now the world of the fictional work is no longer contiguous with ours; its ethic is implicit in the Subject alone.

Literary adaptation need not involve the wholesale recasting of a mythical story, but it is immediately sensible to the modern reader, for whom the mythical narrative is inevitably devoid of literary value. Because "producer's desire" is essentially unrealizable in the real world, the world of myth is one in which the individuality of its hearer plays no role: its content is beyond the possibility of anyone. Its organization, as well as its range of possible variation, is determined by preexisting ritual. Lévi-Strauss's myth collections, whether or not we accept the validity of his categorizations, demonstrate the conservatism of mythical discourse over great distances, as well as over the considerable spans of time needed to account for the myth's spread over these distances.

No praxis can be based on desire as such, but resentment is the foundation of all socially significant praxis. There is, consequently, a temporal continuity in literary narrative that myth cannot possess. If I can understand and identify with a literary character on the basis of my own experience, it is because I am able to construct as the referent of literary discourse a fictional world like my own, organized by the temporality of human praxis. In literature, the deferral structure of culture in general becomes, as it never could in myth, included within the lives of the characters, where it is motivated by their own appreciation of their real and desired social status.[8]

The authority of the literary Subject, unlike that of the Old Testament God, is confined to the imaginary universe we construct on the basis of the text. The Hebrew God could be postulated as having his believers' welfare at heart because he was, after all, conceived for that purpose. His role, as we have seen, was to be the mirror of the resentment of the community, acting to justify the real ethical order—including the often humiliating relations of Israel with neighboring peoples—as a necessary result of and protection against this resentment. God's will can be anticipated, as by the prophets, on the basis of moral principles, but in any case it always corresponds to reality, however incomprehensible this may appear from our moral standpoint. In contrast, the literary Subject's intention embodies no abstract moral principle. The imaginary universe of the literary text is governed by an ethical conception the crucial elements of which are realized in the destinies of the characters. The difference between this fictional ethic and real-world morality is perhaps the most significant difference between Greek and Hebrew culture; even Greek philosophical discourse does not abolish this difference but rather codifies it.

At first glance, "poetic justice" is not dissimilar to morality: the characters are expected to get what they deserve, and the Subject will be held responsible for disappointing the reader's sense of their just deserts. The difference, even in literature composed, as is our own, under the direct influence of Judeo-Christian morality, is nevertheless fundamental. Real morality, like God's will, transcends the ethical order; literary morality does not. In the biblical narrative, resentment is often punished, but it is sometimes rewarded; it is accorded, in short, its full due as the generating force of ethical

structures and of their modification. The prophet's resentment against
the rich and powerful is expressed in moral terms and is, indeed,
the original expression of abstract morality. In contrast, in the literary work, resentment against the ethical order is always punished.
This may be put in more formal terms: if what looks like resentment
goes unpunished, then it was not resentment in the first place. For
the ethical order of the fictional universe is fixed in advance: the
work, whatever its internal temporality, exists as a whole from the
beginning. The character who wishes to change this order is guilty
of *hubris*, and the more we understand and identify with him, the
more effective will be the *catharsis* that his downfall produces in us.

But, by the same token, if literary morality is conservative in
comparison with Judeo-Christian morality, it is also radically non-
normative. The ethical conception of the fictional world concerns
its inhabitants, not the reader. We are able easily to appreciate literary works of other times and places only because we have neither
to accept nor reject their ethic for ourselves.[9] The tragic protagonist
who offends the ethical order of his universe may strike us as more
admirable than the order itself; at the very least, he attracts our
sympathy, for it is with his resentment that we identify. Literature's
moral standing in the Judeo-Christian world has always been suspect, if not altogether unacceptable; the literary depiction of resentment encourages the reader to imagine its fulfillment, all the
more because, in the fictional universe, such fulfillment is impossible.[10]

The esthetic of egalitarian culture remains always dependent on
ritual because appropriative rivalry, unlike resentment, can be evoked
and mastered only in the collective presence of its object. Conversely,
secular culture's independence of ritual makes it the typical form of
culture in the narrow sense of the term. It is no accident that this
second narrowing of the definition of "culture" (the first having been
the passage from the totality of social activities to those centrally
concerned with representation) corresponds both to the original (Latin)
use of the word and to that in common parlance. Religion is no
doubt more fundamental to the social order than esthetic culture in
all societies, with the possible exception of our own; one would
hesitate to make a similar exception even for fifth- or fourth-century
Athens. But it is precisely in the unconstrained, voluntary nature
of the participation they require that cultural pursuits embody a
liberal ideal for human activity. And the relevance of these pursuits
to our lives, the pleasure devoid of appetitive satisfaction that they
provide, is dependent on the resentment we "freely" experience as
members of differentiated—in our own case, almost unlimitedly

differentiated—society. The vicarious pain of the hero's sufferings is for us a unique pleasure, for it signifies our imaginary occupation of society's forbidden central locus.

If it is only by submitting to the will of the transcendent Subject that we can desire the success of the protagonist's impossible resentment, the "end of culture" comes when the character's resentment can no longer be unambiguously distinguished from that of the Subject, when the worldly desires of the author seek fulfillment in the work and provoke in their turn the resentment of the reader. The Subject-reader dichotomy is compromised and eroded by the indefinitely subtle mediations of the modern social order, whose ethical conception can no longer distinguish between resentment and human understanding in general. Thus the epistemology of resentment finally catches up with the artists who had previously, along with their rivals the moralists, found such profit in it. High mimetic art exhausts itself now that the enormous expansion of social differentiation that it has facilitated has made resentment a necessary prerequisite to worldly experience. The Subject cannot survive in a world of competing Subjects. And with the erosion of the opposition between high and popular culture disappears the last vestige of the productivity of irreversible—sacred—difference.

Epic Poetry

Value and the Emergence of High Secular Culture

High secular culture, including, in particular, literature, does not arise as soon as a differentiated social structure begins to generate resentment. Even the highly structured ancient empires were able to do without a secular literature; the *Gilgamesh Epic* constitutes the extreme limit of their literary evolution. The birth of literature proper coincides not with evolution but with regression in ancient social organization. The Greek Dark Age was a period of severe economic decline in comparison with the preceding Mycenaean era. It is thus no surprise that classicists have recoiled from attributing to this "sub-Mycenaean" epoch the most important cultural creation of all. But that attribution is indeed correct. High culture becomes possible, not to say necessary, as soon as resentment comes to be perceived as a necessary social phenomenon. But in contrast with the Jewish (re)writing of human history as at every point transcending this necessity through the agency of divine will, Greek secular culture accepts the necessity of resentment as definitive.

The subject matter of the *Iliad* allows us to understand this necessity more concretely. Achilles, by incarnating the highest abilities of his society, comes into conflict with it. The heroic society creates for the first time what we may already call a "market" for individual talent, restricted, no doubt, to an aristocracy, but at least partially independent of rank. *This* market, and not the market for economic goods, is the first step in the creation of the modern exchange-system. This interpretation both justifies and is justified by Polanyi's assertion that markets in the modern sense played no genuine role in ancient societies before Hellenic times. For the most fundamental characteristic of the market system is not a free market in goods but an ethical structure that encourages the indefinite accumulation of *value*.

Before value can be attributed to goods, and thereby become objectified in the marketplace, it must be a characteristic of individual human beings. Exchange and even trade long preceded this development. For value must be not so much quantifiable as extensible in principle without limit, incommensurable with the constraints of the ethical order even if these ultimately restrain its accumulation. Before money can become a value in this sense, its indefinite accumulation must become an ethical possibility. Individual members of society must, in other words, be assured that their own social value will increase commensurately with the money they accumulate. But this implies that the notion of social value must precede its measurability in monetary terms. For money is the most abstract measure of value; a society that measures its members by their monetary wealth must already long have evaluated them by criteria more concretely related to social utility. And the first, most primitive criterion of *value*, that employed by the heroic society depicted in the *Iliad*, is military *valor*.

The conflict between Achilles and his society is inevitable because this society promotes the maximal possession of valor, while at the same time limiting its rewards by the needs of the ethical order as a whole. Achilles' resentment of Agamemnon is neither contingent nor epiphenomenal; it is an essential condition of life in a society in which individuals are evaluated. For the individual who possesses or acquires the most value cannot be, for all that, independent of the limits of the ethical order. Even the limits of material human existence as such are bound to become an object of resentment in such a society. Because value is, in principle, without limit, the praxis it supports tends to seek satisfaction without limit, independently not only of ethical but even of natural constraints. In effect, such a society encourages its members to believe that it can confer infinite satisfaction, and it thus gives rise not merely to resentment based on fixed differences of status but to a dynamic *generalized resentment* toward every individual or institution that may be perceived as offering a limit to the original "producer's desire" of the active subject, whose praxis is oriented toward a satisfaction he is encouraged to expect. The element of praxis is essential. Value without praxis solidifies itself into fixed status; such a status becomes problematic—that is, productive of generalized resentment—only when changes in the social structure reveal it to be based ultimately on function, which is to say, on praxis.

Achilles is not only by nature the best warrior among the Achaeans; he has proved his mettle throughout the nine years of the war. His wrath is occasioned by the loss of a captive, but this is merely a spark that ignites a potentially explosive situation: his booty, unlike his war effort, has always been far less than Agamemnon's. The contrasting case of Hector is that of the "ethical" individual in a world of value. Hector combines the virtues of warrior and chief; he has no a priori need to base his praxis wholly on his military valor. But (as James Redfield points out[11]) his successes on the battlefield lead him to overestimate his valor; and he eventually falls victim to the man for whom valor, that is, soldierly value, is the sole measure.

Warfare is the most primitive condition of value; it creates a competitive arena in which individuals are measured against each other and where their usefulness to their social group knows no other ethical limitations. Redfield perceives this as a "state of nature" (in a Hobbesian sense), outside of cultural structures per se. But all markets are "states of nature" in this sense, for value is determined within them irrespective of the ethical structures of the social order. The nature/culture dichotomy, the polemic thrust of which always operates to distinguish among what are in fact equally "cultural" sets of phenomena, is too romantically indulgent toward a given culture's own sense of its unity to be of use as an analytical tool.[12]

In its generalized state, resentment becomes an open form in which the positive image of the inaccessible sacred object is no longer replaced predictably by a single central figure (big-man or pharaoh) but by an arbitrary element from an indefinite series of negative images of institutional or individual obstacles to an abstractly defined centrality. In a society with a system of value—we may call this an "advanced" society, one with an "open" ethical structure—as opposed to primitive differentiated societies of the big-man type, or to stable hierarchical societies like the early empires, there is no positive image of centrality. Achilles resents Agamemnon, but neither the king nor even his role provides a model for his desire. Like all literary heroes, Achilles has a clearer image of what he doesn't want than of what he wants.

Because advanced society possesses an open ethical structure, it lacks an explicit ethical conception by which this structure may be grasped. Literature and the other arts provide a universe within which the system of value is finally subordinated to the ethical order maintained by the Subject. Our identification with literary heroes is founded less on a shared image of their ultimate goals than on shared images of the obstacles to their accomplishment. We react negatively to these images because our generalized resentment is always ready to attach itself to any such obstacle, real or fictitious. But in the literary work, as opposed to lived experience, the obstacles the hero confronts are well defined and limited in advance by the closure we attribute to the authority of the Subject.[13]

The contradiction between the value-oriented praxis and the ethical order attains in the literary work a resolution that relocates the hero within this order. The specific obstacles we desire to see removed cease to interest us, either because they have in fact been eliminated or because they have been shown to be secondary with respect to the underlying contradiction. The elimination of the reader's desire at the end of the work is the sign of its formal closure. This closure is not merely discovered at the end; it is anticipated throughout. If it is not accomplished, we feel cheated and reject the narrative as a valid esthetic object. For it is only in the anticipation of such closure that we have agreed to accept the fictional universe as the locus for our desire.

Μηνιν ἄειδε θεά

The first three words of the *Iliad* are also the first three words of Western high secular culture. The second two express the divinity of the literary Subject in the fictional universe, as distinct from the mere humanity of the author or singer who invokes it. And the first word is resentment itself.

"Higher" Homeric criticism has so concentrated on reconstructing the worldview(s) of the hypothetical author(s) of the poems that the exemplarity of the Homeric texts has been all but forgotten. Like all ethnology, Homeric ethnology trivializes the uniqueness of significant cultural phenomena. The more we know about the millenary existence of oral formulaic poetry, the variety of Greek epic material, and the number and chronology of the different contributions to the final text, the less likely we are to take seriously the exemplary status it held in ancient Greek culture. The text recounts, after all, only a relatively brief sequence from the legendary history of the Trojan war; to read most commentators, the author's selection of this particular episode for literary immortality would seem to be of little consequence. That Homer's very first word might have particular cultural significance is not likely to occur to a scholar for whom "the wrath of Achilles" is merely a code name for one of many episodes in the Trojan epic material, one that Homer presumably drew by chance from Hector's helmet.

Yet both Achilles' "wrath" and the events that provoke its outbreak and eventual dissipation are of exemplary significance. The fact that Achilles' grievance against Agamemnon mirrors within the Greek camp that of Menelaus against Paris with which the Trojan War began is not a mere sign of what a New Critic might call the "well-wroughtness" of the poem, or an illustration of what French formalists call *mise en abyme*. This involution of the external conflict is precisely the moment of literary epic, as opposed to the preliterary legend from which it sprang. Although distinct from myth in its content and in its detachment from ritual, heroic legend, in prose or ballad form, clearly distinguishes in motivation between resentment and mere desire.

The story of the Trojan war, from the Judgment of Paris to the abduction of Helen and to the fighting itself, is a tale of rivalries among equals in status: goddesses, princes, military alliances. Open rivalry of this sort may be said to constitute, not a new form of desire, but a form of social action that suspends the structural difference between desire and resentment. As opposed to myth, which concentrates on establishing the internal limitations of societies, the heroic genre celebrates in military and similar (for example, athletic) rivalry the possibility of a human praxis directed toward external, secular desire-objects. Heroic literature, like all secular literature, is the product of differentiated society and of the resentment it inspires.

Desire in primitive society is essentially fantastic; its exercise obeys no human limits because its object, however apparently banal, takes on, through the desire itself, the character of the sacred and the inaccessible. The differences created in myth do not share a common measure with the possibilities of human difference in egalitarian society and may therefore serve to explain otherwise apparently arbitrary differences. In hierarchical societies, on the contrary, the mythical explanation of the meaning of social differences is supplemented by the fictional genesis, on the basis of originally equipotent desires, of new human differences. Resentment may not be the motivation of the heroic rivals, but it is sublimated in the hearer because the victory of one rival over the other is the result of superior merit, not of structural social difference. The more nuanced the superiority, the more both rivals appear as supremely meritorious, the more we identify with the superiority of the one and find consolation for our own inferiorities in the submission of the other.

Like all popular secular modes, the heroic is still very much alive, generally with, but sometimes without, the accretion of the Judeo-Christian moral distinction between "good guys" and "bad guys." But if it remains an essentially popular mode, that is because the symmetry of the desire that separates the rivals makes identification with either one of them contingent on our attribution of significance to a secondary difference. If the sociocritical popular mode discussed above forces the reader to redefine his resentment as dependent on his membership in the "popular" social group, heroic literature obliges him to identify himself with the winning side on the basis of a posited ethical superiority that is irrelevant to the symmetrical roles of both parties in the conflict. The socially unifying value of heroic literature is not, however, to be denied, particularly when its central rivalry is not individual but collective. Here the otherwise abstract identification with winners rather than losers has a communal basis, and when the national rivalries depicted in heroic literature possess an extratextual reality, this identification acquires a patriotic function well recognized by wartime propagandists.

But the *Iliad* is not propaganda, wartime or otherwise; nor is it a piece of popular literature. The point at which the *Iliad* diverges from the heroic narratives that must have preceded it is in its very first word. The wrath of Achilles is no mere reduced model of the Greeks' wrath against Troy for the theft of Helen. It is an expression of resentment, not of heroic rivalry, and its effect is to transform the heroic narrative into literature. Far from an episodic occasion for beginning *in medias res*, Achilles' *menis* is, if we take the *Iliad* itself and not heroic legend as our basis, the source of an understanding that is the archetype of all literary epistemology.

The violence that Homer attributes to the *menis* in the opening verses ("dread wrath, that brought the Achaeans innumerable sufferings and threw so many noble souls of heroes into Hades, while their bodies [literally, "themselves"] were a prey to dogs and all kinds of birds") is that of war. But this violence is less horrible than that which preceded it. At the origin of Achilles' wrath, as of Oedipus's researches, is a plague. The sequence of events that led to it is worth examining in some detail.

Agamemnon had captured the daughter of Chryses, a priest of Apollo; as Achilles later explains in 1.365 ff., this occurred in the sack of Thebes—a Greek, not a Trojan city. His refusal to return the girl to her father had led to Apollo's striking the Achaeans with a plague. Although a legitimate captive according to the usage of war (Chryses himself never contests this), the girl is under sacred protection. Thus Agamemnon has set himself up as the rival of a god; his desire to retain Chryses' daughter is assimilated to the primitive model of desire as sacrilege.

At Achilles' instigation, on the tenth day of the plague (we should recall that the Trojan War is supposed to have lasted ten years), the soothsayer Calchas explains its cause. Agamemnon is angry but agrees to return the girl for the sake of his army. Here the unproblematic difference between god and man does not give rise to resentment. But at the same time, Agamemnon resents Achilles' role in his humiliation and claims as due compensation the latter's own captive, Briseis. Achilles is torn between the heroic act of challenging Agamemnon in combat (in which he would surely win) and submission to the leader's will. On the order of Athena, Achilles submits, with the god-given knowledge that he will one day be offered triple compensation for the affront. Thus it is a deity who forces Achilles to renounce the heroic world for that of resentment. The warrior's respect for divine difference is extended, however reluctantly, to human difference. The social order receives divine sanction; at the same time, Agamemnon's abuse of the position he holds in this order is declared by Athena an act of hubris and will be punished accordingly (1.214).

Achilles' wrath is thus a consequence of the divine interdiction of two preliterary solutions of the problem posed by Chryses' daughter. On the one hand, Agamemnon cannot, as he had originally intended, simply keep the girl in defiance of her father's (and Apollo's) will; on the other, Achilles, confronted with the loss of his own captive, cannot draw his sword and settle his differences with Agamemnon by force of arms. Why, indeed, are these solutions impossible? As for the first, one might say that it is Apollo's divine power that prevents it. But in a more primitive society, there would be no need for the victor to respect the gods of the vanquished. The religious syncretism characteristic of Greek culture from Homer on is the sign of an integrated ritual order that transcends political bound-aries. The Greeks may be pillagers of cities, but their respect for the common gods of these cities reflects at least a rudimentary level of interurban organization and expresses an ethical conception that no longer permits the external discharge of internal tensions that one finds in primitive warfare.

The second case is more critical. Achilles' submission to Aga-memnon is a matter not of external relations but of internal social structure. The necessary choice of "wrath" over violence is an ar-chetypal genesis of resentment, a better model than Hegel's master and slave of the origin of social differentiation. In Hegel's model, the battle between two equals leads to the enslavement of one by the other when the loser agrees to choose life over freedom and to recognize the victor as his master. This is not merely untrue to the facts of the situation. Slavery is the choice of the conqueror rather than the conquered; it implies an economic organization sufficiently differentiated to permit putting the vanquished to work rather than either killing them or adopting them as equals. But, more signifi-cantly, Hegel's dialectic eliminates *ab ovo* the very possibility of resentment by making the slave's recognition of the master the foun-dation of social hierarchy. Social structure is derived from a hypo-thetical interaction without regard for the ethical mechanism that ensures its temporal functioning. This is the central defect of the Hegelian dialectic as anthropology. The characters in this dialectic evolve; but this evolution, based as it is on concepts, is unrelated to the temporality of human praxis. Hegel cannot explain why his historical dialectic is dragged out over millennia when its conceptual framework is accessible to us with a few hours' reading. This is not because he neglects the material basis of culture. For reference to this basis is not a refutation of his conceptual dialectic but merely a supplement to it. Hegel's critical neglect is of the ethical concep-tions that maintain equilibrium in differentiated society—concep-tions that, unlike his moral concepts, arose and evolved on the basis of collective, not individual, experience.

The slave may submit to force of arms, but the submission that is truly crucial for the existence of differentiated society is the *negation* of force of arms—that is, a submission that follows the model of Achilles' submission to Agamemnon. It is this kind of submission that is productive of resentment. Literary epistemology demon-strates here, as throughout the history of high culture, its anteriority to theoretical reflection in uncovering the critical categories of human interaction.

Achilles is condemned to resent Agamemnon rather than challenge him; he can only await his revenge from without. The *Iliad* is
the story of this awaiting and its abandonment by Achilles after its
excessive prolongation leads to the loss of his companion Patroclus.
It is the excess inherent in this awaiting, as manifested in the rejection
of Agamemnon's embassy in book 9, that defines Achilles' attitude
as "wrath." Achilles refuses seven captives equal to the one he lost;
he would refuse, as he says, "riches as numerous as grains of sand
[or dust]" (9.385). Achilles' resentment is without measure. As Odysseus points out, it defies the civic order, which permits two men to
remain in the same city even when one has killed the other's brother
or child, for the anger of the second should be assuaged by the
compensatory payment he has received from the first (9.632–636).

Thus the submission to authority that is the foundation of the
order of differentiated society generates a sentiment that puts this
order in jeopardy. The conditions of battle allow Achilles a freedom
unknown to the ordinary citizen; but this is the illusory freedom of
the pursuit of value, not the uncomplicated freedom of the heroic
narrative. Achilles' refusal to accept Agamemnon's gifts creates an
illusory utopia of resentment. His thoughts on permitting Patroclus
to do battle in his stead exaggerate this utopia into one as fantastic
as any contrived by the Romantics. "But turn back as soon as you
have saved the boats, and let them [Achaeans and Trojans] fight it
out in the plain. Ah! Father Zeus! Athena! Apollo! Let not one
Trojan, not one Argive escape death, so that we two [Achilles and
Patroclus] may emerge from the ruin to undo the sacred veil of Troy
[i.e., to take the city]" (16.95–100). The role of Patroclus, in short,
is to create an equilibrium of forces that will destroy allies along
with enemies. Achilles, in letting him fight, has not relented in the
least; his dream of revenge has, on the contrary, become all the more
destructive.

Yet, as we know, this dream goes unrealized; Patroclus's death
reconciles Achilles to the Greeks and to Agamemnon. Resentment
cannot, as we have affirmed, go unpunished. The war still continues,
but the Achaean social order has been restored. Achilles' last act of
wrath, the defilement of Hector's body, is an external displacement
of resentment that also must be checked; the *Iliad* ends with the
restoration of the body to Priam. No Apollonian plague is necessary
to force Achilles' obedience; the mere counsel of his mother Thetis
suffices. For the ritual order is perceived as less problematic than
the social order; once resentment against man has been vanquished,
resentment against the gods presents no difficulty. At the moment

of returning Hector's body, Achilles expresses to Priam the hope-lessness of such resentment: "There is no use to chilling groans, for such is the fate that the gods have spun for poor mortals: to live in sorrow, while they remain without care" (24.524–526). The differ-ence between Achilles' resignation and that of Job, between stoicism and faith, illustrates the difference between Greek and Hebrew cul-ture. Achilles' gods do not create a sacred history but a literary text; our consolation is not the ultimate justice of God's will but the ultimate conflation of the unrealizable resentment of the hero with the originary paradise of desire.

Thus what has been accomplished in the *Iliad* is not the winning of a war but the arousal and expulsion of resentment. The reader's identification with Achilles in his "wrath" provides his imagination with a utopia of desire, and it is before the backdrop of this desire that the heroic action of the epic unfolds for him. The exploits of the other heroes are of interest only in prolonging the inaction of Achilles and providing models for him to surpass. But no exploits, however extraordinary, could hold for us the interest of his resent-ment, the imaginary satisfaction of which far surpasses any real possibility of the social order.

The *Odyssey*

The *Iliad* is the first major work of secular culture. The second, the *Odyssey*, is both more modern in its outlook and more primitive as literature. It is customary to compare the former with tragedy and the latter with the novel; but this is the novel of chivalry, not the modern novel—*Amadis* and not *Don Quixote*. It is not insignificant that the best-known episodes of the *Odyssey* are the folkloric ones of the Cyclops, the Lotus-Eaters, Circe, and so on, rather than those which directly concern the central theme of revenge on the suitors. Nevertheless, that Homer's second epic is no more a fairy tale than the *Iliad* was a heroic narrative is apparent from both its construction and its thematic emphasis.

Folklore begins as secularized myth that has lost its ritual function and comes to be enjoyed as popular literature. Once this process is under way, folk narrative acquires generative powers of its own, and it becomes useless to seek specific mythical origins for its motifs. In the *Odyssey*, Scylla and Charybdis retain the clearest connection with definite etiological origins—but they are also of slight interest as folklore. The most elaborate folklike episode is, undoubtedly, that of the Cyclops, which attributes to a preagricultural herding society the practice of human sacrifice. Yet the etiological aspect here clearly takes second place to the central Odyssean theme of resourceful vengeance.

We should note that these folktale-like episodes are not included in the Homeric narrative per se. Instead, they are told in a flashback by Odysseus at the court of Alcinous. Rather than episodes of the primary narrative, they are corroborations of its hero's resourceful character. Their relegation to a secondary plane is an indication that, like the purely military episodes in the *Iliad*, framed—via quite different literary means—by the principal theme of Achilles' anger, they correspond to a more primitive stage of literary evolution than the main line of the story. In the *Odyssey* as in the *Iliad*, Homer makes an internal distinction between high and popular culture that appears to have escaped the attention of his interpreters. That the distinction here is more artificial, more dependent on literary form than in the *Iliad* is a sign of its more problematic character. Achilles' anger led to an inaction that framed the actions of the other heroes, devaluing their independent significance while lending them an additional element of suspense. Odysseus is, however, just the opposite of wrathful. His character is adaptable to all circumstances, and only a formal device can emphasize the difference between his primary and secondary praxis.

It was easy to see the relevance of Achilles' wrathfulness for a theory of culture that bases itself on resentment. Odysseus presents a greater challenge. The fact that the contrast between the two heroes later became a commonplace of Greek culture—in Plato's *Hippias Minor*, for example—should, however, indicate to us that not only their characters but their stories stand in symmetrical opposition— one emphasized by their confrontations in both Homeric poems.[14] If Achilles is the archetype of the hubristic man of resentment, Odysseus is the model of practical wisdom. From Roland and Olivier to Julien Sorel and Eugène Rastignac, this opposition has remained present in Western culture, the first group being more sacrificial, the second, more worldly. No doubt the symmetry is not perfect. The tale of a worldly hero always risks falling into the unproblematic realm of popular culture, and this risk is already apparent in the *Odyssey*. But its avoidance is thereby rendered all the more a triumph of literary art; the *Odyssey*, in this sense at least, is already "novelistic."

Odysseus, like Achilles, awaits, but his awaiting is one of calculation rather than obstinacy. His successful revenge on the suitors is a triumph of praxis over self-indulgence. Here it is the latter, not the former, that is based on resentment. Odysseus has no problems in a well-defined hierarchy. His secondary role in the *Iliad* reflects the fact that he, unlike Achilles, "knows his place," just as the secondary position, in terms of both chronology and prestige, of the *Odyssey* with respect to the *Iliad* reflects the secondary nature of the social problematic his story expresses. Achilles resents the insolence of a superior; Odysseus must defend his rightful superiority against the insolence of those beneath him. In identifying with the former, we share his utopian desire for the destruction of the social order; in identifying with the latter, we are on the side of the establishment. It is noteworthy that, of the two poems, the cruelest and most sinister scene of violence takes place in the one devoted not to war but to peacetime civil society. The massacre of the suitors has no counterpart in the *Iliad*.

It is no doubt the essential function of the Telemachus episode that opens the *Odyssey* to characterize the position of the suitors as one of momentarily triumphant resentment against legitimate authority. Because Telemachus is not powerful enough to enforce his right, he is refused the exercise of it; but no one seeks to reestablish order by usurping his rightful place. The suitors are not revolutionaries, but *hommes révoltés*; their satisfaction depends upon the vestigial existence of the very authority-structure they reject. They create a model of egalitarian and therefore "primitive" society, whose leaders are merely *primi inter pares*; but this society exists only as a parasitic growth on the differentiated society that provides it with both food and housing.

This attribution of degeneracy to primitive social form provides the thematic link between the principal plot and the folkloric material of Odysseus's Phaeacian narrative. Homer has no Rousseauean interest in presenting a genetic theory of the social order. Standing at the beginning rather than the end of secular culture, he is concerned to emphasize the incommensurability of primitive and high culture rather than to situate them in an evolutionary framework, let alone one that privileges the former over the latter. The Cyclops or the Laestrygonians are examples, not of what we have evolved from, but merely of what we are not. The human Laestrygonians' indiscriminate slaughter of Odysseus's men in book 10 makes them, indeed, less "civilized" than the monster Scylla, who is satisfied with only six (12.246).[15]

The suitors' inclusion within the walls of Odysseus's *megaron* thus parallels the inclusion of folk material within the *Odyssey*. The hero must respond to the challenge of the suitors as he had done to the

Cyclops or to Circe, but with a difference. In the course of his adventures, he is an interloper whose purpose is merely to escape; at home, he is the master, who must not only escape destruction but himself destroy the society of the suitors. The return of the hero is a well-known folk motif; so is that of the "trickster" who succeeds by ruse rather than force. But the high-cultural element in the *Odyssey* results from the combination of the two motifs. Odysseus is both trickster and hero; he uses tricks to be able subsequently to act heroically. Thus he is neither an unproblematically superior figure who only creates literary interest by his absence nor a powerless individual forced to rely on his wits. Odysseus returns to Ithaca, not as a triumphant king who in the nick of time sweeps away his obstreperous inferiors, but as a victim of shipwreck forced to rebuild his position of mastery on the basis of his judicious estimation of old loyalties and on his manipulation of the resentment of the suitors. The difficulty of precisely defining this conception of the protagonist's role, which is linked, as we shall see, to the moral element of the *Odyssey*, is the underlying reason for at least some and perhaps all of the oft-noted inconsistencies in the details of the hero's return.

Perhaps the most glaring and significant of these concerns the nature of Odysseus's self-revelation to Penelope. As Denys Page has pointed out,[16] the speech of Amphimedon's ghost in the final book (universally assumed to be a later addition, but nevertheless not without pertinence to the plot, at this point at least) suggests a more primitive and folkloristic version of Odysseus's revenge, a version described succinctly by G. S. Kirk[17] as "a simpler and more powerful plot . . . weakened by . . . alterations." In this version, "*everything* conspired to force Penelope to remarry: the suitors themselves, the discovery [by the suitors] of the web-strategem . . . At the eleventh hour Odysseus reveals himself, compounds with her the axe-contest. . . ." "Simpler and more powerful"—than literature. For in this version, where Penelope's web—more famous today than ever in its new role as an allegory of *écriture*—has its *raison d'être*, the whole ambiguity of Odysseus's role would be lacking. If his return were truly at the "eleventh hour," the simple suspense of the plot would deprive his ruse—which would have to be drastically foreshortened and simplified—of more than episodic significance. In league with Penelope in tricking the suitors, Odysseus would control the mechanism of the intrigue too tightly for his disguise as a beggar to modify our perception of his role. The two conceptions of returning hero and beggar would in fact be made incompatible, or at least the cause of an inconsistency far more fundamental than that created by Amphimedon's account or the other textual hints of the simpler version. Similarly, another inconsistency noted by Page[18]—Athena's "transformation" of Odysseus, which is later assimilated to the simple effect of age and his beggar's attire—is attributable to the ambiguity of the hero's assumption of this inferior role for so lengthy a period: from the middle of book 17 to the end of book 21, or close to a fifth of the entire *Odyssey*.

What is at stake here is not so much narrative consistency, or even the character of Odysseus, as the literary effect of the poem, which is to say, its ability to sublimate its hearer's resentment by offering fuel to his desiring imagination. What is crucial is not so much the mechanism of Odysseus's revenge as the length of time it occupies in the text. "Excessive length" is one of the criticisms that Kirk levels against the *Odyssey*. Yet it is precisely in this "excess" that the novellike quality of this narrative is realized. Odysseus's ultimate triumph over the suitors is preceded by his long endurance of their scorn and insults. In this, his role is precisely the inverse of Achilles' in the *Iliad*. Rather than display his "wrath," he patiently dissimulates it. The reader's desire for Odysseus's revenge has none of the utopian quality that Achilles' vengefulness against Agamemnon inspired. On the contrary, the final result obtained by Odysseus is the realization of what for Achilles was the wildest fantasy—the annihilation of all possible rivals within his domain of mastery. What Achilles hopes that war might accomplish, Odysseus accomplishes himself. But before this can happen, the reader's appetite for it has had a long time to be whetted. It is no doubt difficult to call "resentment" the feelings of the master of the house as he plots his revenge. Yet the role endures long enough to make the hearer impatient for the denouement and desirous of the downfall of the suitors, not merely as a realization of justice but as a satisfaction of the resentment he attaches to Odysseus's position. There is, in this impatience, a certain perverse pleasure—a literary masochism, so to speak—which is directly reflected in the violence of Odysseus's ultimate revenge and which is precisely what makes its morality *literary*—that is, not really moral.

It is no accident that this perversity is linked in the *Odyssey*—albeit not always successfully—to a variety of desire that is all but absent from the *Iliad* but that will later come to occupy the principal role in all literature—sexual desire. This permits us to explain another textual difficulty, one related to the inconsistent presentation of Penelope's relationship with her disguised husband. In the 18th book, Penelope, with the help of Athena, makes herself more beautiful and requests gifts from her suitors in view of a forthcoming marriage. Odysseus's reaction to this is described in the following passage: "Thus she spoke; delight came to enduring Odysseus, because she was extorting gifts from them and flattering their hearts with sweet words *while her mind was set on quite other purposes*" (18.282–283). Now if Penelope had indeed been a knowing accomplice of her husband, the underlined words would certainly make better sense.[19] But they are all the more interesting because she is not. Odysseus can enjoy seeing his wife inspire desire in others, regardless of her awareness of his presence, for he knows that her loyalty remains with him. She has, in fact, just regretted his absence, and the "sweet words" with which she encourages the suitors are nothing but a quotation from his own words when he left Troy. Certainly, he cannot really be aware of her "other purposes," and these lines show traces of a more primitive plot-line; but it is far more significant that this whole sequence, by making Penelope a more attractive object of desire, still inaccessible both to the suitors *and to Odysseus*, contributes to the reader's desire and thence to the literary effect. Here, as throughout history, the inaccessibility of the sexual object makes the desire it inspires an antidote to generalized worldly resentment. Penelope's teasing is a perfect example of literary morality: we know that by right she belongs to Odysseus and that the suitors' presumption is destined to be punished; but we enjoy along with Odysseus her arousal of their desire because it adds to the imaginary satisfaction of our own. The slaughter of the suitors inverts this masochistic pleasure into a sadistic one; the massacre avenges us for our loss of desire-object in the final resolution.

The two Homeric epics, so opposite in theme, exemplify the two basic relations of fictional temporality to desire. In the "tragic" *Iliad*, Achilles' awaiting allows us to savor the impossible dreams of his resentment; in the "comic" *Odyssey*, we identify with desires that will ultimately succeed but whose delay and apparent difficulty of implementation are perversely assimilated to the impossible dreams of Achilles. All the major defects of the later poem, including its weak and inauthentic ending, reflect this perversity of the comic, where contingent obstacles to success must be given the appearance of necessary ones, and where the "happy ending" is always a disappointment. Hence the promise of new trials (as at the end of the *Chanson de Roland*); hence the temptation to create spurious new difficulties, like those of the last book, which must nevertheless, like the earlier ones, be resolved. The comic is never so firmly high-cultural as the tragic; the legitimacy of the hero's ambitions makes them a vehicle for our resentment only insofar as we can imagine it to be founded on the illegitimacy of the hierarchy in which we find ourselves, the reversal of which we can hope for only as a collective, not an individual, satisfaction.

The Closure of the Epic Genre

There existed in archaic Greece an epic literature of vast proportions, concerning not only the Trojan War but the stories of the Argonauts, of Thebes, and so on. Yet the creativity of the epic genre did not survive into the classical era, and only the Homeric epics ever acquired cultural significance independently of their legendary content. Perhaps the most striking contrast between Greek esthetic culture and that of the West since the Middle Ages is in the essential unproductiveness of Greek narrative. Only many centuries after the heyday of Greek culture were long narrative fictions, like Heliodorus's third-century *Aethiopica*, again attempted. The quasi-sacred awe in which the Homeric texts were held throughout the classical period may be said to account for this unproductiveness only if we take for granted, as we should not, that no evolution of the epic form like that of the modern novel was possible. What must be explained is both the primacy and the closure of the narrative genre in Greek culture.

The *Iliad* and the *Odyssey* provide two opposite formulas for sublimating resentment, as well as for integrating into this high-cultural sublimation the simpler, nonindividualized forms of popular legend and secularized myth. To claim that these two formulas suffice is, in effect, to deny any importance to their possible adaptation to new content. The epic stands, even for its original audience, in no direct relation to personal experience. The later irruption of such experience into literature, most notably in the lyrics of Archilochus and Sappho, involves the abandonment and, in fact, the rejection of the epic model rather than its prolongation or evolution. With Homer, the high-cultural contribution of epic is closed, and from a modern perspective, in which even the *Aeneid*, like the medieval epic, is of chiefly antiquarian interest, it so remains, until the creation of modern anti-epic narrative by Cervantes nearly two and one-half millennia later. To claim that the narrative ceased to exist or made no progress between Homer and Cervantes is demonstrably false, but there is no doubt that this progress was relatively unproductive of major achievements, and, in the Greek classical era, quite barren of them.

The basic narrative genre may be most simply characterized by the direct communication of its discursive content to the audience by a Subject whose existence is independent of the fictional universe of the work. But such a formal characterization is not only incompatible with later developments like the first-person memoir-novel or the *roman par lettres*—it is too narrow even to include the first-person elements of the Homeric epics, of which Odysseus's lengthy recital of his adventures at the Phaeacian court is the most noteworthy example. The most general characteristic of narrative is the presence of a narrative voice, a subject-of-discourse (who need not be unique), rather than a discursive Subject. The hearer or reader reconstructs in his imagination the objects and actions described by this voice, whose discourse is essentially in the declarative mode. In Homeric epic, as in most narratives, this discourse includes speeches by various actors.

Epic is the first high-cultural departure of narrative from its primitive, popular forms, and this departure is marked in both the *Iliad* and the *Odyssey*. Because, in literary works, we identify with the central figures as individuals, the hypothesis suggested by the closure of the epic genre is that Achilles and Odysseus constitute the sole narrative models of individuality available to the Greeks. This does not mean that the other characters of the epic are not themselves "individuals," but that only in its relationship to the problematic of the two central figures can *any* individuality—that of the secondary characters as well as of the hearer—be guaranteed. Without Achilles, in other words, Agamemnon or Hector, however specifically portrayed, would function only as "types."

In the light of this hypothesis, we may note the obvious: Achilles is the most powerful warrior, and Odysseus the most resourceful intelligence, of the entire fictional universe. That no one can defeat Achilles or outsmart Odysseus is a given of both epics. Nor are these merely specific superiorities, like invincibility in tennis or chess. In the terms of Greek culture in the Homeric era, both heroes are certain victors in any contest of dominance; they incarnate their society's only clearly defined values. Achilles' talent, more concrete, is more primitive and limited; Odysseus's is less heroic but more universal. No direct test of relative strength between the two is conceivable.

This observation provides a clue to yet another doubtful episode of the *Odyssey*, the "Nekyia" of book 11. No doubt various sequences of this episode, like that of the "Boeotian" heroines or the visit to the realm of Minos and the Titans, are later additions. But if, from the standpoint of plot, the core of the Nekyia is Odysseus's conversation with his mother and (more doubtfully) his interrogation of Teiresias, the high point of the scene, which has become proverbial, is Odysseus's encounter with Achilles, in which the latter tells him he would rather be a serf (ἐπάρουρος) in a poor household than the king of the dead (11.489–490). The audience of the *Odyssey*, who must be presumed to know the *Iliad* even though no reference whatever is made to the events therein described, is presumably interested in fixing the contrast between the new hero, who played an important but secondary role in the earlier poem, and the old. In the world of war, Achilles was the greatest soldier, and Agamemnon his chief; but in the world as a whole, of which war is only a part, it is Odysseus who survives both those who had overshadowed him. Thus, in the obviously late 24th book, the funeral of Achilles is described at length by Agamemnon. The poet of the *Odyssey* is concerned to the point of tiresomeness to demonstrate "many-rused" (πολύμητις) Odysseus's superiority to all rivals. The death and regrets of Achilles serve this end. And so, perhaps even more pointedly, does the death of Agamemnon, which is described in the *Odyssey* on no fewer than three occasions.[20] The great king, swiftly returned from the war, could not resist even a single "suitor"; Odysseus, after ten years of wanderings, eliminates a whole flock of them. If the "tragic" Achilles is without peer in war, in an epic written after the great war-epic, the only remaining model of absolute individual superiority is that of the "comic" Odysseus, whose talents permit him to vanquish any obstacle and, most notably, to survive.

These considerations suggest that the closure of epic is due to the fact that it can present only maximal models of human value. If these are to be high-cultural, they must also be models of resentment; and these criteria suffice to determine the themes of both Homeric epics. Achilles' resentment requires his submission to rules of social hierarchy which do not affect his military superiority. Odysseus, whose case is more ambiguous, just as his epic is less clearly distinct from its popular sources, can become a model of resentment only in his feigned submission to the temporarily superior forces of the suitors. Achilles' wrath is the central theme of the *Iliad*, announced from the very first word. For his superior value as such is unproblematic; the mere demonstration of it would provide no point of contact for individual resentment and could only arouse identification on the part of a "popular" hearer for whom the abstract quality of domination can become an object, by definition inaccessible, of desire. In the *Odyssey* it is, rather, the man of many tricks that the Muse should sing (Ἀνδρά μοι ἔννεπε, Μοῦσα, πολύτροπου)—

the man himself, not a specific situation, wrathful or otherwise, because this man is able to use his tricks to extricate himself from any situation, however unfavorable. The locus of desire in the text can only lie *within* one of these "tricks," as indeed it does.

The first step down from myth is the affirmation of absolute worldly superiority. We see this already in the *Gilgamesh Epic*. For this hero, too, is invulnerable to worldly enemies; only his incapacity to attain immortality excludes him from ritual reality and relegates him to the imaginary sacrificial world of fiction. Popular legend develops and vulgarizes the theme of worldly invincibility. In epic, this theme becomes high-cultural by taking into itself the element of resentment. Achilles feels this resentment directly; Odysseus merely places himself in a position where the hearer, in identifying with him in his beggar role, conceives momentarily unfulfillable desires of vengeance. Epic can define individuality only as objective superiority, and individual resentment only as that attached to the position of objective superiority. It cannot incorporate the subjective individuality that will emerge in lyric and dramatic forms, because its narrative Subject remains bound to objectivity.

In antiquity, Homer was considered to be the author not only of the two great epics and the "Homeric Hymns" but of mock-epics like the *Margites* and even the *Batrachomyomachia*. The modern novel, too, is a mock-epic, but one in which the individual subject's inability to attain or even aspire to the absolute superiority of the epic hero has become itself a necessary element of identification. No doubt the classical Athenian, like the reader of *Don Quixote*, could no longer understand the wrath of Achilles as his own because the heroic world, with its one-dimensional criterion of individual value, appeared to him a utopia. But in its quasi-sacred role in Greek culture, Homeric epic bound him to this identification as an article of faith. The high-cultural ethic on its own could not accept or even permit the conception of the novel, and the strength of its principles even in the Christian society of early modern Europe was such that the novel remained a stigmatized genre until the Romantic era. Mock-epic could only be a minor, popular genre in an ancient culture where, in the absence of the abstract moral model furnished by Christianity, objective worldly superiority alone could provide a model for individuality.

The epic model of individuality is that of an absolute individual superiority that must either temporarily or permanently accept a lower place in the social order. The ethical needs of this order must take precedence over the claims of the superior individual. Yet the absolute nature of Achilles' or even Odysseus's superiority is not, for all that, acontextual. Even Achilles can be shot in the heel with an arrow.[21] The context of superior value is, as we have seen, what Hobbes and others called the "state of nature"—human relations devoid of ethical ties. The renouncement of the extra-ethical superiority of warfare or of lawless trickery is imposed as a sacrifice on the civilized individual, whose only real vengeance is imaginary and esthetic. High secular culture, as opposed to narrative monotheism, accepts the permanence of worldly resentment as an inevitable obstacle to the ethical order. Here, too, it is divinity that ultimately enforces this order; the will of Zeus performs the same function as the will of God. But the Jewish tradition makes no concession to the desiring imagination. The reader of Genesis regrets Adam's disobedience and the fall; but paradise is not presented as a mere object of desire but as a lost reality. Conversely, the knowledge Eve seeks in the fruit is, in fact, granted her, and without any interval of literary deferral. Yet the epistemological basis for both cultural developments is ultimately the same.

Polytheism and Monotheism   The Jews, as we have seen, retain their faith in their unique destiny in the face of worldly reversals. This faith is the very essence of monotheism, which, in its original context, meant the denial of divine status to the gods of their neighbors. The Bible is worldly history written from the standpoint of this monotheism. Greek religion was polytheistic. We may then ask in what way polytheism is *essentially* present in epic—and, as a consequence, in the entire lineage of secular culture that is descended from it.

The obvious answer is that a multiplicity of anthropomorphic gods are present in the epics themselves. But it is not the society of the gods that interests us, nor is this society essentially plural. The fifth line of the *Iliad* describes the action as the accomplishment of the design or will of Zeus—Διὸς δ'ἐτελείετο βουλή. The other gods have only secondary powers; calling them "angels" would change nothing in the story. The central locus of pluralism in the *Iliad* is not among gods but among men. To explain the difference between monotheism and polytheism is to explain their respective functionality as ethical conceptions.

The Bible describes in some detail the sociopolitical ground of monotheism in the Jews' refusal of cultural assimilation. It is therefore useful to investigate the question of cultural assimilation in the *Iliad*. Recent research makes it seem at least conceivable that the main events and personalities of the Trojan legend were historical.

In particular, Agamemnon would have been the leader of the Achaean forces, and Achilles a secondary chieftain. What, then, could explain the attribution of individual superiority to the latter? Here we may quote from Denys Page's *History and the Homeric Iliad:*

> . . . The Achaeans did fight the Trojans, and Agamemnon was the name of Mycenae's king.
>
> Achilles is certainly not less historical. Indeed it is probable that *the Mycenaean Epic about Troy, of which the Iliad is the final development, was created in the north of Hellas to glorify Achilles.* It is inconceivable that the court poets of Mycenae should have composed, for recitation to their King, a version of the story in which that king is portrayed in a generally unflattering light; *is roundly abused and insulted by an inferior chieftain from the north;* yet must make humble apology to him. . . . Achilles is preeminent in this story: for that reason, coupled with the fact that the events and the poetical record of the events are so nearly contemporary, he must have been a real person and he must have fought at Troy.[22] [Emphasis added.]

Page's hypothesis is extreme but not unreasonable; it can serve as a useful point of departure. Its most apparent excess is its attributing to a northern source a "Mycenaean Epic about Troy"; it suffices to attribute the *Iliad* alone to this source, especially as there is no evidence for a "Mycenaean Epic" at all, merely of epic *material.*[23] What this hypothesis suggests, and would continue to suggest even in a much weaker version—one that would emphasize post-Mycenaean rather than Mycenaean social divisions—is that the culture that produced the *Iliad* was an alliance among related but separate societies, and that the Achilles-Agamemnon conflict reflects the conflict between specific social groups within this alliance. The origin of the *Iliad* was with the Trojan War, but not simply because wars make for good poetry. It is rather that the necessity of alliance against Troy created an *intersocial model of resentment.* Achilles as king of Phthia was forced to submit to the king of Mycenae's leadership, not as the Hegelian slave submits to his master, but as an ally freely but resentfully submits to a more powerful one in the interest of both. The epic thus generated is a cultural document that functions to transcend the differences among different political units.

Greek polytheism expresses a syncretic cultural unity of independent political units that was well established by the time of the *Iliad.* In myth, polytheism, whether Greek, Babylonian, or even Hindu, emerges only after an internal struggle among the gods leading to the replacement of the old generation (Cronus) with the new (Zeus). In devouring his young, Cronus is acting as a "monotheistic" tribal god more similar to the God of the Hebrews than to Zeus, his son and successor. But Cronus's "jealousy," rather than triumphing, must be overcome in order for a harmonious polytheistic system to be established under the leadership of a new god, who dominates the others without, however, refusing them divine status. This is not a mere allegory of political conflict among the gods' supporters; it reflects a cultural working-out of the already-resolved political problems of state-formation. What distinguishes Greek from Babylonian polytheism is that it survived the states that originally made use of it. The Greek Gods are not local in origin; most of their names are Indo-European. But the specificity of the Greek pantheon reflects both the specific political relations of the early Greek states (Cnossos and Mycenae) and the more general evolution of cultural unity. Zeus may have been "born" (under another name) in Crete, but his triumph maintained itself long after Crete had ceased to be the locus of regional hegemony.

Thus the mere interaction of political units is not enough to explain the *Iliad*. The collective ground of high culture is a necessary but not a sufficient condition. And both "analysts" and "unitarians" on the Homeric question agree that the *Iliad* reached its monumental form only several hundred years after the creation of its putative Mycenaean original, at a time when the political conflicts between Achilles' and Agamemnon's kingdoms were long forgotten. This particular incident from the Trojan War can have evolved into the first high-cultural epic only because it could serve as a model for *individual* resentment *internal* to a single society, which is to say, to society in general.

The original political basis of the *Iliad* is significantly different from the far more ancient base of polytheism in its potentiality for providing such a model. The war alliance creates a temporary hierarchy that is experienced as an ethical necessity but that has not the time—even in ten years—to solidify into a ritual structure. The *Iliad* expresses both the necessity of this hierarchy and the resentment felt toward it by the subordinate allies. A piece of popular literature from the same source would glorify Achilles alone, or show him triumphing over Agamemnon. Popular literature before the existence of high culture excludes the tragic; melodrama develops from tragedy, not directly from myth. Its hearer wants to identify with triumph, not defeat, because his unique individuality is of less importance to him than identification with worldly success. The Achilles of the

Iliad is not a popular hero, because he must accept the limitations imposed on him by the ethical structure of the Achaean camp. In Achilles, a political group otherwise unknown to history is glorified; yet it can only be glorified through him as an individual leader, not as a local god or demigod.

Monotheism exists on a ritual level before the specifically Hebraic development of "narrative monotheism." The Jews could write the Bible only when their temple had been destroyed and their leaders sent off into exile. Their perception of themselves as uniquely chosen by God was an answer to worldly defeat. In contrast with the Greeks and, more particularly, with Achilles' society, their reaction to political subordination was to seek not esthetic but moral compensation. Both accepted their worldly inferiority by including it thematically in their text. But for the Jews, this inferiority was reinterpreted as a God-sent punishment, their superiors being merely God's instruments, whereas in the Greek case, both Achilles' "Phthians" and their superiors were parts of a single culture. The compensatory superiority claimed through Achilles' individual dominance was "natural" rather than cultural, based on value rather than hierarchical order—which is precisely why it can be claimed only in the fictive universe of a literary work. This is a function not merely of national character but of the preexistent cultures and the nature of the dominance-relation between them. Achilles and Agamemnon, hostile or no, were allies against a common foe; the Jews were defeated by enemies. What is of primary interest to us is not the historical occasion for these different cultural solutions, but what the difference of the occasions can tell us about the difference of the solutions. The whole thrust of our previous analysis makes it clear that the locus of expression of this difference must be in the epistemology of resentment.

Zeus may reign over the world of the *Iliad*, but the logic of Achilles' subordination is purely worldly. To grasp the worldly necessity of this subordination is to recognize its arbitrary character with respect to the persons involved. Achilles and Agamemnon act not merely as individuals but as the occupants of socially determined roles, and their mutual dominance is reversed from one aspect of their existence to the other. What is understood here is their underlying symmetry, the interchangeability of resentment and jealousy. In their conflict, they face each other as two angry men hurling similar insults back and forth. And this understanding of symmetry is not limited to this thematically central conflict; it extends as well to the Trojan enemy. True, here too, cultural factors played a role;

Page argues convincingly that the Achaeans and the Trojans—those of "Troy VII"—stemmed from the same racial and cultural stock and probably spoke dialects of the same language. But the equity of treatment of the two sides transcends even this basis. The lesson of literary resentment is the ultimate symmetry of all social roles, hierarchically ordered or not. This "lesson" is not a mere cognitive by-product of the literary work; it is at the very center of its functioning. The purely structural asymmetry of hierarchical social relations is converted in the literary work into an essentially symmetrical relation between individuals motivated by what is not merely seen to be but *experienced* as desire. Resentment learns from literature that, like the jealousy that opposes it, it is nothing but a variety of desire, and that, in consequence, it can obtain only imaginary satisfaction.

This is by no means the lesson of the biblical text. There, difference is essential and absolute. No one could say of the authors of the Bible what has been said of Homer—that "he made his men like gods and his gods like men." All such symmetry is excluded systematically from the outset. The ever-widening gulf between God and man is the result of a series of divine punishments for human presumption; but even walking in the garden of Eden, God is above challenge. His jealousy mirrors man's resentment, but always with man's good in view. No doubt it is possible to suspect the validity of divine difference; this is the contribution of the Enlightenment, when, for the first time, the Bible was read as "literature." The difference between narrative monotheism and secular literature cannot be permanently maintained. But their ultimate fusion, whether it will really take place in historical time or must remain an unattainable ideal of Western culture, is the dissolution of both, not the subsumption of the Bible within the category of literature. At the outset, no one could have understood the common origin of both cultural forms in resentment. It is, no doubt, primary in a study of culture to recognize this origin, but the secondary recognition of their difference is also essential. Without it, the entire history of higher civilization would become merely epiphenomenal.

No doubt the reader of "the Bible as literature" identifies with Adam and desires him to attain immortality. And, in this desire, the reader perceives the ultimate symmetry between Adam and God. But this is a reading that could never have been conceived by the authors of the text wherein the divine difference is defined. The popular Nietzschean dictum, "God is dead," has inspired similar statements about man, notably in the writings of Nietzsche's late disciple Michel Foucault. A more profound understanding of the symmetry of the God-man hierarchy is expressed in Dostoyevski's "You will be as Gods each for the other."[24] The Bible was not written to encourage the conceptualization of this symmetry but to prevent it or, more precisely, to *defer* it as long as possible, that is, to subordinate it to history. The Bible is thus the very opposite of fiction, which offers a utopia in which the ultimate symmetry of hierarchical relations is made present to the imagination.

Literature accomplishes the revelation of new and increasingly fundamental symmetries in the structures of interaction that generate resentment. Such symmetries as that between the superiority of value and that of social hierarchy express a "poetic justice" that is not dissimilar to morality in the Judeo-Christian sense. But the latter is explicit, whereas the former is only implicit. Poetic justice leaves the structures of the fictional world intact; the critical epistemological function of literary resentment is the discovery of the symmetries implied in the construction of this world. The truth-value of such a discovery is not verifiable conceptually. It can only be experienced esthetically, in the maintenance of the object of our desire in its position of inaccessibility throughout the work. We can identify with Achilles' resentment because we know it will be ultimately chastised, just as Agamemnon's excessive jealousy is chastised. Our own experience of resentment may cause us to like Achilles and dislike Agamemnon, but our pleasure in their reconciliation in book 19 comes from our sense of the symmetric unrealizability of both their desires. We desire the one and fear the other (which is to say that we desire the contrary), but our pleasurable absorption in these desires would be disappointed if they were not both ultimately proved unrealizable. As a consequence, the symmetry of crisis is undone, and both Achilles and Agamemnon return to their places in the social order, where the hierarchical difference between the two can no longer be contested by individual value. Our desire for the abolition of this difference has been "purged" by the operation of the narrative.

In the *Odyssey*, the triumph of poetic justice comprises the fulfillment, not the abandonment, of the hero's desire, which only aimed at his restoration to his rightful position. The reversal of his fortunes from victim to executioner may be compared with that promised the "suffering servant" in Isaiah. But Odysseus's triumph takes place within the closed universe of the work, not the open-ended one of history. The suffering servant takes on the sins of his enemies; Odysseus punishes them. In both cases, "sin"—that is, the arrogance of superior position—is eliminated; but God's will leads to universal reciprocity, whereas Odysseus's wreaks general destruction. The biblical text is lacking neither in cruelty nor in vengeance, but the *Odyssey* fosters, on the basis of this symmetry, the desire for vengeance, whereas the Bible excludes all such desire: "Vengeance is mine, saith the Lord."

Homeric epic and the Bible appear at first glance to occupy similarly canonic positions as the central texts of the cultures that grew up around them. But the closure of the Bible is the end of primary textual creation. The closure of Homeric epic, in contrast, gave rise not to massed layers of commentaries but to new forms of literary expression. The closure of the Hebrew canon—although established immutably only some centuries later—corresponds roughly to the period of return from exile (but not of genuine independence) associated with Ezra. Judaism survived as a culture the destruction of its national hopes, but its cultural creativity did not. The productive period of classical Greek culture corresponds as well to the heyday of its political unity, particularly to that of Athens. Yet political decline was marked by no formal closure; no canon of sacred texts was established to keep alive a culture in exile. Greek literary and philosophical texts must be judged by quality, not sacrality. Had the library at Alexandria survived, their quantity would be greater by several degrees of magnitude than what has remained, which is still many times more voluminous than the Bible. This quantity reflects quite a different form of cultural productivity from that, narrow and intensive, of the Jewish tradition.

The epic tradition was never closed in any formal sense. The epic was oral poetry that could not survive in its original form the introduction of literacy. But this does not explain the absence of literary narrative in the Greek tradition. The decline of narrative is the result of the evolution of the Subject of discourse, the "voice" that is responsible for the differences in literary genres. The possibility of such change distinguishes Greek literary culture from the biblical culture wherein the Subject of discourse, whether narrative or lyrical, was merely a reflection of the constant imaginary subjectivity of God. The epic poet spoke at the dictation of the goddess or Muse, as the opening verses of both Homeric poems demonstrate. But this Muse is not Zeus, whose will the poems recount. The sacred objectivity of Homer is that of a cultural memory, not a transcendent will. And the historical basis of this objectivity is the formal guarantee, not the content, of his story.

The ethical structure of the epic is closed, whereas that of the world in which it was composed was open. Thus the closure of epic is of a different sort from that of the ethical structures of simpler societies: it is a closure not inherent in the social relations themselves but imposed upon them by the literary Subject. The popular literature of not-yet-advanced societies is "closed" too, but this closure, in societies devoid of generalized resentment, is guaranteed by the society itself. The obstacles confronted by the hero are as stereotyped as his response to them; only the details allow for the display of individual talent. In a closed society, the plot of a specific tale can be augmented by anyone, just as in a primitive society anyone can elaborate on a myth to explain a new socioeconomic development in cultural terms. In an open society, this is no longer the case.

The openness of the ethical structure need not be exploited in every text; Homer did not spell the doom of popular literature. But, in advanced societies, only in literature and the other arts can the desires generated by generalized resentment achieve resolution. The literary (and, more generally, the esthetic) Subject is the creator of a utopia in which desire may for a time be freely experienced and discharged. In advanced society, the artwork is the only closed universe of experience, and, by the same token, its author, as the creator of this universe, is the only individual to achieve, with respect to his audience, the absolute formal superiority of the big-man at his feast.

The high-cultural work is not merely a pleasurable experience. The desires aroused and resolved within it offer us models of ethical significance in a world in which this significance is no longer given a priori. The epistemology of resentment presents the potential conflicts aroused by value long before values as such can be conceptualized otherwise than in terms of ethical conceptions with which they are ultimately incompatible. The literary work alone gives ethical coherence to advanced societies.

But value is an abstraction whose concrete manifestations are by no means interchangeable. Achilles' resentment is, on the one hand, that of every member of an advanced society, but, on the other, an emotion linked to a specific state of social evolution. Insofar as esthetic experience is sought for the mere pleasure of catharsis, Homer could suffice for all time; but to the extent that this catharsis constitutes an esthetic model of ethically coherent experience, Homer's relevancy is limited to experiences analogous to those of the heroic society he describes. The transformations of social structures can be understood culturally only by means of new texts that express the new conflicts they arouse.

No doubt, Homeric epic was not the definitive end of the epic tradition. Titles like the *Cypria* or the *Argonautica* survive, along with a few fragments, from the post-Homeric era. But the names of their authors rarely do, and most of these works were in fact eventually attributed to Homer.[25] The sub-epical works of Hesiod, composed in the mid-seventh century, are incommensurable with Homeric epic: the *Theogony* is a work of systematic mythology, an abstract variant of creation epics like that of Babylonia (not without interest as a foreshadowing of the theoretical discourse of the pre-Socratics),[26] whereas the *Works and Days* is an example of gnomic popular literature of practical rather than strictly literary interest.

The objective and unproblematic stance of the Homeric subject is that of the popular epic tradition that he transformed into literature. Such a feat could be accomplished only once, and this is the most compelling argument for the unitarian theory. If the *Odyssey* was indeed composed by a second poet in emulation of the *Iliad*, one can only be astonished at the lack of a single word to this effect in the tradition—in contrast, for example, with the fabled contest between Homer and Hesiod. After Homer, the epic became a regressive form, whose literary pretensions could gain their limited credibility only through the use of his name. The precise degree to which the knowledge of writing affected the Homeric epic is unclear, and the theory (developed in particular by Milman Perry[27]) that Homer himself dictated them seems historically untenable. But there is no doubt that the elevation of epic to high-cultural status could not have retained its original significance without writing. High culture requires a system of writing because the individuality of authorship it requires could not otherwise be preserved.

Even if it may be too simple to equate the "naïveté" of the Homeric subject with the oral tradition he brought to an end, this naïveté was at any rate no longer possible in future authors. In Homer, the popular balladeer becomes a central cultural figure; after him, this centrality would lie at the center of every poet's ambition. Histories of culture always neglect the simple fact, well known to every writer and to the historians themselves, of the resentment of the aspiring creator toward the already established figures—dead or alive—who block his path.[28] Homer's was a hard act to follow, for it changed the very conditions under which all future cultural producers would operate, or, indeed, would acquire the very notion of becoming "cultural producers." Homer was the first artist who could take his stand as an individual at the center of his culture. Thus was created a new constitutive ambition for future artists.

But it is not enough to speak of such ambitions in isolation, as though cultural production, with its "anxiety of influence," were an isolated domain. Art is neither independent of nor a reflection of social reality. A society in which Homer could exist was no longer a "heroic" society, either in the sense of the heroic world of the Trojan War that the *Iliad* portrays or in the more apposite sense of the society of Dark Age Greece, where, under conditions of political instability and physical insecurity, military valor had undermined the ethical structure of the ancient order. The very fact of demonstrating the necessity of the conflict between values and the social order is a sign that *these* values no longer obtained, that they had become models for value-in-general in a more peaceful world where colonization and commerce were taking the place of military adventure. The *Odyssey* is already an expression of a postheroic era, and Odysseus is the embodiment of the new, more abstract value of nascent commercial society. Odysseus's infinite resourcefulness is adaptable, as Achilles' is not, to any circumstances, including those of the preexistent social hierarchy. It is this quality that makes him survive where Achilles perishes, and that allows him to reassume his former position in society. His strictly conservative aims contrast clearly with those of Achilles, who would destroy the world if he and Patroclus could be its only survivors. The exponents of Achilles-like valor in the *Odyssey* are, rather, the suitors, whose collectivity is a caricature of the military assembly of the Achaeans before Troy, and whose lives are guided by the need to measure their worthiness as claimants for Penelope's hand. This "comic" rather than "tragic" plot is centered on the representative of the ethical norm, not on those of an extra-ethical value-system. Odysseus, the real soldier, defeats these caricatures of soldiers in a military contest.

Homer's objectivity is a reflection of the primordial status of epic. Homer is the first, minimally individualized literary Subject. But the end of the heroic society that could see its values directly incarnated in the epic heroes was also the end of this minimality. The resentment of a more complex society can identify with that of Achilles and Odysseus, but it cannot be fully expressed in it. In secular culture, the works of the past can never suffice.

Already in the *Odyssey* we hear of bards who sing of the heroes of the Trojan War. Homer portrays himself here not as he was but as he had used to be. Scholars often invoke the shortness of the poems sung by Phemius and Demodocus in the *Odyssey* as empirical evidence of the unique monumentality of Homeric epic. But it would be surprising indeed if they had sung extracts from a pre-Homeric monumental epic, of which they would offer the sole surviving evidence! These singers are subordinate figures, yet he who sings of them is not; and no future singer will be able to take as a given this subordinate role.

LYRIC POETRY

The Birth of Lyric: Archilochus

A theory that grounds culture on resentment can point to few more exemplary figures than Archilochus (ca. 705–640 B.C.), the first lyric poet, known proverbially throughout antiquity for his insults. The illegitimate son of a slave woman, Archilochus boasted about his low birth in his poetry. Himself a soldier, he rejected the heroic ethic, and in one of his most famous surviving fragments, he abandons his shield in order to flee from the enemy.[29] Among Archilochus's fragments are expressions of sexual desire that foreshadow Sappho, as well as a series of popular fables set in epodic verse in various meters. His verses are filled with reminiscences of Homer, whose poems he knew well, but they are never epic in tone or in narrative intent. In his less personal works, generally thought to be earlier than the rest,[30] he attempts to promote the colonial interests of his native Paros and elegizes a disastrous shipwreck that claimed the lives of a number of his fellow citizens.

The beginnings of nearly every genre of the classic lyric—love poetry, satire, fable, the patriotic or personal ode—are to be found among the surviving fragments of Archilochus. The lyric subject here defines itself as capable of everything but heroic narrative. The culture it defines is particularist, not universal. Archilochus's Parian patriotism stands, in relation to the panhellenism of the *Iliad*, not very far indeed from an expression of personal desire. The small and poor island of Paros could assert its interests only within the larger world of Greek commerce. Its chief cultural spokesman expressed within this larger world the significance of a particular loyalty. Yet the general popularity of his poems well demonstrates that, from a cultural standpoint, the poet's role in Parian society was a secondary phenomenon. It is through the expression of the desires of the particular subject, whether individual or collective, that the lyric makes its fundamental contribution to culture.

Archilochus's lyric, like Homer's epic, was not a creation *ab ovo* but a raising of popular forms to a high-cultural level. In Homer, lengthening the poem and presenting the conflict between the hero and his society as essential rather than contingent created the epic as, in effect, a new genre. The extent of Archilochus's innovations with respect to popular literature in literary content and its formalization can less easily be judged, given the extreme fragmentation of his surviving work and our nearly total ignorance concerning his popular sources. But all is transformed once even so traditional a folk genre as the fable is placed within the orbit of the individual subject. Archilochus creates a unique, presumably written text, the Homeric stamp of which is an unmistakable connotative sign, what Barthes called an *écriture*, of the new high literary culture. The literary Subject is no longer a singer of temporally distant heroic deeds but, even in the fables—which are not abstractly moral like Aesop's but are used to chide friends and threaten revenge on enemies—the voice of the poet's personal experience.

The reader of these poems (for this literate poet, the term is already pertinent) is asked to identify not with the desires of an already familiar fictional-historical hero but with those of the poet himself and of his community. The individuality of this identification is a product not of the objectively established superiority of the hero but of the directly given individuality of the poet. This self-expressive role of the Subject was not a precultural given; it had to be assumed in opposition to the epic tradition. Archilochus's poetry appears many centuries younger than Homer's, which it followed in fact by at most three generations, because of its apparently effortless assumption of this role. Archilochus is in no sense a transitional figure; he is arguably the most directly personal lyric poet before the twentieth century.

It is no accident that this expression of ostensibly unproblematic individuality came from a lowborn poet best remembered for his propensity for vicious satire. This is a resentment that can no longer be satisfied by identification with that of Achilles, not to speak of the heroic endurance of Odysseus. But Archilochus's resentment against various figures of legitimate social authority—most particularly Lycambes, who, he tells us, betrayed his promise of his daughter's hand in marriage, perhaps because of second thoughts about the illegitimate birth Archilochus never tired of flaunting—could bear literary fruit only because it was associated with his resentment against the already-established high culture represented by Homer. Archilochus did not deduce Achilles' inadequacy as a model for his personal experience from a rational consideration of the differences between his society and that of the heroic age. What Archilochus attacks is not Achilles but Homer himself, that is, the objective, impersonal stance of the epic Subject. In asserting, for example, his preference for a solid, ungainly general over an elegant one (Lasserre 93), he affirms a truth of personal experience that acquires cultural relevance because it contradicts the aristocratic heroic ethic expressed in Homer. As if in anticipation of Plato's *Ion*, the experience of the real soldier is opposed to that of the mere poet who knows only the outward appearance of things.

The lyric Subject thus places himself audaciously at the center of his cultural universe. The real question is not how he is able to do this but why his readers are willing to accept it. Archilochus exhibits the position of the lyric author in its original simplicity. The Subject is master of his verses but not of the world. He is by his very nature an antihero, a Thersites rather than an Achilles. The resentment of the latter is inevitable, but not constitutive of his being. Were this so, the "wrath of Achilles" would have no meaning. Epic narrative is based on contingency, on a circumstance that reveals contradictions between values and ethical norms. The epic situation is unique because these contradictions are not explicitly present in everyday experience; it attracts our interest because *here* generalized resentment can attach itself to specific obstacles and desire their removal. Conflict is the soul of epic, because in conflict the obstacle becomes personified and symmetrical with the hero. The objective voice of the Subject allows us to witness the conflict from without, to take sides, but also to see both sides, to desire both the satisfaction of the hero and the success of the social order in resolving it. But the imaginary reality of the conflict for us depends upon the reality of its parties' status outside it. They cannot be defined by their conflict; rather, this conflict destroys the solidity of previously held definitions. The discovery that value is not simply an ethical norm among others is made within the text, not presupposed.

Achilles is the most valuable individual; therefore he is bound to become a man of resentment. But Archilochus *defines* himself as a man of resentment. The satiric epodes for which (notwithstanding their present fragmentary condition) he was best known in antiquity define their Subject by his bitterness over a past conflict in which he came out the loser. Lycambes refused to honor his promise; had

Archilochus been able to enforce it, he would not have written about it. The lyric Subject is in a position to crystallize his generalized resentment because he has already experienced the loss of what he thinks he deserves. So, too, has Achilles at the start of the *Iliad,* but Achilles is presented to us by Homer, not by himself. Homer's text recounts Achilles' resentment; it does not express it, save in speeches embedded in the objective discourse. In contrast, Archilochus's invective narrates only to attack; poetry is his only available course of action. Our interest is not in the resolution of the conflict but in the vengeance of the defeated—a vengeance that is only imaginary in the poem itself but whose worldly consequences may be quite real.

The voice of lyric poetry is the unmediated voice of resentment. If epic narrative may be compared to the monotheistic narrative of the Bible, lyric invective should be compared to the invective of the prophets. Archilochus's denunciations of Lycambes and of other privileged members of society are not without parallels in the prophets, who are scarcely sparing with their insults. And the audience for these diatribes is expected to reject the injustice of the privileged in the same way. But the voice of God that speaks through the prophet is quite differently motivated from the voice of Archilochus. The prophet displays the epistemology of resentment, but he does not express personal grievances. God's threats of punishment are based on moral grounds; the victims he defends are the widows and orphans, not himself. Archilochus, too, is something of a spokesman for widows and orphans, but only because, as a penniless illegitimate son, he is one of them.[31] He, too, alleges moral principles in his condemnations, but these are taken from the folk morality of popular fable rather than from an extrapolation of the divine will. And although the reader sides with the author in both cases, his moral conclusions are not of the same nature. In the one case, the evil must be destroyed; in the other, the poet must achieve imaginary revenge. It is the literary Subject whose griefs we espouse, while remaining in the superior position of the outsider. Thus we laugh at Archilochus's literary victims, whereas those of the prophets are expected to inspire us with righteous indignation.

The lyric Subject, even outside of satire, defines himself by what he lacks, not by what he is. The question of value arises, not in its ultimately necessary conflict with the ethical order, but as a problem in itself. The Subject perceives himself as deserving of more than he has, as possessor of a value that has gone unrecognized, as capable of aspiring to objects of desire placed beyond his reach by society or its more influential members. Just as the narrator of epic was, within his fictional universe, the only absolutely central Subject, so the lyric Subject is at the center of his, and this centrality has now become a means of revenge upon the social order that limits his possibilities of action.

The notion of value that finds expression in the lyric is no longer objectively defined in terms of the society; it has been generalized into a justification of desire as such. The lack of fulfillment of the Subject's desire is a scandal because society promotes in each of its subjects an indefinite aspiration toward the acquisition of desirable objects. The dynamic commercial society in which Archilochus wrote encouraged its members to convert their resentment into a praxis oriented toward the acquisition of value, which had already come to be measured largely in monetary terms. Archilochus protests against the still-existing barriers, incarnated in the remnants of aristocracy, to the fulfillment of such a praxis. These barriers are no longer, strictly speaking, ethical structures. In their opposition to "bourgeois" value, they have become contaminated and transformed into values themselves: the value of birth is affirmed in opposition to the value of monetary wealth. Archilochus, of course, had neither, although he could at least dream of acquiring the second. Thus his appeal to divine justice in the first Epode, where he invokes a fable to threaten the traitorous Lycambes, is free from all sociology. Archilochus represents no particular value; he expresses the frustrations of a society free enough to encourage an individualist praxis but not rationally organized enough to reward it.

In Bonnard's chronology, Archilochus, at the age of forty, left Paros for its colony Thasos, presumably because of failure to achieve material security on the mother island.[32] Much of his patriotic poetry dates from this Thasian period and appears to express the political resentment of a popular party in its battles with the aristocrats.[33] The lyric Subject, who expresses an individual desire as significant in itself, can become the spokesman of a political faction—not necessarily a popular one—because, in effect, such a Subject is per se a "political" individual, one whose desires are of concern to the community. The Greek lyric is not, of course, found only on the left, but it is significant that it begins there—just as does Greek politics—in the organized expression of the less fortunate.

Archilochus's resentment leads him to politics, for it was "always already" political. Yet interspersed with the satiric attacks on privilege and pretension are a few fragments of the most universally practiced of all lyric genres, that of love poetry. Archilochus's expressions of sexual desire are powerful and direct, as are his descriptions of female beauty.[34] It is, however, to be doubted that sexual desire occupied in any sense a privileged position in Archilochus's *oeuvre*, or even that he ever wrote love poems in the traditional sense of pleas addressed to the beloved. For Archilochus's poetry is addressed to the community, to his friends and enemies. In Archilochus, the literary Subject has become personal, but the formal mechanism of his poetry remains narrative: where he does not simply recount his adventures and misfortunes, he uses fables to project the just deserts of his victims. Failing this, he may simply paint the latter in abusive terms that themselves constitute revenge. But in no case does the poem create its own fictional universe of lyric communication with the beloved. Archilochus expresses his desires and expects his reader to identify with them, but he does not require us to read them as other than worldly utterances. They persuade us by their rhetoric, not by their poetics; the poetic Subject we sympathize with is always real, worldly Archilochus, not an abstract lyric protagonist whose desires we reconstruct for ourselves. Archilochus's lyric Subject embodies a rejection of Homer's both in objectivity and in values, but all of his poetry could be assimilated to the narrative passages and speeches of a personal anti-*Iliad*. In terms of the creation of poetic form, the true founder of the lyric tradition is not Archilochus but Sappho.

Sappho and Lyric Subjectivity

The lyric Subject is the archetype of the high-cultural individual, abstracted from the specific social values that find expression a priori in narrative and a posteriori in dramatic forms. The lyric Subject is a subject of desire, and, in particular, of sexual desire, the place of which in culture the lyric permits us to understand. Whereas the composition of narrative and dramatic works is a specialized métier, anyone can write poetry, as nearly all literate persons have done at one time or another. The ever-present possibility of the lyric is the ever-necessary possibility of asserting the significance of one's own individuality. The influence of the lyric subjectivity is far vaster than that of poetry; the notion of romantic love that pervades our society, more potent than ever in our era of sexual liberation and easy divorce, is a product of the lyric tradition. In a society that relegates the cultural to a distraction, each individual retreats to an antisociety of intimacy for which the lyric has provided the conceptual framework as well as the vocabulary. "I love you" is not a spontaneous expression of desire; the emotional complex it reflects has been molded by a millennial lyric tradition. The creation of a universal ideal of the couple as bound by romantic love may well be the most important specifically identifiable example of the contribution of secular cultural forms to our everyday lives.

The main thrust of feminism in the cultural sphere has been to oppose the role of the woman placed on a pedestal by generations of lyric poets. Yet the originator of the lyric tradition was a woman— before modern times, at least, the only undeniably great female poet. Sappho's poetry is a further example of the cultural productivity of resentment, and in this example, her sex is anything but accidental. Archilochus expresses the resentment of the outsider against social values that he, for various reasons, does not possess. Sappho expresses hers by the lyrical affirmation of countervalues grounded in an artificial female subsociety.

It is generally conjectured that Sappho was a kind of pagan mother superior, the directrix of a finishing school that prepared the girls of the Lesbian aristocracy for marriage.[35] Unlike Archilochus, who had at least a plausible claim to the hand of Neobule, Sappho had no possibility whatever of retaining permanent ties with the girls she loved. Her creation of lyric form was a reaction to her formal separation from the objects of her desire. Archilochus's claims of injustice are addressed to his fellow citizens; Sappho's claims of affection are addressed to her former charges, who alone may be presumed to understand them. As readers, we are, so to speak, eavesdroppers in a love duet—one that is in reality a triangle, with the legitimate husband as Sappho's rival. But this communication situation is a formal, not a worldly reality. We may never know whether Sappho's poems actually reached their addressees—the best-known of whom, Anactoria, was far off in Lydia with her new husband—but this is unimportant. The poems themselves—and we fortunately possess a few that are nearly complete—re-create an imaginary context for the reader's desire, in which we are asked to share that of the poet while putting ourselves in the place of the directly addressed beloved. By making us await, not a narrative denouement, but a concluding image, the lyric poet, having made herself the master of our desire, persuades us of its "poetic justice" in the face of its worldly impossibility.

The difference between the sexes is marked from the beginning of culture, but this does not suffice to make sexuality itself culturally significant. The primary function of culture is to avert conflict, not to express emotions, and whether such conflict involves a woman or a share in the feast is unimportant so long as both desire-objects retain the same passive role. Whatever the extent of female independence in primitive society, structural anthropology's definition of kinship systems as mechanisms for regulating the exchange of women among different social groups remains justified. When women sit in council, or even go to war along with the men, this involves no modification of the basic cultural structures, and the same is true whether premarital promiscuity or adultery is encouraged or severely punished. Marriage rules and incest prohibitions imply the danger of men fighting over women, just as the rules that regulate ritual feasts imply the danger of their fighting over portions of meat. In primitive societies, and even in the ancient empires—and within Judaism—it is the latter set of rules that are basic and that provide the model for understanding the former.

The specificity of sexual desire begins to emerge only when rivalrous conflict has been assimilated within the dual relationship of the sexual partners. Achilles and Agamemnon quarrel over Briseis, just as Greeks and Trojans fought over Helen—and Odysseus and the suitors still fought over Penelope.[36] Archilochus spares no insults on Neobule, whom he describes as a shameless, decrepit prostitute in the eighth Epode; but his real quarrel is with Lycambes, who rejected his marriage offer. This is not merely a reflection of mores; it reflects the structure of Archilochus's resentment, which is directed primarily at that which prevents his acquisition of the desire-object, not at the desire-object itself.

In Sappho, this is no longer the case. The love relationship constitutes a self-sufficient, intimate universe wherein the lover's resentment may be imaginarily transformed into a desire that sustains rather than destroys the relationship. In Lobel α 5, arguably Sappho's finest extant poem, Anactoria is far away; Sappho does not revile her for her absence but depicts her so as to make her imaginarily present. The presence of the beloved to the lover becomes an internal desire-object for the reader (and, presumably, for the beloved herself as reader) that the poem satisfies, as a sublimated substitute for the worldly satisfaction of the poet's desire.[37] Not content to deny, as Archilochus does, the pertinence of Homer's heroic ethic to real-life combat, Sappho depreciates the military altogether and establishes in the first strophe a radically personal value-system: "Some say that the cavalry, some the infantry, some the navy is the most beautiful thing on the black earth, but I say it is what one loves." This is an *art poétique* that will permit the poet to declare in conclusion Anactoria more beautiful than the famous Lydian army where she is presently quartered with her soldier husband. Sappho illustrates this principle with the example of Helen, who gave up "the best of men" to follow the object of her love. The whole Trojan War, in Sappho's terms, was fought on lyric, not on epic principles; the public value of military glory is a secondary one, because its exercise is dependent on the private value of individual desire. Sappho's resentment here attacks simultaneously the masculine world that marries her charges to soldiers and the Homeric epic that expresses its ethical conception.

This is a radical lyricism that nourishes the entire lyric tradition, although it will not continue to be maintained in open opposition to the social order. Sappho's affirmation of this position depended on the fragile existence of the counter-society of women in which she lived and functioned. Her radicalism is both the beginning and the end of the feminine lyric because it is not adaptable to life experience within the social order. The masculine lyric that follows is both opposed to and in collusion with this order, and this dialectical relation and its evolution effectively exclude women. Sappho's radical lyric demonstrates the fragile freedom of literary forms to recast the world in their own image. Culture is irreducible to empirical sociology. The sociologist, no doubt, would call Sappho's view an illusion, but the whole lyric tradition exists to demonstrate its cultural power. For the private lyricism of each individual member of society continues to be a precondition of his or her successful functioning within the public sphere.

The lyric derives its poetic vocabulary and, in Archilochus at least, its rhetorical form (if not its content) from epic. But the writings of Sappho and of the majority of the early Greek lyricists reveal the more fundamental importance of another source—ritual. It is no accident that, along with her love poetry, Sappho wrote hymns to Aphrodite, or that her fellow Lesbian Alcaeus included a hymn to Hermes among his politically oriented verses (an expression of the resentment of the right rather than of the left: Alcaeus' bête noire was the lowborn leader Pittacus). The nascent lyric genre is not a derivative, through epic, of mythical narrative; it possesses its own links with ritual that are, in fact, more direct than those of epic— more direct, and more problematic as well. The religious element of Homeric epic displays a vast distance in attitude and material— and presumably, therefore, a vast distance in time—from anything that could be used as the mythical element of a ritual. With lyric, the relationship is much closer; the love poem is a kind of hymn requesting directly or indirectly the presence, not of a divinity, but of the beloved.

The first poem (Lobel α 1) in the standard editions of Sappho curiously illustrates this derivation of the lyric: the poet addresses a prayer to Aphrodite to inspire love in an unnamed girl in order to requite her for the girl's coldness. The poem is a prayer to the goddess; but the modern unbeliever will read it as a love poem addressed in fact to the beloved, as was so often the case in the "pagan" poetry of the Renaissance. The goddess may be addressed directly, for she presumably has the welfare of her suppliant at heart; the beloved can only be persuaded indirectly. The imperative function of prayer is, nevertheless, present in both cases, and for similar reasons: the beloved, center of the lover's existence and inaccessible object of her desire, plays for her the role of a personal divinity. The more radically we interpret the autonomy of the lyric subjectivity, the more the intimate world of the love poem may be assimilated to a relationship between worshiper and deity.

The two elements Sappho combines in her prayer to Aphrodite are thus potentially in conflict. That they are not so for Sappho is irrelevant. Secular culture's threat to ritual is all the more dangerous for being implicit, like the nineteenth-century esthetic religiosity that aroused such concern among theologians. The closeness of the lyric to the forms of ritual lends its usurpation by secular aims a more radical effect than was the case for epic. The lyric subjectivity that rejects all socially given values and norms puts in question the significance of the communal activity of ritual. The passage from epic to lyric may thus be understood as the transition from a lower to a higher stage in a process of deritualization.

Despite the considerable interest of inquiries like E. R. Dodds's *The Greeks and the Irrational*,[38] there is no doubt that the strength of Greek secular culture corresponded to the weakness of Greek religion. Polytheism could not truly adapt itself to advanced society; it was an imperial ecumenism without an emperor. Yet, conversely, the literary Subject, once created, possessed a dynamic that precluded the emergence of monotheism. A secular polytheism of literature gradually substituted itself for the old ritual polytheism. As the mortal fictional heroes became objects of identification, the immortal gods became objects of resentment; Achilles' expression of this attitude has already been quoted. Sappho's contamination of sacred and profane is indicative of a further degeneration in the power of the ritual sphere. When she declares that the man about to wed one of her beloved girls "seems equal to the gods" in his felicity, this is not a mere Homeric epithet; religion has become no more than a source of sacred metaphors that emphasize the centrality of an object of worldly desire.

The epic hero railed against the gods as transcendental guarantors of his limited earthly fate; his resentment in this world inspired a resentment toward the other world. This is a classic case of the epistemology of resentment, by which we discover the scandal of our mortality on the analogy with the scandal of the worldly limitation of value. The Jew sublimates his resentment in his submission to God's will; Achilles submits, but without sublimation. Sappho prays to the gods, but, as a literary work, her prayer is addressed to her human audience, and the gods are mere rhetorical devices. In the lyric prayer, the divinity is appealed to as an ally of the poet's desire, whether personal or civic, against a worldly object of resentment. But in the imaginary world of the poem, the reality of the god is irrelevant; if we imagine Aphrodite coming to Sappho's aid, the question of the goddess's extratextual existence cannot be raised without destroying the esthetic closure of the work. Aphrodite's worshipers would not even have thought to raise such questions; their goddess, reduced to an incarnate emotion, had become little more than a figure of speech.[39]

TRAGEDY

Tragedy as we know it, even in Aeschylus, is already far from what we may conceive to be its origins, for example in the works of Thespis listed by Suidas. The difficulty of what might be called the "tragic problem," in contrast with the Homeric problem, is itself a problem. For whoever Homer was or was not, the creation of monumental epic attributed to him involved a transition—perceived intuitively if not conceptually by Homeric scholars—between popular and high culture, between a culture of groups and a culture of individuals. Furthermore, whatever the exact details of this transition, the passage from the original materials—heroic ballads—to the final products—epics—is easily seen to have occurred through a process of elaboration, expansion, and combination. This ease has no doubt beguiled scholars into neglecting the all-important qualitative difference between the epic *topos* "wrath of hero" and the *literary* Homeric treatment of the wrath of Achilles, but that is a matter of interpretation, not of reconstitution.

In contrast, in the case of Athenian tragedy, which evolved several centuries later in the cultural capital of Greek civilization, the very facts of the reconstitution are lacking and are unlikely ever to be brought to light. This is not merely because pre-Aeschylean texts are unavailable—although we cannot avoid reflecting on why this is the case. It is because of the inherent impossibility of defining the status of the protodramatic forms about which we hypothesize. Tragedy, more even than lyric, is linked to ritual, and to such an extent that the creation of prototragic models cannot define their separation. The passage from ritually enacted mimesis to literature may well have been a gradual one that passed through many stages in many places; its specifically Athenian history could hardly have been self-contained. Even with the fragments we possess, we can reconstitute the emergence of what we have referred to as the lyric subjectivity; but the origin of the "dramatic subjectivity" remains a mystery.

The only appropriate approach is, then, to accept the verdict of textual survival. Whatever the hypothesized qualities of pre-Aeschylean tragedy, we must take Aeschylus's work as the first example of tragedy *as a literary form*, assuming that the lack of interest in the texts of earlier plays is a sign of their relative lack of literary value, if not necessarily of literariness per se. The question of formal origins then loses its critical importance for the tragic question. The meticulous scholarship of Francisco Rodriguez Adrados in his *Festival, Comedy and Tragedy*[40] has demonstrated the wealth of ritual elements to be found in extant tragedy; the search for a linear scheme of evolution must be rejected as illusory. Nor can we fruitfully attempt to determine a general structure of "the tragic" by references to Aristotle or to more idiosyncratic critical doctrines. As Adrados affirms,[41] the suffering of the superior hero is the true common denominator of the tragic form, as is borne out by an examination of even the existing corpus.

The abandonment of these illusory aims does not impose limitations on the scope of our analysis; on the contrary. What is important in tragedy, as in Homeric epic, is not the a priori exigencies of the form, but the way in which it is used to formalize a specific content. We need not even consider such matters as the relation of tragedy to hero cults that may have involved mimetic elements. For the existence of tragedy demonstrates the insufficiency of these cults, their lack of resistance to the progressive universalization of high secular culture. Athenian tragedy took place within the ritual context of the Dionysian festival; but this context had become a mere shell enclosing a literary performance. If the epic converted myth into literature and the lyric did the same for choral marriage-hymns and the like, with tragedy, literature penetrated into the very heart of ritual: the sacrifice whose origin is traceable to the originary event.[42] In tragedy, sacrifice becomes wholly humanized, and the victim, an object of sympathy. No doubt a similar development occurred in the emergence of epic from myth. But the epic hero is a god who has been debased to a human level, whereas the tragic hero is a victim who has been raised up. Achilles is "tragic" because, *from the standpoint of tragedy*, humanized god and humanized victim are the same; but this is not the perspective of the epic. Achilles' godlike aspects—his divine mother, his quasi-invulnerability, his armor forged by Hephaestus—are essential to his epic role and altogether foreign to tragedy. Achilles' mortality is, so to speak, "minimal"; he is *all but* immortal, and his knowledge of his fate makes his death appear a scandal, not a normal end.[43] Achilles' resentment is applied to a purely human situation; that is what makes the *Iliad* literature and not folklore. But it is already implicit in the descent from divinity to mortality, as was the case with Gilgamesh.

Achilles' mortality in the *Iliad* is doubled by that of Patroclus on the one hand and Hector on the other, both of whom, in their praxis of error and penalty, are closer to the tragic norm than Achilles. But it is not by accident that tragedy itself ignores these "tragic" figures. No tragic hero, not even the Eteocles and Xerxes of Aeschylus, who attain a maximum of tragic epicality, simply falls on the field of honor as a result of an overestimation of his valor. This is hubris, to be sure, but an epic hubris that only reinforces the military value-structure of the heroic universe. The real problem of this structure, as we have seen, lies in its conflict with the social order, and it is to the resolution of this conflict that death is subordinated. Tragedy is not concerned with value in this sense. In the tragic universe, the victim is given a priori; his incarnation of the highest values of his society—for example, in the case of Oedipus—does not pose the problem of the limitations of value in conflict with the social order, but of the internal limitations of praxis as such. Achilles is the "best of the Achaeans," remains the best throughout, neither suffers because of his valor nor finds it turned against himself. If he suffers, it is because being "best" does not make him *first*. This is quite different from Oedipus's problem.

It may be objected that our distinction between tragedy and epic is based on diachronic considerations foreign to the works themselves: how do we know the difference between debased god and exalted victim when they are both equally human? But are they? This objection may be answered on the phenomenological grounds of the different forms of presentation in drama and epic.

Narrative presents its characters to our imagination, not to our sight. The scene of oral narrative has only one "actor," the reciter, whose centrality is comparable to that of the big-man in redistributive feasts. To the extent that he mimes the characters in their speeches, he makes their presence felt, but in no sense realized. In the agon of debate, say between Achilles and Agamemnon in book 1 of the *Iliad*, the rhapsode must play both parts and continue after the debate to provide the narration. His presence only makes clearer the absence of the personages of his narrative, and his miming them, rather than enhancing the sense of their real presence, only emphasizes by its transitory character that we cannot see, but can only imagine, their being and emotions. The nonpresence of the narrative hero is a sign of his derivation from the transcendental—and immortal—figures of myth. It invites us to imagine him "larger than life," as is consonant with the epic text—and even with the novel, to the extent that the novel begins as, and never entirely ceases to be, a mock-epic.

Because of the freedom of the imagination to transcend earthly obstacles—and we should not forget that, for the original audience of epic, no realist literary tradition had habituated them to lesser expectations—the sufferings of the epic hero are perceived as a fatal limitation imposed from without on desire, a denial of wish-fulfillment under the authority of the central Subject. Because each character exists only within our imagination, we experience his suffering directly, and his downfall as a loss of part of ourself. But, at the same time, we survive the defeat of our desires and emerge strengthened by the renouncement imposed on us by the narrative. This *internal* sacrifice of the infinity of our desire, carried out under the direction of the narrative Subject, leaves us free to admire the humanly limited but still unrivaled greatness of the epic hero. His being remains exemplary, if not his fate; and the bulk of the narrative is devoted to the manifestation of this being in praxis. Achilles' resentment cannot be rewarded, but knowing this, we take pleasure in sharing it. The very length of the monumental epic is a tribute to the joy of its imaginary universe that we leave with regret, strengthened in our individuality through the *askesis* of sacrifice.

Tragedy, in contrast, takes place on the stage among real people. True, these are only actors, but they fix and externalize our imagination just as ritual mimesis had always done. Only the romantic feels an inner exaltation in his identification with the tragic hero. The possibility of romanticism must not be overlooked; but in its nondifferentiation of the tragic from the epic it spells the end of tragedy. Nor is this end to be lamented, for it is a moment of the unification that is the end of culture, the breaking down of barriers between cultural categories that today has reached a far more advanced stage. But although we live in a postromantic era in which even the Bible may be read "as literature," we should not project our cultural ecumenism onto the past. Our phenomenological intuition of the different literary forms can serve us only if we fix our imagination on the concrete differential elements of these forms, without allowing it to wander along the branching paths of modernism. Let us note, not altogether parenthetically, that it is resentment that opens these paths: our desire to be not merely Achilles but Oedipus, Dionysus, or even Jesus is a desire for centrality at all costs that only our modern sense of anonymity could inspire. Antiquity could go no further than Erostratus, but only the most lucid Romantics could resist taking the further step of transforming the sufferings of anonymity into the signs of election.[44]

The tragic hero is identified with not by imaginary choice but by the irresistible attraction of his central position. The limitation that falls upon him as a contingent fate is already present in his very being. The tragic mask dehumanizes but does not glorify: it is the mask of the victim, not of the deity. The action on the tragic stage is not exalting but pathetic. It is not the mere physical limitations of the stage that prevent its being used as a scene of military triumphs and defeats. If the protagonist we meet with is not already a victim—as is the case in *Ajax*, the *Prometheus*, or *Oedipus at Colonus*—he is at any rate never shown in an attitude of heroic triumph. At best, his sufferings may be avenged, like those of Electra. As spectators of tragedy, we undergo *askesis* not in being forced to detach ourselves from our desire but in having to bear witness to the suffering that attends its forbidden realization.

The theatrical triumphs of dramatic heroes are limited to the all-too-human level; the "happy endings" of such Euripidean tragedies as the *Alcestis* (sometimes classed as a satyr play) or the *Ion* are produced by gods, not by the might of the protagonists. The stage is a world of visible limitation, and the action that unfolds upon it consists of the—mostly unsuccessful—pursuit of limited aims. The "heroic" stage is not that of tragedy but of opera; nothing is more foreign to the Greek conception of the theater. The opera, with its rich and often fantastic decor—particularly in its classical heyday in the seventeenth century—expresses a spectacular transcendence of theatrical limitations that is not the original function of the stage but a dialectical reaction to it.

All this may appear to imply the esthetic inferiority of tragedy to epic; in fact, what is revealed is tragedy's greater potential intensity. The literary greatness of tragedy is measured not by the constraints of the genre but by its possibilities for operation within these constraints. The sufferings of the victim may be directly presented as of interest in themselves; this is the case in the early tragedies of Aeschylus, the earliest we possess, which strike us today as "untheatrical." But in the works of Sophocles and, in a very different way, in the *Oresteia*, tragedy goes far beyond the elegiac. The productivity of the tragic formula, its canalization and concentration of the productivity of resentment, gives tragedy first place among all the forms of secular culture.

Tragedy is the most radical form of literature because it is closest to reproducing as literature the structures of the original event. We may even go a step further and claim that tragedy is the most radical form of secular culture; for literature, because of its dependence on language and thereby on the imaginary scene of representation, is the most radical of the arts. The question that remains is the capital one: how did the detachment of the tragic complex from its ritual origin take place? And this question can be answered only on the basis of the evolution not of ritual but of culture—in particular, that of the literary Subject.

The lyric Subject originally expressed the resentment of an individual, whether personal or patriotic. In the poetry of Pindar, this individual element has become linked to the fate not of polity or a faction but of a social group—the aristocracy—and of its value-system, opposed more or less obliquely to that of the "democratic" commercial stratum, which finds its own lyric expression in the civic poetry of Solon. What is lacking on the political level, and what tragedy provides, is a synthesis, an expression of the unity of the *polis* that can offer its own interpretation of the heroic myths that had served as the basis for Pindar's aristocratic separatism. The athlete-heroes of Pindar are not mere citizens; they are made to descend, like Achilles, from the gods. The task of tragedy, viewed in this light, is to demonstrate that this heroic material—precisely what the "progressive" lyricism of Archilochus had rejected—can be interpreted as unifying the contemporary community rather than dividing it.

A similar train of thought inspired Gerald Else to hypothesize that tragedy was instituted by Solon himself for openly civic ends.[45] We cannot comment on the factual element of this hypothesis, which has not received general acceptance. But one aspect at least of the general skepticism toward Else's thesis is based on a theoretical misunderstanding concerning the ritual origin of tragedy. Else's theory, whatever its defects, is alone in facing squarely the question of the existence of tragedy as a *secular* literary form. It may be that he secularizes too much in neglecting the ritual elements of which tragedy is composed. But the composition itself was not a ritual phenomenon.

Yet neither can it be explained politically. The force that brings about the tragic adaptation of mythicoritual content to civic ends is the force not of a political but of a cultural subject. Else's civic tragedy is purely hypothetical; but even if it really existed, we may express doubts concerning its esthetic value. In our present state of knowledge, we must assume that Aeschylus's introduction of the second actor (Aristotle, *Poetics* 1449a) marks the essential transition from the didactic *and* the ritual to the literary. Aeschylus, not Solon or Thespis or Arion, must serve as our model of the original tragic Subject.

Aeschylus

In tragedy, as in all dramatic forms, the Subject has no designated representative in the work. The very notion of the "Subject" is thus called in question. So long as the work was the discourse of a single voice—even if on occasion accompanied by a chorus—the author's human reality guaranteed the significance of his discourse, whether it was the retelling of an old story, as in epic, or the lyric expression of a more or less individualized self. By detaching the author from his discourse, drama refuses independent significance to the personal and collective discourses of which it is composed. From all evidence, this detachment took place gradually within a choral setting through the distinction, first of the leader (coryphaeus) from the remainder of the chorus, then of the first and subsequently of the second actor. It is this last innovation that Aristotle attributes to Aeschylus.

The confrontation of the agon is the central element of drama[46] as well as the point at which the partiality of the individual stance and speech of the characters is definitively established. In the stichomythic agons between the two actors that are a feature of even the earliest extant plays (*Persian Women, Seven against Thebes*), the formal symmetry of the dialogue eliminates any residual centrality that may have remained attached to the coryphaeus. We have observed the importance of the symmetry of the dialogues of the *Iliad*—for example, in the dispute between Achilles and Agamemnon. But in the epic, the partiality of the individual speaker is presented from the standpoint of a narrative center from which the objective difference between the speakers can be maintained.[47] And in the symmetrical responsive form of choral lyric, the center is filled by a ritual object. In contrast, the symmetrical presence of two actors in confrontation, neither of whom can claim absolute possession of the central role, is no longer formal but substantial, that is, mimetic of ethical crisis. Aeschylus's introduction of the second actor, which created the minimal conditions for the radically undifferentiated dramatic agon, should thus rightfully be regarded as the genesis of a new cultural form.[48]

What is revealed in the agon is not the identity of all dramatic roles but the essential symmetry of their *discourse*, that is, of the nonritual language by which each seeks to distinguish the rationality of his position. The agon of ritual reflects the nondifferentiation of the participants at the moment that precedes the return to order realized in the sacrifice and distribution. The passage from nondifferentiation to (re)differentiation occurs in tragedy as well; but the "victim" is not an animal to be killed and eaten, nor even a *pharmakos* to be beaten and driven out, but a member of secular society. From the derivational standpoint, no doubt, the suffering of the tragic hero is a secular version of the sufferings of the pharmakos. But its secularization is precisely what must be explained. Suffering is now presented in the nonritual, profane world as the necessary outcome of the failed rationality of the agon. Nondifferentiation leads to differentiation, but only through the victimization of the one or more of the participants. This is not a mere reassertion of the preexistent ethical order. The tragic protagonist does not return to his former place in the hierarchy, for the agon signifies the breakdown of the old hierarchy, and order can be restored only by a *decision* that replaces the symmetry of combat by a new order. This decision is not an arbitrary ritual act; it must be motivated, and its motivation—its justice—makes tragedy the locus of the highest morality attainable within Greek secular culture.

Whereas the prophetic "suffering servant" is innocent simply because he stands in the role of the victim, tragedy must find the victim guilty in order to justify his victimization. Both these symmetrically opposed positions transcend the domain of ritual and dissolve the link between the human victim and his originally alimentary counterpart. Ritual sacrifice needs a real, edible victim in order to provide appetitive satisfaction to the community. The human victims of Deutero-Isaiah and of Athenian tragedy are both heirs of sacrifice in its most anthropomorphized version, that of the pharmakos or (human) scapegoat. Yet the one is promised future reward for bearing the sins of his tormentors, while the other's suffering is reinterpreted as a justified punishment for an act of hubris. The one case is historical, the other, esthetic. The sufferings of the Jewish people are made a sign of their real centrality; those of the tragic hero, of his fictional guilt. In both cases, an equilibrium is established that annuls all trace of the appetitive asymmetry that ritual retains from the original scene of representation. The tension between periphery and center, multiple victimizers and single victim, has now lost all connection with the precultural distinction between subject and appetitive object. The only further step that can be taken—the step that constitutes modernity—is the decentralization of the whole structure, the elimination of the unique center. But this cannot be accomplished through a return to the indifferentiation of the agon. On the contrary, decentralization is founded on universal differentiation. In a decentralized social order, each subject is his own center and a peripheral element for all the others. To quote Pascal, "le centre est partout, et la circonférence, nulle part."

The prophetic vision of the chosen suffering servant is the product of a resentment that turns present worldly inferiority into future superiority. The point of view of the victim is the source, not the result, of the concept of election. Christianity will extend this role from the Jewish people to the individual human subject in general: in the person of Christ, every person becomes the chosen son of God.[49] For the modern mind—romantic or postromantic—the tragic subject, guilty or not, plays the same role as Christ. But for the original Athenian audience, such an interpretation would have been incomprehensible. The singular position of the victim was not a model to be imitated but an object of envy and horror—envy before the sacrifice, horror afterward. Resentment toward the central position of secular power is converted into its opposite when this position, after passing through the nondifferentiation of the agon, is transformed into that of the victim. The ritual accomplishment of this conversion—for example, in the "dying god" festivals that so fascinated Fraser—is incompatible with the existence of advanced society. The sacrificial figure can have at best symbolic powers; as we have observed, a society that can ritually murder its kings cannot be more than a step removed from primitive egalitarianism.

But Athenian society could murder its kings in the theater. This is the link between tragedy and the establishment of the democratic polis. Tragedy may have been established under the tyrant Peisistratus, but by the time it attains with Aeschylus its genuine independence from its lyricoritual origins, it celebrates the triumph of democratic over monarchic forms. The *Oresteia* ends with the acquittal of Orestes by the Areopagus; but it began with the murder of a king by the "tyrant"-usurper Aegisthus. From kingship to tyranny to democracy, the *Oresteia* recounts the political history of Greece and, in particular, of Athens, through a series of agonic conversions of positive into negative centrality, of power into victimage. The positive ending—the acquittal of the final "victim"— is the necessary outcome of Aeschylus's historical-political vision of tragedy. The world of fiction, and thus of tragedy, abolishes itself in history. This is a less radical vision of tragedy than we shall later find in Sophocles, but it is by no means unfaithful to the tragic premise. The acquittal of the last victim signifies the end of victimage, for Aeschylus's vision of tragedy is not a "tragic vision" eternally applicable to man. In Aeschylean tragedy, the esthetic remains subordinate to the civic; the reality of the polis ultimately abolishes the transitional world of fictional representation.

The *hubris* of the tragic protagonist is fundamentally different from the "wrath" of either Achilles or Odysseus, both of which are foci of identification for the hearer's resentment. It is no accident that it is Agamemnon, not Achilles, who becomes a tragic protagonist. The epic hero is not at the top of the social hierarchy; when he arrives there, as in the *Odyssey*, it is the end of the story. The tragic hero, in contrast, begins characteristically at the top, although this is not a formal necessity. The tragic victim never expresses the resentment of the superior individual toward a stable social hierarchy. For the social order of tragedy is not merely resented but actively called in question. The tragic universe as a whole may be compared to that of Achilles' resentful fantasies. The hierarchy disappears in the agon and must be established anew. Its restoration or even (as in some plays of Euripides) its unperturbed permanence is shown to be dependent on the suffering of the protagonist whose martyrdom, in the absence of ritual sacrifice, creates for it a new, secular center.

The independence of the dramatic scene from objective social hierarchy makes it a possible locus for fantastic solutions to social problems, in which justified resentment triumphs over corrupt reality. This mechanism will later be found at work in the plays of Aristophanes. But in tragedy, the hero's suffering remains the central focus. In Aeschylus's optimistic dramaturgy, resentment motivates not a fantastic transformation of present reality but the historical passage from archaic monarchy to Athenian democracy. Ritual's sacrificial reinforcement of the status quo is transformed in Aeschylean tragedy into a means of political reflection. Aeschylus's presentation of tragic victimage as historically functional is anything but unfaithful to the ritual origins of tragedy, which Sophocles will later deprive of any but their esthetic function.

Prometheus is the simplest, most abstract of Aeschylus's heroes. His sufferings at the hands of Zeus will eventually be ended (in the *Prometheus Unbound*, the lost third play of the trilogy); but his revolt against the king of the gods has brought the permanent benefit of civilization to mankind. The cyclical temporality of ritual, expressed in the original Prometheus myth by the perpetuity of his torture (to which the eagle's gnawing at his liver gives a peculiarly "alimentary" form), is replaced by the irreversible passage from suffering to liberation. This passage abolishes the tyrannical subjection of Prometheus to Zeus, just as the conclusion of the *Oresteia* replaces the tyranny of the Eumenides by the judicial decision of the Areopagus.

Aeschylean tragedy remains, like myth, an expression of institutional etiology; but its mechanism is not the arbitrary desire of a god but the passage of resentment from excess to equilibrium through the suffering of one or more individuals. The final order is the "end of history," because in it, resentment is no longer possible; power relations, whether between Persia and Greece, Prometheus and Zeus, or Eumenides and Areopagus, from really or potentially absolute, have become relative and nonconflictive.

This form of tragedy does not strike the modern reader as good theater. Its generally elegiac character bears witness both to its lyric origins and to its civic function. Its victims are elegiac because their suffering is a ritual *donnée* secularized in lyric; their fates are undramatic because the emphasis is less on the peripateia of their individual lives than on the historical construction of which they are a part. Xerxes is, no doubt, a victim of hubris precipitated from good fortune into bad, but his misfortune is of interest above all in its positive value for Greece. It is not insignificant that the first extant tragedy of Aeschylus—and the only extant tragedy on a historical subject—makes use of the suffering most easily construed as constructive: the suffering of one's enemies.

The esthetic inadequacy of such tragedies as the *Persian Women* or the *Seven* need not be denied on grounds of cultural relativity or excused on those of archaism. Neither argument was necessary for Homer, nor will it be for Sophocles. Tragedy's potential for formal evolution—which significantly distinguishes it from epic—is realized not only in the progression from Aeschylus to Sophocles but in the Marlowe-Shakespeare and Corneille-Racine progressions within modern Europe's major tragic traditions. Not only is tragedy a more productive form than monumental epic; it is a form impelled toward esthetic radicalization by literary rivalry. The competitive nature of Athenian dramatic festivals was, at different times, the source of both Aeschylus's civism and Sophocles' radical individualism. The same need to win popular favor that made Aeschylus glorify the institutions of the polis forced Sophocles to pose his challenge on the point of Aeschylus's vulnerability, that of esthetic closure.

Sophocles

Tragedy first reached a high-cultural level in a period of patriotic fervor—that of the Persian War—and it could surpass this level only by becoming independent of civic considerations. Sophocles' universality is possible only on the basis of Aeschylus's equation of Athenian democracy with the *telos* of history. Here we witness the cultural productivity of organized competition, the agon between creative subjects. Sophocles' movement toward greater esthetic effect is also a cognitive step toward grasping the sacrificial origins of the social order—a step that will later be succeeded by that of Euripides in the *Bacchae*. The Athenian public's search for confirmation of its public achievements thus leads to the discovery of the highest form of esthetic individuality. The greatness and the limitations of Greek culture are revealed by its faith in the decentralized structure of "free market" competition within—and only within—the esthetic sphere.

In Sophoclean tragedy, the suffering of the hero becomes a source of maximal individuation, which may be given a public function (as in the late plays *Philoctetes* and *Oedipus at Colonus*) but which never involves a simple integration into a restructured social cosmos. Aeschylus's heroes lose their tragic individuality in the final reconciliation, as is most clearly visible in the *Oresteia;* those of Sophocles can be reconciled only on the basis of this individuality. No new polis can contain Oedipus or even the body of Ajax. The social order does not change but merely accepts the inclusion within itself of one who can have no ordinary role within it, whose inclusion emphasizes an absolute difference from this order, which is a fictional realization of the sacred. The ritual function of suffering is here fully secularized, which is to say, fully estheticized.

Sophocles' theater is "absurd" in that the fate of his protagonists is independent of their will; it is in their reaction to this fate that they give it human significance. The tragic chaos that in Aeschylus

prepared the institution of a historically new order is resolved by
Sophocles only within the roles of the protagonists. The frequency
of suicide and self-mutilation in this theater (six suicides in seven
extant plays, not counting an attempt by Philoctetes and, of course,
Oedipus's self-blinding) signifies the transfer of ritual violence from
the collectivity to the victim himself. Suffering is brought on by
"fate," but the sacrifice is performed by the self. The only true
murders in Sophocles are those committed by Orestes in the *Electra*.
Otherwise, no protagonist dies unwillingly by another's hand; Antigone hangs herself, and Heracles orders the lighting of his funeral
pyre. The suffering of Sophocles' heroes prepares their apotheosis;
their fate impels them to sacrifice themselves for our esthetic benefit.

Resentment in Aeschylus was ultimately a positive force in the
creation of the new order. We see this directly in Prometheus, but
even Clytemnestra's resentment against Agamemnon was a necessary
stage in the historical transition from monarchy to democracy. The
final world of Aeschylus is one in which resentment is no longer
possible, and it is therefore not surprising that in plays like the *Persian
Women* or even the *Seven*, there is no resentment in the protagonist.
Xerxes may be punished for invading Greece, but his punishment
entails merely that he accept a dichotomous order of (Persian) land
and (Greek) sea that accords both sides an autonomous and noncom-
petitive status.[50] This is not to say that the *spectator's* resentment is
not mobilized. The Persians' sufferings as a result of Greek military
victories afford a transparent outlet for Athenian *Schadenfreude*. If
Persia had been a weaker instead of a stronger power, this could not
be the case: we should be no longer in the world of Aeschylus but
in that of Thucydides. Resentment against Persia is justified, for she
is the aggressor, but it is productive not of destruction but of equilibrium, of mutual recognition. Throughout Aeschylean tragedy,
the spectator's resentment will be transformed into the desire for
justice rather than for unlimited revenge. The sacrifice of the tragic
victim expiates a past crime, and even if it gives rise to a new one
that we desire to see punished, each stage of the process brings it
closer to clarity and resolution. The curse of Agamemnon's house
is an ancient and unfathomable one; Clytemnestra's guilt is patent;
Orestes, even before his acquittal, suffers only as a private person
innocent of public crime. Even in the Oedipal trilogy that ends with
Eteocles' death in the *Seven*, the reconciliation in death of the brothers
brings peace to Thebes and ends the fatal curse that began with
Laius. These original maledictions on royal houses have as their
object the "crime" of difference itself. Their mystery is that of a

resentment devoid of any link to morality; the king's house is accursed merely because as king he draws to himself the resentment of his subjects. In the series of murders that follow, resentment objectifies itself and can finally be expelled.

But in Sophocles, the historical series is condensed into a single life. The original curse has no time to objectify itself in a crime that can be expiated; the hero's suffering expiates nothing but the crime of difference. Aeschylus's plots are edifying; Sophocles' are merely dramatic in their creation of false hopes. The spectator desires to have his cake and eat it too: to admire the sacrificial hero without the sacrifice's taking place. Here it is the protagonist's resentment that attracts the spectator's. The hero is cursed with his esthetic role which, unlike that of the ritual scapegoat, must be borne within a profane world where the absolute difference of the sacred disguises itself in the trappings of an apparently stable ethical structure. The scapegoat's death is, from the standpoint of absolute (Judeo-Christian) morality, *more* unjust, more horrible than that of the tragic hero; but the formal barrier of the sacred deprives its victim of self-expression. The tragic victim's suffering becomes esthetically perceptible as a result of the breakdown of this barrier.

Tragedy defines better than any other literary form the limits of the ethical function of secular culture. It is natural for the reader of tragedy to judge it as a model of the human condition and thus to speak of Aeschylus's or Sophocles' works as proposing "visions" of this condition. The works themselves often contain gnomic statements—usually in the speeches of the chorus—affirming the exemplarity of the fate of their main characters. Yet to speak of "tragic vision" is to forget that the tragic protagonist's suffering, if not his destruction, is an a priori that reflects his secularized sacrificial function. A naively naturalistic interpreter of ritual might assimilate the death of the sacrificial victim to the negative moment of the agricultural cycle, but no one would think to claim that the victim, even when fully anthropologized, typifies the human condition.[51] The victim's death is, on the contrary, supposed to preserve the happiness of the others, whether this is defined as appetitive satisfaction or as liberation from evil forces concentrated in the victim as scapegoat. The literary "victim" is by no means assimilable to that of ritual; but neither has he been converted into a figure of Everyman whose sufferings supposedly typify our own.[52] Tragedy's victims attract our identification without ceasing to be victims, no longer of our desires, but of our resentment. The objectification of the victimage of this resentment in a central figure maintains, in the world of tragedy, a ritual structure even in the absence of the formal separation enforced by the sacred.

Tragedy thus confers a worldly significance upon suffering, not simply because suffering is part of the human condition but because human society is founded upon an institution—the scene of representation—in which centrality and suffering necessarily accompany each other. The sufferings of tragic heroes combine in diverse degrees the mental and the physical; their common basis is simply difference, derived from the original scene but now wholly anthropomorphized. Difference structures the fictional universe, however uncomfortable it may be for the protagonist. If, in Aeschylus, it can on occasion be accepted as fatal and impersonal (Eteocles) or as appropriate retribution for error (*Persian Women*), in Sophocles it is inevitably accompanied by resentment. For although tragedy may be linked to the most fundamental anthropological structure, this link is established only by means of the epistemology of resentment. In Aeschylus, this epistemology is not fully assumed by the tragic character, for whom the sacred still defines his individual fate—just as, in Euripides, the characters are not sufficiently individualized to be able to assume it. The universal presence of resentment in Sophoclean tragedy thus reflects its exemplary esthetic closure.

The Oedipus Tyrannus   Resentment is the contestation of essential difference. This contestation is both necessary and futile; it becomes tragic when exercised by one whose individual difference is essential to the constitution of the fictional universe of which he is a part. Contestation is not essential to the tragic hero; but it is the only possible reaction of the audience to the suffering he must endure as the result of his differentiation. The resentment of the Sophoclean hero marks him as the most fully developed tragic figure because in our identification with him we must contest the structure of the tragic universe from within.

The particular exemplarity of the *Oedipus Tyrannus* lies in the radicality of this contestation; Oedipus alone of tragic heroes suffers as a spectator of his own constitutive difference, which he reconstructs before us on stage. The tragic is exposed as arbitrary at the very moment it is shown to be inevitable. Resentment here attains the structural purity of the original paradox of desire; the tragic difference we would abolish is made to exist in the very act of its abolition. But whereas desire in its purest form is altogether lacking in specific content, the purest resentment is the most concrete. Desire is paradoxical because it conceives an inconceivable fulfillment. The purest desire is the one that conceives the least—the desire to be God. In contrast, resentment begins with real human difference; its most radical form is that in which its contestation puts in question its own basis within human difference—which is, first of all, the biological separation of the child from his parents. This basis is both objective and subjective, for it unites the physical constitution of the human subject with his mental ability to perceive the difference he contests.

The tragic hero is made unique by his suffering. Insofar as we have identified with his worldly greatness, we find it painful to imagine ourselves suffering in his place, and we are thus made to realize the limits of such identification. That enviable greatness is inseparable from disaster is culture's consolation for our resentment. But Oedipus's greatness is that of resentment itself. His intelligence is not, like Achilles' prowess, a socially accepted value; it is not a means that has become recognized as a subsidiary end, but a means pure and simple. The Sphinx's riddle designates an animal monstrous in its differences from itself, without a well-defined nature even in the fundamental animal activity of locomotion. To answer the riddle is not only to see the unity behind the differences but to see man as the only animal that can create such differences; and this is possible only for the spirit of resentment that ever seeks to reduce difference to its common denominator.

Oedipus refuses to let his progress be detained by unessential difference; the Sphinx and Laius both impose difference as an obstacle, and both are destroyed by his reaction. This destruction of differences is the meaning of the oracle, and Oedipus's swollen feet define the suffering entailed by the straight path he follows. This path is a praxis that returns him to his origin, which is to say, to his own given difference that cannot be undone by praxis. The critique of difference defines the most monstrous difference, because it destroys the differences that define the human.

The irony of the *Oedipus* defines its literary exemplarity because it reproduces in the praxis of the protagonist, and consequently in the final epiphany, the domination of the temporal by the atemporal that characterizes the esthetic work in general. For the praxis by which the protagonist attempts to realize his desire exists within a construction predetermined by the literary Subject. The temporality of the literary agon is that of worldly desire, but its outcome exists contemporaneously with it in the mind of the Subject. This double temporality reveals itself in the hero's investigation that only uncovers what was predetermined before he was born.

Thus interpretation cannot choose between fated guilt and arbitrary ritual expulsion. Oedipus is sacrificed at the end, but was
singled out from the beginning. His unique difference is his resentment that destroys difference; but man who creates difference
creates at the same time in all men the resentment that destroys it.
Oedipus kills his father in the ultimate crime of resentment, but we
cannot distinguish between the view that this crime is, as the oracle
says, specifically directed at his father and the view that the murder
occurred because, in his violence, Oedipus rejected any possible
difference between his father and anyone else. Once essential difference exists, resentment exists, and once resentment becomes the
foundation of praxis, we can no longer distinguish between acts that
affirm and acts that destroy difference.

The epistemology of resentment thus leads to the knowledge that
knowledge of difference is impossible. Difference must be accepted
on faith, which is to say, guaranteed by ritual. If we follow Sandor
Goodheart's interpretation[53] and claim that Oedipus "ritually" accepts guilt wihout being sure that he has killed his father, then we
must say that his being guilty of incest—which is the only guilt he
expresses at any length in the play and which Goodheart cannot
claim to be placed in doubt—is equally "ritual." Why, indeed, should
he—should anyone—feel guilty for sleeping with his mother? Certain differences must be respected, but the wisdom that enforces
this imperative is that of ritual, not of science. The sacred differences
Oedipus violates may be anterior to the social distinctions that generate resentment, but once resentment exists, no difference can be
definitively affirmed to be sacred.

But we need not make the specific nature of these crimes the
source of Oedipus's downfall. Even if we rid ourselves of the last
ounce of ritual prejudice, we can still identify with Oedipus's self-
blinding as the penalty for the futility of his entire praxis, of the
straight path taken since youth to avoid the fate destined him by
the oracle. In this sense, killing father and marrying mother are no
more than arbitrary ritual insults; the real crime is that through
trying all his life to avoid certain acts, he has in fact brought them
about. In this most abstract interpretation, we forgo every difference
save one, which is thereupon shown to be the only essential difference: that between hero and Subject, between the fictional world
and the real world for which the former was created. Even if we
acquit Oedipus of patricide and incest, we must convict him of hubris
for attempting to act like a free agent when he is only a character
in a play.

But this difference is precisely the foundation of secular culture. In the open ethical structure of advanced societies, we require someone to construct an ethically closed fictional world in which our resentment can be sublimated. But for this to be possible, the inhabitants of this world must inhabit it as their own reality. For them, resentment is real and praxis is possible. Yet our identification with them is predicated on the fact that their praxis is not possible after all, that whether happy or sad, their end is already determined from without. Oedipus's story realizes this external determination both within the fictional universe and within the consciousness of the protagonist.

The literary work is not a model of life but a model of desire. Its hero's exemplarity is not one that can be followed in life, because life cannot be conceived in accordance with such a model, that is, as the revelation of the impossibility of a coherent praxis based on desire. Oedipus bridges the gap between ritual and the unconscious because his life incarnates the paradox of desire. "Incarnation" is in fact temporalization. The time of the work's performance is that in which the spectator, through his temporary acceptance of the mastery of the literary Subject, can desire the desires of Oedipus. In this secular sublimation of resentment we learn the necessity of the absolute difference between the center and the periphery of the scene of representation as the basis of desire. Whether this desire is fulfilled in the fictional world is secondary. But its nonfulfillment and, more significantly, the revelation of its paradoxicality add to the exemplarity of the literary work as a model for our necessary sacrifice of our own desire. By this criterion, tragedy is the most exemplary literary form, and the *Oedipus Tyrannus* its most exemplary manifestation.

Euripides

It is significant that, although of the three great tragedians it was Sophocles who was the most perfect Athenian, occupying a number of high administrative functions and never, like the two others, leaving to put on his plays elsewhere, his work is of the three the least connected to the historical fortunes of the polis. Only in the *Oedipus at Colonus*, written at the very end of his lengthy career, does Athens come to benefit from the tragic hero's sufferings. But the anomaly vanishes as soon as we realize that the Sophocles' tribute to Athens was made through an *oeuvre* that, by creating the highest form of individuality, demonstrated the polis's capacity to absorb such individuality. In the *Oedipus at Colonus*, it is not the hero's suffering and sacrifice within the play that redounds to the glory of Athens but the fact that he is accepted by the city in full knowledge of his tragic past. Theseus's city—and Sophocles' native village—become beneficiaries of Oedipus's sacred status because they have already witnessed his tragic sacralization on stage. We are far here from Aeschylus's notion of historical purgation through crime and punishment,[54] and even farther from the sacrificial bloodbaths by which Euripides alternately attempts to justify or to invalidate historical reality.

Sophoclean tragedy is dominated by suicide, by self-sacrifice. Euripides' tragic universe is, in contrast, dominated by murder. A play like *The Trojan Women* is little more than a series of executions, and even in a "tragicomedy" like the *Ion*, the main characters are prevented from killing each other only by divine intervention. Suffering in Euripides is justified neither by past injustice, as in Aeschylus, nor by the self-contradictions of desiring hubris, as in Sophocles. As H. D. F. Kitto lucidly points out,[55] many of Euripides' tragedies would fall, in Aristotelian terms, in the category of *miaron*—unclean. Where Aeschylus remains close to ritual in displaying the positive function of suffering, Euripides, by presenting amoral ritual sacrifice in a secular context, inverts its original purpose. Thus if the ritual purpose of Polyxena's sacrifice on the tomb of Achilles was to purify the sacrificers, its effect in the *Hecuba* is, rather, to soil them and thereby to impress the spectator with the evil of military conquest. Euripides' victims, unlike Sophocles', are pathetic, unable to find in their fate more than an occasion for displaying their base or noble character. Their deaths leave us with a sense of injustice that we are moved to project onto real-world situations—such as the Peloponnesian War—that are analogous to those that brought them about. The baseness of Menelaus and Hermione in the *Andromache* is expected to fuel our hatred for Sparta, just as Menelaus's more positive portrayal in the *Helen* may be seen as a token of reconciliation. Here tragedy is no longer even secularized ritual but merely a form of collective image-making.

A number of Euripides' tragedies enact etiological myths and find in the existence of a cult the justification for otherwise unjustifiable deaths. Such is the case with Neoptolomeus's death in the *Andromache* or with that of Hippolytus, in whose play Artemis arrives *ex machina* to offer the establishment of a cult as a consolation to her champion. The contemporaneous existence of these cults being presumed known to the spectators, the plays thus explain the link between arbitrary (that is, ritual) sacrifice and divinization, at least in the partial sense of the hero cults.[56]

The etiological element in the *Hippolytus* thus remains closer to the crassly political annexation of Hercules and Ion (= Ionia) to Athens in the *Heracles* and the *Ion* than to the religious insight of the *Bacchae*. For the latter depicts the etiological function, not of a mythicohistorical event, but of a ritual clearly defined as such. In the *Hippolytus*, it is the hero's failure to sacrifice to Aphrodite that precipitates his demise, but the nature of the goddess of love makes her rites intimate rather than collective; the hero's refusal is allegorical of a psychological trait that leads to catastrophe only through conflict with other human desires—those of Phaedra and of Theseus. In the *Bacchae*, the rites scorned by Pentheus are rites pure and simple, and his conflict is directly with the divinity. Artemis stands as Aphrodite's double in the *Hippolytus*, but in the *Bacchae* it is the human Pentheus who doubles the god's role and whose sacrifice reproduces the *sparagmos* of the Dionysian legend. The etiological element refers not to a hero cult but to a sacred rite, and the death of the human protagonist suggests a sacrificial etiology far more subversive of ritual than Euripides' oft-cited "rationalism." Agricultural festivities associated with the pine tree (in which Dionysus hides Pentheus so that he may observe the Bacchic rites) are mentioned by Pausanias (2.2.5) at Corinth, and A. G. Bather[57] describes a Russian rite in which an effigy in female dress is made to undergo the same ordeal as Pentheus. Pentheus is a sacrificial representative of the "dying god" Dionysus, in whose honor tragedy was performed. The penultimate tragedy of Euripides—and of the classical tragedies preserved for us from antiquity—describes the origin, not of a cult, but of tragedy itself.

The overt presence of ritual, which appears to render further interpretation superfluous, should not obscure the fact that this etiology of tragedy remains nonetheless a tragedy, and a very Euripidean one at that. The hero's suffering may be justified as a punishment for impiety, but this interpretation merely takes for granted Dionysus's divine status, which Pentheus has every worldly reason to question. Pentheus is the quintessential Euripidean hero, for he is at the same time an impious tyrant (like Lycus in the *Heracles* or Eurystheus in the *Heraclids*) and a helpless sacrificial victim; he is punished for his crimes and yet, typically of Euripides, the horror of his punishment is disproportionate to his crime. For however much his dismemberment may be identified with that of the god himself, he will not as a human individual be restored to life. The question of Euripides' piety can never be resolved by this play, which is, by the very fact of its religiosity, the most desacralizing of tragedies. That anthropologists can use it as a source for the study of the Dionysian cult is no sign that its author was any more pious than the anthropologists themselves. The ease with which Western ethnologists can accept the most atrocious practices as signs of piety— including, as we have seen, even those of the Aztecs—blinds them to the fact that tragedy is distinct from ritual in its focus on the finality of human suffering. That man and god are doubles only makes their absolute distinction all the more atrocious.

The ambiguities of the *Bacchae* are complementary to those of the *Oedipus*. The latter is his own double, both victim and executioner. In Sophocles' play, tragedy comes to resemble ritual because worldly interaction reproduces the structures of ritual. In Euripides, it is the ritual that absorbs the worldly, the antagonist of the rite taking on unknowingly the role of the victim-protagonist within it. The common ground of both plays, which is that of Greek tragedy in general, lies in their reproduction of the genesis and structure of desire on the scene of representation. The tragic scene is derived from that of ritual, but we do not have to refer to ritual to understand tragedy. The genesis of desire is the genesis of difference, and difference antedates ritual: it begins, in the original event, at the origin of language.

The animal victim of the original event becomes the tragic hero by passing through a moment, real or imaginary, in which it becomes human, that is, in which only a social difference separates it from its sacrificers.[58] In contrast with "sacrificial" secular literature, the spectator-participant of such a rite has no desire whatever to stand in the place of the victim. The latter takes on himself the sins of his persecutors, which is to say, their resentment; the difference in which he stands confirms the others in their submission to the absolute necessity of social difference.

To identify with the victim, as in tragedy, one must have lost confidence enough in the permanence of the social order to be able to imagine oneself in his place. Yet such loss of confidence is a necessary consequence of generalized resentment, which inspires in the members of advanced societies a wholesale critique of such differences. For the Greeks, the institution of tyranny, as opposed to traditional monarchy, signifies the submission of the entire social hierarchy—with the significant exception of the barrier between citizen and slave—to the critique of resentment. A tyrant's power is never wholly legitimate; its holder is always an at least potential victim of public dissatisfaction. That Oedipus and Pentheus—the latter's hereditary accession to the throne notwithstanding—may both be qualified as tyrants is of no small significance in their tragic exemplarity. For this role places them at the center of their respective societies as foci for the resentment of their fellow citizens.

The tragic hero's sufferings, enacted on a but slightly transformed version of the scene of ritual representation, are transparently analogous to those of a sacrificial victim; and in many of Euripides' plays, including the last, *Iphigenia in Aulis*, the analogy is made explicit. The spectator's identification with the fictional victim distinguishes secular tragedy from ritual, where a real victim is immolated. But the central figure of the victim is not only a potential subject of resentment identified with the public; he is, at the same time, its potential object. In the *Iphigenia*, as often in Euripides' plays, the victim is weak and innocent, and our resentment is directed rather at her executioners. But in the purest example of Euripidean as of Sophoclean tragedy, the two roles of subject and object are combined. Pentheus is, like Oedipus, a man of resentment, jealous of his authority and intolerant of the power exercised by his divine double over the women of his city. We identify both with his resentful centrality and with the periphery from which he is resented, just as we do with Oedipus; what tragedy at its most radical demonstrates is that the two sentiments are inseparable and in fact indistinguishable.

We both see ourselves in the place of the central protagonist and examine him from the safety of the periphery. The tragic hero is a figure of both self and other. The position of the tyrant-victim is that of the potentially highest individuality, because he stands at the central focus in both the subjective and objective aspects of his role. The imaginary sacrifice of this central figure consoles us for lack of centrality; at the same time it teaches us through example the paradoxicality of our own desire for centrality. The praxis of the tragic hero must fail because the ultimate aim of desire is the position of the original victim. The desiring subject wants to possess divinity; divinity, however, is not an individual attribute but a collective category that can be realized only by the unique victim of the collectivity. To wish to be a god is not merely impious and absurd; it leads fatally to the repetition of the underlying mechanism of sacralization, which is precisely that of the original scene. All worldly desire does not lead so far; but the lesson of tragedy is that this is its ultimate consequence.

The tragic hero is destroyed because he can truly desire; we survive because we cannot, although we can identify with the hero's desire. The object of tragic praxis is real and necessary; the hero faces a genuine obstacle that he must surmount in order to retain his central position. Thus we learn that the realizability of our own worldly desires is dependent on our own noncentral position, or in other words, on our—and our desires'—insignificance. We participate in culture as consumers, not producers; we must accept our marginal status because the center, sacred or not, is forbidden us.

Conclusion

All culture is a defense of the social order against conflict, a deferral of violence through representation. What is at the center of the scene of representation is forbidden to the participants at the periphery. From the elementary levels through the establishment of primitive society, the central object is sacralized by the ritual reproduction of the scene and can never be appropriated by an individual member of the community. The unsatisfiable "producer's desire" for the object is consoled by the consumption of a portion of the sacrificial feast. Here, all are equal rivals, their rivalry held in check by the community's hypostasis of its own potential violence.

However much content may later be added to ritual, its basic form remains unchanged; the model of ritual behavior implies an equality of the profane participants with respect to an inappropriable sacred center. Hence, when ritual itself becomes a source of satisfaction for desire, the potential for conflict thus brought about cannot be regulated by ritual alone. The differential satisfaction of the central "big-man" figure gives rise to resentment, and resentment becomes the basis for a new stage of culture.

The culture of resentment has its beginnings in the first differentiated societies and attains the limit of its early development in the ancient empires. The supplementing of myth by popular culture was doubtless not very dramatic, but resentment in early societies was not yet a very powerful force. Hegel's intuition that Egyptian culture expresses itself most fully in its architecture reflects a fundamental truth concerning the means by which such a culture deals with resentment: through repression. Hieratic monumental architecture and sculpture encourage the acceptance of social difference by submission to its sheer power. That, in the later dynasties, important figures below royal rank began to "immortalize" themselves in smaller versions of royal tombs attests to the top-down nature of Egyptian society. The reaction of their second-level occupants toward the divine status of the pharaohs was not to criticize this status but to seek a more modest level of divinity for themselves. The failure of Egypt to develop a high culture in either the Jewish or the Greek sense reflects the invulnerability to criticism of its hydraulically based social structure.

The Jewish and Greek cultures correspond to a postimperial stage of society in which hierarchical difference has become vulnerable to resentment. The Jewish solution guarantees not the social order per se but its moral and legal basis through the appeal to a transcendental divinity. The Jewish God is no longer tribal; he has passed through a period of hominization. For Judaism is posterior to the divinization of the monarch in Egypt and Babylonia. God's laws transcend the social hierarchy, and his rule is never incarnate in a human ruler. The biblical narrative sublimates resentment by posing the difference between God and man as constitutive of the ethical norms of society independently of any hierarchy. Hierarchical society is explained as visited on man as a punishment for his resentment of this absolute difference, the *felix culpa* of Adam's—or the snake's—desire. The promise of restoration with which the Bible ends makes worldly success the ultimate reward of adherence to a moral code independent of specific ethical structures. Abstract, reciprocal morality becomes the definitive sublimation of resentment, for the criteria of human interaction have been made wholly independent of social difference. Yet this constitutes an abdication of religion in the political realm, a disintegration of the unity of morality and ethics. The reestablishment of cultural unity in a more highly articulated form will have to await the radical internalization of the moral/ethical dichotomy in Christianity.

Greek culture reflects not merely a breakdown of the rigid hierarchy of ancient empire but the establishment of dynamic societies involving conflicts among various strata—ruler and aristocracy, landowner and commercial *nouveau riche*, merchant and farmer, citizen and colonial. Rather than sublimating resentment by the subordination of social difference to transcendental difference, Greek literature in its various phases reinterpreted myth, legend, and even history as vehicles for the expression of resentment. The victim of social difference is assimilated to the sacrificial victim of sacred difference, the guilt of resentment to that of desire. Unlike the monotheistic narrative, which carried unique sacred authority, these secular works were subject only to the criterion of esthetic effect. This is true even of Homeric epic, although the Homeric text was not without authority in matters of sovereignty or custom. It is more radically true of Athenian tragedy, which allowed for considerable diversity in the interpretation of even the most familiar mythical material. The literary auditor or spectator submits himself not to a divinity but to a human Subject who is the absolute master of an imaginary universe. In the context of this formal mastery, social difference and its concomitant resentment are also mastered.

The highest achievement of both forms of high culture is identification with the victim as the occupant of the uniquely privileged central position of the scene of representation. In Isaiah, the "suffering servant" becomes a figure of election. His martyrdom reflects his expiation of the sins of others and attests to his own innocence. In this figure, resentment achieves the reversal of worldly values decried by Nietzsche; but this reversal is the submission of historical difference to an abstract reciprocal morality that is thereupon posed as an eschatology—one without which the progressive history of Western culture would be inexplicable. In Athenian tragedy, the privilege of the victim is esthetic, not moral. Whether or not the sins he expiates are his own, his visible suffering forces us to see difference as productive of human sacrifice. In the greatest tragedies, the *Oedipus Tyrannus* and the *Bacchae*, the individual suffers through the agency of his own desire; the worlds of human and sacred difference are as one in the structural centrality of the victim. The deritualized scene of fiction reproduces the structure of the original scene of representation, but now its central figure is merely a desiring subject like ourselves. Tragedy conveys no abstract morality, but it shows us the paradoxical structure of desire that undercuts the absolute claims of difference. Here, too, resentment accomplishes, in a differentiated world, the demonstration of the ultimate identity of all men.

Notes

Introduction

1. Pseudodiachronic because composed of *essentially* synchronic elements.

2. The Eucharistic sacrifice, however real it may be in Church doctrine, is, *as a meal*, clearly symbolic.

3. See Moses I. Finley, *The Ancient Economy* (Berkeley and Los Angeles: University of California Press, 1973), and Jean-Pierre Vernant, *Mythe et pensée chez les Grecs* (Paris: F. Maspero, 1966), p. 247: "La stagnation technique chez les Grecs va de pair avec l'absence d'une pensée technique véritable."

4. Berkeley, Los Angeles, London: University of California Press, 1981.

Part I. The Originary Hypothesis

1. See *La violence et le sacré* (Paris: Grasset, 1972), English translation, *Violence and the Sacred* (Baltimore: Johns Hopkins University Press, 1977), and *Des choses cachées depuis la fondation du monde* (Paris: Grasset, 1978).

2. *Des choses cachées*, p. 109.

3. See "Differences," *MLN* 96, no. 2 (Spring 1981); "Le *logos* de René Girard," in *René Girard et le problème du mal*, ed. M. Deguy and J. P. Dupuy (Paris: Grasset, 1982).

1. The Originary Scene of Representation

1. *Recherches sur l'origine du langage et de la conscience* (Paris: Editions Sociales, 1973).

2. This last is ultimately the fate of the radically nonappetitive theory of Girard, for whom the desire-object is simply designated by the other. The close link between theory of desire and originary hypothesis is exemplarily illustrated in Girard's work, both by its chronological evolution from the triangle of *Mensonge romantique et verité romanesque* (Paris: Grasset, 1961) to the originary mimetic crisis of *La violence et le sacré* and, more pertinently to the present discussion, by the structural identity of the purely derivative object-relation within the desire-triangle and the purely nonappetitive choice of the original victim *as against* an appetitive object. (For a comparison with Derrida on this point, see our "Differences.")

3. Girard's theory attempts to avoid this problem by making, not an act of representation, but the "noninstinctive attention" paid to the cadaver of the emissary victim the originary act of culture. Thus appetitive satisfaction is replaced by the pleasurable passage from violence to peace. But since no further appetitive satisfaction can be gained from the object, its only source of significance must be the "sacred" power attributed to it by the murderers. The body thus becomes *a purely cultural object;* it is this status that permits Girard to call it not the (original) "transcendental signified" but the "transcendental *signifier*" (*Des choses cachées,* p. 112). Hence the reproduction of this "sign" can only be accomplished by the reproduction of the murder. The scene of representation thus created involves no *act* of representation and hence cannot be the origin of language or of desire, not to speak of the "economic" and ethical act of sharing the desired object. But if the sacred as thus defined precedes any form of cognitive act, then there is no way to explain how such acts could arise. For the scene of representation of which we speak is an *other scene* than that of reality, the genesis of which cannot be explained by means of an unmediated relation to a real object, however sacred. In *The Origin of Language,* we attempted to resolve this difficulty by making the body itself occupy the role taken by the appetitive object in the present version of the hypothesis. But in that case, as we had already suggested in the preface to that work, the "mimetic crisis" and "emissary murder" become superfluous, and we have therefore eliminated them from the minimal hypothesis.

4. This is a subject to which Pascal's reflections in *Les pensées* on "diversion" or *divertissement* are particularly pertinent.

5. This does not preclude the exploitation (e.g., in "op" art) of oscillatory nature of the physiological process of perception, or the presence in artworks in general of rhythms sympathetic to those of the human body. The existence of this rhythmic element in art may be said to be predictable on the basis of our theory but not to derive from it as a necessary consequence. For the existence of institutionalized rhythms is not equivalent to the institutionalization of rhythm as such. Poetic or musical rhythms are significant, but this significance depends on the general form of the esthetic, and the relation is in no sense reversible.

6. See Bernhard Laum, *Heiliges Geld* (Tübingen: Mohr, 1924); William Desmonde, *Magic, Myth and Money* (Glencoe, Ill.: Free Press, 1962).

7. See "La différance," in *Marges de la philosophie* (Paris: Minuit, 1972), as well as the broader discussion of philosophical/anthropological issues in *De la grammatologie* (Paris: Minuit, 1968).

2. The Universal Structures of Human Culture

1. We need not overlook the secondary functions of these institutions, which serve to protect society against intracultural as well as extracultural disorder. The social order produces its own metaphysical desire-objects that often far exceed in importance the merely appetitive ones. But appetite is at the basis of all desire; not only does the luxury of metaphysics require that our animal needs be satisfied, but its objects themselves inevitably derive from appetitive values. This by no means implies that appetites do not normally express themselves in a cultural context through representational forms. It merely reminds us that socioeconomic institutions exist primarily to protect us not from these forms but from the unsatisfied appetites they represent.

2. This was indeed the case in the exposition of *The Origin of Language,* where a "second moment" was posited to establish the sign qua sign and the sacred object qua sacred object. The present exposition eliminates this *double emploi* by separating

the earlier hypothesis into two minimal ones. It is then seen that reproduction is a requirement of the sacred but not of the sign, since the latter remains in the significant memory, wherein the scene of representation may be imaginarily reproduced independently of any public event.

3. We might note the relevancy of these considerations to dreaming. Higher animals apparently "dream," at least in the sense of running through the sort of appetitive schemata to which their imagination is limited. Human dreams, of which alone we can speak from experience, take place on the scene of representation, which is in effect the only "other scene" we need to posit. Whatever their physiological function (if any), their relation to desire, rather than being describable, as Freud's early theory had it, as "wish fulfillment," is quite analogous to that of cultural products, particularly literary works. The only satisfactions one has in dreams are of the sort that can be obtained on the scene of representation. And these, including "wet dreams" (which have their parallel in pornography), are always limited to the sort of emotional satisfaction that words can provide.

4. See his *Le système des objets* (Paris: Gallimard, 1968), *La sociètè de consommation* (Paris: S.G.P.P., 1970). The limitations of Baudrillard's view are those of the "alienation theory" of modernity that he shares with so many others. For Baudrillard, interpreting products as signs, that is, elements of a system of representations, is tantamount to denouncing their unreality. Thus he radicalizes the Marxian opposition between (appetitive) use-value and (cultural) exchange-value. In contrast, the entire thrust of our theory demonstrates that man is truly human only on the scene of representation: *le consumérisme est un humanisme*.

5. Because we have not specified that the desire-object must be of an alimentary nature (as the evidence of known rituals strongly suggests), it might be objected that, for example, a sexual object would not require such replacement. The same woman or group of women could thus be "appropriated" repeatedly. But aside from the obvious fact that such repetition could not go on indefinitely, we should remark that, unlike the problems posed by hunting big game, those of sexual distribution are quite well handled by the instinctually based dominance-mechanisms of ape societies, in conjunction with the only occasional sexual availability of females during estrus. It would certainly be difficult to believe that the permanent sexual availability unique to the human female preceded and in some sense caused the passage from ape to man.

6. It is worth noting that the problem we are here discussing has no parallel in the case of the sign, that is, on the scene of representation as such. For we have posited no specific impulsion to repeat the sign. It has rather remained our assumption here, as in *The Origin of Language*, that the evolution of (linguistic) signs proceeds from the beginning independently of that of ritual.

7. See our "Esthétique de la métaphore," *Poĕsie* 1 (1977).

3. Anthropology and the Logic of Representation

1. The more obvious analogy between man and computer with regard to representation, and the only one given any consideration by students of the problem, is ontogenetic rather than phylogenetic: the brain of the child, like the "brain" of the computer, contains "hardware" and "software," the Chomskian influence tending to emphasize the former at the expense of the latter. The learning situation of child and computer with regard to language is superficially similar, since both receive the specifics of language from without; and although the child, unlike the computer, has

no innate bias to one language rather than another, the "hardware" is nevertheless felt to be rather close to the surface. But because nothing is really known about the language-learning mechanisms of the brain, this analogy avoids the problem of the origin of language without even providing a useful model of ontogenesis. Its only justification is that children (and computers) can be observed whereas the original language-users cannot. This is but one typical example of the empiricism without theory that plagues the social sciences.

2. For example, in Margaret Boden, *Artificial Intelligence and Natural Man* (Hassocks, Eng.: Harvester Press, 1977).

3. First published in 1931 in the *Monatshefte für Mathematik und Physik*, vol. 38. English translation (by B. Meltzer), *On Formally Undecidable Propositions of Principia Mathematica and Related Systems* (New York: Basic Books, 1962).

4. See Alexandre Koyré, *Epiménide le menteur* (Paris: Herrmann, 1947).

5. See Ernest Nagel and J. R. Newman, *Gödel's Proof* (New York: New York University Press, 1958).

6. Thus Gödel's statement N° G is "G is unprovable" (in the system), not "G is false"; the terms "true" and "false" cannot enter the vocabulary of the system that simply functions to generate series of symbols. "Unprovable" means, in effect, not generated by the system. See Andrzej Mostowski, *Sentences Undecidable in Formalized Arithmetic* (Amsterdam: North-Holland Publishing Co., 1952), pp. 9, 89.

7. See Piaget's *L'epistémologie génétique* (Paris: P.U.F., 1970).

8. See *The Open Society and Its Enemies* (Princeton: Princeton University Press, 1950).

9. See A. J. Ayer, *Language, Truth and Logic* (New York: Dover, 1952).

10. An easy criterion for determining the metaphysical bent of a logician is whether he gives the word "exist" an ontological sense. Unicorns and round squares, for example, are said not to "exist"—although visitors to the Cloisters museum in New York are familiar with the first and any Parisian can point out several examples of the second. (If this example is felt to be unsatisfactory, one may try plotting the equation $X^{10} + Y^{10} = K$.) St. Anselm might be pleased to know how many thinkers continue to make use of his proof *à l'envers*.

4.   The Theory of Representation as a Fundamental Anthropology

1. It is not the Marxists who today talk the most about "power." Marxism does contain, after all, a structural conception of the economy, even if the articulation of the political and economic elements of Marxist historical models is more an art than a science—one practiced with far more skill by Marx himself than by any of his followers. It is, rather, para-Marxist, Nietzschean writers like Foucault who make the most of the concept of power, which performs a role in their social analyses analogous to that of the phallus in Lacanian psychoanalysis. (This is implicit everywhere in Foucault, nowhere more than in *La volonté de savoir* [Paris: Gallimard, 1976], where we witness the hypostasis of "le pouvoir": "Le pouvoir est partout, ce n'est pas qu'il englobe tout, c'est qu'il vient de partout" [p. 122]. Power thus becomes the basis of all human interaction.) Just as Lacanian phalluses are ideal phalluses, Foucaultian power is ideal power, exercised by an ideal "bourgeoisie"—the exact counterpart of the ideal proletariat in whose name communist parties purport to act. If the two concepts are alike in permitting such abuses, it is because they are both insufficiently conceptualized, more images than models. Except in circumstances of overt physical violence, the notion of "power" explains very little.

2. It is to be regretted that this basic agreement with Chomsky's thesis was not formulated in *The Origin of Language*. The hypothesis of a "language-acquisition device" is superfluous and even tautological, the crucial question being the evolutionary process that originally led to the constitution of our present-day linguistic capacity. But no difficulty would have arisen had we integrated the Chomskian hypothesis into our own, not as an explanation of the existence of fundamental linguistic structures, but as a corollary of our distinction between the elementary and mature stages of linguistic evolution.

3. New York: Random House, 1974.

4. New York: Random House, 1977.

5. New York: Random House, 1979.

6. "Culture as Protein and Profit," *New York Review of Books* 25, no. 18 (23 November 1978), p. 53.

7. Harris, *Cultural Materialism*, pp. 339–340.

8. Ibid., p. 50.

9. "The Biological Basis for Aztec Sacrifice," *American Ethnologist* 4 (1977), 117–135.

10. *Cultural Materialism*, p. 336.

11. "Culture as Protein and Profit," p. 46.

12. Ibid., p. 47.

13. *Cultural Materialism*, p. 340.

14. New York: Oxford University Press, 1979.

15. *The Human Condition* (Garden City, New York: Doubleday, 1958).

16. See Elman Service, *The Hunters* (Englewood Cliffs, N.J.: Prentice-Hall, 1966). In *Cultural Materialism* (p. 81), Harris, like Service, attributes this ethic to the need to maintain low kill rates in the interest of preserving game; hunters, unlike agriculturists, are not given to competitive intensification of production. But the fragility of this ethical equilibrium has been demonstrated by the nearly universal adoption of agriculture by human societies.

17. *Current Anthropology* 7 (1966).

18. "Culture as Protein and Profit," pp. 51–52.

19. I am not familiar with the Hindu's own justification for his practice; but I know that most modern Jews explain the taboos on pork and shellfish as motivated by the danger of disease (trichinosis or food poisoning). This explanation through rationalized "uncleanliness" is halfway between ritual-derived etiological myth and the economic explanations of cultural materialism; it at least serves to show that believers or their descendants are less enamored of the irrationality of their sacred practices than outsiders.

20. *Cultural Materialism*, p. 134.

21. As we have demonstrated in *The Origin of Language*, language is essentially *formal* or, in linguistic terms, syntactic, not lexical. Here we are in full agreement with Chomsky.

22. *Cultural Materialism*, p. 55.

23. Here he differs from Lévi-Strauss, who more prudently refuses to deal with ritual at all, preferring to attack the solidified "structure" of myth. That the Frenchman's is the wiser course is sorely apparent from Sahlins's tasteless descriptions of the "communion" of Aztec ritual. In the absence of any understanding of the social forces involved (the true communion in sacrifice being that of the participants *among themselves* through the mediation of the victim), Sahlins describes the union of captor

and eventual victim with an esthetic relish far better suited to the fictive signs of myth than to the real human actors of ritual.

24. Harris's source is Karl Popper's disciple Imre Lakatos, "Falsification and the Methodology of Scientific Research Programmes," in *Criticism and the Growth of Knowledge*, ed. I. Lakatos and A. Musgrave (Cambridge: Cambridge University Press, 1970), p. 179.

25. This is a first-order principle that should not prevent us from encouraging certain types of linguistic research in preference to others. For instance, the study of linguistic change in a context of social valorization of the variables involved is far more useful than purely formal schemes; we had occasion to refer in *The Origin of Language* to sociolinguistic writings of William Labov. As a research suggestion, if not a "program," we would propose that such studies be carried out not on isolated phonemes or lexical items but on entire linguistic levels, including particularly the syntactic, and that it be made methodologically explicit that *significance* (measurable, let us say, by the presumed heightened attention of the listener or reader) is the independent variable.

26. As for the series of social systems described by Harris in *Cannibals and Kings* and *Cultural Materialism*, we should note that the "retrodiction" of these systems does not involve the confirmation of an a priori hypothetical model but merely a posteriori plausibility. Why at a certain point a state system develops may be thus plausibly explained without any a priori model of the state as an ethical system having been constructed. Our own approach to anthropology is an attempt to introduce such rigor.

27. *Cultural Materialism*, pp. 15–18.

28. This unification is certainly the primary cause of the decline of high culture, both secular and ritual. But this decline parallels the rise and enormous expansion of a mass "popular" culture more completely integrated into the exchange-system.

29. See, for example, Lewis R. Birford and W. J. Charko, Jr., "Nuniamuit Demographic History: A Provocative Case," in *Demographic Anthropology*, ed. Ezra Zubrow (Albuquerque: University of New Mexico Press, 1976).

30. See, for example, Sherwood Washburn, ed., *Social Life of Early Man* (New York: Wenner-Gren Foundation, 1961); Richard Leakey, *Origins* (New York: Dutton, 1977).

31. "Mais je suppose que, quelque temps après le déluge, deux enfants . . . aient été égarés dans les déserts, avant qu'ils connussent l'usage d'aucun signe" (*Essai sur l'origine des connaissances humaines* [Paris: A. Colin, 1924], pt. 2, p. 111).

32. We are here using the word "derive" informally to refer to the process of testing and corroborating positive hypotheses. In the logical sense of the term, one can derive no facts from a hypothesis, whether corroborated or not.

Part II. The Origin of Culture

1. This symmetry was a reflection of the origin of our theory so to speak in dialectical opposition to that of Girard. Our "formal" theory opposed his "institutional" theory in giving preference to ("formal") language where he had chosen ("institutional") ritual. But our preference was presented as a heuristic choice of subject matter, not as the reflection of an ontological priority, whence the symmetry between language and ritual.

2. Readers of *The Origin of Language* will note a considerable change in both terminology and content; in that work, an originary "dramatic" esthetic was opposed

to a "lyric" ostensive-imperative esthetic and to a "narrative" declarative esthetic. In keeping with the more rigorously monistic orientation of the present work, we will not attempt to impose the generic attributes of mature literary discourse on the elementary esthetics, which will be examined rather in parallel with the immature forms of discourse corresponding to the stages of prehistoric linguistic evolution. This procedure implies a considerable modification of the notion of "discourse" outlined in the earlier book.

5. The Elementary Forms of Culture

1. See our "Pour une esthétique triangulaire," in *Essais d'esthétique paradoxale* (Paris: Gallimard, 1977).

2. This conclusion could be drawn simply from the impossibility of expressing such laws in an ostensive language. But it is useful to show that this formal impossibility is associated with an ethical impossibility.

3. The derivation of "negative" from "positive" rituals might explain, for example, the existence of ritual cannibalism, notably that sometimes claimed to have been practiced by early hominids. The category of significance, as expressed by ostensive signs, may be attributed to both positive and negative appetitive objects, and thus it might appear to suffice in itself to explain cannibalism, headhunting, and so forth. This intuitively attractive explanation cannot, however, be originary, if we assume that the origin of ritual acts is communal rather than individual. The powers attached to the possession or ingestion of parts of an enemy (human or animal, even inanimate) must first have been attributed to these acts by the community. It is the *distribution* of brains or scalps that makes them significant, and the origin of distribution, in our hypothesis, is in the "positive" originary event.

4. But ritual can never attain the degree of insignificance or nonviolence accessible to the interpersonal use of language. A ritual always remains a bit sacred, the proof being that it conveys no information.

5. Of course even here the entering or departing member is temporarily noticeable, hence significant and, if one likes, sacred. But this significance is a mere boundary-condition of the well-formedness of the symmetrical group. It is more useful to define sacrality by its transcendence of interactional time, owing to the signifying function of the sacred object or being.

6. We refer the reader to *The Origin of Language*, chap. 3, for a fuller development of these notions.

7. The most elaborate reconstruction of the religious practices associated with these paintings is that of André Leroi-Gourhan, first expounded in his *Préhistoire de l'art occidental* (Paris: Mazenod, 1965). But Leroi-Gourhan's argument for a bipolar symbolism associating different animals with the two sexes has not met with general acceptance. See Peter J. Ucko and Andrée Rosenfeld, *Paleolithic Cave Art* (New York: McGraw-Hill, 1967); Ann Sieveking, *The Cave Artists*, (London: Thames and Hudson, 1979), chap. 3. Leroi-Gourhan's *Les religions de la préhistoire*, 3d ed. (Paris: P.U.F., 1976) offers a more cautious version of his thesis.

8. This characterization is not mere empirical generalization; it follows from the originary hypothesis. Arbitrary constraint is essential to ritual because without it, its ethical basis could no longer be distinguished from that of profane practical action. This remains true in the absence of the sacred, or even of a reverential attitude.

9. As we attempted to show in *The Origin of Language*, the basic form of the imperative is not verbal but nominal, as used, for example, by a surgeon requesting a scalpel ("Scalpel!") from his assistant.

10. The failure to attain a higher form of language—and thus of brain capacity and culture—may well have been the crucial determinant in the extinction of the Neanderthal race—as well, no doubt, as of other pre-*sapiens* races of which we have no trace. The present-day genetic uniformity of man, and the large genetic distance that separates him from his closest relations among the apes, can only be accounted for by the survival of a single line that exterminated all the others. Early humans speaking a language, however rudimentary, could surely have adapted well enough to their environment to survive by themselves in the absence of competition from more advanced human forms.

11. See *L'âme primitive* (Paris: P.U.F., 1963); *Les fonctions mentales dans les sociétés inférieures* (Paris: P.U.F., 1951).

6. The Evolution of Ethical Conceptions

1. The interest in ethological parallels with human conduct has tended to obscure this fundamental distinction between human and animal ritual. An animal ritual is a fixed pattern of behavior containing distinct conflict-averting elements that only appear irrational because, judged by analogy with human ritual, they fail to contribute directly to appetitive satisfaction. We cannot deny the obvious parallel; it is not a mere figment of the imagination. But the parallel between genetic and cultural evolution must not be treated in the same light as evolutionary parallels in the animal kingdom. Cultural evolution differs from genetic not only in rate of speed and mechanism of transmission; one cannot transmit the same content through genes and through representations. Thus it is not sufficient to speak of cultural behavior as "learned"; the category of learning, too, is applied without sufficient discrimination to both animals and humans. Human ritual has a cognitive content; it is never merely *behavior*, but *representation*. Even at its most apparently meaningless, some trace of this representational function remains; the very notion of "meaningless" can apply only to something that should be, and presumably once was, meaningful. Behaviorism in the study of ritual is just as perniciously reductive as it is in linguistics.

2. Speech-act theoreticians have indeed concerned themselves with such equivalences, although rather in the opposite sense. In effect, for them, the *imperative* is the fundamental linguistic form: all speech is an attempt, direct or indirect, to influence the actions (or the thoughts that will motivate the future actions) of the hearer. The imperative is, no doubt, a step closer to the real foundation of language than the declarative beloved of generative grammarians, even if this step must be taken at the expense of the concept of acontextual meaning that gives transformational analyses their power. Our linguistic theory, by beginning truly at the beginning, that is, with the ostensive, can differentiate the domains of validity of both "declarative" and "imperative" linguistics.

3. For a discussion of this point, see our "Differences."

4. It should be noted that the definition of the human is not an issue for Girard. On the contrary, the lack of representational content in his version of the original event is claimed as a guarantee of primitivity: only mimesis is hypothesized, and the primate propensity to mimesis is well known. But Girard's defense of what we would call the minimality of his hypothesis requires that we attribute to mimesis the power to arouse in these prehumans a state of what he had earlier described in *Mensonge romantique et vérité romanesque* as the final stage of "metaphysical desire," in which the object of desire is wholly abandoned in the mimetic conflict with the rival. The originary event would then involve an absolute shift in central focus as well as the creation of significance on the basis of an absolutely arbitrary difference (i.e., that

between the victim and the others). Our hypothesis allows these worldly differences to remain minimal because it locates significance, not in the real world, but in a scene of representation.

5. *Des choses cachées*, pp. 153–154.

6. All quotations from the Bible are taken from the Revised Standard Version (New York: Oxford University Press, 1962).

7. A cultural materialist would probably see in this dietary provision a means of reducing blood cholesterol levels. Fat is, in any event, marginal for dwellers in warm climates; such a distribution would be inconceivable in an Eskimo society.

8. The Athenian *pharmakos* plays a similar role. (See Louis Gernet, *Anthropologie de la Grèce ancienne* [Paris: F. Maspéro, 1968]; Erwin Rohde, *Psyche*, vol. 2 [Tübingen: Mohr, 1925].) The expulsion of a human rather than a goat is more "radical," at the same time as it constitutes an ethical regression. Homer had no pharmakoi. There is no reason to make the moral crudity of this custom a sign of primitivity; the opposite would appear to be the case. We have here a paradigm of the difference between the Judeo-Christian and Greek traditions. The first emphasizes collective guilt and increasingly equates sacrifice with appetitive renouncement; the second, by making use of internal social differences to permit an increasingly intense projection of collective transgressions onto a human victim, will attempt to justify this choice by the retroactive attribution of preordained "tragic" guilt to the victim. Only the Judeo-Christian tradition can attain the understanding of the fundamental innocence of the victim that leads to the abolition of sacrifice.

9. ". . . in the early stages of Israelite civilization in particular, as well as of Semitic civilization in general, first-born children were, beyond all question, regularly sacrificed to the proper deity or spirit as the natural and proper taboo-sacrifice" (Julian Morgenstern, *Rites of Birth, Marriage, Death and Kindred Occasions among the Semites* [Cincinnati: Hebrew Union College Press, 1966], p. 181). Morgenstern admits that this custom "might be accounted for as springing from analogy with the sacrifice of the first-born of animal offspring," in the light of their being grouped together in the legislation of Exodus 22 and 34. He makes light of this "late" parallel, but it seems to us the expression of an accurate anthropological intuition.

10. See *Des choses cachées*, pp. 114–135, especially 114–120. The myths are of Ojibway and Tikopian origin; their text is taken from Lévi-Strauss's *Le totémisme aujourd'hui* (Paris: P.U.F., 1962), pp. 27 and 36. Lévi-Strauss's chief source is Raymond Firth, *Tikopia Ritual and Belief* (Boston: Beacon, 1967), p. 230, although he uses a slightly less explicit version of the myth.

11. This parallel between Girard's and Chomsky's "transformationalism" points up not only the similarity but the difference between culture and language, most obvious in their relative amenability to formal methods. Lévi-Strauss's own formalistic "transformationism" is too rigid and artificial to apply with any rigor even to his chosen corpus of myths. Formalism can only be successful in dealing with the formal relations that occur within the scene of representation, relations that cannot themselves evolve. Culture, unlike language, maintains its evolutionary capacity even after having reached what we have defined as "maturity," and this because of the ever-changing requirements of representation in mediating between ethical conceptions and the desires that work incessantly to erode any well-defined ethical order.

12. We have already alluded to the irreconcilability of the Malthusian and Marxian explanations of social evolution. Malthusian man indulges himself in reproduction but has no economic desires beyond subsistence; Marxian man controls his hedonistic urges in his desire for economic surplus.

13. Chicago: Aldine-Atherton, 1972.

14. *Stone Age Economics*, p. 29.

15. Boserup has made clear that the origin of agriculture is not a matter of technical progress but of the necessary spread of more labor-intensive techniques, presumably under population pressure. This thesis is developed in some detail in Mark Cohen, *The Food Crisis in Prehistory* (New Haven: Yale University Press, 1977). But once the "Malthusian" agriculturist has satisfied his hunger, the fact remains that he is in possession of an instrument that can for the first time permit the accumulation of surpluses in favored times or places.

16. In Sahlins's only passing reference to myth in *Stone Age Economics*, he refers to the breakdown of the Tikopian system of reciprocal distribution with the rise of social differentiation: "An uncommon rift appeared between chiefs and the underlying population. Somber traditions were resurrected—'myths,' Spillius considers them— telling how certain chiefs of old, when pressure on the local food supply became unsupportable, drove the commoners en masse off the island" (p. 143). It is worth noting how ready Sahlins is to treat evolving etiological myths as a mere resurrection of "somber traditions."

17. Harris's comments in *Cultural Materialism* on Stone Age Economics, in contrast with his reply to Sahlins's remarks on Aztec sacrifice and Hindu cow-worship, demonstrate more polemical than theoretical acumen. Harris accuses Sahlins of understating as usual the importance of infrastructural factors in explaining why these primitive societies do not produce up to maximal capacity. But Sahlins's point is not to show how "irrational" this behavior is, but to demonstrate that the *homo oeconomicus* model is inoperative. The big-man case, because it illustrates a transitional stage, is the most revealing example: it permits us to understand why and how modern economic rationality ever developed at all. It is no doubt to be regretted that Sahlins neither grasps the importance of the ritual element nor, more generally, attempts to construct on the basis of this example a more general model of socioeconomic (not to speak of ethical) evolution. But this is a sin of omission that in no way discredits the perceptive analysis that characterizes this work.

18. More strictly stated, modernity is the generalization of the exchange-system to include a professional—and quasi-universal—labor market. Such a market, which in the broadest sense evaluates the work of "capitalists" as well as workers, offers a virtually unlimited field for the socially useful expression of desire, and thus renders ritual control-mechanisms virtually obsolete.

19. This is most apparent in the writings of Lévi-Strauss, who has the honesty to recognize his debt to the author of the *Discours sur l'origine de l'inégalité*. Lévi-Strauss reads Rousseau as Rousseau would have liked to read himself but understood that he could not. Preagricultural society offered Rousseau an anti-model for his analysis of modernity; it was not a subject to be studied nostalgically in itself. Thus, although he was the promulgator of numerous ethnological insights, Rousseau was no ethnologist. Lévi-Strauss's reference to Rousseau is thus only partly lucid; but it shines like a beacon in comparison with the sentimental ethnologism of our "empirical" anthropologists. *Dans le royaume des aveugles* . . .

20. Here again, Harris is merely more forthright than those of his fellow anthropologists who hide behind scientific objectivity in failing to discuss the ethical question. There is, no doubt, a certain wisdom in bracketing the ethical when there is no reasonably rigorous model available for its analysis—when, in other words, the only "ethical" criteria are in fact moral. But the only wisdom here is the wisdom of

ignorance. Most social scientists are not bracketing anything, but merely respecting the tradition of "value-free" social science.

21. Just as our "deferral" is an anthropologically grounded interpretation of Derrida's *différance*, "surplus" here translates his *supplément*—a term already in principle, if not operatively, anthropological in Rousseau. In Derrida's work, philosophy renders up its final insights to anthropology.

22. *Le miroir de la production* ([Tournai:] Casterman, 1973).

23. This point is often made as an accusation by those who oppose themselves to the social order; revolutionaries are not "consumers." Herbert Marcuse emphasized in *One-Dimensional Man* (Boston: Beacon, 1964) the "repressive" nature of consumer society that strengthens its hold on its members by offering satisfaction to their desires. This argument is flawed by the hypostasis of the consumer's role into a form of being. Consumer's satisfaction is not a product of "consumer society," nor, conversely, is this society lacking in producer's desire. The lack of revolutionary action in Western societies is a tribute to their success in satisfying the latter, not in providing the former. Marcuse's book's very existence is self-contradictory; not only is it still possible to have (and to publish) "two-dimensional" ideas, but these ideas, whatever Marcuse's readers may have thought in 1968, have only the most superficial revolutionary potential.

24. The failure to understand the primordially ethical nature of the surplus—a supplementary production that grants not merely differential but uniquely central status to its producer—has led at least one theorist to deny its very existence. See Harry W. Pearson, "The Economy Has No Surplus," in *Trade and Market in the Early Empires*, ed. Karl Polanyi et al. (Glencoe, Ill.: Free Press, 1957). Because everything is consumed, this argument goes, there is never a surplus. We are reminded of Say's law of markets that caused Marx such hilarity: excess production is a priori impossible because the price mechanism will clear the market of whatever is offered for sale.

25. This is not to say that every rite in egalitarian societies must end in a feast. What is claimed is merely that in such societies, no dichotomy can be drawn between ritual and feasting, or, more broadly, that a notion of "ritual" as apart from the appetitive behavior of the community cannot arise. This means, in particular, that there can be no reflection upon the ethical value of "ritual-in-itself" apart from "natural" appetitive satisfaction. Such cultures are aware of themselves as cultures, but they can have no concept of the "cultural."

7.   The Esthetic Element in Culture

1. The French word *public* (German *Publikum*) is perhaps the most satisfactory general term, although it too leaves the relationship unspecified and hence allows for no verbal equivalent.

2. We use this term not literally, to designate the human form, but to indicate the presence of human intelligence. Mythical characters all have at least implicitly the power of speech that is the mark of the human.

3. This contrast is at its most striking in the "bird-man" painting discussed earlier; the bison is an artistic likeness, whereas the human figure is crudely schematic.

4. This is not even to speak of the historical evolution of representational technique over some twenty thousand years. Leroi-Gourhan distinguishes four main styles of cave art, each of which is characterized by a more subtle and accurate naturalism than its predecessor.

Part III.   The Birth of High Culture

8.   The Emergence of High-Cultural Discourse

1. For example, in the case of archaic Greek sculpture: "The familiar archaic statues of young nude males (Kouroi) in stone or bronze . . . are sometimes labeled 'Apollo' by modern scholars and sometimes 'Youth.' But the distinction between god and man is legitimate only when there is external evidence. . . . There is nothing in the statue itself from which to tell" (Moses I. Finley, *Early Greece* [London: Chatto and Windus, 1970], p. 145).

2. As we have already had occasion to remark in *The Origin of Language*, lists of such epithets are often found in liturgies, such as the hymn to Marduk at the end of the Babylonian *Creation Epic*.

3. See Karl Wittfogel, *Oriental Despotism* (New Haven: Yale University Press, 1957).

4. ". . . les égyptologues sont unanimes à considérer *L'Histoire de Sinouhé* comme le plus représentatif et le plus parfait de la littérature égyptienne, celui qui mérite le mieux . . . l'épithète de 'classique'" (Gustave Lefebvre, *Romans et contes égyptiens de l'époque pharaonique* [Paris, Librairie d'Amérique et d'Orient, 1949], p. 1).

5. Examination of the vaster and more complex "hydraulic empire" of China would take us beyond the scope of this work.

6. The status of this hero, two-thirds god and one-third man (!), is nothing if not ambiguous. Because his name appears in a Sumerian king-list, Gilgamesh is sometimes taken for a transfigured real person. Even if this were the case, it would change nothing in the essential progression. Gilgamesh's mother, at least, is a goddess; his father is diversely mortal and immortal. Descent from the gods is also descent of the narrative from god to man. But it is at least a respectable scholarly position that Gilgamesh was originally the name of a deity. "Meiner Aussicht nach gibt es wichtige Gründe für die Annahme, dass *Gilgameš keine geschichtliche Person* ist. . . . Zu unterstreichen ist . . . diese ausdrückliche Betonung seiner Zweidrittelgottheit, . . . ohne dass wir ein einziges Wort zur Erklärung hatten. . . . Hier scheint eben ein Rest einer älteren Vostellung vorzuliegen, nach der er tatsächlich ein Gott war." Sigmund Mowinckel, "Wer war Gilgameš?" in *Das Gilgamesh-Epos*, ed. K. Oberhuber (Darmstadt: Wissenschaftliche Buchgesellschaft, 1977), p. 154–155.

7. The text can of course be extended; further adventures can be added to those already known. Thus a canonical literary work can give rise to any number of secondary texts, as well as figural works in other media. But this productivity remains esthetic; the hero, unlike the god, has no imaginary presence outside of the fictive universe(s) invented for him.

The phenomenon of the hero cult, so widespread in ancient Greece, is an interesting but secondary back-formation—the divinization of a personage, historical or purely imaginary, already celebrated in story, that is, literary discourse. The existence of such mediating figures between man and the gods does not disturb the essential polarity between immortal god and mortal hero, any more than the cult of Christian saints disturbs the essential opposition between man and the transcendental Judeo-Christian God.

9.   Jewish Culture: Narrative Monotheism

1. This progression is accentuated—and from the Jewish standpoint, distorted— in the Christian presentation of the Old Testament, which ends with the prophets who are considered to be foretelling Christ's coming. It is difficult to deny the superior

radicality of this version to the Hebrew, where the story ends optimistically with the reconstruction of the Temple under Ezra and Nehemiah. But Jewish nostalgia and eternal hope for a worldly kingdom—that is, for an ultimate ethical realization of moral principle, less radical than the Christian apocalypse—is truer to modern-day reality, even if it is the Christians rather than the Jews who have been its chief architects. Only the believers in an otherworldly kingdom could construct a reasonably effective moral kingdom in this world.

2. Little attention has been given by theoreticians to the capital distinction between those tribal or local gods whose worshipers must be reconciled within a national whole and such figures as Cronus and the Titans who incarnate functions of merely theoretical importance within the anthropology outlined in such epics. The latter stand for the gods of the pre- or uncivilized, whether they were ever actually worshiped or not.

3. This is the bone of contention between Judaism and Christianity, which conceives of the moral as the simple abolition of resentment and the establishment of reciprocal relations of love divorced from any appetitively satisfying exchange.

4. We use the name "Adam" for convenience; the Hebrew is simply "the man." The fact that Adam becomes a name even in the Hebrew text (e.g., at 4:25) reflects the necessary individuation of man as a subject of desire. Such individuation was not necessary in the Elohist creation-scene.

5. We speak here of the general reader, not of theological interpreters, who a priori cannot understand the text because they maintain as given the absolute difference of the sacred.

6. It is curious that Freud, who was perfectly aware of this development in the domain of religion, failed to apply it to his study of individual desire. For Freud, all dreams are myths, despite the fact that collective "dreams" like the biblical creation-legend are anything but wish-fulfillments. Because Freud failed to grasp the collective origin of individual desire, he situated the collective-paternal superego *outside* the generative mechanisms of desire—the libido as "cathected" through the work of the ego. Thus the dreamer was seen as escaping from his superego, whereas, in reality, his desires, "wish-fulfilled" or not, are wholly dependent on it.

7. The less radical character of Islam, which has remained a socially reactive movement, an expression of external rather than internal resentment, may be demonstrated by the fact that, whereas Christianity has retained the Hebrew Bible as its "Old Testament," only the Koran is scriptural for Moslems. Christianity conceives itself as a historical transcendence of Jewish historicism; Islam merely purges it of its historical element.

8. We may pass over the ascetic Jewish sects like that of the Essene composers of the Dead Sea scrolls, which proved incapable of surviving as a "third way" within the Jewish/Christian dichotomy.

9. We have here used the Jerusalem translation (New York: Doubleday, 1966), which is clearer than the RSV but not substantially different from it.

10.   Greece: Secular Esthetic Culture

1. See Polanyi's essay, "Aristotle Discovers the Economy," in *Trade and Market in the Early Empires.*

2. See S. C. Humphreys, *Anthropology and the Greeks* (London: Routledge and Kegan Paul, 1978).

3. This touches on broad questions of historical causality that lie beyond the scope of the present work, even if they are implicitly raised by it. The question of historical

temporality has not been dealt with adequately by those modern historians who have defined their enterprise to be precisely the expulsion from historiography of the naive, traditional measures of historical time and events in terms of individual lives and interests. Thus we no longer divide historical narratives into periods determined by successive reigns, nor explain wars by the personal ambitions of monarchs. "Cliometrics," as practiced by the *Annales* historians, is only the most recent of a series of developments, traceable at least to Vico, that make the historian's chief aim the study of secular trends rather than individual events. But in dealing with these trends in an ever more rigorous and less speculative manner, historians have lost sight of the need to mediate between long-term secular chronology and the life span by which an individual's participation in these trends is limited. The result of this loss of contact between the long and short term is the attempt to study human societies undergoing historical evolution through small-scale synchronic "cuts" within diachronic trends, rather than as *cultures* collectively aware of their existence in history.

To give the sense of a culture in history remains, no doubt, more of an art than a science. What we suggest is that historians who seek a more rigorous approach to cultural evolution concern themselves with interpreting trends, not only from the standpoint of their effect on the consciousness of the individual members of a society, but from that of the society's cultural manifestations, which more rigorously reflect the effect of these trends on its ethical order. Certainly, explicative models must contain different sets of causes, and hence of ultimate human motivations, according as they deal with temporal sequences internal or external to an individual life. Technological advance may be explained by economic motives in a short-range model (where the innovator seeks to acquire riches), by sociopolitical motives in a middle-range model (where the rise of certain groups to social prominence is attributed to their increased wealth), and by epistemological motives in a long-term perspective wherein man's tendency to seek knowledge appears as an adaptive mechanism independent of the desires of individuals (just as the long-term motivation of reproduction is not the sexual urge but the survival of the species). There is no lack of appreciation of the necessity of different models in the history of technology; it is our hope that a similar appreciation could arise in the history of ethical conceptions, the fundamental constituents of what we call culture.

4. The economic and ritual phenomena of primitive culture are phenomenologically indistinguishable; their explanation as one or the other depends on the positing of fundamental motivations that will only become verifiably distinct at higher cultural levels. Our claim is that ethical constraint is necessarily more rigorous in human society than material constraint, because, precisely, when it is not, "society" has ceased to exist. But ethical constraint, before the emergence of high cultures, remains centered on appetitive concerns. The replacement of desire by resentment as the central source of conflict signals a separation between the appetitive and the ethical that acquires in the high cultures distinct forms of little or no appetitive significance, inexplicable on primarily material grounds. It is our insistence on the long-term causal primacy of these elements that we definitively part company with materialist theories.

5. It is useful to compare the high secular culture of Greece with the practices of those African societies where the king becomes, in reality and not in fiction, a sacrificial victim. (See Victor Turner, *The Drums of Affliction* [Oxford: Oxford University Press, Clarendon Press, 1968]; Girard, *La violence et le sacré*, chap. 4.) These are not high cultures precisely because they do not sublimate resentment but put it into practice, and in so doing purge it in reality and not in imagination. This parallel makes clear the link between high culture and the evolution of social structures in the direction

of differentiation and economic motivation. A society that created kings only to sacrifice them annually is still very close to the egalitarian structure of primitive cultures.

6. As is quite clearly true for the sacrificial African kings mentioned in the preceding note.

7. This point suffices to put in question the attempt to account for the genres of cultural discourse through formal analysis of the texts. The institutional structures of discourse need not be observable on the linguistic level. One might even claim that they cannot be—that, in other words, literary discourse must make use of "ordinary language," and that the specific markers of "literarity" studied by the Russian and Czech formalists are merely secondary residues of literary tradition. For if this were not the case, literature would not truly be a *fiction*. The criteria that distinguish literature from myth are essentially nonlinguistic. To claim that they are, nevertheless, expressible on the *semantic* level is no counterargument, because the category of the "semantic" is merely a *post factum* depository for whatever may appear of significance. To express, for example, the opposition between myth and secular narrative by the dichotomy (immortality of protagonist)/(mortality of protagonist) is not to demonstrate the relevancy of textual semantics except as a system of notation for predetermined categorical differences. And this system is nearly always misleading, because it inevitably reduces diachronic asymmetry to synchronic symmetry. Even worse, the semantic notation-system is commonly projected onto history and taken to imply that the genesis of categories of thought always proceeds—as it in fact never does—by means of symmetrical dichotomies.

8. It is the specificity of this motivation that distinguishes high-cultural narratives from those of folklore, where the protagonist's satisfaction is inevitably deferred, but where this satisfaction, as well as the deferring elements ("tasks," "trials"), are of a conventional and formulaic nature. V. Propp's celebrated investigation of the Russian folktale (*Morphology of the Folktale*, 2d ed. [Austin: University of Texas Press, 1968]) more than confirms these assertions. The tales he studies can be reduced to a small set of basic elements because in no case does the hero's desire put in question the ethical structure of his society. These stories have as their theme not resentment but initiation; the hero must find his place in society through adventures, but this place is already well defined at the outset. The suspense of a fairy tale is only in the most abstract sense that of human praxis; its characters are not individualized, nor is its Subject. We have elsewhere called such works "paleonormative," to distinguish them from the "neonormative" works of literature proper, the ethical structure of whose fictional universe is not given a priori but remains implicit in the literary Subject. See our "Vers un principe d'indétermination en critique littéraire," *Revue romane* 9, no. 2 (November 1974).

9. No doubt our tolerance even of fictional ethical conceptions has its limits. But what we find intolerable are not the ethical conceptions themselves but the morality of the Subject as implicitly or explicitly expressed in the text. This moral criticism of the Subject is a direct consequence of the radical reciprocity of Judeo-Christian morality, which we apply to works that appear to deliberately reject it rather than simply to ignore it. Thus we find anti-Semitic or racist works difficult or impossible to read "esthetically."

10. Our resentful imagination may even function retroactively, as in our appreciation of such primitive artworks as the cave paintings. The modern viewer probably does not hunt buffalo; but his regret at not possessing the animal's strength and purposefulness as portrayed in the paintings is nourished by resentment. The image,

because its contemplation is independent of human time—which it structures only as a perception, that is, on a precultural and, indeed, preconscious level—is independent of the praxial temporality of the literary narrative. It therefore retains the same esthetic value, whether the qualities its contemplation inspires us to desire would normally be sought through the collective, ethically mandated activity of the hunt or through modern man's individual praxis. Both forms of action are attempts to realize "producer's" desire; but the qualitative difference in their temporality would make it impossible to reproduce the universal appeal of the figural image in discursive form.

11. *Nature and Culture in the Iliad* (Chicago: University of Chicago Press, 1975).

12. Redfield's Rousseauean dichotomy bears the trace of the influence of Lévi-Strauss. That warfare is "natural" in the *Iliad* may explain the significance of the dogs and birds that threaten to devour the bodies of the slain; but value-related disorder, figured here by the "natural," will later appear to critics of capitalism in the guise of a criminally unnatural "anarchy of production," with "nature" on the side of the traditional order's peaceful acceptation of human limitations. The nature/culture distinction is always used *ad hoc* as a secular form of ritual accusation. Cultural universality means just that: everything is part of culture.

13. To the extent that life experience in modern society can acquire a specific praxial focus, we may indeed say that life comes to resemble art. See *The Origin of Language*, chap. 7.

14. In the *Iliad*, we have already noted Odysseus's presence in the embassy scene (book 9), where he presents the case for "law and order." In the *Odyssey*, they meet in the underworld (book 11); "short-fated" Achilles is opposed to Odysseus, the eternal survivor.

15. The appropriate parallel is rather with the Cicones (9.60), who kill six men from each ship (just as Scylla would have done had more than one ship remained).

16. *The Homeric Odyssey* (Oxford: Oxford University Press, 1955), pp. 119 ff.

17. *The Songs of Homer* (Cambridge: Cambridge University Press, 1962), p. 247.

18. *Homeric Odyssey*, pp. 88 ff.

19. Cf. Page, *Homeric Odyssey*, p. 127.

20. 3.234–275; 5.510–547; 11.387–464. In the Nekyia of the 11th book, Agamemnon remarks (line 444) that Penelope would never commit a crime like that of Clytemnestra.

21. A provocative parallel suggests itself between Achilles and the descendants of Eve, whose heels are vulnerable to the serpent's bite (Genesis 3:15). In both cases, the heel is a privileged locus of mortality. "Achilles' heel" is not, however, mentioned in either Homeric epic.

22. Denys Page, *History and the Homeric Iliad* (Berkeley and Los Angeles: University of California Press, 1959), p. 254.

23. Page's indifference to this distinction reflects his "analytic" perspective which, far less sensitive than that of, for example, Kirk to the specific qualities of oral poetry, emphasizes the multiple authorship of the *Iliad* and thereby its supposed place in a continuously developing "Epic." In fact, the existence of heroic ballads about the Trojan War is not equivalent to the existence of an epic. Students of the Homeric question might profit from acquaintance with the work of Menéndez Pidal on medieval epic, which he hypothesizes to have developed from ballads or *cantilenas* more or less contemporary with the events they describe. (See his *La Chanson de Roland et la tradition épique des Francs* [Paris: Picard, 1960].) The more we learn about Troy and Mycenae, not to speak of oral poetry, the more the genesis of the *Iliad* begins to resemble that of the *Chanson de Roland* or the *Cantár del Mio Cid*.

24. The epigraph to Girard's *Mensonge romantique*, taken from *The Possessed*.

25. Thus Aristotle was obliged in the *Poetics* (1448b) to limit Homer's authorship to the two great epics, the hymns, and the satiric *Margites*.

26. See Bruno Snell, *The Discovery of the Mind* (Cambridge: Harvard University Press, 1953).

27. See his *The Making of Homeric Verse*, ed. A. Parry (Oxford: Oxford University Press, Clarendon Press, 1971); Albert Lord, *The Singer of Tales* (Cambridge: Harvard University Press, 1960).

28. The pre-Homeric naïveté of literary history is demonstrated *a contrario* by the celebrity acquired by Harold Bloom's doctrine of "influence," with its decorative Freudian and Cabalistic accretions. The germ of common sense in Bloom's vision of poetic influence not as a cheerful *je prends mon bien où je le trouve* but as a structure of resentment and its eventual transcendence is deserving of praise, for criticism has always been blind to these all too basic realities.

29. Lasserre 13. We make use of the excellent Belles Lettres edition of 1958, with text established by François Lasserre and a French translation by André Bonnard.

30. Lasserre, p. x.

31. Although illegitimacy did not prevent him from acquiring Parian citizenship, it deprived him of any share in his father's estate.

32. Bonnard (p. xiv) quotes Critias (A17) as his authority that "poverty and deprivation" were the causes of Archilochus's departure.

33. These texts are extremely fragmentary. One suggestive fragment (Lasserre 25) reads, "O starving citizens, comprehend my words."

34. For example, fr. 266, "Miserable, I lie breathless from desire, pierced to the bones by terrible pains sent by the gods" or fr. 38 ". . . With perfumed hair and bosom such as would have inspired desire even in an old man."

35. See C. M. Bowra, *Greek Lyric Poetry* (Oxford: Oxford University Press, Clarendon Press, 1936), p. 187.

36. We have noted in Penelope signs of a more active role; it is she, after all, who is asked by the suitors to choose one of their number. If we took away Odysseus and made Penelope's choice among the suitors the focus of the story, we would indeed have a plot specifically based on sexuality; and the same would be true if we focused our attention on Odysseus's relationship with Calypso or Nausicaa. But these sexual temptations are rejected by the epic. Nor does their presence imply the real possibility of a work centered on sexual relationships. The intimate world of sexuality is, rather, held up in opposition to that of the epic. It has no independent existence within it, much to the regret of the romantically minded readers who deplore Homer's failure to develop the Nausicaa episode.

37. We have developed these ideas at greater length in "Du féminin au masculin: Naissance du moi lyrique," *Poétique* 46 (Spring 1981); English translation in *Helios* 8, no. 1 (Spring 1981).

38. Berkeley and Los Angeles: University of California Press, 1951.

39. This could not have been the case in primitive Greek religion. But primitive religions have no pantheons; their gods, less anthropomorphic, are also more transcendental. As the gods divide up their powers, their anthropomorphism provides a set of esthetic figures for the specific activities and desires of the human subject. The *reductio ad absurdum* of this specialization was found in Rome, where individual "gods" supervised each function and object. In this truly productive (and not merely syncretic) polytheism, cultural universality became opposed to causal understanding in a kind of immanent occasionalism. Gilles Deleuze describes these phenomena in his *Logique du sens* (Paris: Minuit, 1969), while resisting the necessary conclusion that this

mindless ritualism constituted the extreme decadence of classical religion shortly before its surrender to Christianity.

40. Leiden: E. J. Brill, 1972; original Spanish ed., Barcelona, 1972.

41. *Festival, Comedy and Tragedy*, p. 61.

42. As its name implies, tragedy was the first dramatic form to distinguish itself from ritual lyric, with comedy retaining the undifferentiated name of the *kommos*, or ritual chorus. (See Adrados, *Festival, Comedy and Tragedy*, pp. 39 f.) The more sacrificial form is, at the same time, the most distinctive, for ritual is, in fact, always "comic," resulting as it does in the reaffirmation of the social order for the participants in the fulfillment—albeit as "consumers," not "producers"—of their desire for participation in the sacred.

43. This is not to say that these quasi-divine aspects put in doubt his mortality, any more than they did in the case of Gilgamesh. Homer has toned down the superhuman element by eliminating the legend of the heel and by ascribing his hero's short life to a choice of glory over longevity. But even this choice between two fates is not one open to ordinary mortals. Because the heroic role in epic narrative derives from an immortal one, Achilles' humanization, no matter how thorough, is still a downward one, whereas that of tragedy is upward, whatever height it reaches.

44. We may compare the pathetic protagonist of Sartre's ironic *nouvelle* "Erostrate" with Musset's Franck, who exclaims in *La coupe et les lèvres:* "Erostrate a raison!"

45. *The Origin and Early Form of Greek Tragedy* (Cambridge: Harvard University Press, 1965).

46. "[The] central element about which all the rest is organized is the agon . . ." (Adrados, *Festival, Comedy and Tragedy*, p. 30).

47. The absence of stichomythy from epic may be explained on historical grounds by its derivation from responsive elements of lyric, or the impracticality of rendering such dialogue in narration. But these grounds only confirm our substantive interpretation.

48. Of course, Aristotle may merely have been repeating a traditional attribution. But even if Aeschylus did not in fact introduce the second actor, the attribution of this innovation to him, the most prestigious tragedian of his generation, demonstrates that it was indeed regarded as the turning point in the emergence of tragedy as a high-cultural form. The history of tragedy has perhaps been simplified by the omission of transitional figures, but its fundamental pattern will in no way have been altered.

49. This subjectivization establishes a paradoxical relation between the individual subject and abstract reciprocal morality. On the one hand, all men are to love one another indifferently; on the other, each subject is an absolutely central source of love for all the others. The striving of each for the universal equality of mutual love is, at the same time, a striving to attain the central position of Christ; absolute self-sacrifice is at the same time the achievement of absolute recognition. The theologians' attempts to reduce or disprove this paradox have been proved vain, in the last analysis, not by the superior power of secular philosophies but by the evolution of secular society.

50. The difference between epic and tragedy may be measured by that between Aeschylus's treatment of the Persians and Homer's of the Trojans. Both enemies are respected, but the order of Greek society is made to depend in the one case on domination, in the other on equilibrium. The opposition between value and social hierarchy that is at the heart of the *Iliad* requires the pursuit of the war to a successful conclusion, lacking which neither element would be justified. In epic, values come

into conflict with the ethical order—in the most primitive case, in war. Tragedy is not concerned with values as such, but with the productivity of the suffering which the belief in their validity may bring about. Achilles is an epic hero because he incarnates the highest degree of value; Ajax is tragic because his own expression of this same value is not recognized. When Achilles comes to externalize his resentment in action, he kills Hector; Ajax can only kill himself.

51. Northrop Frye's attempt to assimilate literature to its underlying ritual patterns in *The Anatomy of Criticism* (Princeton: Princeton University Press, 1957) and elsewhere might be thought to contradict this statement. But Frye's analyses are based on high-cultural texts—literary and, on occasion, biblical—not on ritual ones. His vision of ritual makes it, in true Frazerian fashion, primarily dependent on man's interaction not with his fellows but with his natural environment; hence his attachment to the annual agricultural cycle. The use of this cycle as an archetype of the human condition leads Frye to privilege the pancyclic genre of "romance" over those genres, like tragedy or comedy, that he attaches to particular moments of the cycle. For a discussion of the contradictions into which this leads him, we refer the reader to our "Northrop Frye's Literary Anthropology," *Diacritics* 8, no. 2 (Summer 1978).

52. This "existentialist" reading of Greek tragedy inspires the compelling interpretations of Jan Kott in his *The Eating of the Gods* (New York: Random House, 1973); but the underlying pathos of these readings is anachronistically political. Zeus is never for Aeschylus, not even in the *Prometheus*, a mere equivalent of Stalin. The interest of Kott's interpretations lies in their affinity to the reworkings of tragic themes so popular during the *entre-deux-guerres*. That the Greek originals themselves may be made to support such readings is a curiously perverse demonstration of their relevance. For this relevance is only possible to the extent that the modern political universe has abandoned Judeo-Christian morality. The Greek tragedies may then be made to condemn the cynicism of this abandonment under, for example, communist regimes. But this recuperation of tragic suffering as political martyrdom requires a totally immanent, desacralized model of human interaction that is itself dependent on Judeo-Christian morality and, consequently, incompatible with Greek culture. The tragedies may, no doubt, be read in this perspective, but it is inconceivable that, had this perspective been shared by their authors, they could ever have been composed.

53. "Ληστάς Ἔφασκε: Oedipus and Laius' Many Murderers," *Diacritics* 8, no. 1 (Spring 1978), pp. 55–71.

54. At the conclusion of the *Eumenides*, Orestes' *departure* from Athens cleansed of his guilt illustrates precisely the antipodal form of consecration from that realized in the *Oedipus at Colonus*.

55. *Greek Tragedy*, 2d ed. (London: Methuen, 1950), pp. 188, 269.

56. In his provocative volume, *The Best of the Achaeans* (Baltimore: Johns Hopkins University Press, 1979), Gregory Nagy claims that the great cultural works of the pretragic era, notably the *Iliad* and the poems of Archilochus, as well as the more explicit case of Pindar, were inspired by hero cults. But these cults, although their extraliterary existence permitted an interlacing of desire within the fictional universe with the worldly desire discharged in ritual observance, are not themselves literary themes. If we regard Achilles' "untimely" death, as portrayed by anticipation in the *Iliad* and concretely in the lost cyclic poems (*Little Iliad, Iliou Persis*)—the loss of which, as Nagy astutely remarks, is precisely due to their link to local cults rather than to panhelladic customs and interests—as an etiological justification for the existence of his cult at the Hellespont, then it may indeed be compared to that of Euripides' Hippolytus, whose cult existed at Troezen. But the obvious difference is

that, in the *Iliad*, the establishment of the cult does not become the conclusion of the literary work. We can integrate Achilles' eventual death into our understanding of individual desire without requiring for it a collective expiation. And the same may be said, more curiously perhaps, of Archilochus, whose "martyrdom" at the hands of Lycambes is avenged for us independently of hero worship. Nagy's controversial suggestion that Lycambes and Neobule are purely conventional figures, whether true or not, has at least the merit of emphasizing the primacy of the needs of the *literary* Subject over the worldly context he affirms in his work. *Si Lycambe n'existait pas, il fallait l'inventer.*

57. *Journal of Hellenic Studies* 14 (1894), quoted in Henri Grégoire's edition of the *Bacchae* (Paris: Belles Lettres, 1961), pp. 218–219.

58. We should distinguish between human sacrifice as a social institution and the sacrifice of prisoners of war in primitive societies. The social difference affirmed by the latter is inter-, not intrasocietal; sacrifice is merely an extension of war. The Aztec sacrifices, a transitional case, made use of prisoners of war in religious roles internal to Aztec culture. Such phenomena as the pharmakos involve no intersocietal element.

Bibliography

Adrados, Francisco R. *Festival, Comedy and Tragedy*. Leiden: E. J. Brill, 1972.

Aeschylus. *Tragédies*. Edited by P. Mazon. 2 vols. Paris: Belles Lettres, 1920–1925.

Archilochus. *Fragments*. Edited by F. Lasserre and A. Bonnard. Paris: Belles Lettres, 1958.

———. [Works.] Edited by M. Treu. Munich: Ernst Heimeran, 1959.

Arendt, Hannah. *The Human Condition*. Garden City, N.Y.: Doubleday, 1958.

Arens, W. *The Man-Eating Myth*. New York: Oxford University Press, 1979.

Aristotle. *Poétique*. Edited by J. Hardy. Paris: Belles Lettres, 1932.

Ayer, A. J. *Language, Truth and Logic*. New York: Dover, 1952.

Baudrillard, Jean. *Le miroir de la production*. [Tournai:] Casterman, 1973.

———. *La société de consommation*. Paris: S.G.P.P., 1970.

———. *Le système des objets*. Paris: Gallimard, 1968.

The Bible. Jerusalem version. New York: Doubleday, 1966.

The Bible. Revised Standard Version. New York: Oxford University Press, 1962.

Bloom, Harold. *The Anxiety of Influence*. New York: Oxford University Press, 1973.

Boden, Margaret. *Artificial Intelligence and Natural Man*. Hassocks, Eng.: Harvester Press, 1977.

Boserup, Ester. *The Conditions of Agricultural Growth*. London: George Allen and Unwin, 1965.

Bowra, C. M. *Greek Lyric Poetry from Alcman to Simonides*. Oxford: Oxford University Press, Clarendon Press, 1936.

Cohen, Mark. *The Food Crisis in Prehistory*. New Haven: Yale University Press, 1977.

Condillac, E. Bonnot de. *Essai sur l'origine des connaissances humaines*. Paris: A. Colin, 1924.

Deleuze, Gilles. *Logique du sens*. Paris: Minuit, 1969.

Derrida, Jacques. *De la grammatologie.* Paris: Minuit, 1968.

———. *Marges de la philosophie.* Paris: Minuit, 1972.

Desmonde, William. *Magic, Myth and Money.* Glencoe, Ill.: Free Press, 1962.

Dodds, Eric R. *The Greeks and the Irrational.* Berkeley and Los Angeles: University of California Press, 1951.

Durkheim, Emile. *Les formes élémentaires de la vie religieuse.* 4th ed. Paris: P.U.F., 1960.

Einzig, Paul. *Primitive Money and Ethnology.* Oxford: Pergamon, 1966.

Else, Gerald F. *The Origin and Early Form of Greek Tragedy.* Cambridge: Harvard University Press, 1965.

Erman, Adolf. *The Literature of the Ancient Egyptians.* London: Methuen, 1927.

Euripides. *Tragédies.* 6 vols. Paris: Belles Lettres, 1925–1961.

———. *Tragedies.* 2 vols. Chicago: University of Chicago Press, 1958.

Finley, Moses I. *The Ancient Economy.* Berkeley and Los Angeles: University of California Press, 1973.

———. *Early Greece.* London: Chatto and Windus, 1981.

Firth, Raymond. *Tikopia Ritual and Belief.* Boston: Beacon, 1964.

Foucault, Michel. *La volonté de savoir.* Paris: Gallimard, 1976.

Frye, Northrop. *The Anatomy of Criticism.* Princeton: Princeton University Press, 1957.

Gans, Eric. "Differences." *MLN* 96, no. 2 (Spring 1981).

———. "Du féminin au masculin: Naissance du moi lyrique." *Poétique* 46 (Spring 1981). English translation in *Helios* 8, no. 1 (Spring 1981).

———. *Essais d'esthétique paradoxale.* Paris: Gallimard, 1977.

———. "Esthétique de la métaphore." *Po&sie,* 1 (1977).

———. "Le *logos* de René Girard." In *René Girard et le problème du mal,* edited by M. Deguy and J. P. Dupuy. Paris: Grasset, 1982.

———. "Northrop Frye's Literary Anthropology." *Diacritics* 8, no. 2 (Summer 1978).

———. *The Origin of Language.* Berkeley, Los Angeles, London: University of California Press, 1981.

———. "Vers un principe d'indétermination en critique littéraire." *Revue romane* 9, no. 2 (November 1974).

Gernet, Louis. *Anthropologie de la Grèce ancienne.* Paris: F. Maspéro, 1968.

The Epic of Gilgamesh. Edited by N. K. Sandars. Baltimore: Penguin Books, 1964.

Girard, René. *Des choses cachées depuis la fondation du monde.* Paris: Grasset, 1978.

———. *Mensonge romantique et verité romanesque.* Paris: Grasset, 1961. English translation, *Deceit, Desire and the Novel.* Baltimore: Johns Hopkins University Press, 1965.

———. *La violence et le sacré.* Paris: Grasset, 1972. English translation, *Violence and the Sacred.* Baltimore: Johns Hopkins University Press, 1977.

Gödel, Kurt. *On Formally Undecidable Propositions of Principia Mathematica and*

Related Systems. Translated by B. Meltzer. New York: Basic Books, 1962.

Goodheart, Sandor. "Ληστάς Ἔφασκε: Oedipus and Laius' Many Murderers." *Diacritics* 8, no. 1 (Spring 1978).

Harner, Michael. "The Biological Basis for Aztec Sacrifice." *American Ethnologist* 4 (1977).

Harris, Marvin. *Cannibals and Kings*. New York: Random House, 1977.

————. *Cows, Pigs, Wars and Witches*. New York: Random House, 1974.

————. "The Cultural Ecology of India's Sacred Cattle." *Current Anthropology* 7 (1966).

————. *Cultural Materialism*. New York: Random House, 1979.

————. *The Rise of Anthropological Theory*. New York: Crowell, 1968.

Herder, Johann Gottfried. *Abhandlung über den Ursprung der Sprache*. Munich: C. Hauser, 1978.

Homer. *L'Iliade*. Edited by P. Mazon. 4 vols. Paris: Belles Lettres, 1937–38.

————. *L'Odyssée*. Edited by V. Bérard. 3 vols. Paris: Belles Lettres, 1947.

Humphreys, S. C. *Anthropology and the Greeks*. London: Routledge and Kegan Paul, 1978.

Kaster, Joseph. *Wings of the Falcon: Life and Thought in Ancient Egypt*. New York: Holt, Rinehart and Winston, 1968.

Kirk, G. S. *The Songs of Homer*. Cambridge: Cambridge University Press, 1962.

Kitto, H. D. F. *Greek Tragedy*. 2d ed. London: Methuen, 1950.

Kott, Jan. *The Eating of the Gods*. New York: Random House, 1973.

Koyré, Alexandre. *Epiménide le menteur*. Paris: Herrmann, 1947.

Lakatos, Imre. "Falsification and the Methodology of Scientific Research Programmes." In *Criticism and the Growth of Knowledge*, edited by I. Lakatos and A. Musgrave. Cambridge: Cambridge University Press, 1970.

Laum, Bernhard. *Heiliges Geld*. Tübingen: Mohr, 1924.

Leakey, Richard. *Origins*. New York: Dutton, 1977.

Lefebvre, Gustave. *Romans et contes égyptiens de l'époque pharaonique*. Paris: Librairie d'Amérique et d'Orient, 1949.

Leroi-Gourhan, André. *La préhistoire*. Paris, P.U.F., 1966.

————. *Préhistoire de l'art occidental*. Paris: Mazenod, 1965.

————. *Les religions de la préhistoire*. 3d ed. Paris: P.U.F., 1976.

————. *Treasures of Prehistoric Art*. New York: Harry N. Abrams, 1967.

Lévi-Strauss, Claude. *Le cru et le cuit*. Paris: Plon, 1964.

————. *La pensée sauvage*. Paris: Plon, 1962.

————. *Le totémisme aujourd'hui*. Paris: P.U.F., 1962.

Lévy-Bruhl, Lucien. *L'âme primitive*. Paris: P.U.F., 1963.

————. *Les fonctions mentales dans les sociétés inférieures*. Paris: P.U.F., 1951.

Lord, Albert. *The Singer of Tales*. Cambridge: Harvard University Press, 1960.

Malraux, André. *Les voix du silence*. Paris: N.R.F., 1953.

Marcuse, Herbert. *One-Dimensional Man*. Boston: Beacon, 1964.

Menéndez Pidal, Ramón. *La Chanson de Roland et la tradition épique des Francs*. Paris: Picard, 1960.

Morgenstern, Julian. *Rites of Birth, Marriage, Death and Kindred Occasions among the Semites*. Cincinnati: Hebrew Union College Press, 1966.

Mostowski, Andrzej. *Sentences Undecidable in Formalized Arithmetic*. Amsterdam: North-Holland Publishing Co., 1952.

Nagel, Ernest, and J. R. Newman. *Gödel's Proof*. New York: New York University Press, 1958.

Nagy, Gregory. *The Best of the Achaeans*. Baltimore: Johns Hopkins University Press, 1979.

Nietzsche, Friedrich. *The Birth of Tragedy* and *The Genealogy of Morals*. In *The Philosophy of Nietzsche*. New York: Random House, n.d.

Oberhuber K., ed. *Das Gilgamesh-Epos*. Darmstadt: Wissenschaftliche Buchgesellschaft, 1977.

Page, Denys. *History and the Homeric Iliad*. Berkeley and Los Angeles: University of California Press, 1959.

————. *The Homeric Odyssey*. Oxford: Oxford University Press, 1955.

Parry, Milman. *The Making of Homeric Verse*. Edited by A. Parry. Oxford: Oxford University Press, Clarendon Press, 1971.

Piaget, Jean. *L'épistémologie génétique*. Paris: P.U.F., 1970.

Polyani, Karl. *Primitive, Archaic, and Modern Economies*. Garden City, N.Y.: Anchor, 1966.

Polanyi, Karl, C. Arensberg, and H. Pearson, eds. *Trade and Market in the Early Empires*. Glencoe, Ill.: Free Press, 1957.

Popper, Karl. *The Logic of Scientific Discovery*. London: Hutchinson, 1979.

————. *Objective Knowledge*. Oxford: Oxford University Press, Clarendon Press, 1972.

————. *The Open Society and Its Enemies*. Princeton: Princeton University Press, 1950.

Propp, Vladimir. *Morphology of the Folktale*. 2d ed. Austin: University of Texas Press, 1968.

Redfield, James. *Nature and Culture in the Iliad*. Chicago: University of Chicago Press, 1975.

Rohde, Erwin. *Psyche*. Tübingen: Mohr, 1925.

Rousseau, Jean-Jacques. *Discours sur l'origine et les fondements de l'inégalité parmi les hommes*. Cambridge: Cambridge University Press, 1947.

————. *Essai sur l'origine des langues*. In *Mélanges*, vol. 6. London, 1782.

Sahlins, Marshall. *Culture and Practical Reason*. Chicago: University of Chicago Press, 1976.

————. "Culture as Protein and Profit." *New York Review of Books* 25, no. 18 (23 November 1978).

————. *Stone Age Economics*. Chicago: Aldine-Atherton, 1972.

Sappho. Edited by Max Treu. Munich: Heimeran, 1968.

Sartre, Jean-Paul. *Réflexions sur la question juive*. Paris: P. Morihien, 1947.

Service, Elman. *The Hunters*. Englewood Cliffs, N.J.: Prentice-Hall, 1966.

Sieveking, Ann. *The Cave Artists*. London: Thames and Hudson, 1979.

Snell, Bruno. *The Discovery of the Mind*. Cambridge: Harvard University Press, 1953.

Sophocles. *Tragédies*. Edited by A. Dain and P. Mazon. 3 vols. Paris: Belles Lettres, 1955–1960.

Trân Duc Thao. *Recherches sur l'origine du langage et de la conscience*. Paris: Editions Sociales, 1973.

Turner, Victor. *The Drums of Affliction*. Oxford: Oxford University Press, Clarendon Press, 1968.

Ucko, Peter J., and Andrée Rosenfeld. *Palaeolithic Cave Art*. New York: McGraw-Hill, 1967.

Vernant, Jean-Pierre. *Mythe et pensée chez les Grecs*. Paris: F. Maspéro, 1966.

———. *Mythe et société en Grèce ancienne*. Paris: F. Maspéro, 1974.

———. *Les origines de la pensée grecque*. Paris: P.U.F., 1962.

Washburn, Sherwood, ed. *Social Life of Early Man*. New York: Wenner-Gren Foundation, 1961.

Wittfogel, Karl. *Oriental Despotism*. New Haven: Yale University Press, 1957.

Zubrow, Ezra, ed. *Demographic Anthropology*. Albuquerque: University of New Mexico Press, 1976.

Index

Abel, 202, 232

Abraham, 206, 207; sacrifices Isaac, 139–140, 226

Achilles, 241, 242, 260–261, 269, 275, 282, 283, 284, 296; Archilochus on, 270; conflicts with society, 240; mortality of, 280; Odysseus compared to, 249–250, 252, 255–256, 257, 267; resentment (wrath) of, 240, 243, 244–245, 246, 247, 248, 249, 250, 252, 253, 256, 257, 259, 263, 265, 270, 271, 277, 278, 280, 281, 287; as tragic hero, 280

Adam, 258; fall of, 190–191, 194, 195–200, 202, 210; mortality of, 190, 262; passivity of, 199; sin of, 210

Adrados, Francisco Rodriguez, 279

Aegisthus, 287

Aeneid, 254

Aeschylus, 278, 280, 283, 284–289, 292; innovations of, 284–285; produced first tragedy, 279; Sophocles compared to, 290–291

Aesop, 269

Aethiopica, 254

Agamemnon, 252, 255, 260, 263, 275, 281, 284, 287, 290; Achilles resents, 240, 241, 242, 243, 246, 247, 252, 259, 261; captures Chryses' daughter, 245; death of, 256; hubris of, 245; as king, 259

Agriculture: origin of, 151–152, 197, 202; surplus in, 148, 149, 151, 156–158, 161–162

Ajax, 289

Ajax, 282

Alcaeus, 276

Alcestis, 282

Alcinous, 249

Aleichem, Sholom, 208

Amos, 213, 214, 215, 216

Amphimedon, 251, 252

Anactoria, 274, 275

Andromache, 296

Anthropology: Bible as, 192; on causality, 80; generative, 95; historical, 78–79; positive (empirical), 97–101, 122; radical, 71–72; relevance in, 91–92, 93; Rousseau on, 230; speculative, 69–70; on theory of representation, 35–38, 62, 64, 65, 69–70, 95–96, 98

Anthropomorphism, 115, 231; of desire-object, 136; of God, 186, 200, 201, 223, 258, 321–322 n. 39; in sacrifice, 142, 143, 144

Antigone, 290

Aphrodite, 276, 277, 278, 297

Apollo, 245

Appetite: as basis of culture, 75–76, 121; and conflict, 14; and desire, 15, 24–25, 26–27, 53, 134, 306 n. 1; and desire-object, 20, 24–25, 26–27, 53; motivates representa-

331

Designer:	U.C. Press
Compositor:	Publisher's Typography
Printer:	Braun-Brumfield, Inc.
Binder:	Braun-Brumfield, Inc.
Text:	10/12 Janson
Display:	Janson